Visual Communication

Integrating Media, Art and Science

Visual Communication
Integrating Media, Art, and Science

Rick Williams and Julianne Newton

Left: Hidden Mind by Melissa Szalkowski. Original in color.

LEA Lawrence Erlbaum Associates
Taylor & Francis Group

New York   London

Omniphasic Theory © 1996 Rick Williams.

Ecology of the Visual Theory © 2001 Julianne Newton.

Images © Individual artist or copyright holder for each image. The authors gratefully acknowledge all who contributed work to make this book truly visual. For a list of contributors, please see page 421.

A number of Rick Williams's photographs were previously published in his book *Working Hands*, College Station: Texas A & M University Press, 2000.

A number of Julianne Newton's photographs were previously published in her book *The Burden of Visual Truth*, Mahwah, NJ: Lawrence Erlbaum Associates, 2001.

Cover Image: Bonnie #1 by Adam Grosowsky.

Original Illustrations throughout book by Janet Halvorsen.

Design: Julianne Newton

Prepress Production: Julianne Newton and Rick Williams.

Body Type: Univers

Display Type: Electra

Typesetting and Layout: Julianne Newton, using Macintosh PowerBook G4; Quark XPress 6.52, Photoshop CS2, Acrobat 6.02 Professional, and Acrobat Distiller 7.0.

Image Production: Rick Williams and Julianne Newton, using Canon and Nikon film cameras, Epson and Nikon scanners, Canon 350D camera, Photoshop CS2, and GretagMacbeth Eye 1.

Prepress: Penny Eberlein, using Macintosh G4.

Book Production Editors: Claudia Dukeshire, LEA, and Jay Margolis, Taylor & Francis Group, LLC.

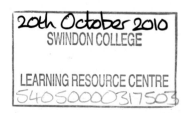
Lawrence Erlbaum Associates
Taylor & Francis Group
270 Madison Avenue
New York, NY 10016

Lawrence Erlbaum Associates
Taylor & Francis Group
2 Park Square
Milton Park, Abingdon
Oxon OX14 4RN

© 2007 by Rick Williams and Julianne Newton
Lawrence Erlbaum Associates is an imprint of Taylor & Francis Group, an Informa business

Printed in the United States of America on acid-free paper
10 9 8 7 6 5 4 3 2

International Standard Book Number-13: 978-0-8058-5066-6 (Softcover) 978-0-8058-5065-9 (Hardcover)

Visit the Taylor & Francis Web site at
http://www.taylorandfrancis.com

DEDICATION

For Jim Tankard and Max McCombs: Mentors, colleagues, and dear friends who were the first to find merit in this work and the first to support its publication.

And for Molly Ivins: Our friend and champion of truth, courage, and laughter.

An intelligent and beautifully illustrated book on how visual communication helps us achieve intellectual and intuitive literacy. A well-researched treatise that instantly shows what Omniphasism and Integrative Mind are all about. What Fritjof Capra tried to do in the Tao of Physics three decades ago, the authors have accomplished here: to bring rational and intuitive intelligences into balance and to help us reconcile our inner and outer vision for a higher state of awareness and a richer state of life.

Prof. Emeritus Herb Zettl, San Francisco State University
Broadcast & Electronic Communication Arts Department

Drawing on their extensive experience as visual artists, educators, and researchers, the authors have produced a book that will inform and stimulate any reader who wants to gain a better understanding of the ways in which our minds make sense of visual images. This is a work of mature scholarship, containing a new theory of visual communication as well as a synthesis of prior research. A valuable addition to the visual studies literature.

Paul Messaris, Lev Kuleshov Professor of Communication
The Annenberg School, University of Pennsylvania

This is an important and truly beautiful book, one that is personally and professionally useful, as well as theoretically advanced. Williams and Newton synthesize key theories in neurology, art, and visual communication as a platform for the concept of an integrative, balanced mind. Filled with insights and practical exercises to achieve this balance, this book suggests that the truly integrated mind finds an equilibrium between intuition and reason that leads to both a fuller way of life and a philosophical outlook with vast educational and cultural implications.

Prof. Ann Marie Barry, Boston College
Visual, Media and Advertising Communication

A challenging book because it presents a thorough review of theory and research in visual communication. An eloquent book because it demonstrates the beauty and process of visual communication through illustrations and many creative exercises. It integrates the art and science of visual communication and is a testimony to the power and insights of Omniphasism — the underlying theory on which this work is based and which explores an integrative balance in ways of thinking and knowing, both rational and intuitive.

Visual Communication breaks new ground in textbook writing by bringing alive the creative and mind-stretching classroom exercises that these professors have developed for their own instructional use. It helps rational thinkers learn to break through to their intuitive side through experiential learning. You have to do more than read about it to open up the intuitive side of the brain. Every student, whatever the learning or thinking style, expands individual potential in a personal and private journey through these broadening exercises.

Prof. Emeritus Sandra Moriarty
Integrated Marketing Communications Program
University of Colorado

Rick Williams and Julianne Newton are two of the most accomplished theorists in the wide field of visual communication. Their years of experience as educators and photographers combine in a well developed and important theory of intuitive intelligence. Additionally the exercises they have created and tested in their own courses illuminate for students ways to access visual intelligence, creativity and the whole mind. The book is a strong argument for inclusion of courses in visual communication and visual literacy in the liberal arts curriculum. Especially valuable are the examples and historical review of the intersections between science and art as performed in the highly mediated culture in which we live and learn. All of us have something to learn from this text.

Diane S. Hope, William A. Kern Professor in Communications
Rochester Institute of Technology

In addition to being a fine textbook and a dynamic practical discourse, the Williams-Newton book has combined rational scholarship and intuitive literacy into a vigorous call to enrich all of humankind as we plummet into and beyond the virtual world of the future. Leading by example and including critical lessons to empower visual growth, the authors have employed imagery, sensitivity, interdisciplinary sensibility, and authentic vision to provide an elegant opportunity for transforming people's lives for the better. It was Adams (Douglas, not Ansel) who once remarked that "you can't help jumbling metaphors when language tries to keep up with music," and so it must be in describing the creative arc of the present volume. Few books today have the insight and ability to energize one's mind, uplift your heart, and make us all a little less vulnerable than we were before experiencing it. This is one of those rare books.

Roy Flukinger, Senior Curator
Harry Ransom Humanities Research Center
University of Texas at Austin

CONTENTS

Contents

PREFACE
Knowing Before Words

No form of communication has a more profound effect on the private minds of individuals or the development of the public mind and culture than the visual imagery of today's media. Images are the primary carrier of media messages produced by the most sophisticated handlers of media-savvy politicians, corporate public relations campaigns, and product advertising. Visual images produced and delivered by television, print media, movies, video games, and the Internet are so pervasive that they touch and profoundly affect the lives of all citizens of 21st-century global cultures.

Before and beyond the ability of words, visual images communicate complex and complete concepts instantaneously to the whole mind. Advances in neuroscience and psychology indicate that the human brain uses imagery, as well as other information perceived by the senses, to guide our actions subconsciously before sending information to the neocortex, the center of words and rational thought. We also have evidence that our nonconscious brains do not distinguish between mediated images and what we see in real life. The brain encodes both forms of imagery into memory as if they are real and as if we have perceived the information directly from real-life experiences. This research, along with other work in brain science, education, art, and communication, has catapulted visual issues to the forefront of scholarship in such seemingly disparate fields as science, art, and media studies.

To become an educated person in the 21st century requires not only verbal and mathematical proficiency but also the ability to interpret, critique, create, and use visual communication on sophisticated levels. In today's visual world, most individuals — even those with advanced education — are ill equipped to distinguish their own perceptions of reality and the behavior those perceptions generate from realities generated by mediated messages. Furthermore, even navigating contemporary culture with conscious awareness of external perceptual influences requires at least minimal mastery of the basic techniques of image production, distribution, and consumption. Most important is appreciation for

Left: Figure P.1. Undiscovered Self by Jerry Uelsmann. Original in color.

the profound effects of imagery on individuals and the communities in which they live. Visual and media literacy are as important to the 21st-century mind as verbal and mathematical literacy have been and continue to be.

This book focuses on cultivating integrative mind processes that facilitate visual and media literacy from both consumption and production points of view and across the boundaries of traditional academic disciplines. We do this by helping you become aware of and use your intuitive cognitive processing abilities. That, in turn, will help you better understand and use visual communication to enhance your intelligence, creativity, problem solving, and performance in education and in life. Two points are significant here. One, by *intuitive cognitive processing abilities*, we refer to those ways we know and understand without the need to consciously or purposefully seek that understanding. One way to think of intuitive processing is as a powerful form of mental activity that occurs before and beyond consciousness and that guides our perceptions of reality and our behavior. Our purpose here is to focus on ways we can access those powerful parts of the mind that are primary guides of everyday life — and we call that process intuitive cognition. We will more fully explain these terms as we work through the book. Two, by *literacy*, we refer to the ability to use (write or create) a means of communication effectively, as well as to the ability to understand (read and interpret) the symbols of that system. Our goal with this book is to integrate the complex, multidisciplined fields employing visual symbols into an easily understood model of balanced intelligence and visual communication. To do that, readers must focus attention on their visual processing skills. Ultimately, we want readers to use the ideas and skills presented in this book to better use all of their cognitive abilities as integrative complements.

As a primary text for introductory-level courses focusing on the visual, *Visual Communication* grounds you in current visual research and visual means of communication. Creative exercises teach you how to apply these new ideas to enhance both your understanding of and work with images. Used as a supplementary text, *Visual Communication* can enhance courses in which new ways of creative thinking and living are a major focus — ranging from the physical and social sciences, through new and traditional arts, and through media studies.

Key Reasons to Read This Book

First, within these covers lie ideas and practices we believe are significant to the future of human life — and more specifically, to how individuals can live informed, creative, and balanced lives that sustain rather than drain personal and communal resources. The contents of this book are the result of our work with close to 10,000 individuals over the last 30 years in four institutions of higher learning, as well as more than 100 conference and workshop presentations throughout the United States and in Australia, Brazil, Canada, France, and

Mexico. Both current and past students tell us the positive impact our work has had on their lives. What we present to you also results from our own personal and scholarly growth experienced during that time. We do not claim to have all the answers. We know our goals are ambitious and idealistic. We do believe, however, that we have wisdom to offer — wisdom that can help anyone who wants to make life better at any level.

Second, we feel compelled to address a void in the preparation of tomorrow's global citizens — whether professional communicators, artists, social scientists, physical scientists, or everyday users of media, art, and science in various forms. A remarkable research movement in neurobiology and cognitive studies is cutting a path through what before seemed impenetrable — understanding how human beings perceive and know, and why they act the ways they do. Central to this new research is clarity about the significance of visual communication and intuitive processing to ways of knowing, creative problem solving, responding to the world, and interacting with one another. We believe we all can use this new information to further the conscious evolution of humans toward a socially responsible and sustainable global culture. We do have choices, as individuals and as collectives. We make these choices — on conscious and subconscious, rational and intuitive levels — every day.

From a neurobiological perspective, our intuitive intelligences, which include our visual intelligence, represent at least half of our cognitive abilities. Our intuitive processing abilities are equally as complex and far faster than are our rational intelligences. Scientific evidence supports the idea that our intuitive intelligences influence and guide rational intelligences. In fact, according to recent experiments, without access to our nonconscious abilities, it may not be possible for an otherwise normal human being to make advantageous decisions based on reason.

This new understanding of how nonconscious processing of both new and previous experiences affects our behavior has yet to be incorporated throughout even the most advanced societies. Our educational, scientific, economic, political, and cultural systems continue to ignore the great, untapped potential of our intuitive intelligences. The result is what we call intuitive illiteracy, a pervasive lack of ability to access intuitive intelligences on the sophisticated levels that can facilitate creative problem solving and advantageous decision making on the most advanced levels of cognition.

However, the power of intuitive cognition has not been completely ignored. Media practitioners and educators in media, advertising, and public relations work hand in hand with researchers in cognitive neuroscience, psychology, art, and communication. Their quest is to understand how best to use media processes to influence public attitudes, and perceptions of reality. Ultimately, the result is persuasive communication that subtly shapes the public mind and public behavior.

We believe this sophisticated use of intuitive communication techniques on an intuitively illiterate culture is the fundamental reason media messages have such influence over our lives. Media messages regularly encourage us to seek personal meaning through wealth, the consumption of products, and the collection of material objects. In such a culture, the environment; intrapersonal and interpersonal relationships; physical health; spirituality; and care for the elderly, the poor, and the disadvantaged too often take a back seat to the quest to attain goods, wealth, and individual and corporate power.

It is important to note here that we are not saying that all media are destructive. Contemporary media, including advertising, produce some of the most creative art in our culture. In fact, a great deal of advertising supports prosocial aims, such as providing revenue for a free press and free media. Nevertheless, an educated person needs to be aware that he or she sees an estimated 3,000 to 4,000 media images every day. According to Robert Coen's "Insider's Report," world advertising revenues were expected to be $604 billion in 2006. Since 1950, product manufacturers have used more of the world's natural resources than were used by the entire world throughout the rest of history.

Our point is that most media are highly intuitive in that they are visually, musically, and psychologically provocative. Media imagery often associate such qualitative values as love, family, friendship, beauty, freedom, wealth, and happiness with material goods. Advertising, for example, appeals to the intuitive mind to sell values and lifestyles, and then associates the purchase of products with the fulfillment of these human values, needs, and desires. We see these values and lifestyles not only in advertising but also in nearly all other forms of media communication. Logically, we know that buying a certain product will not fulfill our needs for friendship, love, or family, yet we buy the products at record levels while genuine self-esteem plummets and social problems soar.

Whether by intention or ignorance, our educational systems and our societies in general have oppressed the development of intuitive intelligence, leaving the populace intuitively illiterate. Using highly intuitive messages, media both support and feed on our intuitive illiteracy. The media are primarily owned and dominated by such multinational conglomerates as General Electric, News Corporation, Disney, Viacom, CBS Corporation, and TimeWarner. Many corporations have taken advantage of our weakening antitrust laws and our political system to build companies that now dominate both media and government. If current trends continue, they will soon dominate formal education. Our collective intuitive illiteracy allows corporate-dominated media messages to shape our perceptions of reality and thus guide our behaviors. The ultimate purpose of the messages is exploitation of economic and cultural systems on a vast scale. In such a culture, dominant values will be corporate values, and activity will be governed by the economic bottom line. Often forgetting its mission to educate at "higher" levels, higher education increasingly prepares students to become cogs in a largely corporate world. Those who pursue careers in newspapers, for example, are likely to land jobs with media chains, whether those jobs are news oriented or marketing oriented. Should they be creatures of great conscience, they will experience enormous conflict between their ideals of practicing socially responsible communication and the realities of profit-driven media companies. Artists, scientists, and business people alike face similar conflicts.

What You Can Do About It

These are strong words. By using the abilities of your whole mind to look at our world with clear vision and personal reflection, we believe you will see that our concerns are warranted. Whether you agree with us about issues of corporate influence is not essential. We ask that you read our ideas about your visual and intuitive intelligences with a mind that is open to possibility — the possibility that you can draw on the enormous potential of your own fully developed intellectual abilities to live a more fully and meaningfully balanced life in our complex world.

As scholars, artists, and educators — and concerned citizens of this earth — we offer you the means by which you can learn to discern and rectify imbalances within yourself, your community, and society at large for the common good of humankind. This we believe is the mission of education. Our goal is lofty, yes, but much can be gained in its pursuit. Consider the alternative — not to try?

We seek to arm you, our readers, with the knowledge and skills to change the way you live and interact with the broader culture. We are not alone in this pursuit. Many independent and alternative publishers, highly aware editors and writers, perceptive visual communicators and business people, soulful scientists and artists, conscientious parents, and other like-minded professionals, scholars and educators seek to educate the whole person and facilitate socially responsible, conscious living in a globally sustainable culture. This book is our way of contributing to that end.

At the heart of this book is a new, balanced approach to the study of intrapersonal, interpersonal, and mass communication. Communication is shared meaning. In its best sense, it aspires for universal understanding — the idea that every person can share meaning with, or understand, every other person. But understanding alone is not sufficient. Sharing is a process, a continual exchange of messages in many forms, a continual seeking to understand ourselves and how we interact with the world around us. And that exchange of messages results in the actions of everyday life.

We focus our new approach on developing intuitive intelligence through increased understanding of and skill in visual communication. It is estimated that more than 75% of the information our brains process is visual. Obviously, when we see with our eyes, we communicate visually. When we read words on a printed page, watch a sitcom on television, interact with an Internet site, take pictures at a birthday party, notice a look on someone's face, or remember what a friend looks like, we communicate visually. When we write, type, draw, paint, film, or photograph, we communicate visually. One of the discoverers of DNA, Sir Francis Crick, chose visual perception as the path for subsequent study of what makes us human. We also know that the blind develop vast visual systems within their minds. Yet most communication schools emphasize writing with words. Most colleges and universities stress verbal mastery with only peripheral attention to visual mastery.

We do not advocate lessening the commitment to learning how to write well as a foundation for good communication in any field of study. We do advocate balancing the commitment to words with a commitment not only to the visual but also to cultivating each individual's potential for balanced and holistic learning, thinking, problem solving, communicating, decision making, and doing. To do otherwise keeps us anchored in the past, while all around us whirl multidimensional media driven largely by profit motives with little regard for consequences to life on this earth.

Visual communication is a core function of the human organism and its interactions with other entities. We want you to understand how ingrained habits of seeing, knowing, creating, and behaving limit potential for living full, satisfying, and socially responsible lives. We want you to learn how you can improve your thinking and creative problem-solving processes through conscious perception of natural and mediated stimuli and through conscious creation of visual messages grounded in awareness of the reciprocity of life. We want you to learn how to use your whole mind — verbal and visual, rational and intuitive — to fully understand your self and the world in which you live and create.

The good news is that you CAN develop and cultivate your whole mind toward a holistic perspective that balances quantitative and qualitative issues that serve everyone, not just a small portion of the people of our world. The problems are serious and pervasive. The time for change is now. We believe there is hope for change. This book is filled with that hope.

R.W. and J.N., Eugene

ACKNOWLEDGMENTS

The essence of this book emerged more than twenty years ago as the authors began to teach and write about visual literacy in the late 1970s. So many individuals and institutions have contributed to our work during that time that it is impossible to fully know or explain how it all came together or to name every source of an idea or inspiration. Each time we found what we believed was the earliest reference to even the most basic concept of a balanced, integrative mind, we later discovered even earlier sources. This book is our best effort to put into one volume all that we have learned — from our experiences, readings, research, art, friends, family, and colleagues — about visual communication, media, the arts, and the sciences in the understanding and shaping of reality, behavior, and culture. This book truly is a collaboration of hearts and minds. Our personal goal is to continue our own paths toward balance and creating sustainable communities.

One thing of which we are certain is that the research, theory, and outcomes are moving targets. They are a life process. Our hope is that this work will provide a flexible framework for continued advances in the many disciplines that are influenced and supported by educational and cultural models that contribute to the development of balance through visual communication and the arts toward the integrative mind.

Our deepest thanks go to our family members, Josh and Bryn, Kate and Graeme, and Matt and Abby, and our parents Vivian Hickerson Reagan, Fred and Iris Williams, and Eva Henley, and to the thousands of students who have been essential to the development of our theories and applications in visual communication and the arts.

We also express deep gratitude to those — especially the students — who gave us permission to include their work in this volume. Their images and words bring the book to life.

At St. Edward's University in the late 1970s and early 1980s, Dean Jean Burbo and Sister Ann Crane strongly supported our work in visual communication and publications. As past presidents of the Texas Photographic Society during the 1980s, we both received extensive help from TPS board members Ave

Bonar, Carol Cohen Burton, Mary Lee Edwards, Bill Kennedy, Bob Haslinger, and Bill Wright, and from Bob O'Connor and Francis Leonard at the Texas Commission on the Humanities and the Humanities Resource Center.

In the 1990s colleagues and friends from many institutions and organizations supported our work. At The University of Texas at Austin College of Communication, Jim Tankard, Max McCombs, Wayne Danielson, J.B. Colson, Janet Staiger, Nick Lasorsa, and Bill Korbus provided unwavering friendship, support and guidance. Roy Flukinger, Senior Curator of Photography and Film at the Humanities Research Center, was instrumental in helping us locate visual artists, scholars, and collectors who contributed to the book and offered constant encouragement for our work. Diane Hope guided us into the National Communications Association Visual Communication Division, where we were awarded for our research, and to the Rochester Institute of Technology Visual Rhetoric and Technologies Conferences. Our dear friend Ann Marie Barry put her soul into this work, line editing the entire manuscript and giving us rest at her lake home in New Hampshire. Herb Zettl, Craig Denton, Larry Mullen, Sandy Moriarty, Ken Smith, Paul Lester, Paul Messaris, and Mary Stieglitz, among many others, contributed and extensively reviewed, critiqued, and advanced our work over many years through the annual Visual Communication Conference and beyond. Lance Strate and Sue Barnes introduced us to the Media Ecology Association, which published our work.

Our editors and publishers at Texas A&M Press and Lawrence Erlbaum Associates, particularly Linda Bathgate, made it possible for all of this to come together. Flukinger, Mary Ann Fulton (then at the George Eastman House), Barbara McCandless at the Amon Carter Museum, and Anne Tucker at the Houston Museum of Fine Arts collected and supported our work. Dean Tim Gleason of the School of Journalism and Communication and Doug Blandy, Associate Dean of Architecture and Allied Arts, at the University of Oregon have provided more support in terms of time and funding than any faculty member could expect. Other institutional and organizational support came from Advanced Micro Devices, Austin Arts Commission, Houston Center for Photography, National Endowment for the Humanities, Meadows Foundation, Brown Foundation, Houston FotoFest, PhotoLucida, PhotoAmericas, NAFOTO, Universidad Autónoma de Mexico, Instituto Culturo Mexicano, Instituto Culturo Peruano, and the Instituto Culturo São Paulo.

Friends of The Old Jail Museum in Albany, TX, supported Rick's work for many years. They include: Reilly Nail, Betsy and Don Koch, Bob and Nancy Green, Bill, Elizabeth, Billy and Liz Green, A.V. and Pat Jones, Watt Matthews, Benny Peacock, Gary Hebel, Melvin Gayle, and all of their extended families.

The people of Zaragoza, Coahuila, Mexico; people in the Kinney Avenue neighborhood in Austin, TX., and Terry Newton were core to Julianne's work for many years. Russell Lee, Stanley Farrar, Frances Leonard, Pete Holland, Bill Wright, Bill Stott, Roy Flukinger, and April Rapier offered feedback, encouragement and exhibition and publication venues for Julianne's work.

Colleagues at the University of Oregon who have been essential to our success include Bill and Jan Ryan, James Fox, John Russial, Al Stavitsky, Carol Ann Bassett, Janet Wasko, Leslie Steeves, Debra Merskin, Duncan McDonald, Andre Chinn, Tom Lundberg, Ryan Stasel, Sue Varani, Greg Kerber, Kathy Campbell, Glenn Morris, and Erik Palmer. Hillary Lake, Ellie Bayrd, and Sharleen Nelson plowed through early versions of the manuscript to edit, create image databases, seek permissions, and set up Quark files. More recently, Lane Community College and LCC colleagues have supported the work. They include Mary Spilde, Sonya Christian, Adam Grosowsky, Patrick Lanning, Rick Simms, and Mary Jo Workman. Jan Halvorsen contributed enormous energy, time, and creativity through her art, illustration work, and synergistic dialogues.

In both Texas and Oregon, so many friends prodded, cajoled, nourished, and encouraged us that we cannot list all. Here is a partial list in no particular order: Steve and Gwen Clark, Bill Witliff, Dave Hamrick, Steve and Ann Taylor, Nancy Springer-Baldwin, Marilyn Schultz, Alice White, Molly Ivins, Betsy Moon, Mike and Julie Murphy, Jim and Cosette Wood, D.J. Stout, Tim McClure, Steve Gurasich, Judy Trabolsi, Fred Baldwin, Wendy Watriss, Sharon Stewart, Jean Caslin, Scott Lubbock, Keith Lawson, and Nancy Boyett.

Thanks to Nancy Golden and the Springfield Public Schools, Rosaria Haugland, the Rosaria Haugland Foundation, and our friends at North Eugene high schools for continuing to support and enrich our current work in integrative arts learning.

Thank you to the friends and scholars of choice — Larry Mullen, Craig Denton, Sandra Moriarty, Herb Zettl, Ann Marie Barry, and Roy Flukinger — who read and edited first and later drafts of this manuscript and thus helped make it what it is.

And to Janet and Richard Reed, kindred souls and forever friends, we could not have made it without you.

Undoubtedly, we have left out the names of beautiful people who helped make this book happen.

We thank you all.

Next Page: Figure P2. Detail from class self portrait made in Rick's first visual literacy class featuring omniphasism in 1995. Original in color.

I would like to support the idea that there could be a universal set of biological responses to moral dilemmas, a sort of ethics, built into our brains. My hope is that we soon may be able to uncover those ethics, identify them, and begin to live more fully by them. I believe we live by them largely unconsciously now, but that a lot of suffering, war, and conflict could be eliminated if we could agree to live by them more consciously.

Michael S. Gazzaniga, 2005

Figure I.1. The Circus, by Julianne Newton.

INTRODUCTION
The Integrative Mind

The brain is naturally integrative as it creates mind. By becoming conscious of its integrative modalities and by developing one's abilities to use those modalities on more sophisticated levels as complementary processes, one can achieve a state of dynamic cognitive balance that facilitates the highest order of cognitive creativity, problem solving, and performance in educational, professional, and life endeavors.

R.W.

This book is written using words to describe a part of the mind that knows *before and beyond* words. This powerful component of human knowing represents at least half of our cognitive abilities, including our visual, musical, psychological, and physiological abilities. We call these cognitive abilities *intuitive intelligences* because they are linked and differentiated by their unique ability to attain knowledge directly without words and without evidence of reason. These intuitive intelligences often use their primary knowledge on nonconscious levels to shape our perceptions of reality, solve problems, make decisions, and guide our behaviors before the conscious mind is activated.

Using words to describe cognitive processes that operate beyond words may seem like a contradiction. However, it is not. We attempt through words and images to provide a clear, working understanding of how you can fully develop and consciously integrate the processes of both your intuitive intelligences and your rational intelligences to create a state of Integrative Mind. This dynamically balanced state of mind will enhance your creativity and problem-solving abilities to work at more sophisticated levels of cognition and to accomplish more than by using only your rational abilities.

As you work through the book, stop to contemplate the images. Each image has been carefully selected and placed in order to communicate to you in ways that words cannot. Determining how each image complements and enhances words in the text is essential to understanding.

The study of visual communication has come full circle as an essential component of becoming an educated individual. During the 19th century, cultivating artistic ability was standard: People considered "educated" were "visually literate" in the sense that they could "read and write" a visual language. Often, that "language" was one or more of the fine or performing arts: A well-educated person could interpret and discuss works of art, as well as paint, or draw, or perform music or poetry — at least on basic levels. In today's world, however, college students usually take a minimum number of arts area courses as part of their undergraduate curricula. Few learn to use a visual medium with proficiency, and even fewer extend visual learning at graduate and postgraduate levels. Ironically, as visual education has been pushed to the periphery of the core curriculum in higher education, the need for visual literacy has grown exponentially.

One has only to glance at the contemporary environment to note the plethora of visual forms that we all must navigate in the course of daily life: road signs and maps, subway and bus schedules, video arcades, limitless Internet sites, blatant brand advertising on clothing, tattooed and pierced bodies, heavily stylized makeup and hair, all supported by 150+ channel television, Internet, and print media that blur entertainment, editorial, and advertising boundaries. It is estimated that the average person in the United States views some 3,000 to 4,000 media-generated images daily. Those images critically influence our lives and our culture. How does a person intelligently negotiate this environment through a word-based education that emphasizes skills that are neither visually nor intuitively sophisticated?

Visual Communication addresses this dilemma by introducing a holistic approach to education in order to integrate visual and verbal and intuitive and rational proficiencies. We wrote this book for a wide range of audiences in various disciplines operating at multiple levels of the educational system. As you read the book, you will follow a carefully planned course of study that teaches you to cultivate your intuitive and visual intelligences in tandem with traditional, verbally based rational intelligences. A major theme throughout the book is the role of the visual as the primary pathway to integrating intuitive and rational cognitive processes. The book integrates our original, holistic approach to learning and knowing with the work of other scholars. Thus, *Visual Communication* expands and bridges traditional approaches to the study of visual communication, liberal arts, and social and natural sciences by embracing intuitive and rational intelligences as equivalent, complementary, and mutually essential cognitive processes.

This integrative approach is called *Omniphasism,* which means "all in balance." Omniphasism teaches balanced, whole-mind cognition strategies by strengthening visual communication and other intuitive processing abilities. Another way to think of omniphasism is as *Integrative Mind Theory*.

Figure I.2. Focusing on consciousness, by Rick Williams.

Clarifying Terms

Let's begin with the simple terms *visual* and *verbal*. Scholars and educators often use these two seemingly opposing terms to represent the two primary systems our brains use to process information into knowledge. In the 1970s Roger Sperry and Joseph Bogen introduced the concept of right- and left-brain hemisphere specialization to explain the same processes. In their model, the right brain was predominately visual and the left brain was predominately verbal. Since then neuroscientists have discovered that the brain is far more complex and integrated than the right/left, visual/verbal model implies. But Sperry and Bogen's basic concept of two primary cognitive-processing systems — one that analyzes information in rational, linear formats and one that synthesizes information in intuitive formats — has stood the test of time and science. The term *cognitive* simply refers to the process of knowing.

To clarify these ideas and facilitate applying dual processing systems to a broader arena of cognition and intelligence, we characterize the two primary cognitive modes in terms of the way they process information — either *rationally* through analysis (dividing something into component parts to understand it) or *intuitively* through synthesis (spontaneously relating different elements to create something new), rather than by their location in the brain. Thus, we call the *analytical* cognitive processes rational and the *synthesistic* cognitive processes intuitive. Each cognitive mode uses particular intelligences in specific ways to understand and respond to the world. These intelligences also can operate intuitively or rationally on basic cognitive levels. The result is an integrated system of complementary cognitive processing modes — each equally significant to whole-mind knowing. We discuss the relationship of these various intelligences to Howard Gardner's multiple intelligence theory later in the book.

Understanding and developing integrated mind processes is fundamental to studying the visual, because visual intelligence is the primary intuitive intelligence. Further, all intelligences, whether predominantly intuitive or predominantly rational, have significant visual components that operate on both physical and cognitive levels. It is estimated that more than 75% of all information the brain receives is visual. Therefore, it is important to explore cognition and multiple intelligences to fully grasp how significant visual communication is to our understanding of the world around us and of ourselves, as well as the behavior that this understanding generates.

The term *cognition* refers to the brain processes we use in the act of knowing.

The term *intelligence* refers to the ability to use cognition (the processes of knowing) to understand and act on what one experiences. For instance, visual intelligence uses imagery we gather through our eyes, as well as imagery we create in the mind's eye, to make meaning, solve problems, make decisions, and determine actions. This process occurs on both conscious and nonconscious levels.

We use the word *intuitive* to describe those primary cognitive processes and intelligences that operate in a synthesistic manner at their most basic cognitive levels. *Intuitive intelligence* means the ability to attain knowledge directly through cognition without evidence of reason. In this sense, intuitive does not refer to extrasensory or paranormal perception. However, intuitive can refer to preconscious awareness or barely conscious perceptions that guide our behaviors toward certain decisions before we have rationally decided to make those decisions. For instance, if someone unexpectedly throws a ball at you, you may see and catch it using intuitive cognition before you have time to rationally, verbally analyze the situation.

Although we also use these processes as part of rational ways of knowing, their primary cognitive function is intuitive and therefore operates *before and beyond reason.* On the other hand, *rational* cognitive processes and intelligences use logic and reason to *analyze* information over time.

Synthesis means bringing disparate pieces of information together to form new understanding. *Analysis* means taking something apart to understand it. So, intuitive intelligences process information from a holistic, nonlinear perspective. To say it another way, intuitive processing often is *preconscious* and *prerational*, meaning it occurs before we are aware of it and before we can use it to make conscious decisions. It synthesizes information across space and time to initiate behavioral responses before the rational mind has had time to use the slower

Williams and Newton

process of analysis to receive, interpret, and respond to the information. When we use the term *consciousness* in this book, we mean a state of *awareness*. In other words, you are conscious of something when you are aware of it or thinking about it. Most often, consciousness involves words. The *nonconscious* mind, on the other hand, refers to the parts and processes of our minds of which we are not aware.

Preconscious processes bring information stored in the nonconscious mind into consciousness, either through the behavior they initiate or through processes of the conscious mind. Thus, the idea of preconscious information includes nonconscious information in the process of moving forward into consciousness.

Visual intelligence, as we use the term here, is a primary example of an intuitive intelligence that uses both nonconscious and preconscious information to initiate behavior. Our eyes move approximately 20 times every second to gather information. We neither are conscious of this movement nor can rationally consider and analyze every image that the eyes see. Nevertheless, selections of this visual information are received by the visual processing center of the brain, which first synthesizes visual stimuli on preconscious, nonrational levels before initiating a behavioral response. In other words, by the time we become conscious of what we are seeing, the intuitive mind has already synthesized the significant information and set a response into motion. Of course, if the rational mind becomes conscious of the information and behavior, it can then use the visual information to analyze what has been observed and adjust behavior as it deems necessary. Thus, visual cognition is equally significant to both intuitive and rational processes in an integrated and complementary format, and vice versa.

Listed below are several categories of intuitive intelligence, along with a brief explanation of each. Please note that in each category of intelligence we emphasize a strong, common visual component. That visual component does not diminish the other properties of the intelligence; however, it does allow us to consider and understand intuitive intelligence as a whole from a visual cognitive perspective. The organization below draws in part from Gardner's theory of multiple intelligences and Ann Marie Barry's theory of visual intelligence. We discuss both of these theories in detail as we work through the book. The purpose of *Visual Communication* is to extend these and other theories with our own original work through a model for developing an integrated mind.

•*Visual Intelligence*

The ability to observe, understand, and respond to images, light, symbols, shapes, patterns, colors, contrast, composition, and balance. May involve physical sight, mind's eye, meditations, metaphorical imagery, imagination, drawing, photography, and gestalt comprehension and response.

•Musical Intelligence

The ability to hear and understand pitch, rhythm, timbre, and the emotional power and complex organization of music. May involve physical hearing, mind's ear, mind's eye, musical instruments, imagination, voice, and emotional and physical responses.

•Psychological Intelligence

The ability to know, understand, and respond to a detailed awareness of one's self and others. May involve sense perceptions; emotions; imagination; visualization; nonconscious mind and memory; dreams; physical, mental, and emotional relationships with self and others; and gestalt comprehension and response.

•Physiological Intelligence

The ability to know, understand, and respond to one's body and its relationship to the self, to others, and to objects. May involve visual and spatial awareness, physical movement, coordination, sense perceptions, emotions, nonconscious mind and memory, meditations, dreams, and gestalt comprehension and response.

All of us are familiar with such rational intelligences as mathematical and linguistic ways of knowing and communicating. We use them every day to name, categorize, count, and logically explain our activities and conscious thought processes. We spend most of our school years learning to read, write, and work mathematical equations — to use our rational intelligences.

We also all use such intuitive intelligences as visual, musical, psychological, and bodily kinesthetic ways of knowing thousands of times everyday. We use them so much, in fact, that we take them for granted. Because most of us are born with the ability to see, hear, and move, we assume that these intuitive abilities develop without need for the intensive formal training or practice that we give our rational intelligences. To some extent, they do develop on their own, without conscious attention. However, we have much to gain if we recognize, develop, and nurture our intuitive abilities beyond the rudimentary levels that enable us to function on basic levels in everyday life.

Not all intuitive cognition is nonconscious or preconscious. Visual memory, for example, can be brought to consciousness and integrated with our rational processes to help us make informed decisions consciously, or it can be deeply embedded in the emotional systems so that we become aware only of the intense feeling that nonconscious visual memories generate. Seeking information in our preconscious minds for guidance in rational decision making can add a cognitively balanced perspective to our experiences and our behavior.

Two active ways to access the preconscious, intuitive mind include meditation — sometimes called active imagination or visualization — and dreams. The first creative assignment that follows chapter 1 asks you to use an ancient technique of visualization. You will work with dreams in creative 9.

Underscoring a Key Point

Before going further, we need to make clear that we are talking about two different, yet integrated, cognitive-processing systems — one rationally dominant and one intuitively dominant — in one brain. Both our intuitive and rational cognitive systems, though operationally different, are integrated and operate together all of the time. Although a particular intelligence does not work alone, it may be dominant for a given task or process. For instance, the rational, mathematical mind might be dominant when we are balancing checkbooks, though the intuitive mind might clue us to the fact that something is wrong with our figures, even when they seem to add up. The intuitive mind might dominate while we draw or dance, but we need the rational mind to study and learn new dance steps or drawing techniques. Learning to use the complementary, integrative nature of cognition in conscious, intentional ways to enhance intelligence and creativity is a primary focus of this book.

The problem today with this integrative-mind scenario is that we live in a culture that has become so rationally biased that our intuitive systems remain underdeveloped and operate primarily on basic, nonconscious levels. Yet they influence both our conscious decision making and our actions. Because our educational, scientific, economic, political, and cultural systems do not focus on or

Figure I.3. One type of knowledge source, by Rick Williams.

emphasize the intuitive mind, few of us have developed a significant, much less sophisticated, ability to recognize and use our intuitive intelligences. This is not to say that intuitive intelligences have gone unnoticed or unused by all. Many sophisticated executives in major corporations, and particularly in advertising and media, have recently learned that practicing visualization and other intuitively centered techniques improves creativity, problem solving, and decision making and thus enhances productivity. But this has not been incorporated into our educational system or our overall culture on a broad scale.

The very fact that you, as an individual within a society, have been taught so little about your intuitive intelligences is itself a testimony to the rational bias of our culture. This bias against the development and nurture of our intuitive intelligences suppresses and oppresses the very cognitive processes that bring creativity, problem-solving abilities, deeper meaning, quality, compassion, and an integrated spirit to the facts and dogma of our lives and communities.

This book is written in words about ways of knowing that operate beyond words to influence and guide our lives. We have organized the reading so that the book flows between theory and practice, and between rational processing and intuitive creating. Chapters 1 to 6 integrate our own work with theories in neurobiology, psychology, education, neuropsychology, and visual and media literacy. This provides both historical and contemporary support and context for various aspects of the omniphasic model of intuitive and rational intelligence and their relationship to visual literacy. Chapters 7 to 11 add new dimensions to traditional approaches to visual and media literacy by introducing and applying omniphasic, integrative-mind techniques. Chapters 12 to 15 illustrate how the media use intuitive communication techniques and offer suggestions about how you can use omniphasic techniques to overcome media manipulations and to create socially responsible visual messages for mass and personal media.

This book teaches you how to use your intuitive intelligences, especially the visual component of those intelligences, as equal and complementary to your rational knowing processes. In this book, you will explore both facts and theory, from a primarily visual perspective, to help your rational mind understand the power and significance of its intuitive complement. You also will work though a set of creative assignments to become more aware of your intuitive abilities, to enhance them, and to integrate them with your rational abilities. In the process, you will expand your cognitive abilities to help you find new solutions to old problems in ways that enhance both meaning and quality of life. You will be well on your way to becoming an excellent visual communicator — one who can both interpret and create visual messages for the 21st-century world.

PART I.
VISION AND INTELLIGENCE
Understanding Intelligence
as Intuitive and Rational

Part I integrates our new ideas with established theories in neurobiology, psychology, education, neuropsychology, and visual and media literacy. This provides both historical and contemporary support and context for various aspects of the omniphasic model of intuitive and rational intelligence and their relationship to visual literacy.

Figure 1.1. Sitting Bull holding peace pipe, by D. F. Barry, 1885, Bismarck, Dakota.
Photographic print on cabinet card, courtesy of the Library of Congress
Prints & Photographs Division, LC-USZ62-111147.

CHAPTER ONE

Seeking Dynamic Balance:
The Shaman, The Scientist, and the Theologian

*Let us put our minds together and see what life we can make
for our children.*

— Sitting Bull, Lakota Sioux, 1877

She-Bear: The Power of Integrating Visual and Verbal Communication

Let us tell you a story, a parable yet, as it was given to us by Bear Faces the Wind. In this story of the soul, Bear Faces the Wind tells the story of She-Bear to a theology professor and to a scientist.

Figure 1.2. Standing Holy, Sitting Bull's Daughter, by D. F. Barry, 1885, Bismarck, Dakota. Photographic print on cabinet card, courtesy of the Library of the Congress Prints and Photographs Division, LC-USZ62-117642.

"Hidden in a den deep beneath the frozen ground in the mountains, She-Bear awakens from her winter sleep and gives birth to two tiny cubs. The bear cubs are blind, hairless, somewhat shapeless creatures weighing less than two pounds each. As the spring sun melts the snow, remaking the fertile world outside, She-Bear uses her tongue to lick her shapeless cubs into the image of bears. Thus, when the melted snow has filled the rivers and the forest floor has flowered, the cubs will be ready to face the outside world in the fullness of their Bearness."

The scientist, considering the meaning of the story, focuses on the idea of bear cubs being shapeless and ponders the idea of how the mother can lick them into the image of a bear. Questioning this, the scientist follows She-Bear to her den the next fall. Later, when the bear is comfortably hibernating, the scientist returns to make a peephole in the den so he can apply scientific observation to the formation process after the cubs are born. Of course, being aware that scientific observations are always challenged, the scientist increases the reliability by following 10 bears and digging 10 peepholes to expand the sample size. To increase confidence further, the scientist adds five more observers to the team. Naturally, in the spring, the team records that in 10 of 10 dens the cubs, though hairless, apparently blind and somewhat shapeless at birth, do in fact look like small bears and, though the mother does lick them, this does not literally change their shape or image. Thus, armed with quantitative scientific evidence, they denounce the story as inaccurate, and therefore invalid, and not to be taken seriously.

Thinking the scientist has missed the mark and that there must be some deeper meaning to the story, the theologian looks to the book of wisdom that she reveres as the word of God and finds the idea of discipline and spiritual growth in a passage about sparing the rod and spoiling the child. Obviously, the theologian challenges, this story is a parable and means that the mother disciplines the cubs until they conform to the image that she has picked out for them as bear cubs.

Bear Faces the Wind, who has told the story from generation to generation, smiles at the scientist and the theologian and tells them, "You are both completely correct and you are both completely wrong."

"Of course," says Bear Faces the Wind, "the cubs physically look like baby bears when they are born. That is what they are. It is good though to confirm that they are hairless, blind, and shapeless." The scientist smiles. But Bear Faces the Wind continues, "Yet what they look like on the outside is not all that the story is about."

"And," says the Bear Faces the Wind, "the story is a parable, and the mother bear will certainly use her own form of discipline to teach the cubs what she wants them to know." The theologian smiles. Bear Faces the Wind continues, "But using physical force to make the cubs in her own image is not the whole point of the story either."

Bear Faces the Wind explains, "This is a story of the soul that teaches both the Rational and the Intuitive mind. It does this by using facts as symbols or metaphors for reality that exists beyond the facts alone."

"For example, it is within the cave," continues Bear Faces the Wind, "that She-Bear, who represents the mature, life-giving, nurturing, feminine spirit within each of us, begins the preparation for the cubs to enter the outside world. Thus, at the beginning of the story, the idea of shaping the cubs has to do with shaping their inner selves, not their actual physical shape.

"Also, bears use their tongues to both lick and heal wounds and to show affection. So, the idea of licking is a symbol of protection and nurturing of the immature until their own inner sense of themselves as bears matures. Because of this shaping, the cubs are able to protect and care for themselves inside before they move into the outer world."

This story, *She-Bear*, is significant to us as individuals and as a society. It clearly illustrates the advantage of holistic application of the rational and the intuitive intelligences of our minds. In addition to using our logical, rational intelligences to establish certain facts about bear cubs, the story draws on our symbolic intuitive intelligences to look beyond the facts. Seeking this deeper meaning is the key to developing creativity and values that ensure quality of life for the individual and, subsequently, for the relationships the individual develops within the community.

The story also parallels and symbolizes the way that mass communication, driven by rationally biased, educational, social, economic, and governmental systems, can effectively ignore the whole story to perpetuate their own, limited, linear, hegemonic systems upon a half-literate society. In this way, they are able to significantly shape our values and, therefore, our behaviors, relationships, and lives.

This symbolic story is significant to the teaching of visual literacy, art, journalism, mass communication, and other disciplines because media messages produced by symbolic prose or visual craft have the power to communicate instantaneously and profoundly to both the conscious and the nonconscious, the rational and intuitive intelligences. Thus, they leave lasting impressions that shape our lives on levels of which we are not always consciously aware.

And these deeply felt intuitive metaphors can be, and are, misinterpreted and misused by gifted, intuitively literate communicators in these same mass communication, educational, social, economic, and government systems. The visual communicators behind these powerful systems use the media to produce and disseminate intuitive image metaphors that are constructed to persuade and manipulate our preconscious cognitive states. Subsequently, these intuitive messages, operating from our preconscious memory, form preconscious biases that guide our problem-solving and decision-making processes. This is the most popular, effective, and powerful art of our time. It shapes our lives in specific ways that exalt the intent of the systems but rarely foster the quality of our being. They teach us to focus our energy and our behavior to use physical, external rewards to nurture and satisfy our deepest inner needs for human understanding and relationships. Of course, this produces an overwhelming quantity of objects in our lives but very little quality in the form of relationships or a sense of community integrity.

Because our educational systems have focused on rational intelligences rather than intuitive intelligences, intelligences that are powerful and equally as complex and effective as our rational intelligences, we are left as intuitive illiterates, vulnerable to sophisticated media manipulations. The use of sophisticated, intuitive communication techniques establishes the mass media as the educators and exploiters of the intuitive intelligences. As such they are positioned to unduly influence our perceptions of reality, our values, and thus our lives and our culture. The film series *The Matrix* suggests what a continuation of this model might look like in the future.

Only when, as did Bear Faces the Wind, we integrate the intelligences of our whole minds to shape our lives and our culture do we embrace the balance that reaps the benefits of the whole story, so that human beings enjoy both appropriate quantity and optimum quality of life.

If you want to become fully educated, both in theory and practice, you must move beyond the limited educational model, which emphasizes mathematical and linguistic intelligence, to study and apply the full capacity of your intelligence. You must move beyond rational bias toward a balanced cognitive perspective that develops and nurtures your intuitive intelligences as equally significant to your rational intelligences. Omniphasism proposes one way to begin making this critical transformation individually and as a culture.

A Theory of Integrative Mind

Omniphasism, which means "all in balance," is a holistic approach Rick Williams developed in 1995 to cultivate and use the varied abilities of the mind. Before we explore the omniphasic theory in detail, it will be helpful to get on even ground in terms of the meanings of basic concepts and words that inform the theory. Tables 1, 2, and 3 at the end of this chapter outline the key terms, ideas and basic theory underlying the view that rational and intuitive intelligences are complementary cognitive processes at work in the integrative mind. We explore the ideas and concepts further in the next few chapters. It is critical to the understanding of omniphasism that you also develop and practice your intuitive abilities. The creative exercises that follow each chapter of this book are designed specifically to help you recognize, practice, and develop your intuitive intelligences in concert with your rational abilities. They will help you understand and apply the theory that is explained in each chapter. For that reason it is important to do the exercises in order, after you have read the chapter. You may discover your own rational bias as you do the creative exercises. This means that you may find some resistance to doing them, or may initially think they are too simple, or that you are not getting enough out of them. Do not let that discourage or stop you. You have spent most of your school life developing your rational abilities in the rational realm of logic, mathematics, and linguistics. If you spend the required time to complete all of these exercises, we feel certain you will have a new and deep appreciation of your intuitive intelligences. Not only will you become visually and intuitively literate but you will be better prepared to apply your whole mind to creatively solve problems and make advantageous decisions for your work and life. The first creative exercise that follows provides a relaxing, intuitively oriented break from the rationally dominant theoretical ideas in the chapter. Enjoy.

Figure 1.3. Winter, by Rick Williams.

Table 1. Key Terms

Cognition (W)*

The act or process of knowing, including awareness and judgment, or a product of this act.

Knowing (W)

Having information or understanding.

Intelligence (W)

The ability to learn or understand and apply knowledge advantageously.

Process (W)

A continuing activity or function marked by gradual changes that often proceed toward a particular result.

Rational (W)

Relating to, based on, or agreeable to reason.

Intuition (W)

Attaining direct knowledge or cognition without evident rational thought or inference.

Rational Intelligence (A)**

The ability to learn or understand and apply knowledge through a process relating to, based on, or agreeable to reason.

Intuitive Intelligence (A)

The ability to learn or understand and apply knowledge directly and non-consciously without the intervention of conscious rational processes

Rational Cognitive Process (A)

A knowing activity that is related to, based on, or agreeable to reason.

Intuitive Cognitive Process (A)

A knowing activity based on attaining direct knowledge or cognition without evident rational thought or inference.

Omni (W)

All

Phase (W)

To adjust until balance is achieved.

Omniphasism (A) / Integrated Mind Theory

All in balance. An interdisciplinary theory that integrates the rational and sintuitive intelligences toward balanced, whole-mind knowing activity, which leads to balanced lives and cultural systems.

W = from Merriam-Webster's Dictionary (10th Ed., 1993)
**A = Authors' Extension*

Table 2. Key Ideas

One

- Human intuitive and rational intelligences complement one another as equal and parallel cognitive processes that operate independently but are integrated.

Two

- Intuitive and rational intelligences are equally complex and equally significant to the balanced, whole-brain functions of a human being.

Three

- A significant bias exists against the development and maintenance of intuitive intelligences throughout our scientific, economic, educational, and cultural systems.

Four

- The rational bias has created an experiential and psychological intuitive intelligence void in our cultures that promotes intuitive illiteracy and leaves us unbalanced, lacking, and longing for completion as whole beings.

Five

- Intuitive illiteracy has opened the door for the media to be used as the educational/exploitation system for intuitive intelligences. The power of the media to persuade and shape lives and cultures lies in their ability to develop intuitive communication processes that effectively fill this intuitive void.

Six

- The development of a holistic educational model that embraces a balanced curriculum, developing both intuitive and rational intelligences as equivalent and complementary, has the potential to enhance creative problem-solving and decision-making abilities and prepare a more balanced, fully educated, self-determining individual, less susceptible to manipulative media influences and better prepared to apply classroom experiences to life experiences in ways that generate balance within the individual and thus within the cultural systems subsequently developed.

Table 3.
Primary Intuitive and Rational
Cognitive Processes*

This table briefly describes some of the basic cognitive processes used by the intuitive and rational intelligence systems. The definitions highlight complementary characteristics of, and differences among, the main processing functions of the two primary cognitive systems. This list, selected from the Bogen and Ornstein list in chapter 6, is not meant to be an exhaustive account of all cognitive processes or all intelligences. Primary intuitive intelligences are discussed in detail in chapter 6.

Intuitive Cognitive Processes

Visual/Spatial - Direct knowing based on seeing, either with the eyes or with mental vision.

Intuitive - Direct knowledge or cognition without evident rational thought or inference.

Holistic - Knowledge of whole things working in groups or as systems; perceiving patterns and relationships.

Synthesistic - Knowledge gained through awareness of the interdependent relationships or connections among things; putting things together to form wholes.

Analogic - Knowledge gained by seeing likenesses between things; understanding metaphoric relationships.

Timeless - Knowing without regard or awareness of time.

Primal- - Knowledge of a primary, fundamental, firsthand nature; often based on perception.

Rational Cognitive Processes

Verbal - Knowing based on how to use words to name, define, describe, label, and categorize.

Rational - Knowledge that is related to, based on, or agreeable to reason.

Linear - Thinking in terms of linked ideas, one thought directly following another.

Analytic - Knowledge gained by separating things into component parts or constituent elements; figuring out step by step.

Abstract - Knowledge gained by taking out a small bit of information and using it to represent the whole.

Temporal - Knowing in relationship to time; sequencing based on time.

Derivative - Knowledge derived from something primary or basic. Often based on conceptualization.

List drawn in part from Bogen, 1975, p. 25, and Ornstein, 1972, p. 37.

Figure I.4. Eloina's Mother, by Julianne Newton.

CREATIVE ONE
The Intimate Eye: Accessing Your Inner Vision Through Creative Visualization

The Goal: Enhancing Your Creative Abilities

When people think of visualization, a meditation technique, they may think of dark-robed monks sitting cross-legged for hours chanting monophonic syllables while staring at candles or, eyes closed, drifting off into other realms of consciousness. Yes, this is a form of visualization or meditation that has been used by devotees of a number of religions for thousands of years. As we mentioned earlier, visual intelligence uses both images we see with our eyes and images that are created from the mind's eye. The mind is able to create visual images from within — that is how we dream. These processes are intuitive and represent a form of creativity that is also used regularly by artists and by executives in advertising, media, and major corporations to help employees focus and enhance creativity, problems-solving, and decision-making abilities.

There are many forms of visualization. All of us have experienced the preconscious, integrated state of mind associated with meditative visualization thousands of times in our lives. Anytime you daydream, for example, you shift into a visual/meditative state of mind. This simply means shifting from the control of your more logically oriented, word-oriented, conscious state of mind to a more introspective, integrative, centered state of mind. In this state, images, instead of words, tend to be the primary means of communication, though words can be part of this state, such as the use of a mantra. For instance, when you use a mantra, such as counting sheep or the word *Om*, and repeat that mantra over and over, the repetition keeps the rational mind directly involved in the process, yet the simplicity of the repetition opens the intuitive mind to the visualization process. This is an example of how creative visualization can be integrative. In the process that we use in this exercise, you focus on your body and your breath instead of using a mantra. Just as when you daydream

Left: Figure C1.1. Reflection, by Rick Williams.

or when you draw, when you visualize or meditate, you may feel peaceful and very connected to your sense of being. At the same time, you may feel very energized and vibrant and fully engaged in the process. You may find that seeing is enough — that words fade from consciousness. You may become so involved with your process that you lose track of time.

If you have never purposefully visualized or meditated before, you may feel resistance to the idea. You may think it is silly, pointless, or even something you cannot or do not want to do. Those feelings are completely normal, because what we have come to know as the dominant rational mind is all about organization and labeling with words, not about seeing. But as you learn to recognize the advantages of this process to your overall intelligence and to your ability to solve problems of various types (as many creative executives in this country have learned), you will see why it is so important to develop your intuitive intelligences along with your rational thinking processes. All we ask is that you give the experience a chance for a very short time — you have everything to gain.

Getting Started

In this particular creative assignment, your goal is to experience the transition from your rational, word-centered, conscious mind to a more integrated state that blends your conscious mind with your visually centered, preconscious mind. Do not set yourself up for failure by trying to preconceive or control the outcome of your efforts. The effort of trying to experience the transition is itself admirable and sufficient. The best way to begin is with an open mind and a willingness to accept whatever happens as appropriate.

The preconscious mind communicates primarily in visual symbols or flowing colors. These symbols are rarely literal depictions of events to come. Instead they are metaphors for events of an interior nature that are happening within your preconscious mind. For instance, if you envision a snake biting you during your visualization, this does not generally foretell your demise (though your rational mind may think it so). One interpretation could be that this image links you to a snake, which, because of its ability to shed its skin and start over, is a symbol of transformation and new life. As in dreams, the preconscious mind often uses images of friends or of real events as metaphorical symbols. So, if someone does something that they shouldn't in your visualization, do not assume that they will do the same thing in real life. Instead, ask yourself what part of you the person and action represent. What message is your preconscious mind trying to communicate to you about yourself through the process of the visualization?

Now, focus on opening your mind. Try not to expect anything specific. Experiencing the intuitive mind in this way is usually simple, enjoyable, and relaxing. You can do it as often as you want and almost anywhere that you are.

This time is just one of those times, not the only time. Many people use short visualization periods during the workday as a way to relax and center themselves, thus regenerating their energy and creativity. You might recall an experience of studying at your desk, rubbing your tired face, and letting your head rest in your hands as you drifted off into a daydream. That was a form of visualization, a way to relax your conscious mind and ask your preconscious mind for inspiration and energy. In this creative exercise, you will enter that state intentionally, rather than accidentally. We also want you to extend the state for a longer period of time. You may or may not see clear images or meanings in each session. So you do not have to go there seeking anything in particular. Simply enjoy the relaxation and experience the sense of awareness. Whatever happens, just happens. Either way, you will benefit from relaxing and refreshing yourself.

We have used this process for more than 30 years. Sometimes we see, in the intuitive eye, clear images with meaning. Sometimes we just see colors and shapes. Sometimes we just listen to the endless, internal dialogue about our problems. Do not try to control the integrative state. However, if you make the effort to engage the intuitive mind and are receptive to its symbolic communication, you can benefit from its insight and wisdom. It is part of your mind and your intelligence. Remember — no one is trying to tell you what to think or do. You simply are learning to listen to and respect your intuitive self.

Figure C1.2. Kelsey finds quiet time in the back yard, by Rick Williams.

Figure C1.3. Josh Daydreams, by Rick Williams.

Part I: The Process

Read through this description of the process completely once or twice before you start. It is simple and you will be able to remember it once you have read it. And you don't have to do it perfectly. These are simply guidelines that work for us. There is no strict process or right or wrong way. Once you start, simply follow this process as well as you can remember and adapt it as is best for you. If you need to scratch your nose in the middle of the meditation, just do so if you like.

You can reach this integrated state in many ways. If you already have a method you prefer, feel free to use it. Even though you are trying to move into a more integrated state, you are not leaving your rational mind completely out of the process. Remember that omniphasism is about integrating the mind. You are using your rational mind to choose to visualize, to select the process you will use, and to focus yourself on whatever technique you choose. This is a holistic process. Once you make the decision to do it, learn the techniques, and practice the process, everything else becomes automatic. It is much like dancing, or driving, or drawing. Once you have learned and practiced the basics, you reach a point where they all just come together and the process works.

Before you begin, find a quiet place where you can be comfortable and undisturbed for 20 to 30 minutes. Put your drawing pad and pencils, crayons, markers, or whatever you want to have with you within reach so that you can make a visual or written record of your experience when you finish. Turn the answering machine on, unplug the telephone, and turn off your cell phone. If you have a favorite place to sit or recline, that will probably work well. Either inside or outside is fine. Some people prefer to sit cross-legged on the floor, perhaps on a pillow. Others prefer to sit erect in a chair or recline in a lounge chair or on a sofa. Most important is to be comfortable in a place that you like, but not quite so comfortable that you fall asleep.

You may want some very soft background music. Music can help you ease away from the mental, verbal chatter that pulls your focus away from the integrated state. If you use music, choose something that does not have words, because words can draw your attention away from the intuitive, back into the verbal. Once you are set up, start the music and sit or lie down. If you are cross-legged or sitting up, lay your hands open on the floor or chair beside you or open on your knees or thighs, or lay one on the other in your lap in an open position. If you lie down, keep your head slightly inclined on a comfortable pillow. Keep your feet uncrossed and your hands open beside you. These open-hand and nonrestrictive body positions are important because they help you open to the process.

When you are comfortable (and the music is softly playing if you like), ask your rational mind to open to the wisdom of your intuitive mind. Ask your intuitive mind to welcome the whole mind and to show you whatever it will. This may feel odd at first, but go ahead and try it. Just say, "Intuitive mind (or inner self or preconscious mind), please help me know what you would have me know." Don't forget that although we are talking about the rational and intuitive as if they are separate entities, they are simply parts — different cognitive-processing systems — of your one mind. Shifting from the dominance of one part of your mind into a more balanced, integrated state to perform a specific task is not an affront to the normally dominant mode. It is dominant only because of the rational bias of our culture.

Now, find a spot on the wall or ceiling that is just above your line of sight so that your eyes (not your head) are looking up. Stare intently at it and take three full, deep breaths, allowing time to let each breath out slowly and fully. Continue to stare at the spot until your eyelids flutter or become heavy and begin to close naturally. You may experience a strong pull or a little nudge, but let your eyes close naturally when you are ready.

When your eyes are closed, begin to relax your body and mind. As you breathe slowly and deeply, think about your feet. Flex and tighten your toes and arches. Hold the flex for a few seconds and then release the flex. Do this as slowly as is comfortable. Visualize the muscles and cells in the part of your body that is relaxing. This process includes both your body and your rational mind in the process as you focus consciously on relaxing your muscles and limbs and visualizing that relaxation. Now, do the same with your ankles by first pointing your toes downward — hold and release. Then point your toes toward your head — hold and release. At each release, notice and visualize the feeling of relaxation and the release of tension and energy in that area.

As the visual, intuitive mind opens you may visualize this relaxation process as actual images of your body or the muscles and cells in your body — or you may visualize it as flowing colors or as anything else. The intuitive mind uses visual symbols to represent other things, so when we say *visualize*, do not try to be too literal or to understand this rationally.

Just relax and enjoy. Take what comes. Move up your body, tightening, holding, and releasing various groups of muscles: calves, knees, thighs, hips, abdomen, lower back, upper back, chest, biceps, elbows, forearms, wrists, hands and fingers, neck, jaw (open wide and hold, relax), eyes (first squinted and then opened wide, hold and relax), forehead, and top of head. *There is no right or wrong way to do this.* The point is to acknowledge your body, relax, and experience the flow of energy and any visualizations that occur. This will ease tension in your rational mind, helping it integrate into the visualization process as you name and organize various parts of your body (the rational mind loves to name and organize things). As you work your way up your body, tensing and releasing muscle groups, notice how you can feel the couch or chair or floor supporting you. Allow your body to sink fully into that support so you can release pent-up energy and feel the surge of new energy flowing through you as you move into a deeper state of relaxation.

Also notice your breathing. As you become more relaxed, your breathing will become smoother and more regular, though it may not be as deep. As you finish relaxing your body, gently shift your attention to your breath. Feel the breath come into your nose, down into your lungs. Feel your chest and abdomen rise and imagine the fresh life your breath draws into you. Feel your lungs full of breath and life. Notice how your abdomen and diaphragm contract to release the breath. Feel your breath as it leaves through your mouth and joins the air that surrounds you, carrying into your surroundings breath and life that, just moments before, was inside your body. Envision bringing breath from the universe into your body to become part of you. Focus on your breathing. Let all else fade into the background with your consciousness. As words or concerns about the day move into your awareness, do not fight them. Just notice them and refocus on your breath.

Sometimes this process is difficult at first because the rational mind is used to using words to be in control by consciously describing and categorizing your experiences. With practice, however, the process will become easier. You will develop your own way of letting the words flow by without interrupting your more visual intuitive state. If you still experience resistance to trying this visualization process, you might remind your rational mind that it will have an opportunity to write down the meditation when you finish but that there will be nothing to write down if it keeps focusing on words now. We know this all seems silly to some of you. Just try it. Remember, the goal of omniphasism is to integrate your whole mind. Do not neglect any part of this process. The conscious decision to focus on your breath is quite rational as is the intention to return to that focus when you drift from it. In the final part of this exercise, you will get to use your rational mind to write about your experience. First, however, complete the visualization. Move deeper into the wordless, visual awareness of the intuitive.

Figure C1.4. Watercolor by Grant.

During this state you often will begin to see or imagine or daydream. You may drift in and out of this state. Do not try to control what you see or hear. You may go into a deep meditative state, you may remain just below the state of consciousness, or you may drift in and out of both. Simply notice what you see and imagine. If rational thoughts of daily concerns distract you, refocus your attention to your breath. Notice the images, scenes, colors, characters, animals, or whatever your intuitive, preconscious mind brings forth. Do not feel you have to remember what happens. You will automatically remember what you need.

You will know when you are ready to return to a fully conscious state. When you are ready, give yourself a little while to exit the deep state. Move your limbs slowly and stretch before opening your eyes. Sit up or move slowly and give your body time to readjust to gravity and balance. You may feel reflective and relaxed. Now is a good time to pick up your pad and drawing or writing instruments and record something of what you experienced. Put a date at the beginning. You may want to write about what you saw in your mind's eye or what you did or felt during the experience. You may want to draw or just doodle. If you don't remember much about your visualization, try picking up a drawing instrument and start to doodle or write down words, ideas, phrases, sentences, or stories that now flow naturally into your conscious mind.

Don't try to make something happen. Just let it happen. If nothing happens that makes sense or that appeals to you, then just write down what you did and what it was like. Describe your experience in as much detail as you can.

Whatever the case, don't judge your experience. This is a very personal experience, and no two are alike. What may seem silly and useless to you at the moment may be, at a later time, the core of something quite profound or meaningful. Remember that this is not a highly logical or linear process that works in a specific way. It often takes practice to understand the significance of a symbol or word or image. After using visualization techniques for more than 30 years, each of us has had a wide range of experiences. Sometimes one of us will finish a session feeling profoundly aware of something important to our lives. Other times we feel a little more relaxed. And sometimes we even feel somewhat frustrated because we have a heightened awareness that we're struggling with a personal issue. All effort to deepen your process of personal awareness is useful. Appreciate whatever level of experience you have. After all, it's you, right now.

When you finish writing about and drawing your meditation, give yourself a few more minutes to emerge fully from the intuitive state of mind. Stretch a bit more and move your limbs slowly. Do not drive or ride a bicycle or take on other complex tasks that require your full attention until you have acclimated.

Part II. Connect With Media

Next, relate the visualization to the mediated world. Look through books, magazines, or on the Internet or TV for an image that seems relevant to your visualization. Think about the image and why it draws your attention at this moment. What in the image reminds you of your visualization? Write a description of the connections between your experience and the media image.

Part III. Reflect On Your Experience

Now write a separate assessment of your overall visualization experience, including your experience with the media image. Explain what you did and experienced in such a way that friend will understand it. Note what worked or didn't work for you in this creative exercise. What did you learn? What might you do differently next time?

Summary

- Read the introduction and instructions carefully, all the way through.
- Spend time visualizing.
- Describe your experience on paper in images and words.
- Find a media image that relates to your visualization.
- Cite the source of the media image.
- Describe in words how the image relates to your meditation.
- Assess your overall experience.

Example #1 (Andrea Schneider): *Description of Visualization*

Figure C1.5. Word description and representation of visualized images, by Andrea Schneider.

The image I found was "Iceland," by Mark Kohlman, *Transworld Snowboarding*, March 2005:143. What first struck me about the image was the lighting. In my visualization light was significant and similar to that in the magazine photograph. The light I visualized, breaking through the trees and spilling out the cracked doors, possessed the same ambiguous golden glow as in the picture. The ambiance created by this light made it hard to determine the setting in my visualization, and the overcast sky and environment I saw appeared more like twilight than darkness created by cloud cover. I also felt a sense of tranquility and warmth during my meditation that is echoed by the warmth of morning light in the image I found. Also, the image of light coming through the trees reminded me of snowboarding in the morning and may have influenced my choice. My perception of the soaring bird matches the snowboarder flying through the morning sky. The snowboarder in the picture points toward the right with his right arm like the hand I visualized. The immediate similarities between both images resulted in my choosing this picture, but with closer consideration, my intuition played a large part, too.

Assessment

I experienced more success in this assignment than I had anticipated. I'm a very visually oriented person, and I feel I could reach an intuitive state dominated by images. My main challenge was eliminating verbally dominated thoughts, particularly current concerns. I also tended to put what I was imagining into words so I wouldn't forget. Ultimately, I did not feel it was necessary, and I did recall what I needed. I learned more than I had known about visualization methods and how they can bring forth subconscious thoughts. I was surprised how much my intuition influenced my image selection from the media. Once I examined the images for similarities I found several other than those that immediately struck me. I discovered that intentionally engaging in visualization could be a useful tool professionally in terms of ideation and breaking creative blocks. My best ideas usually do not surface while I sit at my desk. They come when I'm more relaxed and reflective as when I'm driving, in the shower, or falling asleep.

Example 2 (Cayla Campbell): *Description of Visualization*

I've actually been meditating on the same thing for quite a few days. Every night before I go to sleep, it keeps me awake and every morning I wake up way before the alarm goes off, just thinking.

For this meditation, I decided to try clearing my mind and letting it wander. I put on an Enya CD, lay down on the couch, and just started breathing slowly, like the instructions said. At first I stared at a spot on the ceiling. But then my eyes started to close. A fight with my boyfriend kept coming to my mind. I could see him looking so angry at me, and I had a hard time focusing on breathing deeply and trying to stay calm. I told myself to just "go with it" and see where my thoughts would go. I started thinking about past relationships and other arguments I've had with boyfriends and with my dad.

Then a realization came to me, sort of like a light turning on. I figured out that I had always made it through the tough times, even though the last one really hurt. I survived.

I suppose love is one of the torments of youth. It is a sweet torment, but troublesome nonetheless. Feelings and emotions begin to swell and build like a storm at sea. I've always thought of love as the deep, fathomless sea. It can be calm and beautiful, it can be passionate and stormy and it can swallow its victims into its bottomless depths. My love stories always start calm, but when emotions start to gather like dark clouds on the horizon, my vision becomes blurred. I can't find the way. Last time I nearly drowned in my blindness. Sometimes sinking into the numbing passion is easier than confronting the waves and fighting the sensations.

This time I was again tempted to ignore the storm, but I chose not to be blind. Although my feelings and emotions tossed and rocked me around, I searched for that light that I knew would guide me. Actually, the signals had been there the whole time. I had merely ignored them. You see, even if I am lost in the storm, He is watching for me. He is shining His light out like a beacon, waiting patiently for me to come home. God's light is like a lighthouse to me in times of storm.

At night amidst the raging waves of the sea, the darkness stretches endlessly. All I can see is the flashing glimmer in the distance. I have to rely on that light to guide me. It's called faith. Sometimes it's scary to trust the small light rather than rely on my own knowledge, but it's never failed me. Finally, the darkness and the storm give way to the light of the day. And I realize that even though I was scared and confused, He never was — He was in control. He had a plan, a path for me to follow. I know there will be more storms in my life, whether it be love, pain or hardship, but no mater how dark the night is and how high the waves loom above me, His lighthouse will guide me back to safety.

When I came out of the meditation, I saw myself in the ocean, reaching upward toward a bright light. So I drew a picture of that scene as best I could.

Media Image

My media image is a copy of a painting by Thomas Kinkade called "Clearing Storms." Many of his works have lots of light and color in them, which would be better represented if this copy were in color. He's called the "painter of light." This lighthouse stands out to me as a beacon in stormy times of life. I can see myself in the scene, maybe in a boat tossing and turning in the waves, trying to keep the boat away from the rocks. The lighthouse stands strong to guide me home safely.

Assessment

The meditation helped me focus on my fears in a way that turned out not so scary. They had really been bothering me. Letting me wander while also allowing myself to look for an answer to my problems helped me figure things out. I realized that I knew how to deal with my relationship problem, but I had not been wanting to admit it. I thought I was trapped. The meditation exercise freed me to acknowledge the problem and figure out a way to solve it. It also helped me realize that I'm a lot stronger than I thought and that I know what's good for me.

Figure C1.6. Drawing of visualization, by Cayla Campbell. Look for a media image that relates to Cayla's drawing.

CHAPTER TWO
Abu Rocks: Integrating Perceptual and Conceptual Realities

For a few moments, use your mind's eye to look inside of yourself, into your mind's imagination. In this world of fantasy, imagine an image of yourself as Abu, living in a time before time was known, before minutes and hours, before days and language existed. As Abu, you are an early human being. You roam the earth foraging for nuts and roots for sustenance. What you see with your eyes, feel with your skin, hear with your ears, smell with your nose, and taste with your mouth are the sources of the only reality that you know. You live, moment by moment, in a sensual reality of experience and perception.

All around you, the forest vibrates with life. Your senses are keen and you are aware of your environment and all that transpires around you. Even while you stoop to scoop water with your hand from the stream at your feet, all your other senses are intuitively aware of sounds and scents and movements that surround you. You peer into the stream and see the same boughs of the forest above you suspended in the water below you. You look up and see them above you and down again to see the white clouds floating above the trees now floating in the liquid sky at your feet. You have no verbal language and thus no names for these images. They are not trees or sky or clouds or water. You have no letters to represent sounds to describe them. You have no verbal thought process to compare the reality of the clouds in the sky with the reality of the reflection of the clouds in the water. The images below you are as real as those above you. All that you see and sense is vibrant and alive. Your intelligences are sensory and intuitive, and this critical perceptual intuition drives your actions.

As you kneel to sip water from the creek, your own reflection comes to meet you at the surface where your lips meet and you both drink. Your eyes focus through the reflection into the depth beyond, and you become entranced with the dance of waving fronds of water plants and darting fish. All the while, you

Figure 2.1. bang comics! impulse number one, by Erik Palmer.

are aware of the sounds and scents and the feel of the forest about you. You are acutely aware of all because at times not only are you the hunter but you also become the hunted. Bird wings flutter through the brush. Smaller animals shake the tree leaves. Behind you, something claws at the earth for bugs. You drink deeply. The wind ruffles the hair on your back. The same wind carries a scent, faint but certain and full of danger.

Suddenly, in a single motion, you rise from the water to face the wind and breathe deeply of its message. Others, downwind from you, catch the scent and do the same. In unison, without signal or sound, the clan begins to move together, through the trees, across the open meadow, and up into the high rocks and caves in the hills across the valley.

Here, in the safety of the high rocks, with your belly full, you lie back in the nook of a low branch and rest. Above the forest below and in the distance, you can see the white clouds darkening. You sniff the air and smell rain before it begins to fall. You shift for comfort, and the breeze and the play of sunlight through the leaves lull you near to sleep — more like a daydream trance. In your semiconscious dream state, you see the rain and you dream of the youth of your clan playing in the rain, and the red-clay mud left in puddles in front of the caves. They scoop up handfuls of mud and sling them at one another. They roll in the puddles and slap each other with hands full of clay, leaving momentary red handprints on each other's backs and stomachs. Though seen only in your mind's eye, your dream vision is as real to you as the waking.

A crack of thunder and flash of lightning startle you, pulling you from your dream. You slide from the branch as the first rain splatters cold against your cheek. Around you, darkness envelops the landscape, and you look up to see that the sky is dark as well. Rain drops heavily on your face and your lips. You close your eyes and open your mouth, licking the water as it falls and drips down your face.

Wiping the palm of your hand across your face, you turn and walk beneath the rock overhang, the entrance to your cave. You stoop and lean against the curved wall and watch the waterfall. Stretching an upturned hand from the cave, you let the rain fill your cupped palm so that you can drink. When the lightning strikes across the sky, you mimic its jagged path, tracing its pattern with your extended finger. Thunder rumbles long and loud close by, and you cover your ears with your hands.

As the rain slows, you follow its dripping patterns down from the sky to the earth. With outstretched arm reaching skyward and pattering fingers, one at a time, downward, your hand descends and then rises again to start over. You slow your mime with the slowing rain until a single finger follows one drip from the cave overhang to splash in the mud hole it has bored near your feet.

Slowly leaning forward on all fours, you watch the drops drip into the puddle, and rings move outward from the center to the edges of the basin. You slide your fingers into the cool water and down to the bottom where you can dig hard, sharp fingernails into the slippery, wet, red clay. Leaping across space and time in your mind's eye, you embrace an intuitive connection between the fantasy of your dream image of the children and the reality of the present moment. You pull a handful of clay from the basin and wipe three red finger marks across the back of your other wrist, just as the children did in your dream-trance.

Figure 2.2. Photogram by Bill Westheimer, 2001.

Enchanted, you roll over onto your back and hold the imprinted hand up against the sky, examining the finger marks. Insight traces new patterns in your mind, synthesizing thought, provoking relationships. Your heart races as excitement swells. You roll over, jam both hands deeply into the basin, and bring them up covered with red clay. A slap to each wrist leaves bright red finger impressions there, and open hand slaps to your chest imprint whole hand images on your torso. Beyond simple perception, increasingly conscious, discovery evolves into visual associations. Ecstatic at your discovery, you roll over and over on the wet ground, wallowing in the mud hole, covering yourself in the primal ooze before standing erect, stretching hands skyward, looking down to survey the handprints on your chest and falling to plunge your hands back into the paint pot. When you bring your hands upward this time, instead

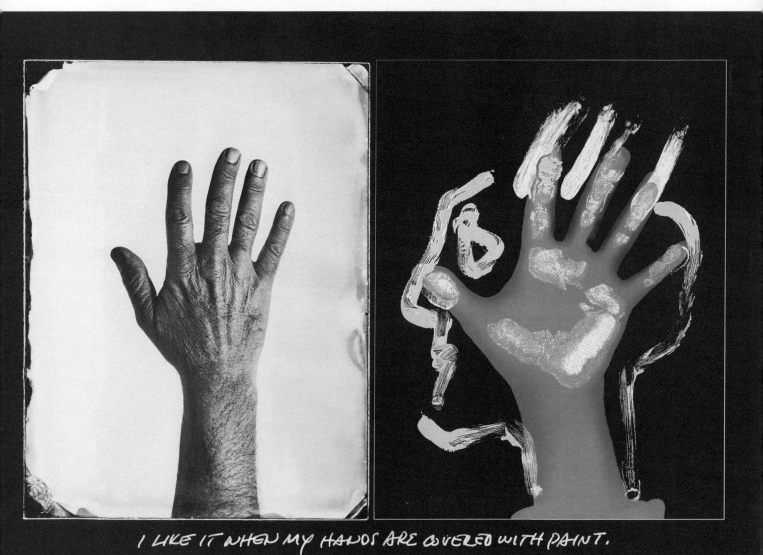

I LIKE IT WHEN MY HANDS ARE COVERED WITH PAINT.

Figure 2.3. Ian Summers, from Manual: The Personalities of Hands, *by Bill Westheimer, 2005.*

of slapping your muddy chest, you slap them repeatedly on the smooth rock surface of your cave wall, leaving multiple red prints of your own hand's image on the rock.

Staggering back, thrown by the power of the wall's message, falling to the ground on your back, breathing heavily of the wet air, you survey the wall. You blink your eyes in disbelief, looking from the handprint on the wall to your own hand. Back and forth you look, awestruck at the recognition of the symbol of your own hand, both attached to your arm and standing alone, of its own power, on the cave wall. You stand slowly and place your own hand on a hand on the wall. You look from one to the other and back again. You slap the wall hard and slap your chest with your hand, and then the wall, and then your chest. In an instantaneous synthesis of intuitive knowing into conceptual knowledge, in a conscious act of rational recognition, you know that you have extended yourself beyond yourself so that others can see that you have been even when you are no longer present. You have created art and a new form of communication by using one thing to represent another.

Of course the story of Abu is fiction, though it is fun to imagine that similar events actually happened. The intention of this story is to introduce us to the idea of a transformation in the experience of reality from intuitive perception to rational concept formation. This omniphasic experience integrated the intuitive process of Abu's dream with the rational concept of a physical symbol or hand-print as an external representation of the self on the cave wall. In this process, both intuitive and rational experiences are equally significant. Today, art and communication media use visual symbols in this way to help us share a sense of experiential, intuitive understanding and reality. Yet we hardly give the process — or what it means in our lives — a second thought.

Although visual symbols are a condensed representation of our experience of reality, and therefore limit or diminish the essence of the experience, they allow us to communicate a sense of shared reality, even if it is not identical to the sense of reality of the person or persons with whom we share it.

Where do the symbols that we use to define a common sense of reality originate? They come from our experiences, from our bodies and our minds. When we see, or hear, or feel, we often create an image in sight or sound that symbolizes our experience.

For instance, when Abu experiences the wind for the first time with newly developed rational abilities and wants to describe it to someone else, Abu might pass a hand quickly through the air or make the sound of the wind by blowing out between pursed lips, or draw a mud wind symbol as three wavy lines on a cave wall.

As Abu develops other symbols and agrees with others of the clan about what they mean, the members of the group continue to define their reality in external ways. They use the tools and concepts that are available to them — motion, sound, shaped objects, and visual symbols — to communicate. Consider that motion (bodily movement) and sound both have visual components. Through this scenario, Abu uses primarily intuitive expressions — bodily movement and gesture, sound, and visualization to represent rational, reasoned concepts. This is an omniphasic blend of intuitive and rational intelligences.

Over time, Abu's descendants expand their symbolic expressions into an intricate and sophisticated communication system that embraces an ever-expanding world of experience and cognitive development. They develop symbols that not only represent wind but also distinguish between a gentle breeze and a raging storm. They add rain (raining fingers), lightning (slashing hand), and thunder (cupped hands pounding ears) by expanding their intuitively based visual, aural, and gestured symbols. They draw in the air and the dirt with their fingers, and they expel air from their lungs to make sounds.

Later, with the discovery of mud and berry mixtures, they make paint to transform air and sound symbols into more permanent visual symbols on the walls of caves, on animal hides, and later on tree bark. Symbols of gesture, touch, drawing, and sound become the accepted signs of reality for their communication system.

Over thousands of years their descendants string together different sounds in logical, linear sequences to tell stories, developing the oral tradition. Sounds and representational objects evolve into systems of letterforms and numbers that can be logically arranged into a progression of concepts so that systems of communicating, counting, and recording history develop. Cave walls and hand-shaped objects give way to parchment, canvas, ink, paper, and the printing press. The experiences of communication as predominantly intuitive expressions of experience — through representational movement, sound, and sight — change to predominantly rational representations of experience through words. The primal intuitive nature of communication is transformed into derivative, rational, logo-centric and numerical, symbolic systems.

Even later, just as our ancestors did in the beginning, we bring the intuitive techniques of vision, sound, and gesture together as mass media books, television, newspapers, films, and computers.

As these mediated forms of our original, personal understandings of real experiences become more pervasive, the sense of reality that we share is defined, perhaps created, more by the persuasive techniques of modern mass communication than by our personal experiences.

The major areas of media in modern communication — print, radio, film, television, and computers — all are primarily intuitive and visual in the way that they communicate. Although radio initially is dependent on aural, verbal communication, it relies heavily on developing intuitive, interior mind images to achieve meaning.

Oddly enough, in this visual world the need to fully understand and develop intuitive, visual communication abilities is basically ignored in our schools,

Figure 2.4. Believe, by Bill Westheimer.

careers, and homes. Because the media are such pervasive and powerful influences in our lives, it is important that we begin to educate our intuitive, visual intelligences as equal and complementary processes to our rational intelligences. To do so not only develops defenses against the eloquent seductions of intuitive mass media messages but also lets us use our whole minds to shape and balance our lives and solve the problems of our growing global culture. In subsequent chapters, we discuss specific intuitive intelligences in detail. However, it is important to note now that our emphasis on visual intelligence as a primary intuitive intelligence is significant for several reasons. Our brains process more visual information than any other form of information. As we noted earlier, our mass media are predominately visual and highly intuitive. In addition, all of our rational and intuitive intelligences — visual, musical, bodily kinesthetic, psychological, mathematical, and linguistic — have strong visual components. Thus, centering our study of balanced cognition and intelligence on visualization provides the opportunity for the broadest comprehension and development of intelligence within a specific framework that is familiar.

With this in mind, we turn to one of the most basic forms of visual communication, the process of creating a personal symbol. As Abu integrated intuitive and rational intelligences to create an artistic and useful symbol, symbol making and drawing can be used to integrate and develop both your intuitive and rational abilities. Many of you have probably forgotten how to draw, or you may have even been embarrassed by your perceived inability to draw. You may believe you cannot draw. In chapters 3 and 4 we discuss how our rationally biased educational and cultural systems help create word- and number-based ways of knowing and communicating. The nearly exclusive use of these systems significantly diminishes your connection to your intuitive intelligences, including your drawing skills. You will also learn how to overcome these systems by accessing your integrated intelligences on deeper levels through symbol building and drawing techniques. Most students discover quickly that learning to use drawing techniques to integrate their natural, intuitive interests in line, shape, and tone with their rational interests in perspective, angles, and accuracy can help them access their integrated intelligences in new ways. After introducing you to these new concepts in personal symbol building and drawing, we move on in chapters 5 and 6 to explore research in cognitive science, psychology, education, and communication that supports the idea of rational and intuitive intelligences as complementary cognitive processes. We further define and explain the intuitive intelligences that you can develop and use to enrich your life.

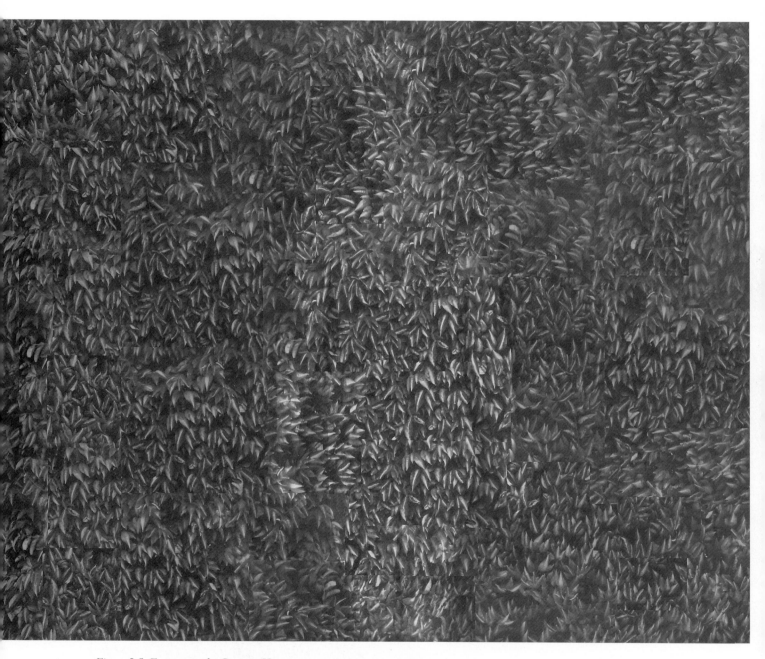

Figure 2.5. Emergence, by Germán Herrera.

An open mind is freedom

Figures C2.1-3. Students' personal symbolic portraits. Upper right by T. Adams.

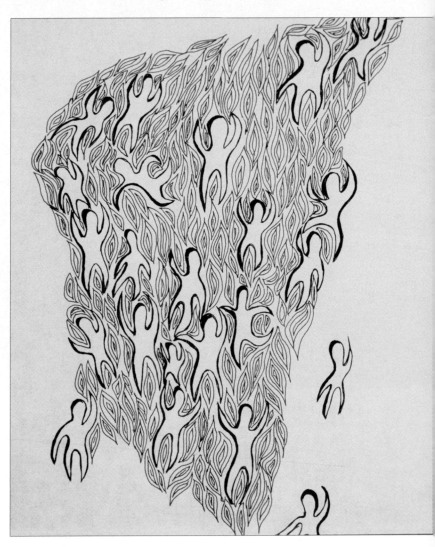

CREATIVE TWO
Visualizing a Personal Symbolic Portrait

The Goal: Creative Problem Solving

This creative exercise helps you learn to consciously integrate the intelligences of your whole mind as you create a symbolic portrait of yourself. Your rational mind communicates primarily through words and complex concepts, which it uses to organize and categorize different qualities that represent who you are. Your intuitive mind most often communicates through visual symbols, feelings, and metaphors that arise from your nonconscious memory to shape a sense of who you are.

Most of the time the integration of rational and intuitive intelligences is nonconscious and seamless. This exercise will help you understand that you can choose to use and integrate them consciously. By purposefully blending your rational and intuitive abilities to create a visual symbol that represents the whole of your being, you also will create a reminder that you live and think on more than one level. You will become more aware of how your various cognitive abilities can cooperate to create something new.

The Process

In the story that began the previous chapter, Abu does just this when he or she uses a dream to make a symbolic portrait that rationally represents Abu. The handprint on the cave wall is Abu's personal symbolic portrait. Read all of the instructions below before you begin to work on Creative 2 to discover and create your own personal symbolic portrait.

Describing Verbally

To begin this creative experience, sit down in a quiet place with pen and paper and think about yourself. Who are you? What things are important to you? What do you like and dislike about yourself, about others, about the world around you? What makes you happy or sad? What animals are you attracted

Figure C2.4. Personal symbol, by Crissy M.

to? How does nature fit into your life? As answers to these questions come to you, write them down in a list. Make the list as long as you want, but at least long enough to give you a strong idea about what things are important to you. Make different lists if you want. This is a linear process that stimulates and uses the rational mind to provide a concise description of yourself in words.

Go over the words several times in your mind. Add to the list or delete items if you wish. Review what you wrote down until you have a full, reasoned idea of what you are about. Write up the finished list. When you finish this very rational, linear process, put the list(s) away and plan an hour or so to begin working with the intuitive processes.

Two of the primary ways to actively access the intuitive mind are meditative visualization or active imagination and dreams. We discuss both briefly below. Each will help you integrate the logic of your verbal description with the images of your intuitive mind to search for your personal symbolic portrait.

Meditating/Visualizing

As you learned during Creative 1, meditative visualization often takes you to a place in your mind in which images communicate better than words. In Creative 2, we want you to look for a visual symbol, which may or may not include words but which represents your current sense of the whole of who you are. You have already made a word list that provides a reasonable description of who you think you are. Now, with that list in your memory, we want you to use the visualization process to help you develop a visual, symbolic self-portrait. If time has elapsed between making your list and starting the visualization process, just before you begin to visualize, spend a few minutes reviewing your list. Then put it away and start the visualization.

Reread the description of the visualization process in Creative 1 completely before you start. Remember that there is no right or wrong way to do this. Adapt our instructions as you need or want to so that the visualization process works for you.

When you are comfortable (and music is softly playing if you like), ask your integrated mind to help you develop a personal symbol. This may still feel a little odd at first, but give it a try. Just say to yourself, "Integrated mind (or inner self or nonconscious mind), please help me know what my personal symbol is." As before, find a spot above your sight line and stare intently at it until your eyelids begin to close naturally. Let them close slowly. Breathe very deeply three or four times, slowing inhaling and then slowly exhaling. Remember the process. Relax your body and mind. Begin at your feet and flex (curl) your toes and arches. Hold the flex for a few seconds and then release the flex. Work your way up your body tightening, holding and releasing the various groups of muscles. Focus your attention on your breath. Feel the breath come in through your nose, into your lungs, enlarging your chest and abdomen, filling you with fresh life. Follow your breath as it leaves your body and joins the air in the room, carrying breath into the universe that, just moments before, was part of your body. Then bring breath from the universe into your body again to become part of you. Focus on your breath. Let all else fade into the background of your consciousness. As words or concerns about the day move into consciousness, do not fight them. Just notice them and refocus on your breath.

You may drift in and out of awareness. Remember that you do not need to control what you see or imagine. Simply notice what is in your mind. Do not try to find your personal symbol, simply let it find you. You may or may not know what it is when you return to consciousness.

When you are ready, return to full consciousness. Remember to give yourself a little time to shift out of the meditative state by moving your limbs slowly and taking a deep, conscious breath. Readjust to gravity and the feeling of balancing your body in connection with the floor. Now pick up your pad and drawing instruments, regardless of whether you are aware of a personal symbol. If you have a sense of your symbol, go draw it or make sketches of it. New ideas may come to you as you draw, so it's fine to start over on a clean sheet of paper and refine it. It is okay to draw the symbol again and again. It is fine to change the symbol and try different interpretations until one seems just right. If you draw a symbol or several symbols and are not sure which is best, just stop and wait awhile, and then look at your drawings later. One probably will seem most appropriate to you, or you may have a new idea that works better.

If you don't yet have a symbol, try writing down what you recall of your meditation. That will often generate an idea. If you don't

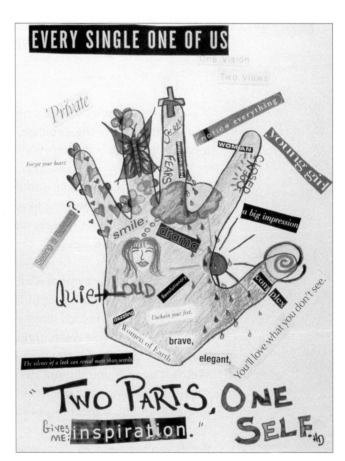

Figure C2.5. Personal Symbol, by A. D.

Figure C2.6. Personal Symbol,
by Jaci Sonnenburg.

remember much about your meditation, try just picking up a drawing instrument and starting to doodle or write words or phrases or stories that flow naturally into your mind. Don't force it. Just let it happen. If nothing happens that makes sense or that appeals to you, then put the paper or pad away and move on. A symbol may come to you later, or you may find a symbol through the dream process below. Repeating this visualization process on another day also may help.

Whatever happens at this stage, try to accept it. Don't be discouraged, and try not to judge your effort or compare your work to someone else's. This process is unique to each person. Even people who have been doing visualizations for many years have very different experiences each time they do it. The key to success, as with music, sports, or art, is practice. The more you practice, the more the process will work for you and seem natural to you. A symbol can come to you at any time, and you can change it at any time.

Make notes about your experience visualizing in search of a personal symbol. Write a description of your experience.

Dreaming

If you already have created a personal symbol through meditation, go ahead and do this part of the exercise, also. You may find clarity about the meaning or look of the symbol through a dream.

When you go to bed, take another piece of paper and write a note to your integrative self. Say something like this: "Tonight I would like to dream about a personal symbol that represents me." That's it. Now put the paper and pen by your bed and go to sleep.

If you dream and a symbol idea comes up in your dream, try to wake up and write it down or sketch it right then. Immediately after dreaming is the best time to recall and record what you dreamed. If you are unable to record the idea then, when you wake in the morning, pick up that piece of paper and pen and, if you dreamed a clear symbol, draw it or make notes so you can draw or sketch it later. If you did not dream a clear symbol, write down whatever you dreamed. You may need to wake up a little early, because this is likely to take longer than you expect — perhaps 30 minutes or more.

If you can't remember what you dreamed, then just begin to write down whatever is in your mind. Often this process will generate information from a dream or the nonconscious mind, or even an idea for a personal symbol.

Sometimes an idea for a symbol will just pop into your mind later when you reread or think about your dream. Make notes about your experience searching for a personal symbol by dreaming. Write a description of your experience.

One More Try

If you did not get an idea from this process, then wait until you have another hour or so and sit down in a quiet place that you like. Again, ask your integrated mind to provide a personal symbol. Then do whatever you do to relax. Be patient. Visualize, meditate, daydream, listen to music, or drift off to sleep.

Some people are most creative while exercising or doing physical labor. One theoretical physicist actually digs ditches to help him think. The activity helps

Figure C2.7. Personal Symbol, by Patrick Healy.

integate the rational, conscious mind and the intuitive mind to enhance creativity. Write a description of your experience.

Finishing Your Symbol

It is important to be open to whatever comes to you. If you see or think of something that seems right, then follow that idea. If it is not clear, then just start working with it. Write, draw, or just doodle using the idea as inspiration. Generally an appropriate symbol will evolve. Remember, the intuitive mind does not work in a linear fashion. It is more likely that the idea for a personal symbol will just come to you at some time when you are not trying to think about it specifically.

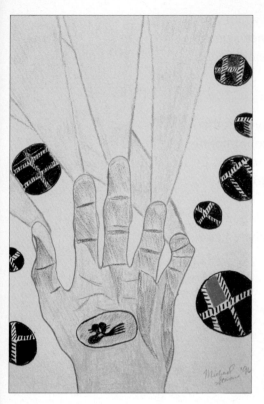

Figure C2.8 Personal Symbol, by Michael Stevens.

You might find it helpful to bring out crayons (yes — crayons!), markers, colored pencils, regular pencils, pens, watercolors and brush, or any other drawing tools that you like. Think of how you liked to draw when you were a child. It might be worth buying a new box of crayons and dumping them out on the table with a lot of blank paper. Nigel Holmes, who designs graphics for such publications as *Sports Illustrated* and *Newsweek*, advises people who feel intimidated by drawing to doodle on newsprint, paper sacks, or other scraps of paper. You can always transfer your design to good paper later, after you have worked intuitively on scratch paper. Remember, don't get uptight about creating this symbol. It does not have to be the perfect symbol that represents every phase of your being for the rest of your life. It is just a symbolic portrait of you at this time. You can change it any time you want or keep it for as long as you like. Once you have settled on a symbol, represent it as professionally as you can on a full sheet of paper.

Summary

- Read the instructions carefully.
- Plan to make notes and doodle as you work.
- Make a list of words.
- Spend time visualizing your personal symbol.
- If you discover a symbol during your meditation, draw it.
- Dream about a symbol.
- Write down your dream and draw the symbol.
- Visualize again, if you want to, or try other ways — such as exercising. dancing, or even taking a long shower — to access your intuitive mind.
- Create a final version of your symbol on a clean sheet of paper.
- Reflect on and assess your overall experience.

Figures C2.9. Personal Symbol, anonymous.

Figure 3.1. Carrie's Dance, by Rick Williams.

Williams and Newton

CHAPTER THREE
Art and Personal Development:
The Quest for Balance

Remember the last time you attended a class in art, creative writing, or music appreciation? How many classes have you taken since that have encouraged you and taught you to develop your intuitive intelligences and your creativity? How does this compare with the number of courses you have taken in grammar, math, science, and the social sciences?

We don't have to look very far into the organization of our educational system to find that rational bias dominates our learning. Even in the "creative" classes, you may be taught basic, linear techniques rather than techniques that engage the whole mind. Unless you are majoring in a creative field, you are seldom required to pursue intuitively centered activities that reach beyond basic understanding and technique into the realm of integrated cognition that generates aesthetically compelling expression. Too rarely are you encouraged to experiment and move outside of the rational model of knowing and learning. This is true not only in our educational system but also in our scientific, political, cultural, and economic systems as a whole. To see this rational bias at work, we need only explore the development, or lack of development, of our abilities to visualize, appreciate, or play music; meditate; dance; write creatively; act; sculpt; paint; or even draw.

Drawing is a primal skill that integrates intuitive intelligences, such as visual/spatial, psychological, and bodily kinesthetic, with rational intelligences, such as verbal and mathematical. In addition to artistic development, drawing assists understanding and representation of geometric relationships, angles and perspective, shadow and light, and spatial relationships.

As children, most of us spent hours living in the inventive world of drawing, delighting in our creations. As we saw in chapter 2 with Abu, drawing evolves from the intuitive perceptual process of seeing and feeling and is a primary component in the development and use of personality, relationships, verbal language, and intelligence in children. Because vision, drawing, and bodily kinesthetic (eye–hand coordination) abilities are such primary intuitive process-es, they provide an excellent means to learn more about and to further develop our intuitive intelligences. Because drawing also involves accurately interpret-ing the relationships of one line to another, the interplay of light and shadow, and conceptual ideas about how to use one symbol to represent something else, it can be used to help develop logical thinking and mathematical relation-ships as well. Drawing is omniphasic in that it blends highly intuitive cognitive and bodily processes with rational thinking processes toward a more fully inte-grated experience. The sort of cognitive integration that art education provides tends to be marginalized in our rationally biased educational and cultural processes.

That is why, if you are like most people, talking about learning to draw causes you to repeat the rational mantra, "But I can't draw." If you can't draw to your satisfaction, it is not because you can't draw but because you have not learned how to use your basic intuitive, visual, and perceptual skills and to integrate them with your rational abilities. It is likely that in your drawing efforts you have come to rely primarily on your simple, rational, schematic, childhood sys-tem of visual representation according to art scholar Viktor Lowenfeld. That is why you probably draw the slight variations of the same eye, nose, and mouth for every face you try to draw.

There are many reasons that you draw this way. Most adults do. Fortunately, this is not difficult to overcome, because learning the intuitive/rational integra-tion of skills that allow you to draw realistically requires no more than recogni-tion and practice. Let us look briefly at the way drawing generally develops in our culture so that we can see why so many adults draw the way they do — like young children — and find out what we can do to overcome that problem. If you already know how to draw, we still recommend you read this section and do the drawing exercises.

Art and the Integrated Individual

Artists, psychologists, and educational scholars have long recognized the sig-nificance of artistic expression and drawing to both the creative and psycho-logical development of individuals. In 1947, Viktor Lowenfeld, a pioneer in the creative and mental growth of children, wrote that "the double function of art in the elementary school classroom as self-expression and as a means of self-adjustment appears evident" (p. 4).

The 1940s and 1950s ushered in an explosion of research about the use of art as a critical educational tool in the development of the whole individual. Lowenfeld traced the artistic development of children and, based on scientist Jean Piaget's earlier work on the stages of childhood psychological develop-ment, linked artistic development to psychological development. Lowenfeld

Figure 3.2. Matt, age 4, painting and painted, by Julianne Newton.

stressed that successful artistic growth both parallels and contributes directly to healthy psychological growth and self-adjustment.

Other leaders in this field, including Florence Cane, Edward Hill, and Betty Lark-Horovitz, concurred and advanced art theory through the development of highly successful curricula and artistic methods in the public schools. However, their primary aim was not to create artists but rather to develop healthy, well-rounded individuals.

Florence Cane, director of art for the Counseling Centre for Gifted Children at New York University, produced a seminal work that forms the basis on which therapeutic art theories and practices are built. Her theoretical work preceded (and perhaps forecasted) the neuroscience and art education work of Bogen, Sperry, Edwards, LeDoux, and Damasio. However, her work grew out of educational, psychological, aesthetic, and intuitive perspectives, rather than from

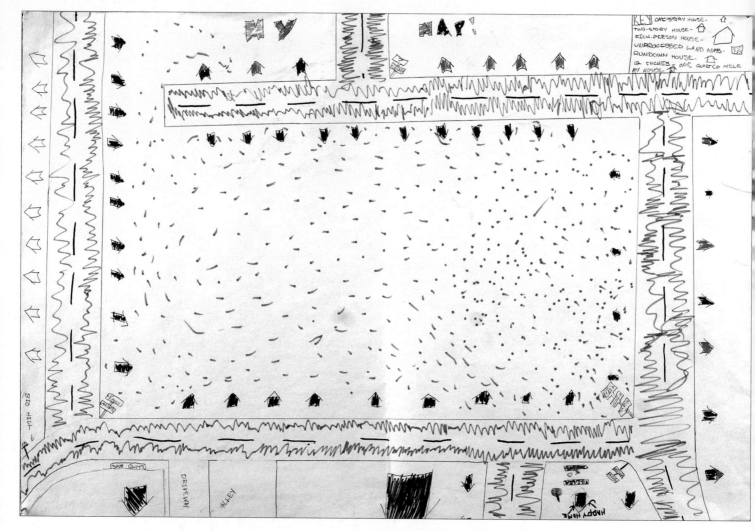

Figure 3.3. My Map, by Matt Newton, age 10.

neurobiological and cognitive perspectives. Her work prepared the ground for the principles of the omniphasic theory and the concept of balancing complementary cognitive modalities as rational and intuitive intelligences. Cane wrote:

> Nature and art have this in common — a form comes into existence by the union of two opposites. In nature, male and female create a new life. In art, two opposite states of being within the artist are needed to create form. The active and receptive states must alternate to produce and complete a work.
>
> The idea of consciously — rhythmically — alternating the process of giving out and taking in is so simple that it seems obvious, but few people make use of it. The tendency is to work to the point of fatigue at which nothing fresh can be contributed. If the student learns to proceed in rhythm, he will find a new energy, a fresh productivity; he will, in short, be following the law of nature. (p. 21-22)

Cane's methods supported her theory and enrich the omniphasic idea of integrated mind and balanced cognition rather than the dominance of one cognitive modality over another. She suggested that there are many ways that pairs of opposites balance each other in artistic and aesthetic practice, as in the way that "the relation between near and distant objects creates a tension which gives a sense of space; the play between dark and light builds form; the juxtaposition of warm and cold colours intensifies their values, the use of movement into, and out of, a picture establishes living form." Cane related these insights to the idea of a balanced, integrated mind by suggesting that "to be aware of the two simultaneously implies balance and understanding" (p. 24).

It is also clear that during this critical period Cane and other scholars were influenced by Swiss psychiatrist Carl Jung in their recognition of the significance of the interplay of the fantasies of the unconscious mind with the conscious mind to the psychological development of the individual. As Cane observed, art is "a means of activating all of one's functions; the simultaneous use of these functions assists in the integration of the personality" (p. 33). Cane echoed Jung, suggesting that too many teachers fail to recognize that "change, the transcendent function, lies buried in the unconscious and that only by coaxing it up through fantasy, play, rhythmic movement, and other indirect means can it be released for union with the conscious" (p. 35).s

Cane's thesis was later supported by Lark-Horovitz, Hilda Lewis, and Mark Luca who suggested, "The aim of art education is not the production of works of art but the unity of the entire growing personality. Learning is not the incorporation of something alien, something imposed on the child. It is an increase in his capacity to bring forth what is within him" (p. 4).

Cane boldly asserted that the basic aim of her method was not the creation of artists but rather "the development of the pupil's body, soul, and mind through art experience. Therefore, the method becomes a series of ways and exercises to awaken and train these essential parts of the child's being" (p. 37).

Edward Hill eloquently supported this transcendent idea in *The Language of Drawing:* "To empty one's mind of all thought and refill the void with a spirit greater than oneself is to extend the mind into a realm not accessible by conventional processes of reason" (p. 5). Lark-Horovitz et al. expressed a similar idea:

> The goal in teaching art to children is not to train artists but to offer experiences that contribute to the growth of the personality. Experience with art heightens his sensitivity to the physical world and leads to a greater appreciation of his environment. It helps him to give order to his sense impressions, and enlarges his capacity for enjoyment. It opens a way of expressing imagination and feeling. (p. 4)

Following Freud's and Jung's lead, these luminaries of art theory and method paved the way for the integration of dual cognitive modalities and artistic and personal development that has evolved since the early 1970s. Cognitive neuroscience continues to reveal more evidence of the significance of the integration of unconscious and conscious, intuitive and rational cognitive functions.

In the following passage Cane made clear the importance of integrating these processes to the development of the individual and to education in general:

> Art is of first importance in education, for the adult as well as for the child, because the problem of adjustment and the full realization of one's potentialities is fundamental in all education.
> We apprehend the world through three chief functions: movement, feeling, and thought. . . . An integrated individual is one who makes a well-balanced use of each of these three forms of activity. Art has three precepts, which must be followed if one is to obtain its fullest expression. There is a correspondence between these functions of the human being and the underlying principles of art. The function of movement is related to the principle of rhythm; feeling, to dynamics and harmony; and thought, to balance. Since the principles of art correspond to human functions, one may therefore gradually integrate functions through the practice of art. By this fortunate relation, the teaching of art can be a valuable method for the growth and integration of the individual. (p. 34)

It is significant, yet unfortunate, that these early concepts about the importance of art to the development of the whole mind and the whole individual have not been universally, or even minimally, integrated into our educational system. In fact, most adults today have little arts education and still draw as they did when they were adolescents — or even young children. Few have developed the skills to recognize and use the multiple intelligences we now know are available to whole-mind cognitive functioning. The centrality of art to education has been severely marginalized by the conventional "wisdom" in much of academia that anything that cannot be measured is to be distrusted.

Fortunately, new research and applied work in Integrated Arts Learning at Harvard and in Minneapolis, Chicago, and Tucson may be expanding this limited approach to pedagogy. Though it is early in the application process, this research suggests that proficiencies learned in the artistic process increase intelligence, creativity, problem solving, communication, and decision making in ways that also enrich performance across all disciplines and life processes (Rabkin & Redmond; Eisner).

Lowenfeld's stages of childhood artistic development may hold the key to understanding why most adults draw like children. They may also reveal something about the rational bias in our educational system and culture that explains why we are not taught to use our whole minds. Reviewing these stages of development will help you understand why learning to draw seems so difficult when, in fact, it is very simple and anyone can do it. Understanding these stages also helps you understand why learning to use your greater cognitive skills and creativity is so important and how drawing and other arts processes will help you do so. The following review draws primarily from Lowenfeld's work, though others, including Cane, Lark-Horovitz, and Kellogg also made significant contributions to understanding childhood artistic development and the significance of art in education.

The Stages of Artistic Development

> *Drawing comes naturally to the child. It begins with the discovery at about two or even earlier that certain substances leave marks on surfaces. The child has found a way to express himself. (Lark-Horovitz et al., 1967, p. 3)*

Children begin to draw when they are about 1 to 1-1/2 years old. A child usually begins holding a crayon or chalk in a clenched fist, making lines or dots or circles that look like random marks on the page. According to Lowenfeld, this initial scribbling stage is purely derivative of bodily kinesthetic movements with no thought process connecting the movement of arm and hand with the marks on the page. As this progresses, perhaps after about 6 months, the child will begin to recognize the causal relationship between the arm and hand movements. This is followed around age 3 or 4 with the first significant shift in the type of thinking the child employs. At about age 3 or 4, children learn the same thing that Abu learned: Drawn lines, circles, and dots suggest something else seen or perceived. This is a cognitive shift from purely intuitive, bodily kinesthetic thinking to a more rational, verbal, though still imaginative, thinking as the child begins to tell stories about and name parts of the scribbling. The scribbling becomes representative in the child's imagination and can be described with words even though the scribbles still do not look like the objects the child says they represent. Lowenfeld suggests that this significant shift in thinking from visual kinesthetic to visual verbal will become a dominant part of the individual's cognitive preferences, as most thinking from this point forward will be characterized by thinking in pictures that are described in words.

It is also around this time that picture books become a daily part of a child's life. In today's culture, this regularly occurs at an earlier age, as parents try to help their children get a step up on competitive educational pressures to read. In this stage, with the help of parents, children begin to expand their basic vocabulary. They look at the pictures and name not only the figures of boys and girls and dogs and cats but also their eyes and fingers and toes and noses.

This integration of pictures with words is significant in that it reinforces the development of the rational symbol system that later supports the development of the rational bias. Of course, integrating words and pictures is a useful exercise in the development of language and complex associations and is not an example of the rational bias itself. The bias develops as the pictures, drawings, and creative activities are marginalized in the learning experience, and words, symbols, and rational meaning are emphasized.

At some point, usually around the age of 4, children begin to develop the desire to expand the relationship between bodily kinesthetic drawing and visual representation. In this *preschematic* stage, the child explores many ways of visually representing the various objects or parts of objects that are important to them. At this stage, circles become heads, dots become eyes, and curved lines become mouths. Not long after this revelation, arms, hands, and feet are added, generally coming straight out of the circular head. But eventually the child loses the fascination with simple and multiple representations and begins to search for definite concepts to visually and verbally represent the important things in his or her visual environment. The child is working here to create a direct visual and verbal relationship between his or her drawings and reality.

As a child's world becomes more complex and her words and symbolic associations more sophisticated, usually around the age of 7, she moves from the preschematic to the *schematic* stage. She begins to add a body to the head and fingers and toes to the feet and to draw more complex faces. Lowenfeld suggests that after a long search for definite concepts of many elements in her environment, the child develops a highly individualized visual symbol for a person and for other visual elements of the environment. These "schema" are used anytime a particular object is called for. In other words, when the child is instructed to draw a man or a dog, the symbol will be the same regardless of what the object actually looks like.

Children also practice their art by drawing these schema, or symbols, over and over, just as they point to and name the same parts of the same pictures in the same picture books repeatedly. In these exercises, their art is slowly transforming from an expression of their primary intuitive, perceptual, and kinesthetic experiences to repetitive, rational learning experiences that develop simple visual symbols to represent objects and concepts from their environment. It is interesting to note that this parallels the evolution of language from visual to verbal discussed in the Abu story. This linear learning process is so pervasive that it influences our drawing into adulthood.

Because this process is directly related to the verbal naming of drawn objects, the repetition represents a distinct and primary process of the rational mind: to be able to recognize and name everything it sees. Still, there is nothing biased about this process of learning symbols as long as we are also taught and

Figure 3.4. "This is my brother. He is hiding in Sudan. He is not happy. . . . He wants to learn, to go to school, but he has nothing. Our school was burned."
Drawing by Nur, age 9, Darfur. Courtesy of Human Rights Watch, 2005. Drawing not only helps children develop balanced mental processing but also can help them express deep emotion and communicate memories and concerns.

encouraged to see and draw the immense variety of eyes, hands, feet, and even trees that exist beyond this limited set of symbols. If we are not taught this, then our ability to draw what is before our eyes is replaced with the singular ability to draw schema or symbols that look similar each time we draw them. The problem is that this system developed for organizational purposes, not for drawing. Because of this, its symbols are simple and seldom realistic or aesthetically pleasing to us as drawings. This transformation of complex, intuitive experience and knowledge into rational symbols is not a rapid process. It happens over many years as we are taught to draw within the lines of our coloring books, to write only within the conventions of grammar and composition, and to use only rational logic as the final judge of knowledge and merit.

It is important to again stress that learning the basic, rational techniques of visual and verbal expression is an essential part of our intellectual and psycho-

Figure 3.5. "I am looking at the sheep in the wadi [riverbed, or oasis]. I see Janjaweed coming — quickly, on horses and camels, with Kalashnikovs — shooting and yelling, 'kill the slaves, kill the blacks.' They killed many of the men with the animals. I saw people falling on the ground and bleeding. They chased after children. Some of us were taken, some we didn't see again. All our animals were taken: camels, cows, sheep, and goats. Then the planes came and bombed the village." Drawing by Abd Al-Rahman, 13, Darfur. This drawing and Figure 3.3 were collected by researchers, who asked Darfur children to draw while the researchers talked with their parents. According to Human Rights Watch, the children offered researchers "hundreds of drawings in the hope that the rest of the world would see their stories as described in their own unique visual vocabulary of war." The children received no instructions. Courtesy Human Rights Watch, 2005.

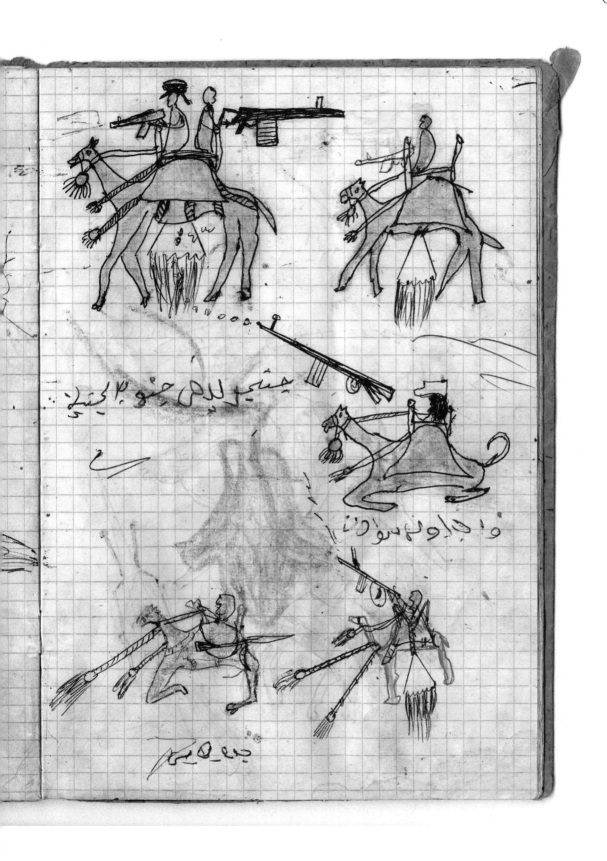

logical growth. In itself, this linear process does not represent the rational bias. However, these processes are only part of the learning process. Limiting our educational processes and cultural expressions to rational, linear techniques creates rational bias. In doing so, we deprive our culture and ourselves of holistic development of our intuitive intelligences and of our ability to transcend basic technique and to express ourselves with creative and aesthetic sophistication in drawing and in other problem-solving activities that require creative thinking.

The effect of this limitation of cognitive abilities is profound. It reaches far beyond art and limits our abilities to use our whole, creative mind to solve problems and to create things of significance to all people. But the limitation of drawing abilities is one of the first, most easily distinguishable and correctable forms of the rational bias. So, noting that this is not an argument *against* the development of *rational* education but an argument *for* including the development of *intuitive* intelligence toward an integrative cognitive model in our educational process, let us return to our discussion of childhood artistic development from Lowenfeld.

As the child's world becomes more complex, often in the fourth or fifth grade, the child begins to expand her drawings to include new expressions of her expanding perceptions. Some gender differences are noted. Traditionally, many girls draw flowers, hearts, and rainbows, whereas many boys draw cars, weird faces, and weapons. We don't yet know if these differences are the result of genetics or culture — or both. In other words, do parents and teachers draw flowers and hearts for little girls from infancy, so girls become inclined to draw such figures as they grow up, or has there always been something in little girls that makes them particularly interested in hearts and flowers? Here again, we see a strong emphasis on accuracy and realism. It is often during this stage that a natural sense of composition begins to give way to the emphasis on realism.

Between the ages of 9 and 11, children move into the stage of realism. By this age, children depend strongly on their schematic symbol system for drawing information. But these schema are merely symbolic with little means for depicting the details needed to realistically represent a subject. Although their symbol system has probably grown more sophisticated by this point, it is not developed enough to satisfy their growing desire to draw realistically. The complexity of a child's world and experience outstrips the young child's ability. Here, the child often tries to overcome the inability to draw realistically by substituting a large variety of details for realism. The child is drawing from concepts of object "schema" instead of from the visual perception of the object in front of them. Nearly all children's art scholars agree that this is the crucial point at which most children give up drawing altogether or continue drawing like children into adulthood.

Self-criticism at this age becomes severe. If the right direction is not given, the child may stop drawing altogether because of dissatisfaction with his or her efforts, Cane said. Caught between the desire to draw as a mature artist and the inability to do so, young teenagers tend to remain fixed on a plateau, the threshold of realism, according to Lark-Horovitz. It has been shown that the drawings of half of all adults are at the schematic level and can be compared to the schematic representations of 6- to 10-year-old children.

So, what is the "right direction" to which Cane referred that can offset the child's dissatisfaction by teaching her to draw realistically? How can an individual, whether child or adult, be taught not to substitute his rational, schematic symbol system for his natural, intuitive ability to draw what he perceives? The answer is to learn to use intuitive cognitive processes, such as visual and bodily kinesthetic intelligences, in concert with rational processes, such as conceptual thinking and exploring mathematical relationships. We have used this integrated, omniphasic process with more than 5,000 students, whose drawings

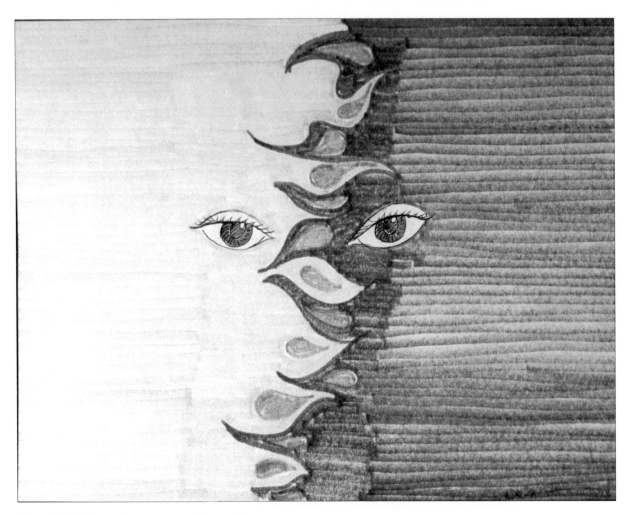

Figure 3.6. Self portrait, anonymous 18 year old.

became more realistic and whose drawing experiences became more enjoyable. Although drawing realistically was not the final goal of the exercises, learning to draw more realistically often gives adults more confidence about drawing in any form. Even more important is that our students also learned to "see" and to use their whole minds to create and interpret visual messages of all kinds — from classical art to video to theoretical models to better writing.

By now you may be getting the idea that the point of the creative exercises is to help you not only learn to visualize, draw, or write creatively but also, and perhaps more important, appreciate, develop, and nurture your intuitive intelligences as essential components of an integrated mind and a balanced sense of self. This is an area where practice perfects. The more you practice, the faster you learn. Each creative exercise builds on the previous one to help you better experience and recognize the nature of your intuitive and rational intelligences.

By practicing the drawing exercises in Creatives 3 to 6, you will learn to tap the immense potential of your whole mind to enhance your creativity and problem-solving abilities. It is likely that you will also discover that you can, in fact, draw what you see. Indeed, this is a major step toward developing the integrated intelligences required to understand and create today's media images and to successfully negotiate today's visual cultures.

Figure 3.7. An Artist, by Erling M., age 6, Kolbotn, Norway. Color pencil. Natural Child Gallery.

Figure 3.8. *Poppa Take Me to the Moon, by Megan A., age 7, Ontario, Canada. Watercolor and collage. Natural Child Gallery.*

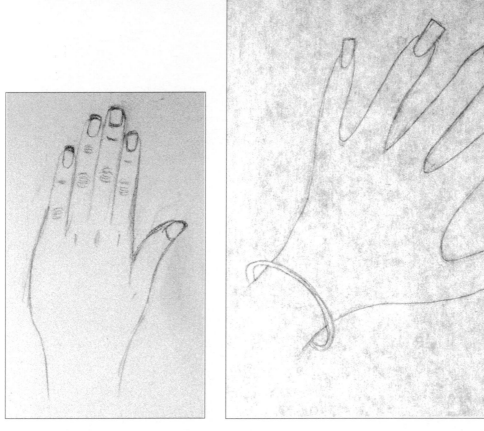

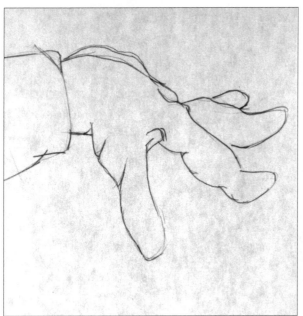

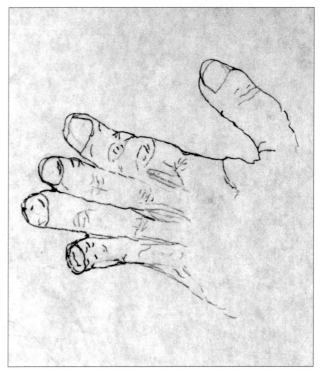

Figure C3.1-4. Examples of first drawings. Clockwise from top left: by Abel, Beason, Fowell, and Harrell.

CREATIVE THREE
The Perceptual to Conceptual Leap:
First Drawings

The Goal: Creative Decision Making

Abu made the leap toward integrating perceptual and conceptual cognition by learning the basic principle of representation and symbol making — that something painted or drawn can stand for something else. In Creative 3, you will integrate your own perceptual and conceptual abilities to learn to use drawing techniques to access deeper levels of your mind. This exercise is simple and will take about 1 to 2 hours. It can also be fun if you can set aside your rational judge and just draw the best that you can draw right now. One way to do that, and one of the most important components to successful drawing, is to go very slowly.

The goal is simply for you to make a record of your drawing skills so you can compare them to your skills after you have finished all of the drawing exercises. You will come back to these drawings later to see how much you have learned about the integrated mind and how it has affected your drawing in Creatives 4, 5, and 6.

You will make two drawings to the best of your present ability. Make each drawing on a clean piece of drawing paper using a No. 2 pencil or a medium drawing pencil. We suggest spending at least 30 minutes per drawing. Use a full sheet of paper for each one. You may do both drawings one after the other or do them at different times.

Do not worry if your drawings are not good enough to satisfy your inner critic. No one but you will judge how well you draw. However, do the best you can. Take the exercise seriously. No matter what your ability, this exercise is important for your development as a professional as well as for your personal development. It is important to your progress and needs to be done before you move on to the next chapter and creative exercise.

The Process

1. Read the instructions before you start drawing.
2. Spend time relaxing before you begin. Doing a visualization works well.
3. Now, draw a picture of your hand in any position that you want — the more complex the position, the better. Use a full sheet of paper for the drawing. Use a pencil to draw. Do not put your hand flat on the paper and trace it. After you begin drawing, do not move your hand or the position of your head. You need to look at your hand from the same angle throughout the drawing.
4. Draw a second picture of your hand in a different but complex position. Try to proceed at an even slower pace this time. Look carefully at the lines of your hand and the angles that are made as a finger bends, and transfer those lines and relationships to your paper just as your eye sees them.
5. Now, pause to look at your work. Do not be critical — that is not the purpose of this exercise. Just note the lines and shapes in your drawings.
6. Sign and date both drawings.
7. Reflect on and write an assessment of your experience.

Summary

- Read the instructions carefully.
- Spend time relaxing before you start.
- Make two drawings in pencil or ink, using a full sheet of paper for each.
- Ponder your drawings.
- Sign and date each drawing.
- Reflect on and write about your overall experience.

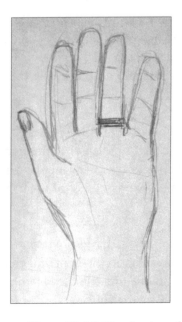 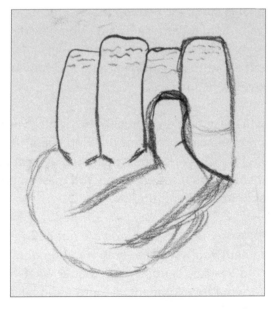

Figures C3.5-6. First drawings of hands. Above Left: By Almeida. Above Right: By Jackson.

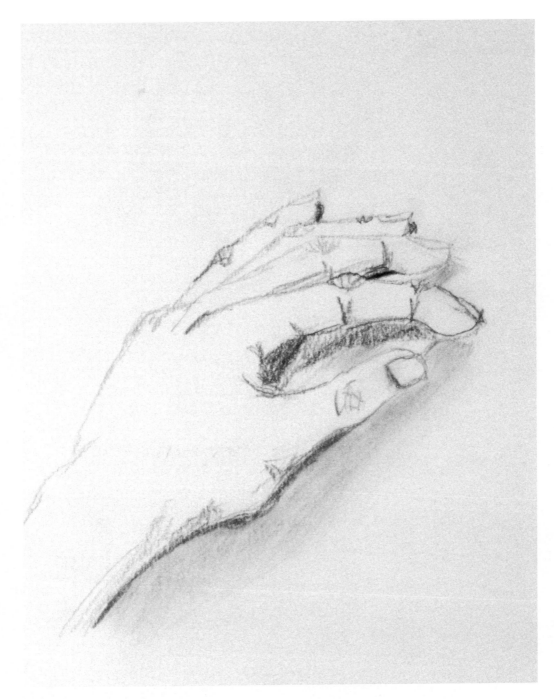

Figure C3.7. First drawing, artist unknown.

Figure 4.1. Mood Lifter, 2001, by Maggie Taylor. (Original in color)

Williams and Newton

CHAPTER FOUR
Overcoming Intuitive Illiteracy: Accessing Your Whole Mind

The impulse to draw is as natural as the impulse to talk.
Kimon Nicolaides (p. *xiii*)

From the earliest days of the Renaissance, the primary method used to teach students to draw was to copy directly from masterworks, both drawings and paintings. Vincent Van Gogh copied Rembrandt drawings of hands over and over until he had mastered them. Traditionally, repetition has helped students learn to "see" what is before them — to see as an artist sees, in great detail, with attention to line, light, and shadow; visual relationships; and emotional content. By focusing deeply and experiencing the character and feeling of each line and shape as if it exists independent of the rest of the composition, you can learn to draw what you perceive rather than rely on preconceived childhood schema or ideas.

Repetition Techniques and Perception

A number of repetitive techniques have developed since the Renaissance to achieve this artist's kind of "seeing." These include gesture drawing, segmented detail drawing, dot drawing, circle drawing, blind drawing, contour drawing, duplication exercises, differentiation exercises, vase-face drawing, mirror-imaging, and many more. Another technique that art teachers have used to teach seeing and composition is to turn the work upside down to get a fresh perspective of the elements within the frame. This technique helps the student move away from a literal, representative perspective and focus on the arrangement and juxtaposition of specific visual elements within the composition — such as line, form, relationship, direction, eye movement, and emotive qualities of line and shading.

As early as 1544, the camera obscura was used to pass light reflected from a subject through a pinhole into a darkened room and then project an upside-down image of the subject onto the wall opposite the pinhole. Originally, this

*Figure 4.2. Camera Obscura, 17th century. Note that the artist entered the camera obscura,
or dark room, through a hole in the floor. Images of external objects passed through small openings and
were projected upside down on the walls to use as drawing aids.
From "Ars Magna" by Athanasius Kircher (Amsterdam).
Oxford Science Archive, Oxford, Great Britain. HIP / Art Resource, NY.*

early camera was used to view solar eclipses and later was redesigned to be
used by artists to draw subjects realistically by tracing the upside-down images
as they were projected onto etched glass surfaces in portable versions of the
camera obscura. The same instrument was again adapted to take the earliest
photographs. With further adaptations and refinements, the view camera was
developed and used as the primary camera for photography for nearly 100
years. In this camera, the photographer focused and composed the upside-
down image on an etched glass plate under a large black hood.

Nicolaides adapted and integrated many of these historical drawing exercises
in his 1941 book, *The Natural Way to Draw*, which is still in print today. One of
the first statements that Nicolaides makes is, "The knowledge — what is to be
known about art — is common property" (p. *xiii*). Indeed, this is witnessed by
the plethora of art instruction in books and now on the web that use these
basic techniques to teach people to draw.

By the 1970s, researchers had shown that the two hemispheres of the
brain process information in different ways. Their work indicated that the
left brain is primarily verbal and that it processes information using analytical, linear cognitive processes. The right brain is primarily visual and

processes information using synthesistic, global cognitive processes. Further studies in cognitive neuroscience have confirmed that the brain processes information in two distinct ways (analytic and synthesistic) much as earlier researchers suggested, but that the hemispheres and cognitive processes are more integrated than originally thought. Our integrative theory of mind builds on this work but reframes it to focus on cognitive function as rational and intuitive rather than as right brain/left brain. We believe that drawing exercises help teach students to overcome their schematic symbol systems, as Cane suggested, and to focus on perceptual details that are important to draw-

Figure 4.3. Illustration of two children looking at a table camera obscura, taken from E. Atkinson's "Natural Philosophy," 19th century. Camera obscuras were known to the ancient Chinese and Greeks, and were used by Arab astronomers in the 10th century to observe the sun. Note that in this camera obscura, a reflex viewing system projects the image right side up. Science Museum, Science & Society Picture Library.

ing accurately and, perhaps more important, to authentic seeing and knowing. We also believe that the exercises work in ways similar to the repetition of a mantra in meditation, the rhythmic beating of a drum in dance, or the reiteration of kinesthetic movements in sports, to integrate and focus rational and intuitive cognitive processes rather than separating out the intuitive. We discuss this process further in creative 4.

Omniphasism suggests that drawing is a cognitively integrated process that uses rational intelligences, such as finding mathematical relationships and using verbal metaphor and abstractions, as equal and complementary processes to the visual, perceptual intuitive processes, such as seeing, eye–hand coordination, and focusing on and integrating independent details.

Through the visualization, drawing, and other exercises in this book, you are learning to integrate rational with intuitive processes toward whole-mind cognitive experience. As Hill and others suggested, our purpose is more about teaching you how to use complementary ways of knowing than about teaching visualization, drawing, creative writing, or dream interpretation (though each is useful in and of itself). The exercises are steps along the path toward cultivating a balanced mind with new, creative problem-solving and decision-making abilities that outperform more segmented, rationally biased models.

The drawing exercises combine traditional approaches of repetitive, mirror, and contour drawing techniques to help you transcend the habit of drawing schema and learn to see as an artist. If you practice, not only will you learn to integrate your rational and intuitive abilities intentionally but also you will learn to draw more realistically — if you choose to do so. Fortunately, many of the creative processes that educators such as Rubin, Nicolaides, and Simmons and Winer developed to help students learn drawing and graphic design have the added advantage of helping practitioners learn to recognize and integrate other abilities, including visual, physiological, mathematical, logical and abstract, and psychological intelligences.

You have already begun to learn how to access and appreciate your intuitive

Figure 4.4. Untitled, by Jan Halvorsen.

Figure 4.5. Jan's Sketchbook, by Jan Halvorsen.

intelligences. By practicing a few basic exercises, including some that have been used by artists for centuries, you can learn to recognize, use, and develop your intuitive abilities more effectively.

Because visual stimuli are processed primarily in the right hemisphere and visual cognition takes place before and without the need for reason, visual intelligence is a highly intuitive process. However, reason can be part of visual cognition. We can, for example, see the outline of a hand on a cave wall and rationally speculate about its meaning. We can see words on a page and use our rational knowledge to understand their meaning. Yet the original process of seeing the hand outline on the wall or the words on the page does not require a conscious reasoning process for you to derive knowledge from the seeing experience. One of the primary purposes of using particular fonts in print design is to impart visual meaning to the typeset words before and as you read the words and without conscious analysis of the underlying font structure. We discuss this in detail in chapter 13. Visual communicators and designers use colors, shapes, composition, shading, and other techniques to attract our intuitive responses before we can think about messages on a conscious level. In fact, a great deal of media communication is never processed by the conscious, rational mind. Yet the messages affect us emotionally and become part of the nonconscious memory system that guides our behavior.

Figure 4.6. School Children Pondering, by Julianne Newton.

Rational Bias and Visual Response

Further compounding the difficulty of learning to draw is the rational bias of educational systems and subsequent oppression of the intuitive ways of knowing in everyday life. The effect of the rational bias is that we most often use and value a certain kind of information processing — the conscious processing that is best expressed in words or numbers. Verbal and mathematical classification is the language of the dominant rational mind. Sometimes we sense other ways of knowing and become aware of the intuitive mind, which operates without words all the time. When we hear music and move spontaneously to the beat; when we see art and respond with delight or sorrow or inspired actions; when we catch a football or spike a volleyball or return a difficult tennis serve; when we drift off into daydreams or into the visuals stimulated by a good book; or when we drive from point A to point E without being aware of points B, C, and D, we are experiencing types of intuitive intelligence at work.

However, because of the rational bias of our culture, we do not generally understand these abilities as forms of intelligence. More often, we assume either that such experiences are the result of practice or that they are aberrations or experiences in which we have lost control. To some extent, this loss of control is accurate because, in these intuitive experiences, conscious processing does not dominate. Even when the rational mind is dominant, it is guided by intuitive cognitive processing. Yet, often when we become aware that the intuitive mind has guided a behavior, such as driving, instead of accepting the experience as one of knowing and understanding, our conscious, rational mind "assumes control" and warns us that we could have caused a serious wreck or missed an important part of a lecture as our thoughts drifted elsewhere. Many of our parents and teachers trained our rational minds with such well-intentioned verbal cues as, "Be sure to color within the lines," or "Think about what you're doing — stop daydreaming." Such skills are helpful to develop self-discipline. Yet coloring outside the lines and daydreaming can stimulate the creative thinking processes that help us make decisions in innovative ways.

Remember: We believe that the bias toward rational processing is a learned, cultural bias and that the natural state of cognition is a balanced integration of cognitive modes. Remember, too, that cognitive balance is dynamic, constantly shifting, and achieved when rational and intuitive intelligences are equally valued and developed. When we seek and achieve a dynamic balance as a regular part of life, we are best prepared to draw on the whole mind to solve problems.

The Second Nature of Consciousness

Practice and repetition certainly improve skills, but there is a point at which the skills become integrated into the whole, when we transcend technique and the skills become second nature. Notice the term *second nature* in the preceding sentence. Our *first nature* is our nonconscious, intuitive mind responding intelligently to stimuli. The stimulus might be a loud noise or something moving

Figure 4.7. Marion Jones (left) finishes just behind Gail Devers in the 100-meter dash in the 2004 Prefontaine Classic at the University of Oregon's Hayward Field. Photograph by Collin Andrew.

quickly toward us, or it might be a media image, music, or a human gesture. At those points, the intuitive mind responds more quickly than the rational mind by instantly telling the body to respond in the most appropriate manner.

Great artists, musicians, dancers, actors, athletes, other highly skilled individuals such as policemen, firemen, medical professionals — and even writers — also transcend the rational learning of technique when they soar into the realm of intuitive creativity, performance, or action. Within this realm people certainly use practiced techniques. However, we do not think about those techniques rationally as we improvise a musical arrangement, as poetry spontaneously flows from pens or lips, as we hit tennis balls moving toward us at 90 miles an hour, or as we throw out an arm to protect a child in an automobile. These are intuitive responses integrated with practiced technique in an omniphasic symphony of expression. This is the integrated mind. Most of you have undoubtedly experienced the feeling of "being on a roll" while writing, or "being in the

Figure 4.8. Dancing at Lane. Photograph by Rick WIlliams.

zone" while playing a sport, only to be dashed out of the "roll" or "zone" when you stopped to think consciously about what you were doing. Our goal is to help you learn to tap into those zones and balance your conscious and subconscious processing experiences through omniphasic practices.

Consider visual intelligence, for example. Most of us are born with the ability to see, and we do enhance visual communication by using it constantly. But we also can say that we are born with the ability to make sounds. We can even learn to speak other languages by spending time with other people who are speaking them. Yet children spend many years learning to recognize letters and their combinations as words. Children also have to learn to form the letters on paper in meaningful sequences. However, just as learning to read words does not necessarily mean someone fully understands what he is reading, learning to negotiate life visually does not mean we always understand what we see. It also does not mean we can effectively create, or write, visual messages.

We spend 18-plus years of our lives learning predominantly rational processes to the exclusion of our more intuitive abilities. We experience the loss constantly. We experience the loss of our intuitive intelligences in the boredom of classrooms where we memorize dates and data that have no evident relationship to our lives. We experience the loss in the dissatisfaction with our real lives in comparison with glamorized media images of freedom, independence, sex, and beauty. We experience the loss through imbalances of wealth and political power, through lack of concern for dwindling natural resources, through intolerance for cultural differences, and through violent oppression. We experience the loss through shallow relationships, disintegrating families, devaluing everyday labor, and in the very heart of our being.

The good news is that we can learn to bring balance to our lives by consciously choosing to cultivate our intuitive intelligences — and we can have fun in the process. The *synthesistic* nature of intuitive intelligences means they rapidly integrate many diverse pieces of information to make a new whole. We do not have to train them using the same laborious formats we use to learn such rational processes as grammar and spelling. Visualization, for example, is a global skill that uses one of the primary intuitive intelligences, visual intelligence, to synthesize information across space.

One way you can nurture your intuitive abilities and integrate them with your rational abilities in a very short time is to practice the drawing skills described in the next three creative exercises. Additionally, as you learn the basic components of drawing that help you integrate rational and intuitive intelligences, you can also improve your drawing skills dramatically. If you use them regularly, the basic component skills will become integrated into global skill and drawing will become automatic. Soon you will be able to draw the things that you see to the satisfaction of even your worst critic, which is most likely your own rational mind.

Figure 4.9. Music Instructor Ron Bertucci conducts the Lane Symphonic Band.
Photograph by Rick WIlliams.

It seems obvious that educating and using our whole minds would be advantageous — and it is. Learning to access intuitive intelligences and use them in sophisticated ways opens corridors to knowledge, helping us "break-set" from habitual approaches to problem solving and living. In the process, we learn to tap our creative potential. We also learn to understand how media messages influence our thinking and behavior. Advantages of developing our intuitive abilities include greater creativity, better problem-solving abilities, enhanced aesthetic abilities and appreciation, better communication skills, more balanced living, and more sophisticated understanding of influences on our own thinking and how we influence others.

As you enjoy the next three drawing exercises, remember that the main purpose is the same as the visualization and other exercises — to learn to recognize and use the power of your integrated mind. In chapters 5 and 6 we discuss the historic and contemporary science underlying the ideas of Omniphasism and Integrative Mind.

Williams and Newton

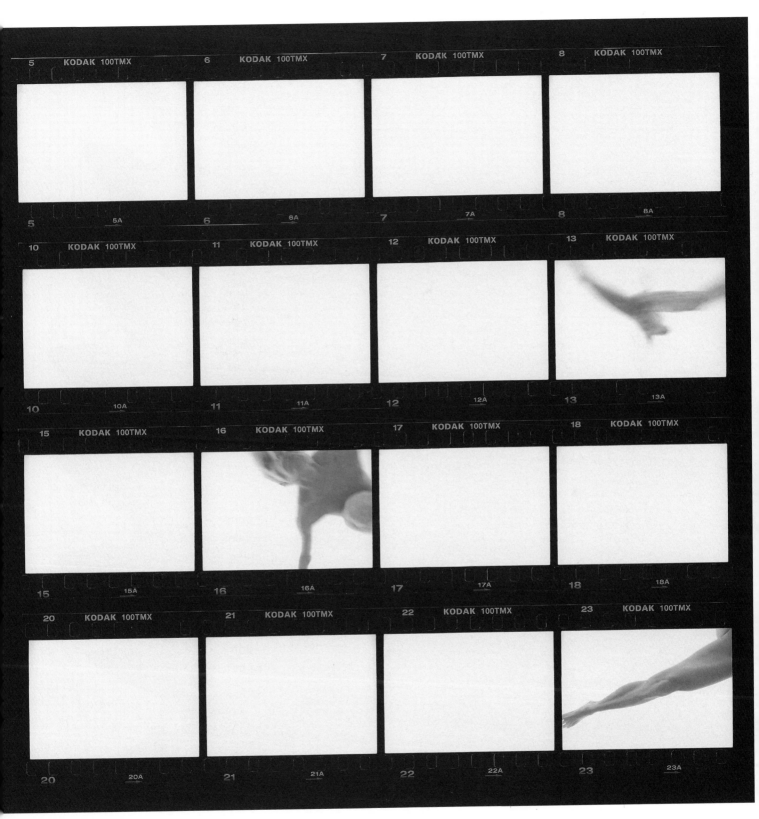

Figure 4.10. bang comics! nightwing number fifty three, by Erik Palmer.

Visual Communication: Integrating Media, Art, and Science   83

Figure C4.1. The Sawblade, by Rick Williams.

Williams and Newton

CREATIVE FOUR
The Yin/Yang of Drawing:
Drawing Contours, Not Features

The Goal: Integrating Ways of Seeing and Knowing

Before you continue reading, take a minute or two to draw an eye on a piece of paper without looking at an eye. Just draw from memory. No one is going to judge your work, so just draw an eye as you normally would.

Unless you are a practiced artist, the eye you have drawn is most likely an adaptation of your schema for an eye. As both Lowenfeld and Cane suggested a half century ago, the main impediment to drawing realistically for most of us is that when we try to draw a feature such as an eye or a hand or flower or butterfly we revert unconsciously to our schematic system of simple symbols for those subjects that we learned as children. When we revert to our automatic schema rather then seeing the individual character of each line that makes up a feature, we lose many of the important details that an artist needs to see and copy in order to make an accurate drawing.

For instance, many of us have a schematic for an eye that involves a complete circle inside of an oval. You've just doodled an eye. Now turn the page and look at the photograph of the eye in Figure C4.2. Notice that you cannot see the entire circle of the iris. On most people you cannot see the entire iris even if the eye is open wide. The schema we use to represent an eye works fine as a visual symbol but does not begin to represent the details of an actual eye.

Take a few minutes to look more closely at the photographed eye in order to see it as an artist sees it. While you are looking, notice the beautiful curved line of the upper lid where its edge (or *contour*) appears to touch and follow the curve of the eyeball below. Notice how the lashes make the edge a dark and wide or heavy line at times. Slowly follow that curve with your vision. The line starts near the nose, curves upward in a long arch, and then slopes gently downward. The left arch is slightly longer than the right arch before it reaches

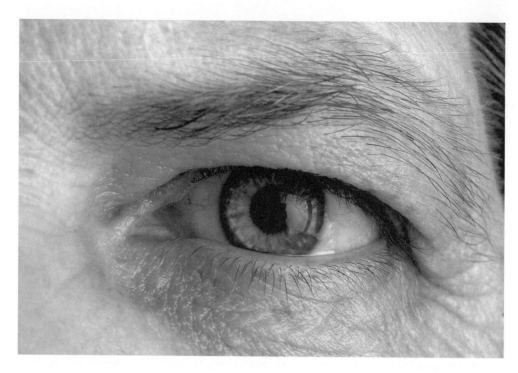

Figure C4.2. Rick's Eye, by Julianne Newton.

the middle of the iris. It slants more dramatically to the lower lid. Notice how close the line is to the black pupil of the eye and how large the pupil is. Notice the size of the pupil relative to the size of the iris. The size of the pupil is also a subtle clue to how bright the light is on the subject. Does the pupil sit in the middle of the iris or is it closer to one side and/or to the top? Is is wide open or closed?

Now look above the iris and notice the line made by the entire upper lid as it folds and rests just above the contour you just followed. The line of the upper lid is longer and reaches closer to the nose than the lower line. Follow this second line slowly with your artist's vision from one end to the other. Did you notice that it is thicker in some places than in others. Look at the distance between the upper and lower lines. Are they equidistant from one another all the way across?

Now look at the edge of the lowest lid beneath the eye. Notice how it intersects with the upper lid that you have been following in the preceding paragraphs. Again notice the slope and length and character of the line as you follow it slowly with your own vision. How far is this line from the bottom of the pupil compared to how far the upper line is from the top of the pupil? This distance will help you define the arch of the bottom line, which you can see is different from the arch of the top line. Look carefully at the point where the upper and lower lines meet near the edge of the nose. Notice the angle that is created by their separation and consider how wide or narrow that angle is. Look at the same corner on the other side of the eye. Is the angle the same?

Now look at the corners again. Do you see the tiny flap of skin on the inside of the left corner? Notice how that little flap helps give the impression that the eyeball is behind that skin and the lid. Notice also all of the tiny lines that come out of the corners and onto the face and notice the other lines above and below the eye that tell you something about the person's age and the condition of his skin.

You have probably just spent more time seeing and understanding the physical appearance of an eye than you have ever done before. This is the way an artist sees any subject as they draw it. In doing so you have used your integrated intelligences to experience and understand the dynamics of the eye in ways that are far more complex and meaningful than a simple schematic under-standing. You used mathematical intelligence to compare line lengths, direc-tion, angles of rise, and intersection with other lines. You used your linguistic intelligence to describe and understand these relationships to yourself and to develop a sense of the feeling and character of the eye and individual. You have used your intrapersonal and interpersonal intelligences to understand the emotions you feel when you look at another person's eyes, and you have used your visual intelligence to see and encode all of this meaning into your aware-ness and your unconscious memory.

Learning to see in this way not only will help you draw better but also will help you to consciously integrate your multiple intelligences, in turn making you more aware of the world around you and more engaged in life experiences. The process helps you understand life on more sophisticated levels and from multiple perspectives. Enhancing your visual perception also helps you be more creative and solve problems using you whole mind. By seeing the com-plex system of contours that make up a subject and by drawing those lines, you move beyond your early schematic system to a new vision of your world.

Before we move on to the drawing exercises that are specifically designed to help you learn more about the process of seeing and accurately drawing the lines of your subject instead of focusing on the subject's features, let's practice using an artist's view by studying one more subject that has been a standard for teaching contour drawing for centuries, the hand.

Look at the photograph of the hand in Figure C.3. As mentioned earlier, artists refer to an edge that defines part of a subject as a *contour*. Look at the contour that defines the bottom edge of the pointing finger in this photograph. Do you see the edge of the finger that separates it from the darker background? Just as you did with the eye, notice how that contour starts. Look at the wrinkles that the bend of the finger creates at the uppermost point of the finger. The shadow in between the folds creates a contour on either side as it moves upward into the hand. Notice the angle of that contour as it intersects the bot-tom of the finger. Now let your gaze move along the bottom contour down the

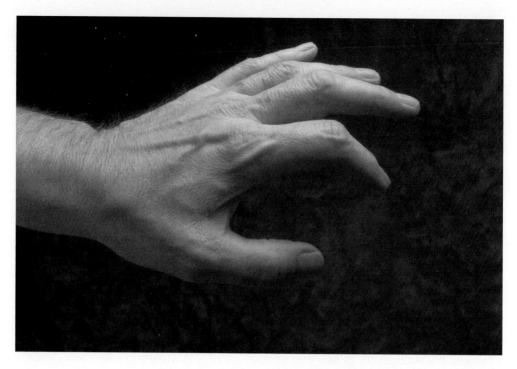

Figure C4.3. My hand, by Rick Williams.

finger. Do you see how that first contour arches and slopes slightly downward before it intersects the next vertical contour below the knuckle? It is not a straight line. This contour is really divided into sections of different lengths that move in different directions. Here again look at the angles created by bends in the contour. Notice how long each is compared to the other. These comparisons are one of the bases of proportion that will make your drawing realistic.

Now pull back and look at the dark background space between the bottom of the forefinger and top of the thumb. Focus on that space so that the hand goes out of focus. Look at the shape of that space and see the contour or edge it creates against the finger and thumb. To draw this part of the hand, you can either draw the contour of the finger and hand or you can draw the contour of the space. You will end up with the same contours either way.

Finally, move away from the photographic image and hold up your own hand in front of you in a similar pose. Follow the same contours on your own hand that you did on the image. But now, move your hand around and, one at a time, notice all the contours that make up your different fingers, your hand, and your wrist. Look at the veins and see the contour lines on either side of them. Look at the hairs as lines or contours. Look at the wrinkles in the knuckles and bends in the fingers. When you do this, you are translating the features of your hand into lines or contours. If you simply copy those lines *as you see them* without defining them as *finger* or *knuckle* or *fingernail*, you will move beyond your schematic system and learn to draw what you see — just as

Lowenfeld and Cane suggested more than sixty years ago before cognitive neuroscience became part of our understanding of the processes of seeing and drawing. More important, you will help bring your cognitive system into a balance of integrated mind that will serve you on many levels of your life.

But before you start trying to draw realistically, it is important that you take your new understanding of contours a step or two further so that you can truly understand the importance of the character of lines to drawing. The following exercises are designed to help you do just that. If you practice these two exercises and those that follow, the drawings you will make later will surprise and delight you. At least that has been true for thousands of people before you.

One final idea before you start the exercises. These two exercises focus on the character of lines or contours, not on representational accuracy of features. So relax and focus on seeing and copying the lines in your subjects. Do not judge the drawings. Again, just enjoy these exercises and do not worry about what the drawings look like. Learn to draw lines as you see them.

Part I. Drawing Contours

This exercise is as old as art schools. Nicolaides described this process in his 1941 book, *The Natural Way to Draw*, but it has been used for centuries by artists and art teachers to help students access their artistic vision and draw accurate contours. Notice we said draw *accurate contours*, not draw *accurate pictures*. The point is to focus on the *character of lines* and simply *copy* that character. The character of a line is its *length, angle, direction, thickness or thinness*, and *emotional impact*. That is all we are interested in because it is truly all that is needed to draw accurately.

Once you learn to see and draw contours accurately, we will teach you to put those contours together to create realistic interpretations of your subject. Do not skip or skimp on the practice of these exercises. You have been drawing in the schematic stage for many years, and you must learn to see and draw contours before you move on to realism, creative expression, and visual communication of concepts. As you draw, do notice how you feel. Look for that same integrated state of mind that you experienced in the meditation and visualization exercises — that enjoyable, engaged state of being in which all else seems to fade into the background.

You will need a pencil, a blank piece of paper at least the size of computer paper, and four short pieces of tape. The most important part of this exercise is to see and draw *slowly*. Each drawing should take you about 30 minutes. Before you begin drawing be sure to look at the examples in Figures 4.4-7. You will note that the drawings are not accurate representations of their subject's features, but are expressive and intriguing contours. That is what you are after.

Situate yourself at a comfortable table that is large enough for you to put the paper to the side of your dominant hand and your subject to the other side. When you draw in this exercise, you will look at the subject but never at the paper. When you are situated, tape the paper to the table so it will not move as you draw. Place your non-dominant hand in a comfortable position where you can easily see it but so that you cannot see the paper when you are looking at your hand. Arrange your hand in a fairly complex position so that your fingers overlap and bend somewhat.

Now look at your hand and find a contour that interests you. It can be a line along the edge of a finger or fingernail or a line on your hand. Pick a point on that line at which you want to start drawing.

Before you start drawing, focus on the point of a contour where you decided to start drawing. Move only your eyes along that contour and move them very slowly from one end of the contour to a natural ending point for that particular contour. This might be where the contour intersects another contour or where it curves to go in another direction. As you move your eyes slowly along the contour, pretend that your pencil is touching that point and moving along just as your eye moves. Repeat this on the same line several times. Notice the direction and thickness or thinness of the line, its smoothness or bumpiness, and where other lines intersect it.

When you have done this, look at the paper and pick the place where you think your chosen contour should begin if you are going to draw your whole hand on the paper. Place your pencil on this point and keep it there as you shift your eyes back to your chosen contour. *Do not look at the paper again* until you have drawn your entire hand by moving from contour to contour.

Focus again on your chosen contour. This time, as you begin to move your eyes along that same, familiar line, move your pencil along the paper as if it is following the same line, at the same pace as your eyes. When you come to the end of the contour, *do not pick up your pencil and do not look at the paper.* Move your eyes to an adjacent contour and then, without looking at the paper, move your pencil to the point where you think that contour should begin. In the same slow way, begin to move your eyes slowly along the new contour and move your pencil as your eyes move. Imagine your pencil touching the edge of a contour just where your eyes are looking.

If you have trouble focusing on the line of a part of your finger or hand, try shifting your attention to the space behind, between, or around your finger or hand. Draw the contour of that space instead. This will direct your attention to something other than your hand, making the background the focus of your vision. This process makes use of *figure/ground* relationships, a phenomenon of visual perception. When you focus your attention on your hand, your hand is

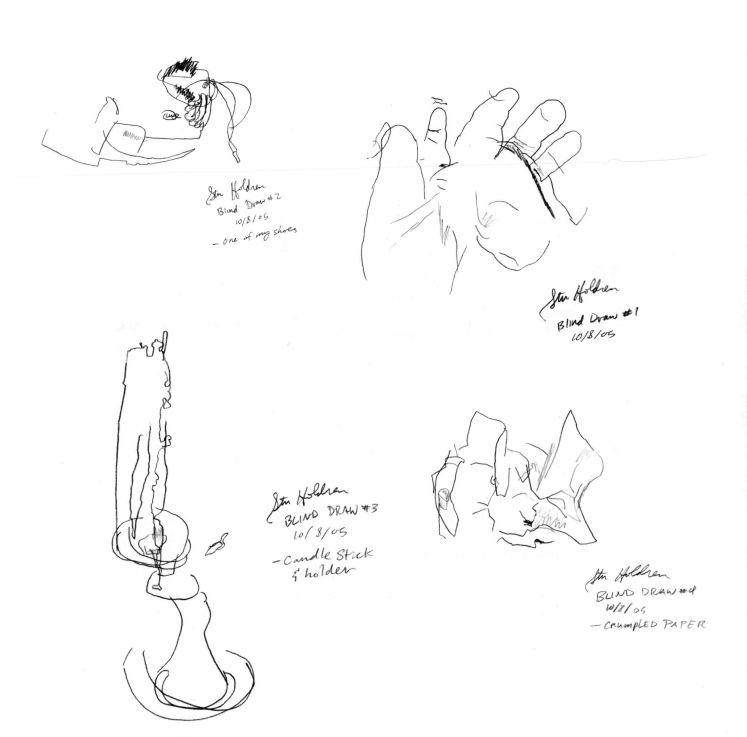

Figures C4.4-7. Clockwise from top left:
One of my shoes, Blind Drawing #1, Crumpled Paper, Candle Stick & holder, by Stu Holdren, 2005.

Figure C4.8. High-contrast detail of "The Sawblade," shown in Figure C4.1, accentuating figure/ground relationships. Focus alternately on a white space and then on the black pattern, bringing one forward in your vision and using the other as background. Note the shifts your eyes make as they move from one space to the other.

the *figure* and the space behind it is the *ground.* When you focus your vision on the space behind your hand, you are reversing the visual relationships so that the space becomes the figure and your hand becomes the ground. You cannot focus on both figure and ground at the same time, but you can reverse your visual focus on one or the other. Concentrating on what you originally perceived as ground can help you focus on contours.

The same principle applies to perception of Figure C4.1, "The Sawblade." You alternately perceive the forms of the jagged blade's shadow as figure or you perceive the blade itself as figure. The illustration in Figure C4.4 will help you define the figure/ground relationships of the Sawblade. We discuss more about relationships of figure/ground in chapter 11.

Whether your hand or the space is the focus of your vision, concentrate on the lines, moving from one contour to another until you have drawn all contours on your hand, including the ones on your fingers. Do not just draw the outline alone. You will probably have to fight your urge to look and see what you have done. Remember that the point here is not to draw an accurate representation of your hand but to *learn to look at and draw accurate contours.*

When you finish your drawing, look at it with an artist's eye to examine the contours. Compare a specific contour to the same contour on your hand, and see how closely you represented the character of that line. Is the line the same length, width, angle, and curve?

Take time to relax and do another contour drawing of something else — a crumpled piece of paper, a flower, a shoe, or anything you like that has complex contours that intersect each other. Each time, focus your attention on the lines only. That is the important subject in this exercise.

Part II. Practice

Part II is the same as Part I — except this time, as you draw two contour drawings of different objects of your choice, glance at your paper each time you move from one contour to the next. Use this glance to place your pencil in the correct position on the paper to start the new contour. Your focus is still on the contours and spaces of your subject, rather than on the paper, 90% of your drawing time. These images will look more like the subject than the one on which you did not look at the paper because of your alignment of each contour. This moves you more toward the drawing technique that most artists use.

Part III: The Yin and Yang Drawings

In order to practice the contour skills you just learned, draw three horizontal rectangles on a piece of paper in the same size and arrangement as the rectangles in Figures C9-11. Then draw the simple contours of the abstract figures in each of the rectangles in Figures C9-11, just as you see them. Be sure to focus on the contour around the space and take your time. Move your eyes slowly and move your pencil along with your eyes' movement as your eyes follows each contour. Remember that you can draw the positive or negative spaces. Shade in the dark areas with your pencil. You may glance at the paper as you draw. But focus primarily on the contours and spaces. Do this now.

Part IV. Completing the Circle.

When you have finished Part III, turn to page 98, but *not until you have finished the drawings* or you will spoil the effect. As you can see, each of the abstract drawings you just made is a section of the yin and yang horse logo created by graphic designer Maggie Macnab. Each rectangle you just drew is 1/3 of the entire drawing, and they were rearranged so the horses were not so obvious. In addition to practicing your new contour drawing skills, the point of this exercise is to illustrate that what you have learned about drawing contours instead of figures actually works. If you cut out your drawings and put them in the right order, they will complete the horse pattern even though you did not intend to draw two horses at all. In this same way, looking at your subject as an arrangement of lines that you copy onto paper will help you draw better.

Using your new contour drawing skills, draw a circle the same size as the one in Figure C4.12. Then copy all of the simple contours into the drawn circle to complete the entire design. If you have trouble focusing only on the contours in the area you are drawing, try covering the lower 2/3 of the circle with paper to isolate the lines as you drew them in the first part of the Yin/Yang drawing. Then you can slide down the cover sheet and draw the next section. The more you practice drawing contours in this way or in the contour exercises you did in Part 1, the better you will see and draw as an artist does.

Look again at Maggie's design in Figure C4.12. She derived the logo in part from the ancient *I Ching* symbol for yin/yang. Note that you cannot see both horses at the same time. Your eyes shift between figure and ground: either the white or the black horse will be outlined as figure against the background of the other.

When you finish, reflect on your work through all processes of this exercise and write an assessment of your experiences.

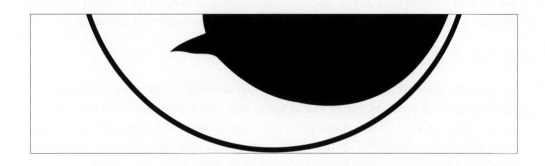

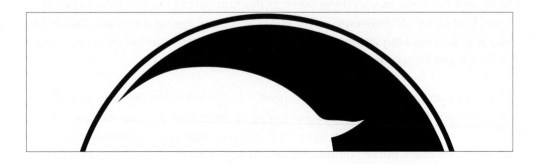

Figures C4.9-11. Yin/Yang drawing exercise

Summary

- Read the instructions carefully.
- Spend time relaxing before your start.

Part I. Drawing Contours

- Draw your hand, using a full sheet of blank paper for each drawing.
- Focus on contours and spaces. Do not look at the paper as you draw.
- Make as many contour drawings as it takes to become comfortable with the process — at least two.
- Sign and date each drawing.

Part II. Practice

- Follow the process as in Part I except draw different subjects and glance at the paper to position your pencil each time you move from one contour to another.
- Sign and date each drawing.
- Reflect on and write an assessment of your experiences completing parts I and II.

Part III. The Yin and Yang Drawings

- Use a full sheet of blank paper.
- Draw three rectangle about the size of those on p. 94.
- Draw the contours and spaces you see in each of the rectangles.
- Sign and date each drawing.

Part IV. Completing the Circle

- Use a full sheet of blank paper.
- Draw a large circle.
- Turn to page 98 of this book and look at the Arabian horse logo by Maggie Macnab.
- Draw the contours inside the circle.
- If you have trouble focusing on contours instead of features, cover part of the drawing with a clean piece of paper.
- Sign and date each drawing.

Reflection

- Reflect on and write an assessment of your experiences completing all the exercises.

Figure C4.12. Logo design for Maddoux-Wey Arabians, by Maggie Macnab.
To learn how Maggie created the design, look in chapter 11.

Figure C4.13. Grand Canyon from South Rim, Arizona, 1941, by Ansel Adams. Vintage print. Records of the National Park Service (79-AAF-8), National Archives and Records Administration. Adams composed most of his great landscapes upside down due to the viewing system of the large-format cameras he used. For fun, try studying the image upside down, looking for figure/ground relationships and contour lines. Then turn it right side up again and notice how your eyes shift to determine meaning patterns.

Figure 5.1. Sea Sprite, by Rick Williams.

CHAPTER FIVE

Ulysses in his Right Mind:
The Historical Intuitive Mind

*Until now, we have supported the fiction that adult roles
depend largely on the flowering of a single intelligence. In fact,
however, nearly every cultural role of any degree of sophistication requires a combination of intelligences.*

Gardner (1993, p. 26)

By now, we hope you have experienced enough of the excitement that comes with the intentional use of intuitive and integrated processes to have both a sense that they are real and a desire to learn more about them. If a part of you is still a bit skeptical, consider that quite normal. So far, we have primarily used stories and creative exercises to facilitate an introduction to the rational, intuitive, and integrative mind. In this chapter and the next, we present a rational, scientific argument to complement the intuitive processes you have experienced. A historical framework is a good place to begin to situate omniphasic theory within the larger context of communication, art, philosophy, psychology, neuroscience, and education.

Julian Jaynes: The Bicameral Mind and the Ancient Intuitive Mind

Evidence of the two major cognitive-processing systems of the human brain, operating in tandem but in separate and distinct ways, is recorded in written language as far back as 600–1000 BCE, the approximate time of the first written version of the *Iliad*. Psychologist Julian Jaynes theorized that people living in the era of the *Iliad* functioned as though human nature was split in two.

For the Myceneans, Jaynes proposed, this bicameral (two houses) mind operated so that one half seemed directly connected to a divine source (gods and goddesses), serving as the admonitory guide and director of all human activities. The other half was connected to the corporeal world, directed activities to carry out the guidance of the admonitory (divine) mind. Jaynes reasoned that

Figure 5.2. Odysseus and Circe, illustration from the Nuremberg Chronicle, a 15th-century book by Hartmann Schedel. Courtesy of Morse Library, Beloit College. Note that the names Odysseus and Ulysses refer to the same main character of Homer's Iliad and Odyssey.

this left humankind without conscious decision-making abilities. Because the gods directed all decisions, there was no need for conscious reflection about life.

Jaynes's other contribution with significant relevance to integrative mind theory is his assertion that the evolution of the rational, linear, conscious mind and the development of written language during the Greek Golden Age of Reason led to the origin of consciousness in humankind and, subsequently, to the demise of the bicameral mind. When humankind began to use reason for introspection, self-determination, and consciousness, rational thinking processes

Williams and Newton

began to take control over the divine (intuitive) mind. This initiated the development of a disabling bias against intuitive intelligences in society.

In his updated Afterword to the 1990 edition of *The Origin of Consciousness in the Breakdown of the Bicameral Mind,* Jaynes asserted that the results of research in asymmetrical hemispheric function (Bogen and Sperry's right/left-brain research), "even conservatively treated, are in agreement with what we might expect to find in the right hemisphere on the basis of the bicameral hypothesis" (pp. 455-456). He pointed out that the superior ability of the right hemisphere to process information in a synthesistic manner and in a way that uses spatial intelligence to add clarity to cognition is, indeed, the same synthesistic process in which the divine voice of the gods gave clarity of direction in the early bicameral mind. Jaynes further suggested a relationship between asymmetrical hemispheric function and the bicameral mind, stating that hemispheric specialization of the brain is the contemporary neurological model of the original bicameral mind.

We want to suggest a correlation between Jaynes's explanation and current neurological thought in which the reason-generated demise of the synthesistic–intuitive dominance in the 10th- to 6th-century BCE bicameral mind parallels the subjugation of the synthesistic, right-hemisphere processes to the logical, left-hemisphere processes described in the 20th-century research of Sperry and Bogen. This correlation provides a context for understanding our rational/intuitive cognitive model by placing the origin of a rational bias about 600–1000 BCE, the advent of the Greek Golden Age of Reason.

Figure 5.3. *School of Athens — detail of Plato and Aristotle, by Raphael (1483-1520). Notice that Plato, on the left, gestures toward the metaphysical, while Aristotle's gesture asserts the real. Location: Stanza della Segnatura, Stanze di Raffaello, Vatican Palace, Vatican State. Photo Credit: Scala / Art Resource, NY.*

Bogen and Sperry and Distinctive Cognitive Processing

To understand the significance of the Bogen and Sperry research to integrated mind theory, it is initially necessary to understand the basic structure of the human brain. The brain is physically divided into two major parts, the right and left hemispheres, which are connected by the *corpus callosum*, a structure that facilitates communication between the two hemispheres. When Bogen and Sperry began their research in the early 1960s, it was generally thought that the left hemisphere processed verbal information and the right hemisphere processed visual information and that this information was integrated by the corpus callosum. Until the late 1960s and early 1970s, the left hemisphere, the seat of language, which we link to linguistics, logical thinking, and reasoning, was considered to be the dominant or major hemisphere, and the right hemisphere was thought to be the subordinate or minor hemisphere, in terms of both complexity and function.

In the 1960s, Bogen performed a series of innovative neurosurgical procedures at the University of California at Los Angeles to sever the corpus callosum in patients suffering from incapacitating chronic epileptic seizures. After surgery, the patients' hemispheres continued to operate independently but did not communicate with each other. These individuals were the perfect "split-brain" subjects for Sperry and his student, Jerre Levy, at California Institute of Technology, to test their ideas about hemispheric specialization.

By administering a series of tests to these patients, Sperry and his colleagues were able to confirm their hypotheses that each hemisphere experiences reality in its own way and each has its own way of experiencing and processing information. He also discovered that the processes of the right hemisphere are as complex as the processes of the left hemisphere. Sperry was awarded the Nobel Prize in medicine for his groundbreaking work.

Most significant to integrative mind theory is the Bogen and Sperry characterization of the processes of the left brain

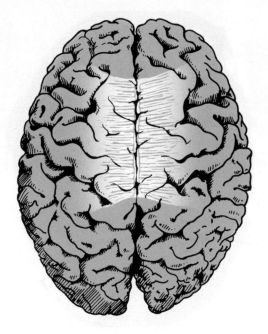

Figure 5.4. Brain from above showing left and right hemispheres. The connecting lines represent the corpus callosum, which actually is embedded within the two hemispheres. Illustration by Janet Halvorsen.

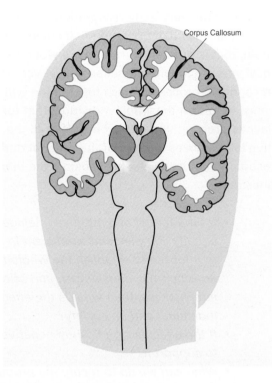

Corpus Callosum

Figure 5.5. Two hemispheres of the brain shown from the front, with the connecting corpus callosum. Illustration by Janet Halvorsen.

(rational) as verbal, analytical, logical, linear, and the processes of the right brain (intuitive) as synthesistic, global, perceptual, metaphorical, visual.

Jerre Levy, who worked and published with Sperry on the experiments, discovered that the mode of processing used by the right brain is rapid, complex, whole pattern, spatial and perceptual, and it is comparable in complexity to the left brain's verbal, analytical mode. Levy, in fact, suggested that the language of the left, logical hemisphere is inadequate for the rapid, complex synthesis achieved by the right hemisphere. Levy described the left hemisphere as analyzing over time and the right hemisphere as synthesizing over space.

In addition to these findings, Sperry's own comments on his research indicate that he clearly recognized both a societal and an educational bias against right-hemisphere processes, biases significant to integrative mind theory. Sperry wrote:

> The main theme to emerge . . . is that there appear to be two modes of thinking, verbal and nonverbal, represented rather separately in left and right hemispheres, respectively, and that our educational system, as well as science in general, tends to neglect the nonverbal form of intellect. What it comes down to is that modern society discriminates against the right hemisphere.

Although contemporary brain research has challenged Sperry's view of isolated left/right hemispherical specialization, it has upheld the concept of *distinct cognitive processes.* Integrative mind theory is concerned with the distinct processing systems originally associated with left and right hemispheres. As noted earlier, to transcend the issues related to left/right definition, we refer to the cognitive mode and processes that Sperry assigned to the left hemisphere as *rational* and the cognitive mode and processes he assigned to the right hemisphere as *intuitive.*

Thus, it is the very early recognition of a dual brain — half synthesistic, half analytical, each half operating in its own unique way to make up the whole brain, that is of interest in Jaynes's work. And it is the Bogen/Sperry idea of a local versus global, rational/analytical versus intuitive/synthesistic perspective in cognitive processes, each functioning with equal intelligence and significance to inform the whole individual that forms the correlation. Further, both Jaynes's recognition of the beginning of the demise of the synthesistic, intuitive intelligences in favor of the rational during the Age of Reason and Sperry's recognition of a societal bias against the intuitive processes suggest important questions:

- *If the rational and intuitive intelligences of the brain are equally complex and significant in their cognitive abilities to inform and establish the whole individual, and if there is an economic, educational, and scientific bias against intuitive intelligences, then what is the effect of this bias on the individual and on society?*
- *If the effect is significantly negative, why do we continue to support it?*
- *What can we do to rectify the problems generated by this bias?*

As individuals, we are equipped with minds that, as a society, we are half educating at best. We are leaving a major portion of our cognitive abilities out of the equation of cognition. We have created a culture that wonders (with our analytical/logical half-mind) why society is so out of balance, why we all seem to struggle — under the influence of a rapidly growing, quick-fix, self-help industry and a corporate agenda to substitute consumerism for self enlightenment — toward some rational solution that remains just out of our grasp.

We believe that the emptiness and longing that so many feel in their lives is directly derived, at least in part, from our half-headed educational and cultural systems that ignore the growth toward individual and cultural wholeness that educating the whole mind could provide. Perhaps the void many individuals experience and the many personal, cultural, economic, and scientific problems we face are in reality an inner recognition of the untapped potential of our intuitive intelligences and a suggestion of the possibility of a fully integrated mind to creatively solve problems in new ways that support a sustainable future.

Figure 5.6. Outside Contact, Applied Materials clean room, by Rick Williams.

Figure C5.1. Portrait I, by Janet Halvorsen, 2006.

CREATIVE FIVE
Drawing the Figure:
One Contour, One Space at a Time

*You cannot govern the creative impulse; all you can do is elimi-
nate obstacles and smooth the way for it.*

— Kimon Nicolaides

The Goal: Drawing What You See

By now you should have a strong sense of what the integrative state of mind
feels like in both meditation and drawing: that sense of deep awareness and
engagement as time passes without notice, words flow but mostly in the background or as a source of support, and you feel a sense of unity and purpose.
You also now can recognize and draw contours and negative space as you see
them. You have already seen, with the yin yang horses, how drawing contours
effectively represents your subject, even if you do not focus on what the subject is. Now you have an opportunity to draw a person realistically by drawing
the contours and spaces as you see them in a line drawing.

Part I. Pure Seeing

First, focus your mind on achieving a state of "pure seeing," a way of looking
at what is before you "for itself," as art theorist Donald Weismann believed (p.
20). Weissman distinguished three types of seeing. One is *operational seeing*,
which we use to get through everyday life without thinking much about the
process. Chances are you picked up this book and opened it without really
looking at the characteristics of the book — its paper, colors, size, thickness,
and so forth — in part because you have now become familiar with the book
as an object. You placed yourself somewhere — in a chair or couch in a quite
place perhaps — without realy seeing the chair or couch. Weismann's second
way of seeing is *associational seeing*, which is a key way we interpret meaning
from the information that enters our eyes. Looking at a photograph of your
lover, for example, triggers "a chain reaction of associations" (p. 20). You might
recall a kiss, an argument, a certain smile or laugh. In other words, looking at
the picture brings thoughts to consciousness and you begin to "see" and think

about more than is actually in the photograph. We talk more about this kind of seeing in chapter 12.

Right now, we want you to focus on practicing the third kind of seeing — *pure seeing*, stopping to consider what you are viewing just for the sake of noticing details with your eyes. Look at Figure C5.1, which opens this creative exercise. It was drawn by artist and instructor Janet Halversen, who created many of the illustrations in this book. Notice the variation of thin and thick edges, and the spaces and shapes created when lines intersect. Let your eyes wander over the image slowly. Notice the details of the woman's eye, lips, nose, and ear. Stop to see each line that forms those features. Notice how far the line goes from the top of her forehead at the hairline. See that the contour is the same length as the contour edge from her chin to the end of the neck line. See the space formed by the intersection of her hair, forearm, and bicep, and another space formed by her neck, upper arm, and forearm. See the large area of space made up by the contour of her back and the edges of the drawing. To draw the woman's back you can draw the contours of that big space. Look at the dark thickness of the line that forms the contour of her back and compare it to the thinner, broken contour that runs down the side of her bodice. Follow the contour of her hair line from the lower lobe of her ear to where it touches the bend of her elbow. Follow it very slowly and see how it is more than one line. It is a series of broken lines that start and stop and that parallel each other.

Part II. Drawing

Now it is time to draw this figure one contour or space at a time. Place the drawing on the table in front of you where you can see it easily. Place a clean sheet of paper next to the drawing so that you can comfortably see both and glance from one to the other. Take a moment to note and make a small light mark at the point where the top of the woman's head should be on your paper. Mark the spot where the contour of her back touches the left edge of the paper. Mark another spot where her right wrist should start and another where her right elbow should be. Each of these is the beginning of a contour line. Locating the general position of those lines in advance will help you keep the proportions of your drawing accurate. Now pick a contour you want to draw and find the spot on the paper where that line should begin. If you like, you can lay your pencil on its side and measure the distance from the edge; then transfer that to your drawing paper. Just as you did in your earlier contour exercises, look at the contour you are going to draw and imagine that your pencil is touching that line and moving along it as you eyes move along it. Move your eyes and your pencil slowly and copy that contour accurately. Now simply move from contour to contour, glancing at your paper for position but looking *mostly* at Jan's line drawing as you follow the lines with your eyes and pencil. Keep your focus on a small area, the contour you are drawing, and on its relationship to adjacent contours. If you have trouble staying focused on an area or seeing just the lines, try covering part of the whole drawing with two sheets of paper so the section you are working on is all you can see. Spend at least 30 minutes on this drawing. Then take time to enjoy your work and reflect on your experience. Sign it with your name and date it. Write an assessment of your experience and summarize your relections.

Before you finish this exercise, find another line drawing and draw it in the same way as you did the first one. There are a number in this book, and you can find many on-line under names like Picasso, Rembrandt, Van Gogh, Degas, and John Lennon. Cartoons make excellent drawing practice. Note the artist, sources, and other information about the drawing you use. Sign and date your drawing, and write about your experience.

Also, take a look at Figure C5.3. It is the same drawing you just studied first, except Jan added shading that implies light, shadow areas, and tones. Notice how much depth and feeling these simple shadings done with the side of the lead add to the feeling and dimension of the drawing.

Figure C5.2. Portrait II, by Janet Halvorsen, 2006.

Summary

Part I: Pure Seeing

- Put associations and concerns of the day aside, and just look at the line drawing that begins this exercise.
- Follow the contours — the lines and spaces in the drawing — with your eyes.

Part II: Drawing

- Read the instructions carefully.
- Spend time relaxing before you begin.
- Use a full, clean sheet of blank paper for each drawing.
- Make two complete drawings — one from the line drawing at the beginning of this exercise and a second one of your choice.
- Sign and date each drawing. On the back, include the full citation for the original artist, work title, and source.
- Reflect on and write an assessment of your experiences.

Figures C5.3-4. Above: Shaded version of Figure C5.1. Right: Portrait III, by Janet Halvorsen, 2006.

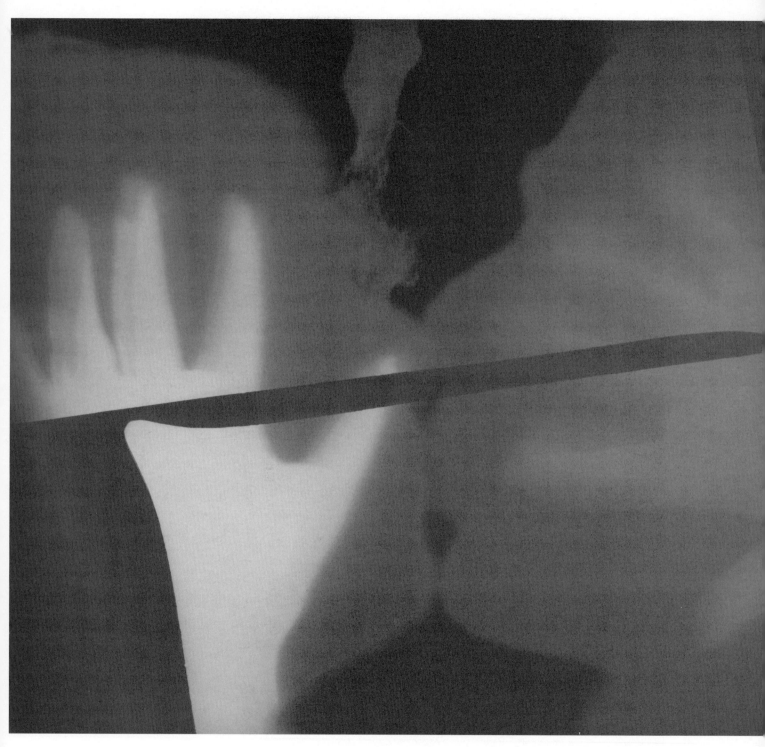

Figure 6.1. Rayograph, The Kiss, May Ray kissing Kiki de Montparnasse, hands face kiss, by Man Ray, 1922. Gelatin silver print (photogram). © 2006 Man Ray Trust, Artists Rights Society (ARS), NY / ADAGP / Paris; Digital Image © The Museum of Modern Art/Licensed by Scala / Art Resource, NY.

Williams and Newton

CHAPTER SIX
Multiple Intelligences and Nonconscious Biases: The Contemporary Intuitive Mind

The factual knowledge required for reasoning and decision making comes to the mind in the form of images.

Antonio Damasio (1994, p. 96)

Distinguishing the nature of the principal cognitive systems as either *rational* or *intuitive* organizes their respective processes as predominantly analytical or predominantly synthesistic. Rather than dichotomous, however, this distinction should suggest complementary interdependence through parallel and integrative processes. It is important to remember that even this approach is an overly simple way to distinguish the complex cognitive patterns of the human mind. Certainly, in terms of identifying specific locations, or in terms of mapping the interaction of rational and intuitive processes, a dual system of this nature cannot tell the whole story. However, this kind of organizing framework does facilitate discussion and comprehension if one thinks in terms of *both/and* — two kinds of processing operating together in synchrony and in complementary ways.

Howard Gardner: Multiple Intelligence Theory

Harvard Educational Psychologist Howard Gardner (1993) defined intelligence as "the ability to solve problems or fashion products that are of consequence in a particular cultural setting or community" (p. 15). He suggested that "except for abnormal individuals, intelligences always work in concert, and any sophisticated adult role will involve a melding of several of them" (p. 17). Gardner (1999) described eight independent intelligences and separated them into two distinct categories, those that are testable by logical, linguistic, and mathematical means (tests such as college entrance exams) and those that are not. Thus, Gardner used a parallel/dualistic organizational model and noted a strong cultural/educational bias against the development of those intelligences that are not testable by logical, linguistic instruments. There seems to be a clear parallel between the educational bias Gardner cited against nonlogical/

Table 4. Comparison of Integrative Mind and Gardner's Multiple Intelligences

Integrative Mind Model	Rational Intelligences	Intuitive Intelligences
Gardner's Multiple Intelligence Model	Logically Testable Int.	Non-Logically Testable Int.
	Linguistic	Spatial/Visual
	Logical/Mathematical	Musical
		Bodily Kinesthetic
		Intrapersonal
		Interpersonal
		Naturalist

nonlinguistic intelligences and the bias cited by Jaynes and Sperry against synthesistic cognitive processes. Gardner's linguistic and mathematical/logical intelligences correlate with the integrative mind definition of rational intelligence. Gardner's spatial, musical, bodily kinesthetic, intrapersonal, interpersonal, and naturalist intelligences correlate with the integrative mind definition of intuitive intelligence. Although Gardner's spatial intelligence does not fully incorporate the concept of visual intelligence, it may be seen as complementary to recent work by Barry and Williams. The work views visual intelligence not as a basic aptitude but rather as a functional process effectively utilizing both rational and intuitive systems in the brain to fully understand and respond to visual information.

The Nature of Holistic Processing

We use the term *intuitive intelligence* to include the six intelligences that Gardner defined as *nonlinearly/logically testable intelligences.* Because Gardner uses the term *intelligence* to refer to specific aptitudes, to avoid confusion, we note that intuitive intelligence also links to the cognitive models developed by Jaynes, Bogen/Sperry, and Damasio. We also use the term *intuitive intelligence* to suggest the kind of processing implied within dualistic cognitive models. To make the relationships clearer, Tables 5 through 10 show how each of the six intuitive intelligences relate to the communication processes of gathering and using information to solve problems and make decisions. Information in these tables is adapted, in part, from the work of Florida A&M University journalism professor Gerald Grow, who has developed ways to teach students who are predominantly visual thinkers how to improve their writing. Though these tables focus on communication, they also imply larger information-gathering processes. Each table defines one of Gardner's six intuitive intelligences, identifies visual components of each, describes how each aids the processes of gathering and using information, and identifies which creative exercises in this book help develop each intelligence. Though not all of the intuitive intelligences are specifically visual, all have significant visual components. The creative exercises in this book develop both your analytical/ rational and your synthesistic/intuitive abilities.

There can be no words without images.

Aristotle

Damasio: Non-Conscious Mind and Behavior

Working from a neurobiological perspective in his book *Descartes' Error*, cognitive neuroscientist Antonio Damasio pairs nonconscious emotion and rationality as complementary aspects of cognition. Damasio asserted that "even after reasoning strategies become established in the formative years, their effective deployment probably depends, to a considerable extent, on a continued ability to experience feelings . . . certain aspects of the process of emotion and feelings are indispensable for rationality" (pp. *xii-xiii*).

Recent experiments performed by Damasio and others at the Iowa College of Medicine present empirical evidence suggesting a causal relationship between

Figure 6.2. Moon Rise, by Rick Williams.

Table 5. Visual/Spatial Intelligence

Definition: Ability to know through visual observation and mental Imaging

Visual Components: Seeing, Drawing, Photography, Dreams, Media, Mind's Eye

How Visual Intelligence Aids Information Gathering:
- Develops keen, accurate sense of observation with details including fact and nuance
- Develops understanding of relationships on multiple levels, from diverse perspectives
- Develops perceptual abilities
- Develops understanding of the gestalt; comprehension of the "big picture"

How Visual Intelligence Aids Communication
- Develops use of descriptive, spatial, and metaphorical techniques in communication
- Develops ability to accurately record and report what is known

Key Creative Exercises:
Drawing, Dreams, Writing from Images and Music, Photography, Design and Semiotics, Personal Impact Assessment, and Six Perspectives Analysis of personal and media images

---

nonconscious memory and overt reasoning. The experimental data shed light on the preconscious effects of unconscious knowledge and memory on behavior. Working with Damasio and others, behavioral psychological Antoine Bechara developed an experimental process called the Iowa Gambling Test to help study how people make decisions and choices. The team reported results from their series of experiments on both normal participants and patients with prefrontal damage and decision-making defects. The experiments found that overt reasoning is preceded by a nonconscious biasing step. This step uses neural systems other than those that support declarative (or rational) knowledge.

The researchers tested both normal participants ("normals") and individuals with prefrontal damage ("patients") in a gambling task that simulates real-life decision making. The researchers measured parallel behavioral, psychophysiological (anticipatory skin conductance responses, or SCRs), and self-account measures of participants' progress during the experiment. Normals began to produce SCRs when reaching for disadvantageous decks of cards and to choose advantageously long before they were consciously aware of which strategy worked best. Patients did not produce SCRs and chose disadvanta-

Figure 6.3. Cindy's Grandmother, by Rick Williams.

Table 6. Intrapersonal Intelligence

Definition: Detailed, knowledgeable, responsive awareness of oneself

Visual Components: Mind's Eye, Dreams, Reflections, Meditations

How Intrapersonal Intelligence Aids Information Gathering:
- Develops sense of one's own inner values, biases, and motivations that help one to be more objective and sensitive to others
- Develops insights or hunches into possible motivations of others
- Develops ability to bring to consciousness, unconscious biases that influence decisions
- Develops sense of integrity, self, and personal ethical standards
- Develops confidence in one's own abilities and insights
- Develops empathy and understanding for others

How Intrapersonal Intelligence Aids Communication:
- Develops depth and insight
- Develops author's voice and presence
- Develops symbols for inner experience including values, feeling, and personal story

Key Creative Exercises:
Drawing, Dreams, Writing from Images and Music, Photography, Design and Semiotics, Personal Impact Assessment, and Six Perspectives Analysis of personal and media images

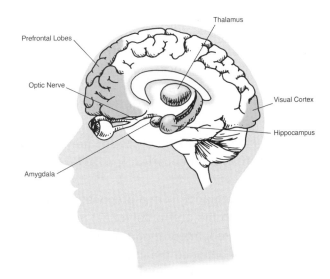

Figure 6.4. Side view of the brain showing positions of the pre-frontal lobes, thalamus, amygdala, and visual cortex. Illustration by Janet Halvorsen.

geously, even after they consciously knew the correct strategy. Thus, patients with damaged prefrontal lobes, who did not have access to nonconscious memory, were unable to make advantageous decisions even after they understood the advantageous strategy.

Bechara et al. reported that "in normal individuals, nonconscious biases guide behavior before conscious knowledge does." They concluded, "Without the help of such biases, overt knowledge may be insufficient to ensure advantageous behavior" (pp. 1293–1295). This suggests that the brain's prefrontal lobes use a memory system that relies on nonconscious biases to guide advantageous, rational behavior — before we engage our rational minds. In this way, it is possible that rational behavior actually depends on access to nonconscious biases as a means of functioning effectively.

The Iowa team's work supports the omniphasic idea that *intuitive intelligences attain direct knowledge* before conscious rational processing occurs. They operate in complementary, parallel ways to both guide and support behavior and rational decision making. Wolfe suggested a similar scenario for visual processes in 1983 when he said:

> Moreover, it appears that because vision is the result of a number of subsystems at work and not just a direct line to the brain from the senses, many of these subsystems function independ-

ently of one another and are beyond all introspective understanding. (pp. 94–98)

In 1986, Joseph LeDoux described this complex visual process from a cognitive perspective that suggests a similarity between the theory of unconscious biases and preconscious visual processes:

> The newer research contradicts earlier thought and reveals how sensory signals from the eye travel first to the thalamus and then, in a kind of short circuit, to the amygdala before a second signal is sent to the neocortex. (pp. 237–248)

Simply put, the eyes see and, from a preconscious mode (using the amygdala, perhaps in concert with the prefrontal lobes) motivate behavior before the rational mind is activated. Integrating the work of LeDoux and Damasio reveals a potential correlation between the intuitive, neurobiological processes between the eye and the brain and the type of intuitive processes that characterize the unconscious memory of our prefrontal lobes. Both processes operate on preconscious cognitive levels to motivate behavior before the neocortex can transform the information into conscious knowledge.

Figure 6.5.
Fisherfolk
Communion, by
Rick Williams.

Table 7. Interpersonal Intelligences

Definition: Detailed, knowledgeable, responsive awareness of others

Visual Components: Observation and analysis of visual world and media

How Interpersonal Intelligence Aids Information Gathering:
- Develops critical understanding of the effects of one's own actions on others, including information gathering and communication
- Develops sense of social responsibility
- Develops critical understanding of the effects of others' communication on the self
- Develops sense of personal responsibility

How Interpersonal Intelligence Aids Communication:
- Develops one's own critical and cultural perspectives in communication
- Develops techniques to enhance human interest in communication, sensitivity to audience, characterization, human meaning, relationships, quotes, anecdotes, and dialogue

Key Creative Exercises:
Drawing, Dreams, Writing from Images and Music, Photography, Design and Semiotics, Personal Impact Assessment, and Six Perspectives Analysis of personal and media images

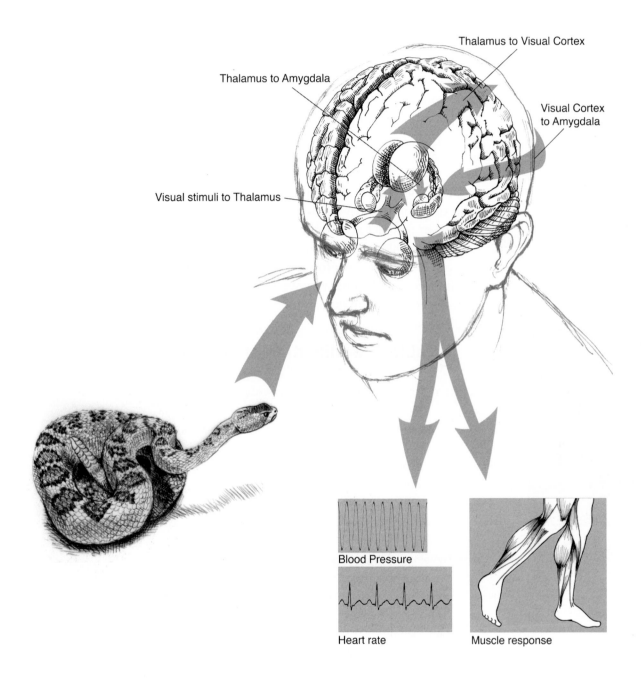

Thalamus to Visual Cortex

Thalamus to Amygdala

Visual Cortex
to Amygdala

Visual stimuli to Thalamus

Blood Pressure

Heart rate

Muscle response

Figure 6.6. LeDoux's theory of visual processing and response. Illustration by Janet Halversen.

If this is true, visual communication, especially visual media images, both pre-consciously motivates behavior and becomes part of nonconscious memory to form the biases that guide future decisions and behavior. This supports the omniphasic idea that visual intelligence operates as a highly intuitive process both before and beyond reason.

In her seminal book, *Visual Intelligence*, Ann Marie Barry addressed LeDoux's work and this preconscious visual phenomenon. Barry suggested that perceptual processes that begin with unconscious emotional bias, and may or may not be checked by rational interference, are the primary motivators of behavior:

> The implication of this is that we begin to respond emotionally to situations before we can think them through. The ramifications of this fact are significant, suggesting that we are not the fully rational beings we might like to think we are. . . . In fact . . . much of [what seems to be rational] cognition is merely rationalization to make unconscious emotional response acceptable to the conscious mind. (p. 18)

Figure 6.7. Frank jumping, by Rick Williams.

Table 8. Bodily Kinesthetic Intelligence

Definition: Control of one's body and of objects, timing

Visual Components: Drawing, Focusing, Eye–Hand Control, Movement

How Bodily Kinesthetic Intelligence Aids Information Gathering:
- Develops ability to draw upon physical/visual resources to produce visual and verbal messages
- Develops eye–hand coordination in photography, computer work, and design
- Develops ability to handle technological equipment
- Develops a sense of natural pace and movement

How Bodily Kinesthetic Intelligence Aids Communication:
- Develops understanding of physicality, sexuality, and ability to communicate such
- Develops sensitivity to movement and understanding of body language
- Develops ability to communicate down-to-earth, organic, grounded, gut feelings

Key Creative Assignments:
   Drawing, Dreams, Writing from Images and Music, Photography, Design and Semiotics, Personal Impact Assessment, and Six Perspectives Analysis of personal and media images

---

Barry also addressed the rational bias of our culture and the power of images to shape our world through sophisticated media. She recognized the need to educate everyone in visual processing and proposed a paradigm shift in thinking "toward a growing awareness that images are a means of communication that runs deeper and is ultimately more powerful than words in its ability to condition attitudes and to form thoughts" (pp. 337–338).

Both Damasio and Barry suggested that emotions are the primary cognitive complement to reason. Working from LeDoux's research, Daniel Goleman explained that emotional intelligence is more significant to decision making and behavior than rational intelligences. Goleman also correlated emotional intelligence with Gardner's personal or psychological intelligences. From an integrative mind perspective, this correlation, and the preconscious character of emotion, place emotional intelligence within the intra/interpersonal framework of what we have called intuitive intelligence.

Further, drawing on the work of LeDoux and Damasio, Goleman explained a relationship between the amygdala and prefrontal lobes, whereby they work together to mediate and guide preconscious behavioral motivations. He

Figure 6.8. Singing at Lane, by Rick Williams.

Table 9. Musical Intelligence

Definition: Sensitivity to Pitch, Rhythm, Timbre, and the Emotional Power and Complex Organization of Music

Visual Components: Mind's Eye, Stimulation of past visual experience related to music, Drawing from music, Music with images, Writing from music

How Musical Intelligence Aids Information Gathering:
- Develops links to deep preverbal flow of thought or unconscious biases
- Develops sense of integrated harmony of parts and resolution of disparate elements
- Develops ability to listen to varying dialects and languages
- Develops ability to perceive different cultures

How Musical Intelligence Aids Communication:
- Develops a sense of rhythm and flow in writing
- Develops ability to integrate complex organization
- Develops ability to develop harmonious solutions to disparate problems

Key Creative Exercises:
> Drawing, Writing from Images and Music, Photography, Dreams. (Music can be used daily to help develop awareness of the ability of music to establish mood and affect feelings in a synthesistic manner.)

explained that the amygdala provides a more spontaneous, rudimentary response and that the prefrontal lobes provide a more sophisticated, synthesistic response — both preconsciously. All of this work suggests that visual communication is clearly a primary provider of information that develops prefrontal, unconscious memory and, therefore, is the primary source of nonconscious biases that guide behavior.

Approaching the subject from a psychological background, Robert Ornstein reviewed 25 years of the hemispheric specialization debate in *The Right Mind: Making Sense of the Hemispheres.* Noting more than 45,000 publications, he concluded his exhaustive survey of psychological, psychiatric, and biological literature on cerebral asymmetry with a statement similar to, though perhaps more poetic than, Damasio's:

> I'd say that there exists in the right side a capacity that updates the different possibilities for action at any time. It's necessary, for the brain to guide us through this complex world, for the different centers of the brain to be put on-line when it is time to analyze sounds, update memory, or decode a new dish of food. So one aspect of the right side's overall or higher view of events

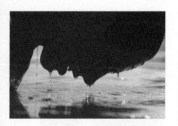

Figure 6.9.
Nancy,
by Rick
Williams.

Table 10. Naturalist Intelligence

Definition: Ability to recognize, appreciate and understand the natural environment.

Visual Components: Observation, experience and analysis of natural world using both visual seeing and mind's-eye memory of naturalist experiences

How Naturalistic Intelligence Aids Information Gathering:
- Develops keen, accurate sense of observation with details, including fact and nuance
- Develops understanding of relationships on multiple levels, from diverse perspectives
- Develops perceptual abilities
- Develops understanding of holistic comprehension of the "big picture"

How Naturalistic Intelligence Aids Communication
- Develops use of descriptive, spatial and metaphorical techniques in communication
- Develops ability to accurately record and report what is known

Key Creative Exercises:
   Drawing, Dreams, Writing from Images, Photography, Personal Impact Assessment, and Six Perspectives Analysis of personal and media images

is that it may well have a measure of influence over which mental module gets activated. Context, in our life, trumps text, not the other way around. "Higher consciousness" is another way of putting it. (p. 159)

In another realm of science, physicist Fritjof Capra (1991) used a dualistic model of parallel perspectives to address the need to develop a more holistic scientific worldview. Capra cited such scientific luminaries as quantum physicist Neils Bohr as he described a contemporary, ongoing paradigm shift in scientific vision that leads away from the concepts and values of an outdated rational, technological worldview that is "severely limited and inadequate for dealing with the problems of our overpopulated, globally interconnected world" (p. 325). He suggested that the paradigm shift currently taking place is toward an ecological view "that will form the basis of our future technologies, economic systems, and social institutions" (p. 325). Capra said, "The ecological paradigm is supported by modern science, but it is rooted in a perception of reality that goes beyond the scientific framework to an awareness of the oneness of all life, the interdependence of its multiple manifestations, and its cycles of change and transformation" (p. 326). This ecological world view embraces an organic, holistic view of the world; it recognizes the limitations of all rational approaches to reality; and it accepts intuition as a valid way of knowing. Capra's *ecological worldview* is dualistic in that it recognizes rational and intuitive thought as parallel and interdependent. Capra also recognized the disabling bias against holistic, intuitive processes in our culture. The dualistic approach of integrated mind theory also draws from centuries of cross-cultural traditions that have explored and defined aspects of everything from human psychology (conscious/unconscious), neuropsychology (left/right brain), and mythology (masculine/feminine archetypes) to academic research (qualitative/quantitative), philosophy (yin/yang), and physiology (male/female).

Table 11 draws from lists in Bogen's (1975) parallel ways of knowing and Ornstein's (1972) two modes of consciousness to indicate how thinkers in a variety of fields have described the dualistic nature of the mind over the centuries. This helps to graphically and conceptually clarify the concept of equal and complementary cognitive processes. In the table, the parallel cognitive modalities are organized by author under the headings of rational and intuitive intelligences.

As we noted earlier, one way of looking at dualism rightfully argues against *either/or* kinds of thinking. Yet dualism can also imply *both/and* thinking. Communication scholars Marshall McLuhan and Bruce Powers, for example, predicted the need for this shift in our understanding in *The Global Village*, which Powers completed and published after McLuhan died in 1989. McLuhan believed humankind had advanced beyond two-dimensional perceptions when we devised such multidimensional mechanisms as television. The blending (or clash) of Eastern and Western perspectives has led us to multidimensional, simultaneous, and holistic ways of knowing, McLuhan argued. He further postulated that we have lived this nonlinear consciousness for most of the 20th century — but that we have only recently begun to understand it.

We need not reach far to find ways that multidimensional, omniphasic mental processing permeate our daily lives. Consider, for example:

- magazines packed with more ads than editorial content
- a sports bar with 27 television monitors lined up in a row showing six different events simultaneously.
- an Internet site with blocks of text, multiple images, and blinking ads.
- a television screen that includes small frames of other visuals and running banners.

Table 11. Complementary/Parallel Systems of Knowing

This is a partial list of key authors who have written about parallel ways of knowing, two modes of consciousness, two types of intelligence, or two cognitive styles. The table draws in part from Bogen (1975, p. 25) and Ornstein (1972, p. 37).

Intuitive	Rational	Author
Divine	Corporeal	Jaynes
Feminine/Yin	Masculine/Yang	I Ching
Unconscoius	Conscious	Freud/Jung
Timeless	Time	Oppenheimer
Gestalt	Analytic	Levy/Sperry
Nonlineal	Lineal	D. Lee
Simultaneous	Sequential	Luria
Spatial	Verbal	Bogen/Sperry
Simultaneous	Successive	Sechenov (per Luna)
Intuition	Intellect	Assagiola
Intuitive	Rational	Maslow/Capra
Divergent	Convergent	Austin
Analogic	Digital	Bateson & Jackson
Metaphoric	Rational	Bruner
Relational	Analytic	Cohen
Primary	Secondary	Freud
Concrete	Abstract	Goldstein
Multiple	Sequential	Neisser
Holistic	Analytical	Ornstein
Synthesis	Analysis	Levy

- children who think they study better with the background noise of television or loud music.
- billboards along the road that we have learned to perceive peripherally.

In fact, we find that McLuhan's idea that the media are so pervasive that they leave no part of us untouched is truer today than when he put it forth in the 1960s. Today, we know that media not only pervade our external lives but also invade our intuitive, preconscious minds as well. Through the simultaneous synthesis of music, movement, color, and metaphoric visual and verbal language, the media develop interpersonal and intrapersonal relationships among actors and their lifestyles. This promotes psychological associations with products, values, media characters, and celebrities on intuitive preconscious levels of cognition. Media fill a large portion of our intuitive needs, affecting every aspect of our conscious and unconscious processing.

In this light, McLuhan's ideas about multidimensional ways of knowing lead us, appropriately, to the next section of the book, which explores the relationship between the rational bias of our educational systems and the development of visual and media literacy curricula. These educational biases helped create, and continue to support, the visual, intuitive illiteracy that make it so difficult to negotiate intelligently the multidimensional, omniphasic messages of our media-centric culture.

This dilemma emphasizes the critical need to adopt an omniphasic *both/and* model that supports the development of both rational and intuitive intelligences as equal and complementary cognitive processes. This synthesis facilitates cognitive balance — the whole-mind application and expression of intelligence that is integral to a balanced individual and the balanced cultural systems she will develop.

Bringing It All Together

In summary, integrative mind theory, grounded in the historical framework of Jaynes's bicameral theory and Bogen's/Sperry's hemispheric specialization research, affirms that the human mind uses two primary cognitive-processing systems (rational and intuitive). The theory transcends the semantic and neurotechnical problems associated with historical right/left-hemisphere research by focusing on function rather than location in the brain and by redefining the cognitive modalities as functionally rational and intuitive. Rational intelligence is the ability to attain knowledge directly, through cognition, without evidence of reason.

Further, the theory integrates interdisciplinary research to suggest that rational and intuitive intelligences represent complementary, parallel cognitive systems. These systems are independent, yet integrated, and are equally significant to whole-mind cognitive processing. The theory also points out a signifi-

Figure 6.10. Sun and Moon, illustration from the Nuremberg Chronicle, a 15th-century book by Hartmann Schedel. From Morse Library, Beloit College.

cant cultural, educational, economic, and scientific bias against the development and practice of intuitive intelligences. Additionally, these postulates are grounded in an interdisciplinary synthesis of recent research and theory, including Gardner's multiple intelligence theory, Damasio's theory of unconscious biases, Barry's theory of visual intelligence, Goleman's theory of emotional intelligence, Ornstein's concepts of text and context, and Capra's theory of an ecological worldview.

Both journalism and entertainment media are visually dominated. Because visual intelligence is primarily intuitive, and because people operate best when using whole-mind thinking, the next generation of media professionals and scholars must enhance their ability to use their intuitive communication skills on more sophisticated and socially responsible levels. Therefore, visual literacy provides a particularly significant area of study for the well-educated individual as well as for the communication professional and scholar.

In Part 2 of this book, we explore the rational biases of traditional visual and media literacy. We also suggest ways you can build on what you now know and expand your knowledge of and use of the visual to embrace omniphasic visual/media literacy. Further, Part 2 begins to explore the consequences of the visual and intuitive illiteracy in our culture. You will develop a working understanding of the techniques of creative, intuitive communication processes in writing, graphic design, photography, film, video, and new media. You will learn how to use your creativity to guide your own intuitive experiences in ways that will enrich life experiences and, subsequently, in ways that will help you build defenses against media manipulations of preconscious cognition.

Theory must be testable. Although we reject the idea of total reliance on linear data support, in keeping with omniphasic theory, we did draw on interdisciplinary, quantitative, and theoretical evidence in neurobiological and psychological studies, as well as qualitative experience from many years of teaching, to structure the exercises in this book and to build theory for further testing.

Application of integrative mind techniques with university students and in ongoing research studies has demonstrated that this holistic approach to visual communication and education can teach you to use your whole mind, and to replace invasive media experiences with self-directed intuitive experiences. Development of whole-mind processes fosters greater creativity, powerful problem-solving abilities, and balance. A more fully educated, self-determining individual who is less susceptible to media influence is better prepared to apply all his or her learning experience in ways that generate balance, both within the individual and within the cultural, economic, educational, and scientific systems of our visual world. You will have the mental tools you need to meet the challenges of the century before us.

Figure 6.11. Bailando, by Julianne Newton.

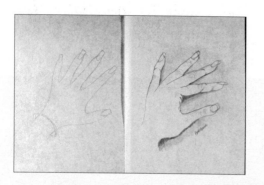
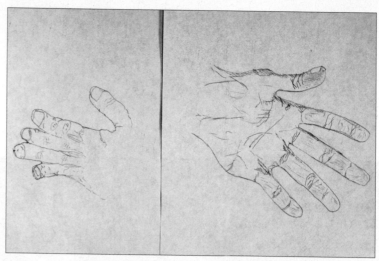
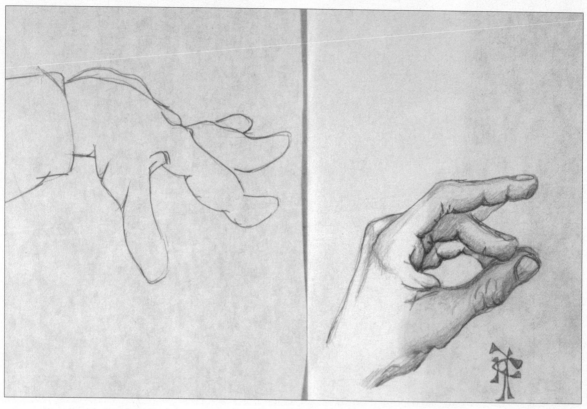
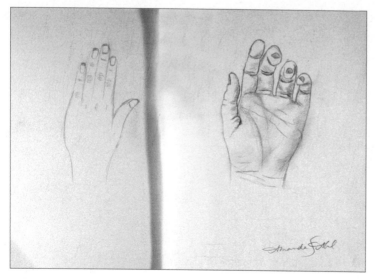

Figures C6.1–4. Before and after work by students who have worked through the drawing exercises. Figures on the left in each pair were drawn for Creative 3. The ones on the right in each pair were drawn for Creative 6. Notice that everyone improved, regardless of beginning skill level. Clockwise from top left: Beason, Fowell, Harrell, Abel.

CREATIVE SIX
Bringing It All Together:
Drawing for Real

The Goal: Seeing Results of Cognitive Balance

This is the final exercise in drawing your hand. If you have practiced all the other exercises as suggested, you should be able to shift easily into your integrated-mind drawing mode. Your goal for this creative exercise is to produce a drawing of your hand that is a great deal more realistic than your preinstruction drawings, which you completed for Creative 3.

How to Begin

Allow at least an hour of free time for each drawing. Begin by relaxing. You might meditate for a few minutes or do a short contour drawing of your hand to help you transition into an integrative state of mind.

When you are ready to begin, place your free hand in a comfortable and aesthetically pleasing posture on the table in front of you. Tape a sheet of blank paper close to your hand. Look at your hand for some time, noticing all of the fine edges and spaces and relationships. Notice how the light and shadows fall, how the fingers curve, and how the edges of your hand meet the table below it to form an edge or contour.

Find the spot on your hand where you would like to start. Place your pencil on an appropriate place on the paper. Just as you did in the contour drawings, begin to move your eyes along a line or edge and simultaneously move your pencil along the paper in the same direction. You should spend most of your time looking at your hand and just glancing at the paper from time to time in order to check an angle or spatial relationship or the width and strength of a particular line, or to find the right place to start a new contour or shape. Draw lines and spaces that are adjacent to one another instead of outlining your hand and filling in the blanks. As always, take your time and enjoy this relaxing process.

You should spend a minimum of 30 minutes on each drawing in this exercise. Because we have not studied proportion or shading, you may find that a finger is a little too long, or you may have some trouble trying to fill in shadows or highlight areas. However, we believe you will find great satisfaction in the result of your efforts, and it should be a peaceful, relaxing time. LIke all other intuitive processes, practice will bring improvement.

When you have finished, sign and date your work and spend some time enjoying your progress. Get out your drawings from Creative 3 and look at the difference. Even practiced artists report that they find this method helpful and enjoyable.

When you finish the first hand drawing, draw *one more complete hand in a different position* using this technique. You can do it immediately or wait until another time. *The more you practice, the more you will improve* and the more easily you will recognize the character of your integrated experience.

Now, reflect on and write an assessment of your drawing experiences. Include a discussion comparing your early drawings with the ones you just completed. Also note insights you have gained by working through the creative exercises in Part I of this book.

Beyond this point there are many ways to continue to improve your drawing. The best way to improve is to practice. Many drawing books are available to help you learn about proportion, shading, and other aspects of drawing.

Summary

- Read the instructions carefully.
- Spend time relaxing before you start a drawing.
- Make as many drawings as you want to but at least two.
- Reflect on your work and write an assessment as described above.

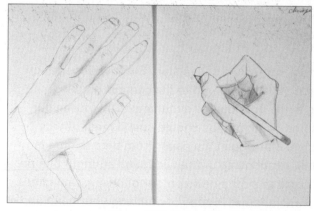

Figure C6.5. Before and after, by Hammer.

PART II.
VISUAL ILLITERACY AND EDUCATION
What We Don't Learn

Part II presents approaches to visual literacy and grounds you in the fundamental visual forms humans use and develop in order to communicate.

Figure 7.1. Grocery Carts, by Ave Bonar.

CHAPTER SEVEN
The Square Peg and the Round Hole: Education and Intuitive Intelligence

> *We have within us a deep wisdom and bondedness with our incredible evolutionary history and a creativity within which we draw, from moment to moment, that has an ingenuity that should astound and humble us.*
>
> Edmund O'Sullivan

The metaphor of trying to fit a square peg into a round hole exemplifies the traditional, rationally biased approach to education in general, and to visual and media literacy specifically. Conventionally, the idea suggests something that doesn't work. Yet a simple, synthesistic shift in perception can turn the metaphor into a symbol for an integrated, whole-mind dynamic.

To explain: In your mind's eye, envision a round hole in the middle of a round piece of wood. Now, envision a square peg. In the usual, logical scenario, the square peg will not fit into the round hole. Now, envision a slightly smaller square peg that will fit snugly but neatly into the hole, which is slightly larger than the peg. In this interpretation, the square-peg/round-hole metaphor can represent the integration of rational/analytic (square, lineal, solid, definable) intelligence with intuitive/synthesistic (circular, global, continuous, noncontainable) intelligence. The peg and the hole together represent integrated, or balanced, cognition, a gestalt synthesis of deeper understanding than either the rational or intuitive symbols would imply independently.

An omniphasic experience blends the rational and intuitive intelligences. In this instance, the rational helps us understand the logic (or illogic) of concepts, and the intuitive helps us envision new possibilities. Though we have neither used external visuals to describe this peg/hole concept nor described a particular peg/hole in detail, it is quite likely that you have a strong image of the metaphor in your own mind's eye at this point. This is a glimpse into the intuitive synthesis of the integrated mind.

Now, let's apply this process to a media image. Consider both the logical concepts and emotional impact of visual images in advertising. Visual logos, for example, not only represent corporate image identity but, when linked with visual imagery, also create emotional associations that encourage viewers to link self-image with the corporate image or product. The Nike Swoosh coupled with the emotional attitude of "Just Do It" and visual images of successful, strong, determined, athletic individuals is one example of this intuitive/rational blend. One relatively simple symbol communicates a complex blend of stimuli to help us remember the association every time we view it. By stressing only logical, linear, rational ways of understanding and interacting with the world, however, many educational systems create citizens who are rationally skilled but intuitively illiterate. They may respond to such stimuli as the Nike Swoosh without being aware of its influence. The one-sided approach to knowing that most of us have learned for most of our lives has prepared us for a singularly rational world — that doesn't exist.

Bogen (1975) noted that "the entire student body is being educated lopsidedly." An educational system based on monetary measures of success, he said, "avoids altogether any concern for the quality of human existence." He believed many students found their courses irrelevant and that they were "concerned not so much with making a living as making a life." Students

> see a world of warring elders, busily Becoming at the expense
> of Being, who want them to be unhappy in the same half-
> brained way. . . . It is time we learn to live within nature as bilat-
> erally educated, whole persons. (p. 29)

Although the renowned neurosurgeon wrote those words in the 1970s, he could write them today. School curricula have, with few exceptions, become even more oriented toward rational skills than they were. Consider, for example, the trend toward "teaching to the test," the practice in which grade-school teachers focus curricula on helping students score higher on standardized tests. Although the "No Child Left Behind Act" of 2001 has the worthy goal of making sure all children can read and do basic arithmetic, it often does so at the expense of holistic learning. As CNN reporter Van Harken noted in 2003, "An unintended consequence is that art and other classes like music, gym, science and social studies get cut or compromised to make the budget focus more on the core curriculum." He cited the experiences of Christi Praeger, a second-grade teacher at Bronx (NY) Public School, who told of the excitement children express when she brings art supplies, which she had to pay for herself, to the classroom:

> "They get so excited," Praeger, 26, said. "They'll ask me all
> day long, 'Miss Praeger, when are we going to get to make art?
> Can we do it now? Can we? Can we Miss Praeger?'"

Figure 7.2. Boy on Bus, by Ave Bonar.

Praeger said she wishes art could play a regular part in her lesson plans. The students' interest [sic] in reading, writing and math increase when she employs creative methods.

But, she can't afford it. She bought the construction paper, markers and glue with her own money because she doesn't have an expense account. (para. 2-4)

The Van Harken article continued:

"I don't disagree that reading and math are the most important aspects of education. But compromising other subjects . . .

Figure 7.3. Los angelitos, by Julianne Newton.

causes us to teach only for the test," Praeger said. If a student's talents lie in art, or music or science, they lose out, she said. "And schools can't force [teachers] to be creative in their approach, especially if all that matters is a test score." (para. 8)

It is important to emphasize here that, as Ms. Praeger noted and recent research concludes, children do better in reading, writing, and math — the skills traditionally considered linear and logical — when they also have opportunities to develop their creative, or intuitive intelligences. And, as we also have stressed, areas long considered reason based, require intuitive-based processing to be explored to their fullest capacity in the human brain.

Our goal in developing an integrative mind method is to help expand the current models of both visual literacy and our educational system toward a balanced perspective by developing curricula that effectively blend the teaching of intuitive and rational intelligences. Ironically, a movement toward visual literacy has been growing since the 1960s. However, because of the rationally biased educational system, visual literacy classes typically rely on groundbreaking but still almost exclusively linear modes of teaching.

Although many people now understand the need for visual literacy, we have few means for learning the holistic cognitive strategies that visual, intuitive thinking makes possible. Even worse, current educational and economic paradigms sustain a disabling bias against at least half of our cognitive abilities. This bias has created populations who are unaware that they are intuitively illiterate, yet who live in a highly intuitive, media-dominated culture. A provocative extension of this idea is that this same bias is a source of oppression and domination in cultures that have historically valued and developed intuitive processes. The rational bias is at least part of what spurred Western European dominance of peoples of India, Africa, and the New World. And it is also the basis for criticism that arrogance on the part of the United States has spread its early policy of "manifest destiny" beyond its own continental shores. The rational bias feeds hierarchical systems of dominance with false notions of superiority in terms of sex, race, class, age, rank, physical and mental ability, and culture.

The Contemporary Vision

> I think that any belief that all the answers to a given problem lie in one certain approach, such as logical-mathematical thinking, can be very dangerous. Current views of intellect need to be leavened with other more comprehensive points of view. It is of the utmost importance that we recognize and nurture all of the varied human intelligences, and all of the combinations of intelligences. If we recognize this, I think we will have at least a better chance of dealing appropriately with the many problems that we face in the world.
>
> Howard Gardner (1993, p. 12)

The phrase *visual literacy* may at first seem an inappropriate pairing because in common usage *literacy* implies the ability to read and write words. Perhaps we use it because the word *literate* links visual knowing to the rational brain process of word play. Perhaps it is because intuitive intelligences, R-Mode processes, global awareness, and synthesistic perceptual intelligences have not worked their way into the mainstream language as easily as the more linear term *visual literacy*. Perhaps it is because a logical interpretation of visual literacy can be more easily and appropriately quantified than intuitive processes, is more easily correlated with rational concepts, and is therefore more readily legitimized. Perhaps all of the above contribute to our casual acceptance of the rational, word-based term *visual literacy* to describe a highly intuitive, non-word process. The complexity of this line of thinking (notice the linear reference to logic in the preceding phrase) relies somewhat on the fact there are few clear, respected, mainstream words to describe intuitive proficiencies in our language. So, we fall back on such readily accepted terms as *literate*, *nonverbal*, or *nonlinear* to describe nonrational processes instead of using such less-accepted but more specific and appropriate terms as *intuitive*, *synthesistic*, *visual*, or *global*.

Another important perspective is that such terms as *intuitive* and *visual* have been degraded as ambiguous, nonscientific, emotional, and even irrational. However, that is exactly our point: Much of living as humans is all those things — ambiguous, nonscientific, emotional, and even irrational. Consider the practice of medicine, for example. As advanced as 21st-centu-

ry medicine is, good physicians will be the first to tell you that medicine is a "healing art" and requires attention to aspects of the body that science cannot "fix." The world's greatest physicists, as they try to define a unified theory that explains the basis of our existence, continue to discover as they delve farther into either the vastness of space or the quantum universe of the atom, that unseen, vibrating strings of energy, not solid objects, may be the basis of all life. This is why Sir Martin Rees, Britain's Astronomer Royal, suggested that scientific explanations remain perpetually incomplete. Rees said, "If we learn anything from the pursuit of science, it is that even something as basic as an atom is quite difficult to understand. . . . This alone should induce skepticism about any dogma or any claim to have achieved more than a very incomplete and metaphorical insight into any profound aspect of our existence" (as cited in Wakefield, 2004).

Figures 7.4-5. Left and above: Looking two directions from the same spot on Texas Highway 166. Photographs by Frank Armstrong.

Figure 7.6. Eloina and the Angel, by Julianne Newton.

Williams and Newton

Cultivating the Intuitive

This brings us to another key point: The best way to deal with these human tendencies is not to deny but rather to cultivate the intuitive processes to better understand and use them. Carl Jung called this process "embracing the shadow," acknowledging parts of ourselves with which we are uncomfortable to use their power to help us grow as human beings. If you have ever watched reruns of the science fiction program *Star Trek*, or movies based on the series, you will recognize these same tendencies in the ongoing battle between the half-Vulcan/half-human Mr. Spock (who symbolizes the rational and highly logical) and the human doctor called Bones (who symbolizes the intuitive and emotional). Throughout the episodes, Spock wrestles with the part of himself that is human, favoring his logical, Vulcan self. Bones, a physician educated in the most advanced medical technology, wrestles with his logical side, favoring his intuitive gift for knowing. Occasionally, Spock and Bones learn from one another, acknowledging their "shadow sides" as necessary complements to their dominant mental modes.

Still another point of view is to consider that the term *literate* also has developed a more inclusive meaning: to be well educated, cultured, lucid, and polished, and to have knowledge or competence. This inclusive meaning reflects the evolution of a more rounded, integrated view that embraces both the intuitive and rational perspectives, just as the square peg/round hole metaphor did. Yet the idea of evolving beyond visual literacy toward an omniphasic perspective larger than reading and creating visual messages focuses attention toward the *integration of the visually intuitive with rational literacy*. In the following sections, we review the ideas of a few key scholars who have paved the way to move *beyond conventional visual literacy*. Understanding the tenets of their work will help you comprehend the challenges you face as you try to use your whole mind. We first review the rational side and then the intuitive side of visual literacy. Then we offer an omniphasic perspective that blends both rational and intuitive intelligences.

The Rational Side of Visual Literacy

Writing in 1973, at a time when the mention of the words *visual literacy* drew questioning stares, Donis A. Dondis helped initiate the quest for an academic foothold for a critical, yet long-neglected discipline with publication of her now-classic work, *A Primer of Visual Literacy*. Dondis, a Boston University communications professor and dean, noted the potential pitfall of comparing visual communication to language and the futility of trying to fit visual intelligence into a logical whole, analogous to language. Dondis also recognized that the intuitive complexity of visual communication, coupled with the lack of methods to analyze or define it, contributed to the paucity of attempts to realize and develop basic visual competencies.

Figures 7.7-8. Morgan and Miller reading and telling stories, by Rick Williams.

Facing this challenge, Dondis developed an approach to visual literacy that was unique but included the same rational purposes "that motivated the development of written language: to construct a basic system for learning, recognizing, making and understanding visual messages that are negotiable by all people" (p. *x*). So, recognizing the complex intuitiveness of visual communication and the need to develop a visual grammar to advance understanding and communication about the visual experience, Dondis began to develop an intuitively based visual syntax:

> There are guidelines for constructing compositions. There are
> basic elements that can be learned and understood by all stu-
> dents of the visual media, artists and non-artists alike, and that,
> along with manipulative techniques, can be used to create clear
> visual messages. Knowledge of all of these factors can lead to
> clearer comprehension of visual messages. (p. 11)

Some 20 years later, communication theorist Paul Messaris of the University of Pennsylvania contributed a strong contemporary voice to the visual literacy debate. In *Visual Literacy: Image, Mind, and Reality*, Messaris suggested that visual literacy's strongest effects are to provide defenses against media manipulation and to increase aesthetic appreciation. Focusing on media imagery, he wrote that "greater experience in the workings of visual media coupled with a heightened conscious awareness of those workings" is often referred to as visual literacy (p. 2). Messaris proposed that we consider four aspects of visual literacy: "1. comprehension of visual media, 2. cognitive consequences of visual literacy, 3. visual manipulation, and 4. aesthetic appreciation" (p. 3). He suggested that these aspects represent a range of positive consequences most commonly associated with visual literacy. Messaris ultimately dismissed the first two aspects, asserting that images, unlike language or mathematics, use cues learned in our basic perception of reality; therefore, visual literacy does not lead to broader cognitive advantages. He suggested that increased awareness of and experience with sophisticated media messages decreases susceptibility to media manipulation and increases artistic appreciation. These, Messaris said, are the primary positive advantages of visual literacy.

Further developing the rational, analytical perspective toward media messaging, visual communication theorist Paul Martin Lester (1995) defined education as "teaching the individual to seek factual information and base reasoned conclusions on those data" (p. 80). Additionally, he stressed that "the first step toward understanding visual communication is to educate yourself about the many ways that information is produced and consumed in a modern, media-rich society" (p. *x).* Lester carefully explored the production aspects of media through sections on typography, design, information, cartoons, photography, motion pictures, television/video, computers, and interactive multimedia. He addressed the need to analyze imagery and develops six perspectives to analyze any image: personal, historical, technical, ethical, cultural, and critical.

Our emphasis here on the pervasive rational perspective employed in traditional visual communication theory is not intended to suggest that these visual literacy pioneers mistakenly neglected the intuitive aspects of visual literacy. Dondis was clearly aware of the intuitive nature of the visual experience and consciously directed the field toward the necessary development of an analytical perspective to establish legitimacy for visual education. Messaris suggested that a great deal of visual learning is primarily intuitive and that one of the primary functions of visual literacy is to enhance artistic appreciation. Lester proposed the personal *gut-reaction* perspective as the initial analytical tool.

Yet each of these thinkers necessarily employed linear, rationally centered processes and techniques to communicate their ideas within the rationally biased educational system. In his 1997 book, *Visual Persuasion*, Messaris stated, "Although the study of persuasive communication has a history of more than two millennia, the focus of this scholarly tradition has tended overwhelmingly to be on verbal strategies" (p. *vii).* Developing an analytical approach to the study of visual communication has been crucial to its acceptance and is critical to understanding the complex messaging systems of visual communication. It also provides a strong basis for the development of new theories and new strategies in visual communication. Yet it addresses only part of the story.

Recognizing this, Lester, a photographer, theorist, and philosopher, included omniphasism and omniphasic techniques in later editions of his book *Visual Communication: Images with Messages*. Lester himself is strongly intuitive, epitomizing the ambidextrous abilities of a whole-mind thinker. His book *The Zen of Photography* is as intuitive as his *Visual Communication* is rational.

The Intuitive Side of Visual Literacy

In chapters 5 and 6, we related the work of a range of scholars to visual communication and the omniphasic theory. We want to expand on a few of those ideas here to support our discussions of the intuitive side of visual literacy.

Gardner is perhaps the most influential contemporary voice to begin to break this pervasive cognitive imbalance. As we noted earlier, Gardner addressed what he considered a rational bias against other forms of intelligence. Gardner addressed the need to integrate the mind: "Any adult and state of any consequence, in any culture, will involve a blend of intelligences that make possible the solving of problems and creation of products of significance." He further addressed the need to restructure both our views and our educational system: "Only if we expand and reformulate our view of what counts as human intellect will we be able to devise more appropriate ways of assessing it and more effective ways of educating it" (1993, p. 9).

On the visual literacy front, communication scholar Arthur Asa Berger supported and expressed an intuitive voice. He created an early, more balanced approach to visual literacy in his book *Seeing Is Believing*. Berger blended a strongly rational emphasis on design, semiotics, and media analysis with intuitively oriented exercises, reaching beyond the linear status quo to suggest "a link between creativity and imagination — our ability to generate images in our minds, images *not* always representational or connected to anything in our experience." Imagination, he said, "refers to the remarkable power our minds have to form a mental image of something unreal or not present and to use the power creatively, to invent new images and ideas" (p. 2). In this, Berger captured the spirit of the intuitive process. Talking about visual thinking, metaphorical/holistic knowing, synthesizing across space instead of analyzing over time, he sees in the mind's eye something like reality that is not reality — imagining things that have never existed as solutions to problems that do exist. Berger recalled Jung's story of how the scientist Kekule dreamed of a snake with its tail in its mouth and from this dream discovered the benzene ring. This creative ability to find new solutions to old problems is a phenomenon common to the state of intuitive consciousness, however generated — through photography, art, music, poetry, meditation, visualization, visions, dreams, or other intuitive processes. Berger made a critical point: "Our emotional states and our creative impulses need some kind of visual and symbolic expression to develop and maintain themselves" (p. 1).

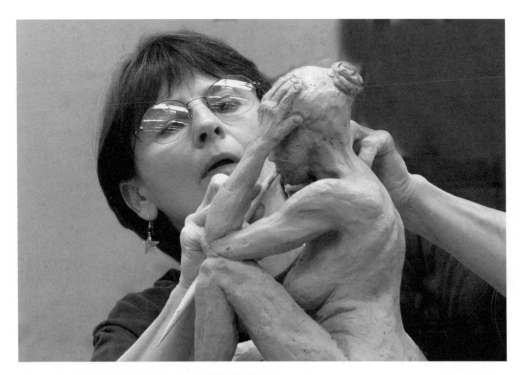

Figure 7.9. Sculpture class at Lane, by Rick Williams.

This states the problem clearly. We, as individuals and as a society, do little to develop and maintain our intuitive intelligence. This may be, at least in part, why we keep coming up with the same old solutions that never work to the same old problems that never get solved. We are not talking about such problems as putting a person on Mars but about how to avoid continuing destructive social and economic systems and how to replace them with sustainable systems.

There seems to be nothing implicit in our systems of government, business, education, and socialization to recognize, or nurture our intuitive intelligence. In ignoring this half of our cognitive abilities, societal systems leave a great creative and qualitative void. Gardner (1993) went so far as to say:

> Perhaps if we can mobilize the full range of human intelligences and ally them to an ethical sense, we can help to increase the likelihood of our survival on this planet, and perhaps even contribute to our thriving. (p.12)

The Need for an Integrative New Approach

New work in visual studies and "multimodal literacy" raises important questions and suggests possibilities for mobilizing "the full range of human intelligences" to which Gardner referred. In his self-described "skeptical" and "reactive" introduction to visual studies, art historian James Elkins called for rigorous visual theory that seeks to do more than critique the visual — "to affect the

Figure 7.10. Singing at Lane, by Rick Williams.

state of affairs outside of academic discourse." Asserting that he wants "to make life harder — and therefore more interesting— for people who love the visual world as much as" he does, Elkins proposed eight visual studies-related competencies to which undergraduates should engage: art history; non-Western visual competencies; past modes of seeing-making images; science imaging; special effects; digital images, graphics, and design based on understanding the effects of design; and a wider range of architectural spaces.

Carey Jewitt and Gunther Kress used the concept of *mode* in "meaning making, including image, gaze, gesture, movement, music, speech and sound-effect," all of which are "equally significant for meaning and communication" (pp. 1-2) Jewitt and Kress asked two sets of questions:

> First, how do modes shape what is represented, and how do the differences in modal representation reshape what is represented?
> And secondly, how are learners, and how is learning affected, changed, shaped, by the differences in mode, the material differences entailed, and the different senses called on, engaged, in the use of a mode? (p. 3)

In his book *Literacy in the New Media Age*, Kress addressed "the profound changes in the social, economic and technological world which in the end will shape the futures of literacy." He concluded: "We are the makers of meaning, and we can move into that period with a theory that puts us and our sign-making at the centre — not free to do as we would wish, but not as the victims of forces beyond our control either" (p. 176). Kress called for theory developing multiple ways of reading, writing, and knowing as a "new literacy" for the "new media age."

This new literacy is also implicit in Barry's idea of visual intelligence:

> What is needed to achieve visual intelligence is a paradigm shift in our thinking away from a logocentric bias and toward a growing awareness that images are a means of communication that runs deeper and is ultimately more powerful than words in its ability to condition attitudes and to form thoughts. Only when we recognize the way in which images communicate can we begin to deal appropriately with the effects of those images

Figure 7.11. Dancing at Lane, by Rick Williams.

and to fully appreciate the horizons that visual thinking opens for creative thought. While the ability of the image to speak directly to the emotions and to the deepest part of the psyche is the great gift of images in the realm of art and literature, and the holistic logic of perception is the key to opening up the mind, it is also a curse to the uninitiated who do not understand the range and profundity of its power. (p. 338)

Edmund O'Sullivan addressed these ideas through his theory of *transformative learning*. Decrying the rationally based, industrialized, and ruinous dominance of Western culture, O'Sullivan called for a revolutionary shift in educational systems throughout the world toward "integral development." "Integral development," he wrote, "must be understood as a dynamic wholeness where wholeness encompasses the entire universe and vital consciousness resides both within us and, at the same time, all around us in the world" (p. 208). In a remarkably hopeful treatise calling for practices of transformative learning, O'Sullivan asserted, "We have within us a deep wisdom and bondedness with our incredible evolutionary history and a creativity within which we draw, from moment to moment, that has an ingenuity that should astound and humble us" (p. 222).

Omniphasic thinking addresses these challenges. By offering direction for the future of education, omniphasic, integrative practices are one way to address the problem of the deep intuitive void felt on largely nonconscious levels by 21st-century humanity. Drawing from the works of those who pioneered the field, we suggest a broader, more inclusive definition of visual literacy as a way for illuminating — and filling— the intuitive void (see Table 12).

Table 12.
Omniphasic Visual Literacy

The ability to perceive, interpret, and create visual messages through the use of intuitive and rational intelligences as equivalent, complementary, and integrative processes of the mind.

This definition blends the rational approaches of earlier proponents and theorists in the visual literacy movement who laid the groundwork for an omniphasic approach to knowing with their holistically centered work. Our goal in teaching and scholarly work since the late 1970s has been to focus attention on the intuitively grounded and visual aspects of music, writing, art, photography, acting, meditation, daydreaming, and any of the multitude of other intuitive

Figure 7.12. Western hemisphere, image courtesy of National Aeronautics and Space Administration.

processes and activities that enrich our lives and our society — if we let them and if we cultivate them toward processes of integrative mind. All of these, in their own ways, have visual components, either visualized in the mind's eye or seen with the eyes in the external world.

Table 13 at the end of this chapter outlines scholars and theories discussed in the first seven chapters of this book and notes their relationships to Omni-phasism and Integrative Mind Theory. The resonance of scholarly thinking through time and across disciplines underscores the significance of these core ideas.

Figure 7.13. Eastern hemisphere, image courtesy of National Aeronautics and Space Administration.

Figure 7.14. Dancing at Lane, by Rick Williams.

In Conclusion

The problem? We don't make adequate room in our cultural and educational systems for sophisticated, self-directed expressions and understanding of our intuitive intelligence. This has created an intuitive void in our experiences and our cultural and educational systems and allowed mass media to shape our perceptions of reality and, therefore, our lives.

The first part of this book sought to introduce you to the key ideas underlying the development of omniphasic theory and to describe the capacity of the conscious and nonconscious mind to see, understand, and express itself in ways that balance rational and intuitive processing. This chapter expanded on ideas that inform omniphasism and stressed a few of the reasons omniphasic thinking is so important in studying the visual.

Our hope is that omniphasic thinking — an expanded, inclusive integration of our ways of knowing — will further both education and research and enrich your own personal life as well. You know part of the secret to fitting the square peg into the round hole. You are about to learn more.

Table 13.
Summary of Theories Relevant to Omniphasism

Omniphasism	Rational Intelligence	Intuitive Intelligence
Williams & Newton	The ability to understand through reason.	The ability to understand through direct knowledge without evident rational thought or inference.
Bicameral Mind	Corporeal Function Brain	Admonitory Brain
Jaynes	Conceptual	Perceptual
Hemispheric Spec.	Left Brain	Right Brain
Bogen/Sperry	Rational, verbal, logical, analytical	Intuitive, visual, synthesistic, gestalt
Multiple Intelligence	Logical Intelligences	Nonlogical Intelligence
Gardner	Logical/Mathematical Linguistic	Spatial/Visual Musical Personal Interior Personal Exterior Bodily Kinesthetic Naturalist
Emotional Intelligence	Reasoning	Feeling
LeDoux/Damasio/ Bechara/Gazzaniga	Conscious Cortical Processing	Nonconscious Limbic Processing/Amygdala
Visual Intelligence	Analytic Judgment	Associative Logic
Barry	Reason/rationalization	Perception
The Right Mind	Left Hemisphere	Right Hemisphere
Ornstein	Text	Context
Science/Paradigm Shift	Technology/Mechanical	Ecological/World View
Capra	Rational knowledge	Intuitive knowledge
Contemporary Visual Literacy		
Dondis	Grammar of VL	Synthesis of Style
Messaris	Four Aspects of VL	Innate Visual Literacy
Lester	Six Analytical Perspectives	Personal Perspective
Berger	Semiotics	Creativity & Imagination
Elkins	Verbal/Other Competencies	Visual competencies
Jewitt/Kress	Monomodal	Multimodal
Barry	Countering Media Influences	Unconscious Perceptual Learning
O'Sullivan	Rational Learning	Transformative Learning

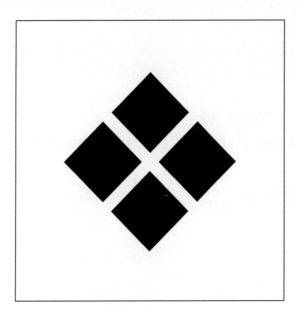

Figures C7.1–3. Example of University of Oregon student Brett Crosse's final product for Creative 7 in Winter 2005. Can you guess the concepts each design communicates? See answers below.

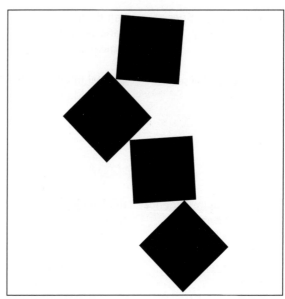

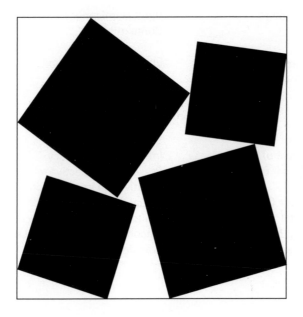

Answers: Top – Order. Middle – Playful. Bottom – Congested

CREATIVE SEVEN
Designing Shapes: Concepts in Visual Form

The Goal: Communicating Concepts Visually

As we move from visual theory and personal drawing exercises into practices where visual forms communicate meaning, it is important to understand how to create meaning with visual forms. In their book *Visual Literacy*, Judith and Richard Wilde presented a series of exercises to "lead students away from traditional thought processes, away from traditional avenues of visual research, and away from 'right' and 'wrong' answers" in ways that encourage students "to look inward for personal design solutions" (p. 11). The Wildes' novel approach reversed traditional approaches to visual design by using concepts to develop techniques, rather than the other way around. In other words, the designer considers the meaning of a project and then works with visual forms to discover effective content and techniques to convey that meaning. In this way, visual communicators intuitively discover design techniques as solutions.

Because the Wildes stress self-discovery as the primary goal of their exercises, students not only learn basic visual design techniques but also solve problems in new ways as they develop personal creativity and self-reliance. Creative 7 adapts one of the Wildes' exercises. It is designed to encourage you to go beyond habitual, learned responses to use a more instinctive, introspective, and spontaneous approach to problem solving. This approach supports omniphasic thinking by integrating conceptual thinking and creative problem-solving techniques. Creative 7 also leads you through the steps a professional designer might take to find a visual way to communicate an abstract concept. You begin by translating your thoughts onto paper through drawing and end with work in a finished form ready for presentation.

How to Begin

Begin by gathering the tools you will need: blank drawing or typing paper, a No. 2 pencil and a good eraser, a ruler, and a pen with black ink or fine-tip marker. If you prefer, you also may use a computer program, though designing on computer is a very different process than when you begin with pencil and paper. You can even do this exercise using the Word drawing tool. You may copy and use the page of squares included with these instructions or you may draw your own. To draw your own by hand, do the following:

- On one sheet of paper, use the ruler and pencil to draw three sets of eight 1-inch-square frames (as illustrated at right).
- Leave about 2 inches of space between each set of eight squares.

Now, take some time to relax and get into your intuitive, creative mode before completing the exercise.

How to Proceed

Within each of the first set of eight square frames, sketch four black squares to create eight different graphic images that all illustrate the concept of *order*. Here is one example.

Continue until you have eight different visual thumbnail, or preliminary, sketches that convey the concept of *order*.

Consider each sketch and select one you think is best. Now, using pencil or a computer, carefully refine and re-create it in a *3-inch-square* box on a *separate* piece of paper. If using pencil, carefully draw the outline of each of the four black squares in the pattern you created that best communicates *order*. Then go back over the lines in ink and fill in pattern squares with black ink.

When you have this, repeat the entire process for *two or more* of the following concepts using the other sets of eight square: *peace, motion, boldness,* and *joy*.

The Exercise

- Read the instructions carefully all the way through and get your supplies together.
- Print or create the page with three sets of eight 1-inch-square frames.
- In the first set of eight frames, illustrate the concept of *order* using four black squares within each of eight frames.

- Pick the best example of *order* and carefully re-create it in a 3–inch-square frame on another piece of paper.
- Repeat the process for at least two other concepts from this list: *peace, motion, boldness,* and *joy.*
- Place each design on a separate page.
- Sign and date your designs.
- Assess your overall experience — what did you feel, learn, think about? How does this creative exercise help you understand intuitive and rational creative processing?

Example: Order, Peace, Movement

Andrea Schneider drew the sketches at right to explore the concepts order, peace, and movement. Here are her final selections, which she drew using an illustration software program. Pen and ink final designs will work well if carefully done. Her assessment is below.

Assessment by Andrea Schneider

I feel that my overall experience was fairly successful. I had fun with the assignment and felt both relaxed and challenged. While doing the assignment I worked in a highly omniphasic state. In terms of creativity, my intuitive abilities dominated, but the difficulty came when I had to apply rational thought to my project. Since we were given a word, a verbal, rational element, I felt as though I flipped between different cognitive processes. Sometimes there were discrepancies between the two sides. With the word "peace" in particular I first thought, "What does peace mean to me?" Ultimately, peace for me was a feeling of balance, harmony, and cooperation that I strove for with my arrangements. Ultimately I felt that "peace" was the most difficult, but I think my final products reflect an accurate visual representation of the words for me, and reflect some successful shifting between intuitively and rationally based thinking.

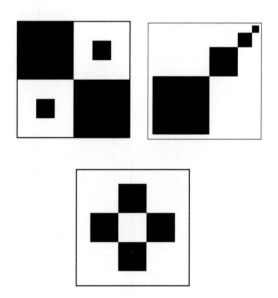

Above: Figure C7.4. Polished design communicating concepts of, clockwise from top left, peace, movement, and order, by Andrea Schneider. Right: Figure C7.5. Schneider's exploratory sketches.

ORDER

Peace

MOVEMENT

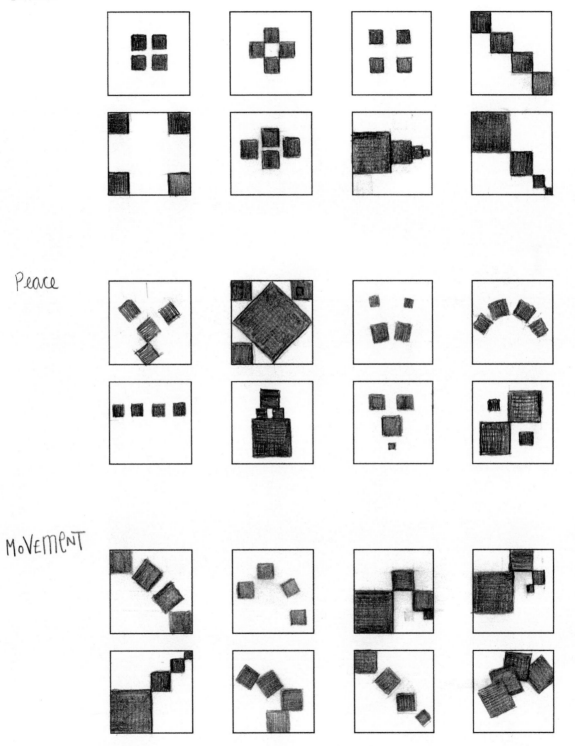

Figure 8.1. Poet's house, 1999, by Maggie Taylor. (Original in color)

CHAPTER EIGHT
Visions in Voice:
Language and the Intuitive Mind

Because integrative mind theory blends intuitive and rational intelligences in a holistic manner, we now turn to a number of other areas of theory and creative activities and processes that do just that. First we explore language and the sounds produced by verbalizing language. Words often are considered both product and process of reason; but recognizing the intuitive aspects of words also can help balance your capacity for using and understanding them.

In the next chapter, as you learn to access your dreams, you will tap the potential of the nonconscious mind to serve as both a motivator of behavior and a guide to understanding. As with our discussion of words, we want to turn the common understanding of dreams on its head, opening up the rational basis of dreaming. In chapters 10 and 11, working with photography and graphic design will help you to express your inner feelings and thoughts and to understand and respond intelligently to the visual meaning of the art you and others create.

In part 3, you will learn how to apply what you know about blending rational and intuitive processing to life experience. To do this, we turn to the media as pervasive life experience for most individuals living in 21st-century culture. Because mass media make available immense quantities of intuitive stimuli, as well as information for the rational mind, they provide a ready resource for omniphasic thinking. We show you how media-generated messages blend words, sounds, and visual imagery into dreamlike symbol sequences to create persuasive messages that shape perceptions of reality in ways that are not always beneficial. You also will learn how to reverse the manipulative effect of these mediated images by using them in positive ways to deepen your understanding of yourself and to expand and enrich your perceptions of reality, your life.

Now, let's move on to new ideas and creative exercises about language, dreams, photography, and graphic design.

Both oral and written languages typically are considered to be highly rational, forms of communication. Yet the ways we speak and write often emerge from highly intuitive perceptual processes that influence how we live, communicate, and think. Grammatical patterns and organizational structures of language may be rational and logical. Yet patterns of sound, inflection, rhythm, and cadence, as well as such figures (note use of the term *figure*) of speech as metaphor, emerge from highly intuitive cognitive processes.

Although we may have moved beyond the idea that gods of ancient mythology bestowed the gifts of speech and writing on humans, we have a long way to go toward understanding how we actually produce, acquire, and use language. We know, for example, as Altmann tells us, that newborns prefer the prosodic, or melodic, characteristics of their mother's voices, having learned the characteristics while still in the womb. "For the infant," Altmann wrote, "language is not an independent entity divorced from the environment in which it is produced and comprehended, it is a part of that environment, and its processing utilizes mental procedures that may not have evolved solely for linguistic purposes" (p. 135). Altmann explains the complexity of the task infants face in acquiring language:

> How are children to know which of the many sounds they hear correspond to which of the infinite range of possibilities before them? For example, children may be able to work out that, among the sounds in the spoken utterance "look, the dog's playing with a ball", the sounds corresponding to "dog" are intended to correspond to the animal in front of them (perhaps because they already know that "ball" refers to the ball, and have a sufficient grasp of syntax to realize that "dog" corresponds to the concept associated with dogs, or with animals more generally, or to things of that shape, or to things of that colour, or to its head, or to all of it. Given the infinite number of hypotheses that children might test, how are they to reject all but the correct one? (p. 136)

Children learn names for objects in categories of similar shape, a phenomenon psycholinguistics call shape bias. Shape bias emerges after children have learned "a certain number of nouns," indicating that associative learning is taking place. Work in psycholinguistics and cognitive psychology supports neural connectionist models of learning and knowing that can be tested through computer simulations of "spreading patterns of activation between" neural-like units (p. 132).

Figure 8.2. Illustration by Soria Moria slott [sic], from William Lunder's Asbjørnsen and Moe: Norwegian folktales, Norway, 1936. MS 2774, The Schøyen Collection MS 2774, Oslo.

Figure 8.3. Kate and J. B., by Rick Williams.

Although we do not fully understand how humans acquire and produce language, we do know humans can distinguish from 60,000 to 75,000 words. Even more impressive, more than half the world's population speaks more than one language. As Altmann concluded, "The adult language faculty . . . is an emergent characteristic of a biological system that, in its initial state at least, is as much a device for acquiring language as it is a device for using language" (p. 157).

Understanding exactly how human language originated or how babies learn to talk and children learn to read and write is not as important a concern to our present discussion as understanding the role of words and other symbol forms. It is most important to understand words as symbols developed by, acquired by, and used by the brain — both the rational and the intuitive parts. It is likely that language developed as a secondary response to our primary experience of reality, allowing us to describe and communicate with each other about those experiences. Language also allows us to think rationally and to communicate abstract thoughts and ideas. As did Abu, before we developed language, we saw, we felt, we acted, but we did not speak in words, though we may have made gestures, expressions, and sounds that represented fear or rage or sorrow or some other primary feeling.

As our human cognitive processes evolved, we grasped the basic ability of visual forms to represent reality and to keep records. We translated our visual and aural perceptions into communication systems, developing sign language, tools, patterned objects, and etchings or paintings of animals or objects on rocks and cave walls, and later as symbols on clay tablets, papyrus, and paper.

Written Language

University of Texas archaeologist Denise Schmandt-Besserat expanded our understanding of how writing came about. Until her work during the 1970s, scholars believed writing began with pictographs — simple pictures that look like objects or living things. Before the 18th century, popular myth had it that writing had been handed down to humans through divine revelation.

Drawing on archeological evidence supported by her own painstaking study of ancient artifacts dating from 8000 to 6000 BCE, Schmandt-Besserat developed a new theory of the origins of writing. She proposed that Neolithic counting devices, small clay objects formed as geometric shapes and animal figures, were the first records of human sounds and thoughts:

> [These tokens] evolved to meet the needs of the economy, at first keeping track of the products of farming, then expanding in the urban age to keep track of goods manufactured in workshops. The development of tokens was tied to the rise of social structures, emerging with rank leadership and coming to a climax with state formation. (p. 7)

Eventually, clay, ball-shaped envelopes were devised to store the tokens. Accountants imprinted token shapes on the outside of a container before sealing it:

> The number of units of goods was still expressed by a corresponding number of markings. An envelope containing seven ovoids, for example, bore seven oval markings.
>
> The substitution of signs for tokens was a first step toward writing. Fourth-millennium accountants soon realized that the tokens within the envelopes were made unnecessary by the presence of markings on the outer surface. As a result, tablets — solid clay balls bearing markings — replaced the hollow envelopes filled with tokens. These markings became a system of their own which developed to include not only impressed markings but also more legible signs traced with a pointed stylus. (p.7)

Schmandt-Besserat noted that the signs were "picture signs." She stressed, however, that "the signs were not pictures of the items they represented, but

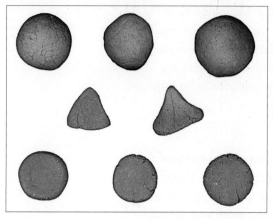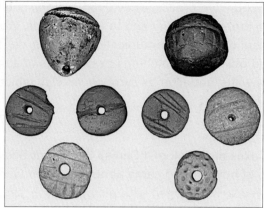

Figure 8.4-6. Top left: Neolithic plain counting tokens, made of clay, "possibly representing 1 measure of grain, 1 animal and 1 man or 1 day's labour, respectively," ca. 8000-3500 BCE. Middle: Complex counting tokens made of stone; top left represented 1 jar of oil, others represented textiles, ca. 4000-3200 BCE. Top right: Bulla-envelope with 11 plain and complex tokens representing an account or agreement, "tentatively of wages for 4 days' work, 4 measures of metal, 1 large measure of barley and 2 small measure of some other commodity," all from Syria/Sumer/Highland Iran, ca. 3700-3200. The Schøyen Collection (from left) MS 5067/1-8, MS 4522/1, and MS 4631, Oslo.

rather, pictures of the tokens used as counters in the previous accounting system …. the token system reflected an archaic mode of 'concrete' counting prior to the invention of abstract numbers" (p. 7). The critical point here is that written language evolved "not only from new bureaucratic demands but from the invention of counting" (p. 7). The tokens, first used in physical "one-to-one correspondence" (p. 7) to animals or jars of oil, initiated the next level of visual communication — transference of literal depiction into abstract form.

On Sounds and Signs

Recognized sounds also became conscious, rational symbols of representational reality. The integration of sound and visual metaphors became the basis of languages that included both visual and verbal components used together. Continuing this tradition in a slightly modified form, humankind developed another kind of visual/aural symbol system — the alphabet.

To form letters we use the basic visual elements of point, line, and shape, which we discuss in chapter 11. We discuss letterforms in more detail when we get to the parts and characteristics of contemporary type in chapter 13. In the Western alphabet, letterforms represent sounds that, when put together in a particular order, form syllables, which form words. We use words to represent ideas as well as things and living entities. The sound and sight of words call forth not only visual symbols from our mind's-eye memory but also feelings associated with past experiences related to the sounds and the visual perceptions. Because language and sound processes deal, in part, with visual images and feelings, language and sound are partially based in our visual, metaphorical, perceptual, intuitive intelligence.

Words in sequence form phrases and sentences to communicate increasingly complex thought patterns. In this way, language utilizes our linear, logical, sequential rational consciousness. Some scholars believe that the ways we developed the visual representation of language have had profound influence on the structures of our societies. Following the ideas of Harold Innis and Marshall McLuhan, Robert Logan proposed that the Western bias toward linear, rational cognitive processing evolved from the effects of the *phonetic* Western alphabet, basically a code representing basic sounds of oral language, on the structures of the brain.

Reading words in a line, as you are doing now, helps create patterns in your brain that in turn influence the way you think about living. Similarly, Logan argued, the logographic or *pictographic* characters of Eastern languages have affected ways of thinking and living in Eastern countries. In such pictographic languages as contemporary Chinese, entire words are represented by unique visual signs that depict them as ideograms or pictograms of about 1,000 basic characters. Syllabic systems of writing, which fall between alphabetic and logographic, phonetically code each spoken syllable into a unique sign. Many languages of North American indigenous people are syllabic systems.

Logan wrote:

> A medium of communication is not merely a passive conduit for the transmission of information but rather an active force in creating new social patterns and new perceptual realities. . . . It is only by studying both the medium as a "message" and the messages that the medium transmits that a full appreciation of cultural and historical processes can emerge. (pp. 24–25)

Logan called this the Alphabet Effect, a phenomenon that he and McLuhan argued causes coevolution of written language thought. The Western alphabet is the most recently developed letterform system, the most abstract, and uses the fewest number of signs — 26 letters. It involves a) coding and decoding, b)

Figure 8.7. Churinga, "3 campsites, waterholes or totem centres (concentric circles) with people sitting facing the centres, guards facing outwards (U-forms of 3 lines), as a part of the Aranda aborigines' mythological landscape," in chalk stone, Central Desert area, Australia, before 500, incised with opossum tooth. According to collection commentary, "There is no certain way to date the old churingas that are from the pre-contact period (before 1780). They can be as old as Aboriginal culture, 40-50,000 years. With the earliest rockpaintings and carvings, the cylcons and churingas represent the oldes form of communication and art, still present, and they represent the oldest religion still observed. The aborigine owner's belief is that his kuruna or spirit is intimately associated with his churinga." The Schøyen Collection MS 4610, Oslo..

Figure 8.8. Churinga in schist-like stone incised with opossum tooth: "Kangaroo tracks in the sand moving around concentric circles; an iconographic emblem of the kangaroo totem, and the movement of his ancestral being around a waterhole, totem centre or a special place in the tribe Aranda's mythological landscape," Central Desert area Australia, before 1800. The Schøyen Collection MS 4629, Oslo.

converting sounds into visual signs, c) thinking deductively, d) classifying information, and e) ordering words. These processes, in turn, contributed to the development of codified law, monotheism, abstract science, deductive logic, and individualism. This idea is given momentum by the thousands of years it took humans to develop oral and written languages through institutions ranging from agriculture to global corporations. Logan argued, "Because the alphabet is so much a part of our information environment, however, we often take its existence for granted and we are blind to its effects, much as fish are unaware of the water in which they swim" (npn). As noted earlier, we discuss letterforms in more detail when we get to the parts and characteristics of contemporary type in chapter 13.

Notice that visual symbols are the basis of both the intuitive and rational processes of language development and use. Both written letters and the rational sequence into which they are arranged to make words and sentences are visual. The verbal sounds and the concepts expressed by letters and words elicit visual imagery in the mind's eye. However, the two visual processes of language construction differ significantly in the quality and use of symbolic

Figure 8.9. Oracle bone: "Cracking made on the Xinhai (Day 48); no quick victory on the yin (Day 51?). Approved. It will rain on Jiahai (?)." Oxen scapula, Xiaotun, China, 14th-12th century BCE, lines in Chinese script, prepared and cracked with burned marks on reverse. "Nearly all known Chinese oracle bones derive from Xiaotun near the ancient capital of the Late Shang Dynasty of Anyang. The oracular use of the bones involved the interpretation of pattern of cracks which appeared on the bones after subjection to heat by the application of a heated metal rod. The text records the interpretation of the oracle and the date of its production. The oracle bones are so far the first preserved evidence of Chinese script in complete meaningful sentences." The Schøyen Collection MS 2103/1-4, Oslo.

information. Visual symbols of the rational mind are used to name and recall objects and to think, speak, and write about them. The visual symbols of the intuitive mind are based in perceptual and emotional experience and are used to recall and create feelings. For instance, the word *child* is a rational arrangement of specific letters in a specific order that names and calls to mind characteristics of a human being of a particular age. But even though the word *child* does not refer to a specific child, because we all have emotion-laden experiences of childhood and children, the word goes beyond its rational meaning to elicit feelings associated with those experiences and perceptions.

One way to think about how language works is to consider that the integration of logic and perception in the development and use of language may be based in the ability to recognize, understand, and respond to the representation of one thing as a likeness or analogy for another thing. This ability is the basis for both art and language. It is also what makes language omniphasic: it is a format through which we can better understand the integration of rational and intuitive intelligences. Language also can help us explore the role of the visual intuitive as a primary motivator of behavior.

For example, considered in one way, words are logical extensions of the rational mind. The English alphabet is linear in character as one word is composed of single letters, one following the other in specific order. Without the rational order, the letters are simply shapes and references to sounds, not words. Without the proper order their meanings as symbols of life experiences or thoughts or images is lost. From this perspective, it is the linear, rational order of words, sentences, and paragraphs that imparts basic meaning. Meaning is what the word is really about.

But the logical aspect of words as symbols designed to name, categorize, and convey basic meaning of experience or thought describes only one limited part of language. The deeper meaning of a word or group of words is carried in the symbolic aspects of the words. The full meaning of a word carries significant visual and intuitive aspects that were part of the original experience that the word represents.

When we read or hear a word, we reach beyond the basic, logical meaning, backward toward the original experience and move across space and time through a cognitive synthesis that connects us, through imagination and memory — including many nonconscious and preconscious memories — to primal feelings. This synthesis moves us away from a general, common understanding of the word toward experiences that are wholly individualistic — experiences that really are not shared by all.

Figure 8.10. Cuneiform script on clay tablet, part of the Sumerian creation story in which a bird and fish "argue for their usefulness in the universe as it was then conceived," Babylonia, 1900-1700 BCE. The Schøyen Collection, MS 2110/1, Oslo.

For instance, when we rearrange the letters *o h e t r m* into *m o t h e r*, we create a common symbol that, on one level, we can generally understand to represent a woman who bears children, perhaps the woman who bore us. But what an impersonal, diminished symbol that common definition is compared to the woman herself, or our experience of the woman.

Your mother and your experiences of her as your mother are unique to you and are the basis of your memories, both conscious and nonconscious, of those experiences. Your essential, primal, visual, physiological, and psychological knowing spans a lifetime in a way that can never be conveyed accurately or completely to another

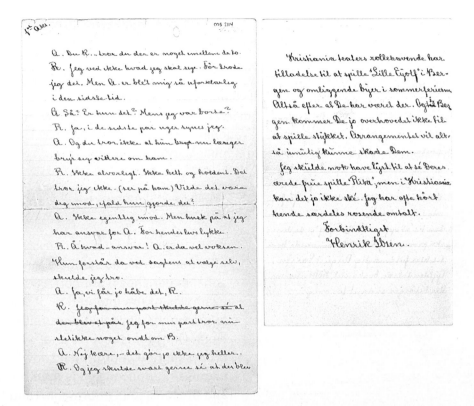

Figure 8.11. Above Left: Renowned Norwegian playwright Henrik Ibsen's cursive script on paper of part of first act of Lille Eyolf, ca 1893. Above Right: Signed letter concerning his right to produce the play and present it throughout most of Norway, March 28, 1895. The Schøyen Collection, MS 2114, Oslo.

person merely by six written or spoken letters. Someone else may have her own experiences of your mother, but the two of you cannot share the same understanding of the same person. Although you can share meaning, that understanding represents only a miniscule part of what you experience when you hear, write, read, or say the word mother.

Thus the intuitive part of your mind, at the mere mention of the word *mother*, can synthesize those primary, experiential memories instantaneously into a holistic sense of your relationship. This cognitive synthesis has the ability to affect the deepest parts of your psyche in ways that guide and change your behavior at any given moment, and it can happen without your rational mind's awareness or controls.

And, of course, that intuitive knowledge and response is different from your sister's or your brother's. This knowledge would bear only schematic resemblance to your father's sense of *mother* or to another person's sense of *mother*. On a predominantly rational plane, we may say the word *mother* as if we all were talking about the same woman. However, underneath, our intuitive intelligences are simultaneously synthesizing meanings with different psychological, physiological, and behavioral nuances.

Of course, humans of similar cultures share ideals of motherhood on some level. We also share archetypal images of motherhood, mother earth, Madonna and Child. Yet our own individual intuitive knowledge of *mother* influences our conscious and nonconscious perceptions. The meanings of most words and other forms of experience and communication are deeper and more meaningful than we are able to consider or understand rationally in any given moment. Although we speak to one another on rational, conscious levels, the fact is that deeply intuitive, nonconscious cognition influences all communication.

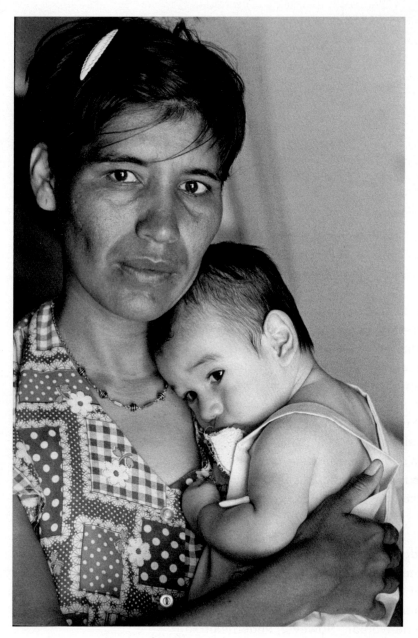

Figure 8.12. Chely and her baby. Photograph by Julianne Newton.

Words as Balanced Ways of Knowing

With this in mind, let us revisit the idea that words, as symbols for personal experiences, are perfect examples of the integration of the two primary ways that our brains work. Our brains receive and process intuitive or primal knowledge using nonconscious memories and preconscious information and perceptual abilities. We use that knowledge, often without conscious awareness, to guide our perceptions of reality and to develop our value systems. Our brains also transform that primary knowledge into rational knowledge that helps us understand, communicate, and evaluate our behavior and respond with reasoned intelligence in our relationships and behavior.

Before going further, we remind you that we are talking about two independent, cognitive-processing systems of our one brain. However, both our intuitive and rational cognitive systems, though functionally distinct, are integrative and operate together. One intelligence does not work alone, though one may be dominant for a given task or process. For instance, the rational mind might be dominant when you balance your

Figure 8.13. Liturgical book script in Latin and French, with illuminated borders, initials, and miniatures on vellum. Book of Hours; Metz, France, mid 15th century. The Schøyen Collection MS 007, Oslo. Original in color.

checkbook, whereas the intuitive mind might be dominant when you draw or dance. Yet the mental processes operate in an integrated manner.

As an example of this interplay, consider the first time you learned a new dance, to drive a stick-shift car, or to type. At first it was awkward and you had to think rationally about where to put your feet in keeping with the beats of the music, or how hard to press the gas pedal or clutch. As you practiced the rhythms of these various endeavors, you moved to a gestalt synthesis of rational structure and intuitive flow, just as you did in the drawing exercise. You experience the global integration of rational and intuitive as you eventually begin to dance without thinking; drive without stalling; and flow through characters, words, and sentences on your computer keyboard.

This is a glimpse of the integrative mind, or omniphasic mental processing. This balance can add deeper dimensions to your writing, speaking, thinking, working, relating, and relaxing and knowing. For now, we are applying it to the written word to see how daily activities are affected by the integration of rational and intuitive language abilities.

Figure 8.14. Left: Oldest known musical notation on a lenticular tablet used as a school text in Babylonia, 2000-1700 BCE. Old Babylonian cuneiform indicates two ascending scales to be played on a four-stringed lute with frets. The notation includes headings "intonation" and "incantation." Below: A modern transcription. The Schøyen Collection MS 5101, Oslo.

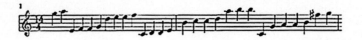

The Sounds of Words

We have discussed the development of language out of experience and looked at its use from a written perspective. But beyond the structured, written use of language, our ability to verbalize language through speaking or singing adds another dimension to this complex concert of cognitive processes. Because letters are visual symbols for sounds, words, and ideas, they are part of the rational symbol system of language. However, the ability to use tone, pace, resonance, volume, and inflection allows the voice to convey deeper and more complex meanings drawn from our intuitive musical/tonal and emotional intelligences. Vocalization of language also draws directly from and simultaneously informs both our intrapersonal communication and our nonconscious memories.

An example of a personal life experience will help clarify. As a child, one of your authors often nestled in the large, warm arms of his great-grandmother while listening to *The Phantom* or *The Cisco Kid* on her bedside radio. As he sat there cradled, rocked, and comforted, and the exciting mysteries unfolded, he felt loved, secure, nurtured, and content. His imagination, aided by voices, inflections, sound effects, and music, was free to create images of the unseen characters and scenarios in his mind's eye. So strong was this experience more than 50 years ago that even hearing the word *radio* today brings back both the inner visions of that experience and the inner feelings of warmth and security. When he is working alone, Rick nearly always has either on the radio, music, or the sound of the television in the background. We all have had these emotional experiences. Not all are so positive, but all tap deep feelings within our psyches when certain words are spoken or read.

Other intuitive processes involve tone of voice, pacing, inflection, and even word choice. You may recall feeling a strong, emotional response when a parent uses your full name in a loud, formal, and stern voice. On the other hand, you probably have a very different emotional response when a significant other calls you by a name that only he or she uses for you. So the language that we read and write, and speak and hear blends perceptual visual and aural processes with the conceptual, sequenced approach of our rational intelligences to communicate to the whole mind. In this, language is omniphasic.

The Form of the Presentation

Of course, this blending of metaphor and fact, of intuition and logic, takes various forms, depending on the intended point of the communication. It can be designed as such a rational and linear sequencing of conceptual thought that, though it makes its points, it is difficult to follow and loses readers' attention. For instance, note that even though the title of the following academic study is *The Nature of Human Arousal . . .*, the form of presentation is such that only research specialists would understand it or find it interesting:

> Hypotheses 1 and 2 were tested by regressing change scores
> for the nonverbal composites on linear, quadratic and cubic
> polynomial change scores for arousal. (p. 240)

On the other hand, linguistic communication can be so intuitively esoteric as to be incomprehensible. The following passage from James Joyce's *Finnegans Wake* is an example of word play that is highly intuitive in its focus, tone, pacing and inflection. The words roll lyrically off the tongue (especially with ans Irish brogue), but the meaning is barely comprehensible to most readers:

> . . . not yet, though venissoon after, had a kidscad buttended a
> bland old isaac: not yet, though all's fair in vanessey, were sosie
> sesthers wroth with twone nathandjoe. Rot a peck of pa's malt
> had Jhem or Shen brewed by arclight and rory end to the reg-
> ginbrow was to be seen ringsome on the aquaface. (p. 3)

These extremes support the idea that a balance of cognitive processes can improve both the understanding and the quality of word experiences. As an example of this omniphasic blend, note the following passage from Henry Miller's *Plexus*. In its rationality, it is grammatically correct and develops a logical theme. Yet, intuitively, it is presented in emotionally powerful, poetic prose. Thus, the passage renders a gestalt experience that integrates technique and aesthetic to create an artistic experience of clear thought and inspiring vision through the use of words and the everyday acts of writing and reading.

> On lonely nights, pondering the problem — only one ever!
> — I could see so very clearly the world as it is, see what it is
> and why it is the way it is. I could reconcile grace and evil,
> divine order with rampant ugliness, imperishable creation with
> utter sterility. I could make myself so finely attuned that a mere
> zephyr would blow me to dust. Instant annihilation or enduring

*Figure 8.15. "My beloved knows my heart, / my beloved is sweet as honey, / she is as fragrant
to the nose as wine, / the fruit of my feelings." Old Babylonian cuneiform script
on clay tablet, only known love poem for this early period, Babylonia, 18th century BCE.
The Schøyen Collection MS 2866, Oslo.*

life — it was one and the same to me. I was at balance, both sides so evenly poised that a molecule of air would tilt the scales.

Suddenly a most hilarious thought would shatter the whole setup. An idea such as this: "However deep one's knowledge of abstruse philosophy, it is like a piece of hair flying in the vastness of space." A Japanese thought, this. With it came a return to a more ordinary sort of equilibrium. Back to that frailest of all footholds — solid earth. That solid earth which we now accept as being as empty as space. (p. 635)

To experience the powerful way in which this integration of technique and aesthetic can communicate emotions within the intuitive mind, try standing and reading the passage aloud several times. Or choose a poem that you like and read it aloud. In either case, as you begin to understand the meaning, use your voice to emphasize tone, pacing, and inflection to enhance the feeling and meaning of the words.

Conclusion

To summarize, the linear, logical design of words in the Western tradition, through alignment of letters locates language in our rational, analytical, cognitive-processing system. This system delivers one kind of knowledge and meaning — primarily logical, factual, naming, categorizing knowledge that generates abstract thought and ideas, and can sometimes alter our behavior.

On the other hand, all of our factual, rational knowledge is derived from experiences and thoughts of a very personal and unique nature, including those of our imaginations and creativity. These experiences are stored in nonconscious memory until something — such as the need to make a decision, or seeing the word *mother* — stimulates specific memories. Then these nonconscious memories are brought forth through our synthesistic, intuitive cognitive-processing system to give unique, personal meaning to the rational facts of our experience. This intuitive cognition may occur on either conscious or nonconscious levels, or both.

Thus, language is an omniphasic blend of rational and intuitive intelligence. It allows us to communicate our experiences and thoughts through commonly held concepts that suggest basic meaning. Language also stimulates deeper, intrapersonal meanings that are drawn from both nonconscious memories and emotions. When we use the global, symbolic imagery of our intuitive intelligence in concert with the logical sequencing of ideas and concepts of our linear, rational intelligence, we use our whole minds in an omniphasic symphony of cognitive unity. The conscious development of this creative process and the abilities associated with it have the power to draw us — mind and heart — into full awareness. From this sense of wholeness, our lives can then become an artistic expression of our creative energy.

Figure 8.16. Dáme una sonrisa. Photograph by Julianne Newton. Language can both prohibit and enhance rational and intuitive knowing. Words draw on and evoke images in the mind's eye. Do images evoke words? When you look at this photo what do you sense? One interpretation is that the image expresses the mixture of emotions children feel in dealing with society: impatience, curiosity, acquiesence, and anxiety. Those empathetic feelings are experienced by a viewer instantaneously, before the feelings were named as words in the conscious mind. What do you see when you look at this picture?

This is Sky

Sky wears costumes.
He wears them everyday,
not just for special occasions.
He is very attached to his mother,
mostly to her thigh.

He will play alone for hours,
then sit and color and do mazes
for still more hours.

I hope he will be able to deal
with the real world
when it is time for him to do so.
What a shame that he must.

Figure C8.1. "This Is Sky," by Mary Lee Edwards.

CREATIVE EIGHT
The Visual Word: Giving Vision to Voice

The Goal: Integrating Visual and Verbal

One way to find your own creative voice in language is to use visual images to inspire creative writing. This very simple process can reap great rewards. In addition to helping you find a unique voice for writing poetry or creative prose, the process can help you improve such nonfiction writing as journalistic articles and term papers. The process also can help "unlock" writer's block.

Another way to find your creative voice is to compare the difference between reading silently and reading aloud. Words read in silence and words read aloud evoke different thoughts, images, and emotions.

In this exercise you will explore the visually creative potential of words.

Part I

Find an image that holds your attention. It is fine to use one of the many images in this book. Other potential sources are magazines, art books, picture archives. Be sure to note the artist (if known), title, source, date, page number, and other reference information so you can fully credit the image.

Take the picture, along with your journal or a few sheets of paper and a pen or pencil, to a quiet place where you can sit comfortably and write.

Spend a little time relaxing. Try meditating or drawing for a short time. Try vase/face or blind contour drawing.

When you are ready, pick up your pen and look at the picture. The idea is to let the picture inspire creative or descriptive writing.

Begin to write immediately. Do not wait and study the image. If nothing that makes sense comes to mind, just start writing the words that come to you. Let them flow and see if they develop into a poem or short story or a creative description of the picture or some part of it, just as you let the lines flow onto the page in blind contour drawing. Initially, do not worry about how it sounds or fits together. As the words flow, see if thoughts begin to emerge that tie the words together into a poem or story, or simply into a vivid description of what you are feeling and thinking after experiencing the image and spontaneous flow of words. If this does not happen easily, look back at the words you wrote and see if they bring up ideas for a descriptive phrase or a sentence or two for a poem or story. Or, try rearranging the words that you wrote and see what develops.

Do this with at least two pictures.

Part II

Find a poem that you like. Read it silently several times. When you finish reading it silently, stand and read it aloud using the tone and volume of your voice to add depth and meaning to the words. Notice the difference between the silent and spoken readings in terms of how you feel and what you think and understand.

Reflect on and write an assessment of both parts of this exercise discussing your experiences and what you learned.

The Exercise

- Read the instructions carefully and select an image.
- Spend time relaxing before you start writing.
- Write what flows out while contemplating the image.
- Select another image.
- Write as many word visions as you want, but at least two.
- Select a poem.
- Read it silently several times.
- Read it aloud at least twice.
- Assess your experiences.

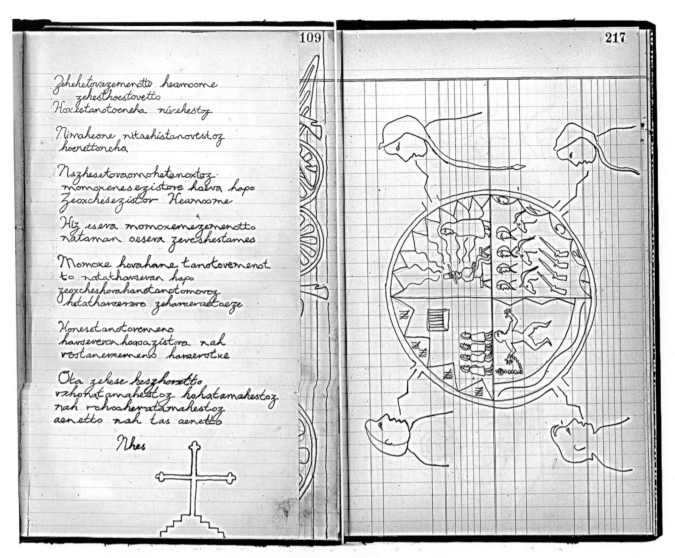

Figure C8.2. *The Bulman Ledger, Cheyenne cursive script, name glyphs and drawings, Oklahoma, 1891-1900. The rare intact ledger includes pen drawings by Bullman of travels, imprisonment, the exchange of a dead golden eagle, a smallpox outbreak, and a marriage proposal. Above Left: The Lord's Prayer, Matthew 6:9-13, the Bible. Above Right: Collection Commentary indicates the page "seems to depict the recounting by 4 men of a collective vision. The vision in a quartered circle shows a man on a bench in the upper quadrant, being addressed by a blanketed figure who may represent Thunder, as power lines are radiating out from a zigzag sky. Similar zigzags in the upper left quadrant have a different connotation with 4 figures in prison and a conventionalised counting device of 5 lines, repeated 5 times. The diagonal slash to denote 5 is a White man's way of counting. The lower left quadrant depicts a man chained to the wall, but surrounded on both sides by lightning symbols. The lower right quadrant is distinguished by the Roman numerals 1-5 in semi-circles, plus 4 rifles, 3 horse heads, and 4 human heads, seemingly the booty of 5 successful raids. In the last 3 decades of the 19th c. Indians of the Apache, Cheyenne, Sioux, Kiowa and other tribes of the Great Plains, often deprived of traditional artistic and ceremonial venues because of their confinement to reservations, turned to drawings in small books and discarded ledgers as a way to make sense of the profound cultural stress to which they were subjected. The indigenous style evolved into a new form of Indian art, characterised by meticulously detailed depictions of clothing and paraphernalia." The art is today represented in most major U.S. art museums. The Schøyen Collection MS 4605, Oslo.*

Figure 9.1. Kate's Fourth of July. Photograph by Rick Williams.

CHAPTER NINE
Insight Out:
Dreams and the Nonconscious Mind

Dreams — windows to the soul, a recounting of the day's events, the voice of the nonconscious mind, a seemingly meaningless firing of neurons, the language of the seer, an escape from the day, visions of the prophets, mental visions, connections to the collective unconscious, messages from the divine. Metaphors for dreams and arguments about their significance to our lives — or the lack thereof — could be used to chronicle human understanding of human imagination and consciousness. Few people seem to be neutral when the subject of discourse is dreams. Yet, whether one sees dreams as significant or not, any history of humankind must include stories of how dreams and visions have influenced individuals and culture. From Jacob to Ulysses, Aristotle to Jung, and Sitting Bull to the Dalai Lama, dreams and visions have served humankind as powerful metaphors for connections between the soul and forces larger than us. Dreams have shaped the lives of individuals and the futures of nations.

With its bias toward scientific measurement of provable facts, contemporary culture has lost touch with ways to use dreams and visions for guidance and clarity in improving the quality of our lives. Just as we balanced rational understanding of words with a discussion of their intuitive roots, we will balance intuitive interpretation of the phenomena of dreaming and visualization with the rational basis of recent scientific exploration of dreams and mental imaging.

The term *pseudoscience* is often used by those who are rationally biased to diminish the significance of theories and processes that do not fit within certain parameters of the scientific method — such as measurability and repeatability — as proof of value. We recall one scenario, for example, in which a group of individuals passed out leaflets about pseudoscience before a presentation by physicist Fritjof Capra at the University of Texas at Austin. Introducing Capra was Ilya Prigogine, a highly respected scientist and recipient of the Nobel Prize in chemistry in 1977 for his contributions to nonequilibrium thermodynamics, particularly the theory of dissipative structures. Prigogine stressed his support for Capra's applications of systems theory in Capra's book *The Web of Life*. Rationally biased members of the audience could not contain their disdain for Capra's provocative and imaginative ideas. Those who could hold rationally and intuitively derived concepts in tandem were mesmerized by both Prigogine's and Capra's presentations. The kind of marginalization attempted by those opposed to Capra's work exemplifies rational bias that establishes quantitative measurement and evaluation as the primary — and often the only — standard of value.

It is important to understand that we are not devaluing scientific approaches to knowing. Some processes and theories appear to have the probability of being precisely measurable and repeatable most of the time. For instance, when you flip a light switch or start your computer, you expect the light or computer to turn on and to function normally, just as they did the last time you used them. On a biological level, if you are taking medication for a medical condition, you want that medication to be exactly the same each time you take it.

However, many things that are important and valuable to our lives and communities are not precisely measurable and repeatable. Physicists tell us that nothing is infinitely repeatable. Therefore, quantification cannot be the ultimate measure of value for all processes and experiences. When methods designed for evaluating quantitative processes become the dominant paradigm, a cultural bias then directs all evaluation toward rational thinking and quantification, even of personal, social, and cultural concerns. How much money do you have? How many home runs have you hit, either real or metaphorically? Will you be able to do it again, and again, and still again? How intelligent are you based on rationally biased tests such as the SAT and GRE? How many facts can you repeat for a test? These questions all use quantitative measurements of success and repeatability and ignore quality-of-life experiences. All things of value are not quantifiable or repeatable.

An Example

Consider an evening when you go to a musical concert and the artists perform extraordinarily well, not only playing their known hits but also improvising and creating new, spontaneous compositions. By the time the concert is over, you are so inspired and filled with excitement that you stand up and applaud and whistle or yell for an encore. You do not want the experience to end.

Now, consider the concert from an omniphasic perspective. A concert is a blend of the rational (quantitative) and intuitive (qualitative) processes that together provide the final experience. The individual musicians practiced, playing notes repeatedly, and developed technique until the integration of their individual performances was tight. The lighting and sound technicians tested the positioning of lights and circuits to set the right ambience for the light and

Figure 9.2. Willie Nelson in concert, Austin, by Rick Williams.

level of sound. The maintenance crew made certain the floors and seats were clean and comfortable and the temperature adjusted properly. These are a few of the rational background processes that had to occur for the holistic experience of enjoying the performance to happen.

So, what happened then? The colors and lighting of the scene on stage set an appropriate mood so that you could, without consciously thinking about them, synthesize ambient, visual features into an intuitively sophisticated, unique experience. The musicians performed beyond the mere playing of notes to create a stirring performance that aesthetically transcended into a unique musical experience. Your intuitive intelligences — visual, musical, and bodily kinesthetic — synthesized the visual array, the musical excellence, the comfort of your seat, and the rhythm of your body to create a holistic, qualitative experience.

So how do you quantify that quality experience? How do you measure your experience? Does an applause meter accurately reflect your experience? And further, would you want to repeat that experience exactly the same way each time you went to a concert? You probably would want the light and sound to work well and the musicians to be practiced and the theatre to be comfortable and clean. But would you want to experience that same concert, in exactly the same way, over and over? Probably not. Even if you did want to, you could not. It is the uniqueness and aesthetic quality of a particular experience that give it value. Repeating it precisely is neither possible, because we cannot quantify and repeat our unconscious intuitive experiences, nor desirable, because the repetition denies the unique qualities that so inspired us.

Much of the quality of such an experience depends on the complex, rapid, synthesistic abilities of the unconscious, intuitive, visual, musical, and bodily kinesthetic intelligences. Your nonconscious mind integrated your various intuitive processes so seamlessly that you were never aware of much of the process itself. How you were relating to yourself (intrapersonal intelligence) and how you were relating to the other concert patrons or to the musicians (interpersonal intelligence) also entered into your overall experience in significant ways.

The Role of Dreams in Human Knowing

Dreams provide one form of visual experience that is not measurable or repeatable — although some psychiatrists now believe they can construct a full description of your personality if you provide them with 100 of your dreams. Dreams can provide insights into the qualitative experiences and issues of our lives. When we consider dreams and visions, we are working on a broader scale with the same intuitive, synthesistic processes of our unconscious minds that are active in musical events, media images, and films. All that is in the unconscious mind has the potential to emerge into consciousness to influence our actions. In this way, dreams build bridges between unconscious and conscious states of knowing, providing preconscious stages on which intuitive intelligence can synthesize perception and memory.

The story of Rene Descartes, the 17th-century philosopher often called the father of rationalism, provides important insight into this discussion. Mathematics scholars Phillip J. Davis and Reuben Hersh told the story well:

> The Modern World, our world of triumphant rationality, began on November 10, 1619, with a revelation and a nightmare. On that day, in a room in the small Bavarian village of Ulm, Rene Descartes, a Frenchman, twenty-three years old, crawled into a wall stove and, when he was well warmed, had a vision. It was not a vision of God, or of the Mother of God, or of celestial chariots, or of the New Jerusalem. It was a vision of the unification of all science.
>
> The vision was preceded by a state of intense concentration and agitation. Descartes' overheated mind caught fire and provided answers to tremendous problems that had been taxing him for weeks. He was possessed by a Genius, and the answers were revealed in a dazzling, unendurable light. Later, in a state of exhaustion, he went to bed and dreamed three dreams that had been predicted by this Genius.
>
> In the first dream, he was revolved by a whirlwind and terri-

Figure 9.3. Jacob's Ladder, 1973, by Marc Chagall (original in color). © 2006 Artists Rights Society (ARS), NY. Photo of painting by Scala / Art Resource, NY.

fied by phantoms. He experienced a constant feeling of falling. He imagined he would be presented with a melon that came from a far-off land. The wind abated and he woke up. His second dream was one of thunderclaps and sparks flying around his room. In the third dream, all was quiet and contemplative. An anthology of poetry lay on the table. He opened it at random and read the verse of Ausonius, "*Quod vitae sectabor iter*" (What path shall I take in life?). A stranger appeared and quoted him the verse "*Est et non*" (Yes and no). Descartes wanted to show him where in the anthology it could be found, but the book disappeared and reappeared. He told the man he would show him a better verse beginning "*Quod vitae sectabor iter*." At this point the man, the book, and the whole dream dissolved.

Descartes was so bewildered by all this that he began to pray. He assumed his dreams had a supernatural origin. He vowed he would put his life under the protection of the Blessed Virgin and go on a pilgrimage from Venice to Notre Dame de

Lorette, traveling by foot and wearing the humblest-looking clothes he could find.

What was the idea that Descartes saw in a burning flash? He tells us that his third dream pointed to no less than the unification and the illumination of the whole of science, even the whole of knowledge, by one and the same method: the method of reason.

Eighteen years would pass before the world would have the details of the grandiose vision and of the "*mirabilis sientiae fundamenta* —"— the foundations of a marvelous science. Such as he was able to give them, they are contained in the celebrated "Discourse on the Method of Properly Guiding the Reason in the Search of Truth in the Sciences." According to Descartes, his "method" should be applied when knowledge is sought in any scientific field. It consists of (a) accepting only what is so clear in one's own mind as to exclude any doubt; (b) splitting large difficulties into smaller ones; (c) arguing from the simple to the complex; and (d) checking, when one is done. (pp. 3-4)

Descartes became concerned that he could not tell the difference between a state of dreaming while asleep and a state of wakefulness. This concern became the basis of his argument that sensory perception could not be trusted. Ironically, Descartes's theories were inspired by the dreams, which, wrote philosopher/theologian Peter Chojnowski, Descartes interpreted as a "divine endorsement":

Having in mind, for a number of years, a project and method to bring all the sciences together within the context of a new universal philosophical "wisdom," Descartes interpreted the vivid dreams that he had on the night of the Vigil of the Feast of St. Martin as a sign from God Himself. From that moment on, Descartes would believe that he had a divine mandate to establish an all-encompassing science of human wisdom. (npn)

The point to relating Descartes's story here is that the very person so often cited as being the father of reason as a way of thinking that became the basis of the scientific method, used his dreams to develop his rational theories. Though he discounted his dreams, they influenced him. All humans have within them various means for deriving knowledge. Dreaming is one of those processes.

Miguel de Cervantes: Another Great Dreamer

The great Spanish poet, playwright, and novelist, Miguel de Cervantes (1547–1616), expressed this position eloquently through the adventures of Don Quixote. One adventure from Part II of *Don Quixote*, published in 1615, is particularly helpful to our discussion of dreams. In the story of the Cave Montesinos, Don Quixote's faithful servant, Sancho Panza, and a guide lower a rope-secured Don Quixote "into the depths of the dread cavern." The guide, described as a "humanist cousin," has urged the don "to observe carefully and examine with a hundred eyes everything that is within there" (chap. XXII). After spending only about half an hour asleep in the cave, Don Quixote believes he has spent 3 days there, experiencing "the sweetest and most delightful existence and spectacle that ever human being enjoyed or beheld." The don describes a scene in which an old man approaches him, embraces him, and says to him:

Figure 9.4. Don Quixote, 1955, by Pablo Picasso.
© 2006 Estate of Pablo Picasso / Artists Rights Society
(ARS), New York; Scala / Art Resource NY.

"For a long time now, O valiant knight Don Quixote of La Mancha, we who are here enchanted in these solitudes have been hoping to see thee, that thou mayest make known to the world what is shut up and concealed in this deep cave, called the cave of Montesinos, which thou hast entered, an achievement reserved for thy invincible heart and stupendous courage alone to attempt. Come with me, illustrious sir, and I will show thee the marvels hidden within this transparent castle, whereof I am the alcalde and perpetual warden; for I am Montesinos himself, from whom the cave takes its name." (chapt. XXIII)

So real were Don Quixote's experiences in the cave (and so strong are Sancho's doubts about their actuality) that Don Quixote goes on to query a number of unlikely sources whether his experiences were truth or dream. Spanish literature scholar Anthony J. Cascardi, of the University of California,

Figure 9.5. Still from Atanarjuat, The Fast Runner, a film by Zacharias Kunuk, Igloolik Isuma Productions, in co-production with National Film Board of Canada. Atanarjuat, which takes place in the Arctic at the beginning of the first millennium, tells the story of an Inuit legend kept alive through oral history. Atanarjuat is played by Natar Ungalaaq. The screenplay was written in Inuktitut and cast with Inuit professional actors and first-time performers.

Berkeley, explained that Cervantes's purpose was "to affirm the role of fiction in our relationship to the world (which, it might further be said, is an affirmation of the role of fiction in the task of philosophy)." Cascardi noted "Cervantes' will to include the imagination and dreams within the range of valid human experience — within what we call the 'world' in the broad sense — free of the caveats of reason." Therein lies "a basis on which a discovery of the world, as such, may begin" (npn). These are similar lessons to those posed to you at the beginning of this book in the parable of the scientist, the theologian, and the shaman. The point is that both science and fiction, rational and intuitive, have value in helping us understand how and why we live.

What Science Has To Say

Fortunately, for those more scientifically than intuitively inclined, contemporary science has come to value dreams as a rich source of understanding human cognitive processing. Recent studies support the idea of a critical affective connection between the preconscious and conscious mind. That connection guides the development of our perceptions of reality and thus our conscious behavior. Jaynes suggested the significance of this connection in early cultures with his description of the admonitory qualities of the visions and nonconscious voices of the bicameral mind. Bogen's and Sperry's description of the processes of the right hemisphere as visual, global, synthesistic, and symbolic parallels Freud's and Jung's theories that describe dreams as visual, global, and symbolic. More recently, Bechara, Damasio, Tranel, and Damasio(1997) demonstrated the significance of the influence of unconscious biases from the unconscious memory of our prefrontal lobes as they guide our rational decision-making processes. This work, together with the significance of dreams and visions as guides for individuals and groups of people throughout history, suggests that the activities of the nonconscious mind are critical to the quality of our lives. In Part III of this book, we explore how contemporary images employed by media — from magazines to the Internet — use dreamlike qualities and processes to affect the preconscious mind to influence our lives. But for now we explore dreams and meditation as primary processes that help one approach and understand the nonconscious mind as guide.

Historical Foundations of Dreams

As early as 1900, psychiatrist Sigmund Freud proposed the then revolutionary concept that dreams are the "royal road" to the unconscious mind and that they reveal, in disguised symbolic form, the deepest elements of an individual's life. Freud's younger associate and later critic, Carl Jung, suggested that all consciousness evolves from the unconscious mind and that the process of individuation, or self-awareness, integrates the unconscious and conscious facets of the mind. He believed that one of the primary problems modern cultures face is the splitting of consciousness from its roots in the unconscious and the subsequent focus on material rewards as substitutes for self-awareness and inner guidance. Jung believed that, although the unconscious breaks into consciousness in obvious ways from time to time, one would have to seek motivations in the unconscious to better understand how they work. He theo-

Figures 9.6-7. Left: North and Central American Indian archetypal art. Right: Milagros, silver icons used to represent objects of prayer. Photographs by Rick Williams.

Visual Communication: Integrating Media, Art, and Science

Figures 9.8-10. Top left: Mesoamerican snake god sculpture.
Top middle: Hopi pot with bear icons. Right: Navajo wedding basket
with star pointing east. Photographs by Rick Williams.

rized that the unconscious mind communicates through visual symbols that represent various aspects of the self, and that accessing and understanding these symbols would lead to a deeper understanding of one's psyche and behavioral motivations. According to Jung, dreams and images from meditation are the two primary ways of accessing the unconscious mind. Thus, he developed a process for better understanding the symbolic meaning of one's dream imagery.

One of Jung's most useful contributions was the concept of archetypes, which he defined as instinctive patterns or imprints to which all humans unconsciously relate. Jung believed that archetypes play major roles in our dreams and are expressed in our myths, art, and stories.

Among Jung's archetypes (adapted from Boeree, 1997) are:

- The Mother — nurturing, life-giving entity characterized by
  Eve, Mary, earth mother, the sea.
- Mana — spiritual power characterized by phallic symbols.
- The Shadow — the dark side of humans, characterized by the
  snake, dragons, monsters, and demons.
- The Persona — the mask one puts on for the outside world.
- Anima — the female aspects of men, characterized by a spon-
  taneous, intuitive young girl, or as a witch or the earth mother;
  the life force itself.
- Animus — the male aspects of women, characterized by a
  wise, logical old man or sorcerer.
- Syzygy — the anima and animus together as a whole.
- Father — a guide or authority.
- Family — deep relationships.
- Child — rebirth, the future, characterized by Christ and the
  child-god.

- Hero — fights the shadow, demons, monsters; represents the ego.
- Maiden — purity and innocence; naiveté who may discover her power and become the anima.
- Wise Old Man — form of animus that guides the hero to the unconscious.
- Animal — human's relationship with creatures.
- Trickster — troublemakers who impede the hero's progress.
- Hermaphrodite — union of opposites, characterized by Jesus as a feminine man and Kuan Yin as a male saint known for feminine compassion.
- Self — ultimate unity of personality, characterized by the perfection of Jesus and the Buddha; represented by the circle, cross, and mandala — a geometric figure often expressed as circles within squares within circles within squares.

Though areas of both Freud's and Jung's work have been criticized by cultural theorists and scientists alike, their discoveries and theories provide the foundation for several mainstream strains of contemporary psychology. Psychologist and Jungian analyst Clarissa Pinkola Estés adapted Jung's theory of archetypes and personality in her classic book of myths and stories, *Women Who Run With the Wolves*. Estés explored the archetype of the Wild Woman through the relationship she sees between women and wolves:

> Wildlife and the Wild Woman are both endangered species.
>
> Over time, we have seen the feminine instinctive nature looted, driven back, and overbuilt. For long periods it has been mismanaged like the wildlife and the wildlands. For several thousand years, as soon and as often as we turn our backs, it is relegated to the poorest land in the psyche. The spirit lands of Wild Woman have, throughout history, been plundered or burnt, dens bulldozed, and natural cycles forced into unnatural rhythms to please others.
>
> It's not by accident that the pristine wilderness of our planet disappears as the understanding of our own inner wild natures fades. It is not so difficult to comprehend why old forests and old women are viewed as not very important resources. It is not such a mystery. It is not so coincidental that wolves and coyotes, bears and wildish women have similar reputations. They all share related instinctual archetypes, and as such, both are erroneously reputed to be ingracious, wholly and innately dangerous, and ravenous. (p. 3)

Figure 9.11. Zaragoza Woman, by Julianne Newton.

Figure 9.12. Ascent, by Germán Herrera.

She went on, of course, to write about woman's deepest nature as sharing psychic characteristics with wolves: keen sensing, playful spirit, devotion, relational nature, great endurance and strength, deeply intuitive, highly adaptable, fiercely stalwart, and courageous.

The Wild Woman archetype is important to our discussion of dreams because it illustrates how patterns and instincts related to the natural world can help us understand our tendency to draw on myths, folktales, and stories for wisdom. It also illustrates how understanding an archetype can help a person understand how a seemingly nonsensical dream, full of creatures and strange-but somewhat-familiar beings, can apply to our everyday lives.

Psychologist Frank Coolidge explained:

As the study of great apes aids in the understanding of early hominid evolution, so too can contemporary dream research help in the understanding of ancient hominid dream life and cognitive evolution. It has been proffered that a major leap forward in the cognitive evolution of hominids may first have occurred in the building of nests, and a second major step may have been the full transition to ground sleep. These two changes may have begun a modification of the quality and quantity of hominid sleep, which in turn may have enhanced waking survival skills through priming, aiding the consolidation of procedural memories, and promoted creativity and innovation. Current dream research with children, adults, and animals, and the dreams of modern hunter-gatherers, appear to support the hypothesis that these changes in sleep may have been critical to the cognitive evolution of hominids from Homo habilis to Homo erectus. (para. 1)

Coolidge, who specializes in personality change, brain–behavior relationships, sleep and dreaming, posed a fascinating theory about the concurrent development of changes in human sleep habits, survival, and dreaming.

Contemporary Research about Dreams

Contemporary work on dreams by neuroscientist Jonathan Winson and others offers support for Coolidge's theory, at least in regard to a connection between dreaming and surviving. Winson's work also supports much of what Freud and Jung proposed about the unconscious mind. We too have found that the core psychological assumption that learning more about the self and intrapersonal motivations through dreams and meditation supports positive self-evolution. Our students report, for example, that the dream interpretation exercise that follows this chapter provides insight to better understand themselves and the motivations behind their behavior.

The work of neuroscientists, evolutionary scientists, and psychologists suggests a correlation between Freud's and Jung's ideas about dreams and LeDoux's and Damasio's work on unconscious memory. The omniphasic emphasis in both yields insight into the effect of mediated images on perception, decision making, and behavior in the individual. By extension it can help us understand the development of cultural norms as well.

Using electroencephalographic information from experiments on mice and rabbits, Winson developed a neurobiological map of dreaming. The map reveals that dreaming uses the same mental processes used to develop waking strategies of survival, learning, and long-term memory. Winson suggested that "dreams may reflect a memory-processing mechanism inherited from lower species in which information important for survival is reprocessed during REM sleep. This information may constitute the core of the unconscious" (p. 60).

Figure 9.13. Swans reflecting elephants, 1937, by Salvador Dali. © 2006 Salvador Dali, Gala-Salvador Dali Foundation / Artists Rights Society (ARS), NY; Erich Lessing / Art Resource, NY.

When integrated with LeDoux's and Damasio's work, Winson's research suggests that during waking activities and during REM dream sleep, life experiences significant to survival are encoded neurologically in the hippocampus and prefrontal cortex as unconscious memory. These nonconscious memories are later activated as the basic cognitive substrate against which experiences are compared and interpreted. Behavior is then motivated from nonconscious cognitive levels. Winson's work demonstrates that dreams are meaningful and useful for survival strategies and memory. In short, dreams are windows into the inner life of the individual, as both Freud and Jung suggested.

In subsequent chapters, we explore how media images parallel dreams in the ways they encode nonconscious memory and guide behavior. We also show how to decode and better understand the effect of those media images on your life by using techniques similar to the dream interpretation process that you will learn in Creative 9. But first, let's look at how your own dreams work to help you understand the world, both outside of you and within your own nonconscious mind.

Figure 9.14. Boys sleeping, from "Street Boys of Haiti," by Maggie Steber.

Figure C9.1. *Unravel, by Germán Herrerra.*

Williams and Newton

CREATIVE NINE
Dream Visions: Insight Out

The Goal: Understanding Mental Imagery

The following is an adaptation of a Jungian/Johnson dream analysis technique that can be used to explore the interior/personal meaning of one's dreams. Robert Johnson, a renowned Jungian psychologist who has practiced, written about, and taught meditation and dream interpretation techniques at retreats and workshops throughout the world, kindled one of your authors' interest and taught him to adapt a Jungian word-association process to interpret dreams. This process is based on that technique. Only you can decide what your own dreams mean, but this procedure can help you access that meaning.

According to Jungian dream analysis, dreams are not literal and should be seen only as symbolic of the interactions of one's own inner dynamics. There are seven basic steps. Although the process is somewhat time consuming, familiarity will increase speed and understanding. An example follows the instructions.

How to Begin

I. Spend as long as it takes writing down a recent or remembered dream in as much detail as you can. It is helpful to write the dream immediately upon waking or, if you remember an important dream or a recurring dream from another time, write it down and work on it now. If you don't remember the entire dream, simply start writing what you remember. Often, the remainder will come to you as you write.

2. Review the dream you have written and list all of its significant parts — characters, places, things, colors/tone, feelings, and so forth — in a column on the left side of your page. We will call these *primary words*. Leave enough space between each primary word on this list to write new words above and below the original words.

3. Look at each of the primary words you have written, one at a time. Start with the first word and, in a circle around that word, write other words (associations that come into your mind as you think about the first word). Write down whatever comes to mind. Finish all of the associations for the primary word before you move on.

4. When you have completed the list of word associations, go back to the first primary word and mull its associative words over in your mind. Try to intuit which is the most significant word on the list and draw a circle around it. Look at the associative words and say them to yourself until one seems most significant.

There are no right or wrong answers so don't let your rational mind overdo this. One associative word will seem right. Circle it. Do this for each main word of the dream you have listed.

5. Make a second list of the circled associative words, perhaps to the right of the primary word list. Then, look at each of these words, one at a time, and consider what part of your inner self that word represents. Create a third list of the inner self words adjacent and parallel to the associative word list. Again, there are no right or wrong answers. It may be helpful to say to yourself, "This word represents my _____ self."

For instance, in the example that follows, the word *home* is the first significant associative word. To Rick, home is a safe place. So he might say, "Home represents my safe self" and then write that down as the first meaning on the inner self list.

6. Now, use the self words to help you write a story that interprets your dream. This will show you how it applies to you and offers insight about your life and behavior. Use as many of the words as possible. You do not have to use the word *self* with each term unless it is helpful to you.

Example of Dream Interpretation: Cave Dream by Rick Williams

1. Write the dream

I am in a *forest* and pick up a *mossy rock* from the side of a hill. *Behind the rock is a hole*. As I look into the *hole it enlarges* and *reveals a path*. I *walk down the path* and *light* follows me and *I can see*. At first I think it is *sunlight*, but *deep within the cave* I can still *see dark, shrouded figures scurrying away* from the light toward *dark shadows* near the *back of the cave*. It is at this moment that I realize that the *source of the light is I* and that *everything* that is *illuminated* by the light *is within me*.

2. Make list of significant parts of dream.

(Note that in some cases two or more words are used to describe a concept.)

Forest
Mossy Rock
Behind Rock
Hole
Hole enlarges
Reveals path
I walk down path
Sunlight
Deep in Cave
Shrouded Figures
Seek Shadows
Back of Cave
Source as I
All Within Me

3. Do word associations

earth   nurture
Forest   home
hide   safe

ancient   cover
Mossy Rock
hard   primal

under   inner
Behind Rock
beneath   hidden

entrance   inner
Hole   space
soul   lost

make room   see inside
Look, Hole enlarges
welcome   beckon

movement   change
Reveals path
life   reveal   unknown

courage   seek unknown
I walk down path
go inside   inner

life   nourish
Sunlight
see   outside

inner   soul
Deep in Cave
hidden   unknown

dark   fear   inner
Shrouded figures
 inside   hidden

hide   run away
Seek shadows
not seen   anger

end   convergence
Back of Cave
 all

outside   knowledge
Light source is I
 knowing

together   one
All within me
 integrate

4. Select most significant associative words by underlining or drawing a circle around them.

earth	nurture		_life_	nourish
Forest	_home_		**Sunlight**	
hide	safe		see	outside

ancient	cover		inner	soul
Mossy Rock			**Deep in Cave**	
hard	_primal_		_hidden_	unknown

under	inner		dark	_fear_	inner
Behind Rock			**Shrouded figures**	
Beneath	_hidden_		inside	hidden

entrance	_inner_		hide	run away
Hole space			**Seek shadows**	
soul	lost		not seen	_anger_

make room	see inside		end	_convergence_
Look, Hole enlarges			**Back of Cave**	
welcome	_beckon_			all

movement	_change_		outside	knowledge
Reveals path			**Light source is I**	
life	reveal	unknown		_knowing_

courage	_seek unknown_		_together_	one
I walk down path			**All within me**	
go inside	inner			integrate

5. Make a list of the significant associative words and then create a parallel list that assigns some inner part of your self with each association.

Significant Associative Words	**Inner Self**
Home	Safe self
Primal	Core self
Hidden	Fearing self
Inner	Spirit/soul
Beckon	Inner voice
Change	Courageous self
Seek unknown	Growing self
Life	Powerful self
Hidden	Shame self
Fear	Broken self
Anger	Destructive self
Convergence	Integrative self
Knowing	Eternal self
Together	Unified self

6. Look over the list of symbols of your inner self and write down a story or interpretation.

Inner Self
Safe self
Core self
Fearing self
Spirit/soul
Inner voice
Courageous self
Growing self
Powerful self
Shame self
Broken self
Destructive self
Integrative self
Eternal self
Unified self

As my core self draws on my inner voice and begins to feel safer, I find the courage to move beyond my fearing self. This is a powerful movement of the part of me that seeks growth toward my shamed, broken self that is destructive. It is the integration of the two, and the acceptance of the powerful and the broken together, that reveals the unified, essential self.

7. Evaluation/Assessment

This dream is consistent with the meditations and inner work that I have been doing in my life recently. But the new revelation in this dream is the suggestion that the constructive and destructive forces within me do not have to be against one another, but can work together. In other words, acceptance of the negative as a real part of myself, rather than trying to deny its existence, will help heal the wounds that created the destructive forces and thus to transform the destructive into constructive power.

Summary

- Read the instructions carefully and review the dream interpretation example.
- Spend time relaxing before you start, and then use the process to interpret your own dream.
- Write down your dream interpretation.
- Reflect on and assess your overall experience.

Figure 10.1. Hand on the Saddle, by Rick Williams. Gary Hebel mounts his horse
for an early-morning roundup on the Green Ranch in West Texas.
Note the soft light and shallow depth of field.

CHAPTER TEN
Sharing the Vision:
Photography as a Medium of Balance

The mind knows more than the eye and camera can see.

Jerry Uelsmann

In many ways, the photographic images we see in media are very much like our dreams. They often represent small segments of life; they are often fanciful and magical; they contain hidden, symbolic meaning; and they reflect their creator's idea of an ideal life. Thus, they shape our own perceptions of what reality is and how we should respond to it. Though they enter our brains through our eyes, they become memory through many of the same cognitive processes as dreams. They may then become part of dreams and daily life.

Painted by light itself, photographic images are material representations of what a person sees when looking at the world through a viewfinder and camera lens. Furthermore, photographic images look like the world we see — so real that people still tend to believe what they see in photographs. However, in much the same way that words can communicate facts and fiction, and logical and intuitive meanings, it is the nature of photographs to produce images that can both stand for the real world and express opinion.

The world's first known photograph (Figure 10.2), taken by French nobleman Joseph Nicéphore Niépce in 1826, reflects the nature of photography as simultaneously objective and subjective. This first image accurately recorded the location and form of buildings on Niépce's estate as he saw them from the upper window of his home. Yet, even if we define an authentic photograph as one that reports what was before the lens during the exposure time, then what this image recorded is complicated. Exposure time lasted at least 8 hours. This means that only those things that stayed still for most of that time were recorded on the image, because light rays bouncing off them had time to change the chemical composition of the coating on the pewter plate. Birds, passing clouds and people, and small trees blurred by the wind would not have been recorded because they moved too fast to affect the light-sensitive process. As the sun traversed the

*Figures 10.2–5. View from the Window at Le Gras by Joseph Nicéphore Niépce, heliograph, 1826.
Top: Figure 10.2. Version most frequently reproduced. Helmut Gernsheim touched up
an unsatisfactory Kodak copy (middle version above) with watercolor to look the way
he thought Niépce envisioned the image. Above from left: Figure 10.3. The framed image
as Gernsheim found it in 1952. Figure 10.4. Enhanced 1952 copy (which Gernsheim considered
a distortion) made by Eastman Kodak's Research Laboratory in England.
Figure 10.5. 2002 copy by the Getty Conservation Institute in California. Gernsheim Collection,
Harry Ransom Humanities Research Center, The University of Texas at Austin.*

sky during the long exposure, highlights falling on both sides of the towers were recorded — a visual effect not seen in real life. There is more to learn about viewing this historic image, however. Collector/historian Helmut Gernsheim first saw the pale, barely discernable heliograph in an elaborate frame (Figure 10.3). Eastman Kodak technicians produced an enhanced copy (Figure 10.4) of the original heliograph. Gernsheim, however, was dissatisfied with the copy print and touched it up with watercolors, producing the version that is most frequently published (Figure 10.2). The Getty Conservation Institute recently made another copy (Figure 10.5) of the heliograph that looks more like Niepce's original plate, which must be viewed at an angle to see the faint image.

Perhaps a more obvious illustration of the representational challenges to photographic reality is an image of the Boulevard du Temple in Paris (Figure 10.6) taken 12 years later by another Frenchman, Louis Jacques Mandé Daguerre, from a window. By 1838, exposure times had been reduced to between 5 and

Figure 10.6. View of the Boulevard du Temple, Paris, by Louis Jacques Mandé Daguerre, 1838. Courtesy of the Bayerisches National Museum München, Germany.

Figure 10.7. Two Ways of Life, by Oscar Reijlander, 1857. Composite photograph by Swedish photographer Oscar Gustav Rejlander (1817-1875) who worked in London. Rejlander created this tableau representing Good (right) and Evil (left) by making a combination albumen print from 30 separative negatives. Rejlander himself is the central figure. National Museum of Photography, Film & Television/ Royal Photographic Society/Science & Society Picture Library.

60 minutes, depending on the light and tones of the subject. Daguerre's image portrays an accurate and sharp representation of the street, buildings, and trees. Yet, only one human figure, a man who stood still as his boots were polished, was recorded in the image. All other activity was too fast to be recorded, as if the image had been made when nothing but stationary objects and the lone man were present. People passing, stopping, talking; wagons and horses moving through; birds flying or landing on roofs; movements of the person who was shining the visible man's shoes — none of these is captured in the photograph because of technical limitations.

Another early technique that illustrates an even greater disparity between the material world we can see directly with our eyes and representations of that world was *composite photography,* or *combination printing.* In this genre, created about 150 years ago, each image became part of an enacted narrative. The photographer made separate pictures of different models, in different areas of a planned setting, at different times. The separate images

Williams and Newton

were then either pasted into a collage, which the artist rephotographed to make a new negative, or printed skillfully onto one sheet of paper in the darkroom. Oscar Gustave Rejlander's "Two Ways of Life" (Figure 10.7), an 1857 visual allegory about the choice between good and evil, comprises 30 negatives and poses by 16 models.

Contemporary photographic artist Jerry Uelsmann (see Figures P.1 and 16.1) developed precise techniques for advancing the 19th-century combination-printing method into 20th-century masterpieces. Uelsmann works with as many as 10 negatives in a darkroom with multiple enlargers, moving the same piece of light-sensitive paper to each enlarger to record a negative in a specific location on the paper. The result is a provocatively surreal photograph that challenges the viewer's perceptions because visual elements in the image do not seem manipulated:

> The visually plausible but philosophically impossible situations presented in Jerry Uelsmann's photographs contradict the essential information we have come to expect from photographs. By subverting the currency of literal fact, Uelsmann releases us from the constraints of photography's mimetic function. No longer burdened by representation, we naturally return to our internal, nonlinear faculties of thought and feeling to savor the inexpressible resonance of his enigmatic visions. Vague, despite their sharpness and fine detail, and ambiguous despite our recognition of their constituent elements, his photographic montages are like dreams that slip past our perceptual defenses triggering a response but never quite revealing their meaning. (Karabinis, npn)

Although advances in digital imaging could make Uelsmann's painstaking work easier, Uelsmann still prefers to use his darkroom method because he enjoys "an element of alchemy . . . like some communion ritual. It's still magical to me," Uelsmann said (Karabinis, npn).

Digital artist Maggie Taylor (see Figures 4.1 and 8.1) uses Adobe PhotoShop to combine photographs into fanciful images. Digital pioneer Dan Burkholder also has advanced a technique for digitally combining elements from separate images and then producing a single high-quality negative of the new image. New digital cameras now produce images of such high quality that photographic artists, as well as photojournalists, find using film to be a matter of choice (and a less-frequent choice at that) rather than necessity. The nonphysical nature of digital imaging frees photographic artists from the constraints of film technology, making possible fantasy compositions of infinite variety. As Uelsmann once said, "The mind knows more than the eye and camera can see."

Right: Figure 10.8.
Tía María 1,
by Julianne Newton.
The photographer observed
this scene repeatedly before taking
the image without Tía María's
knowledge. When Tía María saw
the photo, she expressed concern
that she wore houseshoes and was
sitting by a trash can.
Is this a Visual Document
or a Visual Theft ?
Far right: Figure 10.9.
Tía María 2, a view made
with Tía María's conscious
participation. Note how
the photographer's point of view
changed to equal Tía María's,
indicating a balance of power
between photographer
and subject. Is the second image
a Visual Embrace,
or Visual Theater?

Photographic Truth

The challenge to makers, users, and viewers of any image, whether a direct recording of light rays from a nonmanipulated subject (as with the Niépce and Daguerre images), or a composite of carefully constructed imagery (as with the Rejlander, Uelsmann, and Taylor images) is to consider carefully the many factors affecting perception of truth and fiction. Photographs present both a representational image of the subject, in that they look real, and a *point of view*, established through the physical line of sight of the photographer and through the photographer's perception of a subject. This *point of view* is expressed first by the subject the photographer chooses to represent (and whether that subject be literal or symbolic) and then by the way the photographer represents that subject through technique and style. This involves choices of lens; film or digital mode; camera; angle of view; framing; use of stop action or blur; and use of selective focus, light, timing, and the way a photographer and subject interact.

Point of view also affects the composition of the photograph. *Composition* refers to how a photographer arranges, or composes, visual elements within an image frame. A good composition stimulates eye movement that purposely

directs a viewer's eye to one part of the image, and from one part of the image to another. A professional photographer using a 35mm camera can intuitively place the viewfinder of his camera around the visual elements in a scene for the best composition. A professional studio photographer has time to compose the elements before looking through the viewfinder. This composition underlies aesthetics of an image. (See chapter 11 for guidelines about composition with different media within a frame.)

Many of the aesthetic choices a photographer makes are guided by nonconscious motivations. Further, the image goes through another level of control after it is created: cropping, editing, placement with type or in a layout, literal and symbolic framing, publication, exhibition, dissemination. Finally, once an image is presented to a viewer, the image is interpreted from the viewer's own perspectives, using both rational and intuitive processes. This suggests that photography is a medium in which the rational and intuitive processes are equally significant to the production and interpretation of a compelling and revealing image. Any image is both a representation of something "out there" in the real world and a revelation of the maker's conscious and nonconscious motivations, or that individual's "interior world."

Even the mechanics of photography embrace this rational/intuitive model. The sophisticated technical and mechanical aspects, such as the direct relation-ships between shutter speed and aperture that achieve a correct exposure of an image, serve as creative controls the aesthetic qualities of the image. The photographer must consider these interrelated factors to integrate the correct technical exposure with the desired aesthetic qualities and content.

Consider the idea that people we see in still photographic frames often are people who were in motion when the photographs were made. The moment at which all of the technical and aesthetic decisions come together usually takes less than one second. This means that the photographer had a very short time

Williams and Newton

Left: Figure 10.10. Matt and the Governor, by Julianne Newton. In this photograph of 6-year-old Matt Newton photographing then Texas Gov. Mark White, notice the extended depth of field created with a small aperture, the expanded sense of space created with a 28mm lens, and the strong highlights and shadows created by bright sun. In the photo above, Figure 10.11, taken seconds after the photo at left, you see Matt's response when Governor White pointed to him and asked, "Son, do you know how to work that camera?" Texas Sequescentennial Celebration, Washington-on-the-Brazos, 1985.

to integrate all of the technical and aesthetic elements: choose the correct camera, lens, film or ISO; set the appropriate shutter speed and aperture; point the camera; frame the picture; and release the shutter.

The great documentary photographer Sebastião Salgado said that the 100 or so images in one of his books together represent less than one second of real time in the real world. This means that all of these technical and aesthetic decisions must come together at the precise moment that the action reaches its peak to create a great photograph. Photographic legend Henri Cartier-Bresson called that very instant "the decisive moment." When the action is moving fast, this process occurs over and over very rapidly, although one moment or one photograph from a series usually is better than all the rest because of the unique way in which the elements within the frame were captured. In a more subtly moving scene, there may be only one moment that warrants taking.

Of course, some problems can be anticipated and some decisions made in advance. Yet a photographer often has little control over changing light intensity and patterns, his or her distance from the subject, or the actions of the subject or other elements falling within the camera's viewfinder. For fast action to be translated into compelling images, the photographer must transcend the rational thought processes about the mechanics of technique and allow the intuitive, aesthetic processes to take over. This does not mean that technique is ignored, rather that it has been incorporated into a holistic, creative process in which the intuitive mind is the dominant guide. Just as you don't think about telling your legs to move when you ride a bicycle or your arm to swing the racket to hit a tennis ball, a good photographer develops reflex responses to what is seen. The more practiced the athlete, the better the performance. The same is true of photographers. At the same time, some people could practice forever and never perform an athletic feat on a professional level. Once again, the same is true of photographers. The degree of talent each person possesses affects the degree to which each can integrate intuitive and rational processes into a masterful act. Part of the process of learning about your own multiple intelligences is to discover how, and in what areas, you can best use the processes of integrative mind in your own life.

This rational and intuitive character of photography makes it a medium similar to visualization, meditation, drawing, dream interpretation, and creative writing. It can be used by anyone to learn to recognize and integrate both rational and intuitive processes. It does not mean, however, that everyone can excel at the same level. This integrative character of photography also means that photographs and other visual images are powerful because they communicate to us instantaneously and holistically on both nonconscious and conscious levels. Viewing and understanding images helps generate a sense of cognitive balance often lacking in the onslaught of rationally biased thought and activities that dominate our daily lives.

Technique in Photography

Understanding techniques used to create photographs is basic to making and understanding images in general. Though many media messages on television and the Internet, in films and print media, integrate movement and sound or words with visual images, the basic principles of photography and visual design apply across the various formats. Thus, basic understanding of photography and design prepares you to better understand the persuasive and manipulative techniques of media messages, and it helps you turn the meaning and affect of those messages to your own best advantage.

Figure 10.12. Gary Hebel in the Bunk House, by Rick Williams. Note the natural light from the right highlighting one side of Gary's face and the window light from the left creating a rimlight on the other side of his face.

Our technical exploration begins with a discussion of cameras and light. Then we examine basic techniques of photography that interact to control an image technically while also producing an aesthetically compelling image. We begin each section with a discussion of film cameras because learning in analog promotes visualization and because many students in art and related fields want to learn techniques of film photography. Photojournalists and other artists prefer digital photography because it is less expensive than film and because of its flexibility; speed of use; and, increasingly, its unique aesthetic characteristics. For these reasons we cover both film and digital photography as we go.

The Still Camera

A still *camera* is a light-tight box with a mechanism on one side for holding a light-sensitive substance and a light- gathering opening on the opposite side. The simplest camera, a pinhole camera, can be made by simply putting a piece of film or photographic paper in a light-tight container, such as an oatmeal box, and creating a tiny pin hole in the opposite end to act as lens and shutter. Of course you have to load this camera in the dark and cover the pinhole with black tape until you have the camera in position for the exposure.

In a manufactured camera, a glass or plastic *lens* focuses and controls how much light passes through its opening, called the *aperture*, to strike the *film* or *digital sensor*. A high-quality lens uses carefully designed and arranged concave and convex glass pieces to focus light rays gathered through an adjustable aperture onto the light-sensitive material in the camera. In front of the film or sensor is a curtain, called the *shutter,* that shields it from light until the curtain is opened. The shutter can be adjusted to open and close at different speeds to let in varying amounts of light from the lens. The amount of light that the aperture and shutter speed allow in is called *exposure*. Exposure is a combination of a specific shutter speed and aperture that is adjusted according to the *intensity of the light* available and the *sensitivity of the film* or *sensor*. We measure light intensity with a light *meter*, which can be part of the camera or separate and held by hand.

Film, Film Speed and Digital Ratings

Film is made of a clear, acetate base coated evenly on one side with an *emulsion* containing grains of light-sensitive silver halide. Light allowed through the lens turns the exposed silver black in proportion to the amount of light striking them. The brighter the light reflected from an area of the subject, the darker the film will be in that area. That's why the film is called a *negative* after it is processed; light and dark tones have been reversed. In a black-and-white negative, a white shirt appears very dark, whereas a black hat leaves the film almost clear. In color negatives, green grass looks magenta, blue sky looks yellow, and a red apple looks cyan. *Chemical development* of the film completes this process, converting exposed parts of the film and removing the silver that was not exposed. The unexposed parts of the film are left clear or nearly clear in negatives.

The *speed of film* is a numerical designation for the sensitivity of the film to light. Film speed is determined by the size, and thus the number of the silver crystals embedded in the emulsion. The larger the silver crystals, the more

Table 14.
The Basic Daylight Exposure (BDE) System

All exposures are determined in relation to the Basic Daylight Exposure, which remains constant. The formula for computing BDE is based on the correct f/stop for making good exposures in bright, direct sun: *f/16* for *f/stop* and *1/ISO* setting for *shutter speed* (f/16@1/ISO).

Example:	ISO	100	ISO	400
	Shutter Speed	1/125 sec.	Shutter Speed	1/500 sec.
	f/stop	f/16	f/stop	f/16

Changing the shutter speed or f/stop to make equivalent combinations will give you the same exposure results.

Example:	ISO	Shutter Speed	f/stop	ISO	Shutter Speed	f/stop
	100	1/125	f/16	100	1/1,000	f/5.6
	100	1/250	f/11	100	1/2,000	f/4
	100	1/500	f/8	100	1/4,000	f/2.8

Sunlight - Normal Subject in Sunlight	Use Basic Daylight Exposure
Sunlight - Dramatic Effect or Silhouette Effect shooting directly into the sun	Use 2 stops less than BDE
Sunlight - Bright Snow or Sand	Use 1 stop less than BDE
Sunlight - Backlit Subject, exposing for shadow area, portrait, etc.	Use 2 stops more than BDE
Overcast - Weak, Hazy (very soft shadows)	Use 1 stop more than BDE
Overcast - Normal, Cloudy Bright	Use 2 stops more than BDE
Overcast - Heavy or Open Shade	Use 3 stops from than BDE
Neon Signs, other light signs	Use 5 stops more than BDE
Stage Shows, with Bright Light	Use 5 stops more than BDE
Stage Shows, with Average Light	Use 7 stops more than BDE
Flood Lighted Acts (Ice Shows)	Use 6 stops more than BDE
Flood Lighted Acts (Circus, etc.)	Use 7 stops more than BDE
Brightly Lighted Theater Districts	Use 6 stops more than BDE
Store Windows at Night	Use 6 stops more than BDE
Fireworks - Displays on the ground	Use 6 stops more than BDE
Night Football, Baseball, Races, Track Meets, Boxing, Wrestling, etc.	Use 6 stops more than BDE
Office with Fluorescents	Use 6 stops more than BDE
Brightly Lighted Night Street Scenes	Use 7 stops more than BDE
Basketball, Hockey, Bowling, etc.	Use 7 stops more than BDE
Fairs, Amusement Parks	Use 8 stops more than BDE
Swimming Pool - Indoors, Tungsten Lights above Water	Use 8 stops more than BDE
Home Interiors at Night - Areas with Bright Light	Use 8 stops more than BDE
Home Interiors at Night - Areas with Average Light	Use 9-1/2 stops more than BDE
School - Stage and Auditorium	Use 9 stops more than BDE
Churches - Tungsten Lights	Use 9 stops more than BDE
Indoor, Outdoor Christmas Lighting at Night	Use 10 stops more than BDE
Candlelight Close-ups	Use 10-1/2 stops more than BDE
Floodlighted Buildings, Monuments, etc.	Use 11 stops more than BDE
Distant View of City Skyline at Night	Use 13 stops more than BDE

Adapted from table by J. B. Colson, University of Texas, Austin; and Frank Armstrong, Clark University, Worcester, MA; for UT Austin Photojournalism Program.

sensitive the film. Film speed is expressed in numbers and has been set in the United States by the American Standards Association and thus was called the ASA of the film. ISO, which refers to the International Standards Organization is now the most common designation. A few standard filmspeeds are ISO 100, 200, and 400. The higher the number of the ISO, the more sensitive, or fast, the film's response to light. For instance, ISO 200 film is twice as sensitive to light, or twice as fast, as an ISO 100 film. The faster a film is, the easier it is to shoot in dim light. However, this faster speed also results in larger grain structure and a less smooth transition between tones in the negative. A slower-speed film, such as ISO 100, needs more exposure time but results in a finer grain structure and a smoother tonal range.

Film-speed terminology has carried over into the digital era; most digital cameras indicate light sensitivity in terms of ISOs. Similar effects occur with digital speeds: the higher the ISO the less light needed for exposure. The trade off is lower-quality digital files. ISO speed and its inherent grain/pixel structure and tonal range are part of the technical and aesthetic considerations of choosing a film or digital speed. These factors affect whether you can capture movement in blurred or frozen form and whether a photograph will look grainy/pixelated or smooth and sharp.

Manufacturers make film in different sizes to fit different-sized cameras. For example, the most commonly used camera size, a *35 mm camera*, requires roll film that produces 24 or 36 frames measuring 24 mm x 36 mm. A specialized camera such as a Hasselblad is known as a medium-format camera because it uses 2-1/4" roll film. Film comes in sheets as large as 8 x 10" or even larger for use in large-format cameras.

Understanding different film sizes is important, because film size can affect the ultimate quality of a photographic print. If you start with a small negative, the result of using 35 mm film, small prints (3 x 5" or 5 x 7") may look fine, but quality decreases when you make larger 8 x 10" or 11 x 14" prints from the same negative. If you want to make even larger prints, such as 16 x 20", or you want superior image quality, you may want to use a medium- or large-format camera and hence, larger-sized film. In many cases, advertising photographers typically use medium- or large-format cameras and film because their clients desire the quality and versatility a larger negative can offer them. The trade-off is lack of spontaneity. People often need to be posed in certain positions in advertising photography. Newspaper photographers, on the other hand, use 35 mm cameras because they must capture spontaneous activities. Their trade-off is image quality. News photographs are less likely to be reproduced large and are printed on low-quality newsprint that does not render fine detail.

Right: Figure 10.13. In the Doghouse, by Rick Williams.

As camera and film technologies advance, quality and function are improving in all formats and media. This is particularly true of digital technologies, which have replaced film cameras for popular and journalistic use. Digital cameras use semiconductors to translate light rays into zeroes and ones (digital code) for storage (memory) as picture elements, or tiny graphic points known as *pixels*. Generally, the larger the capacity of the semiconductor device, or chip, the more the number of pixels stored and the higher the quality of the resulting image. A consumer-priced camera, for example, might have a resolution of 3.3 megapixels (or 3.3 million pixels), which is generally considered the minimum number needed to produce acceptable quality small prints. A professional-grade camera, such as Canon's EOS 1Ds Mark II, uses 16.7 megapixels, sufficient to make large prints that some critics say are of better quality than prints made from film negatives.

One major advantage of digital cameras is that changing speed rating in the middle of a shoot does not require changing film. Instead of having to adjust the camera controls — and one's shooting — to match the sensitivity of the film being used (or vice versa), a photographer can adjust the camera's ISO for individual frames. Digital capture also makes it possible for photographers to shoot in less light and still obtain usable pictures. It also means a photographer can set the ISO to shoot in the low light of a bar, for example, and then go outside, adjust the ISO for bright light, and capture an image on the same recording device.

The disposable film cameras you buy for one-time use are already loaded with relatively high-speed, color negative film. Typically, these cameras allow no control other than how and when you frame the subject matter and whether you add flash. Distance from the subject and careful framing are keys to success with these cameras. Lens quality can improve somewhat in more expensive versions of one-time-use cameras.

Single-use digital cameras, available since 2003, are increasing in quality. The camera introduced in 2005 by Jonathan Kaplan, head of Pure Digital Technologies, for example, includes an LCD viewing screen on the back and and a button for deleting images before taking the camera to a store for downloading, printing, and storage on a CD. Other models will allow users to transmit images directly from the camera to the store. The success of camera phones has revolutionized everyday picture taking even more. The main technical issue with disposable digital cameras and camera phones has been image resolution. Even as digital technology advances, concerns about image permanence continue. In 2006, making a permanent, archival negative became a selling feature.

Even though digital cameras use pixels instead of silver grains to record an image, most of the basic components, functions, and principles of still photog-

Figure 10.14. Chute Dance, by Rick Williams.

Notice how this photograph of a Texas cowboy, a figure who exemplifies both myth and reality, captures the power of rugged energy and the grace of a dancer.

Note the stirred-up dust and peak moment caught by a relatively fast shutter speed of 1/125th of a second, the slightly blurred extended boot indicating differential motion, the depth of field caught by an aperture of f/11, the contrast of light and shadow making angular patterns on the ground, and the intuitive framing of the decisive moment by an experienced photographer.

Figure 10.15. Horse Race, by Julianne Newton. This motion of horse and rider were frozen by panning the camera with a relatively slow shutter speed of 1/60 second. Notice the hard, contrasty light, shallow depth of field and blurred background.

raphy camera use are the same for digital and film technologies. For instance, even though pixels have no grain, as the photographer increases the sensitivity of the recording medium, the digital camera creates electronic *noise* rather than grain, often seen as distorted color or contrast.

Most important, however, is that photography — which means *writing with light* — is more about seeing and image making than it is about the image-making device. Good equipment certainly makes a difference to a skilled photographer — but the training and eye of the seer ultimately make the difference between a snapshot and a great photograph.

Photography and Light

Light is the essence of photography — and of physical sight. The quality of light expressed by contrast, direction, color, and brightness conveys its own meaning as we gaze upon the real world and presents particular issues when trying to represent that world in an image. We describe light both in terms of contrast and direction.

Contrast

Hard or High-Contrast Light. Contrast means the difference in tone between the highlight, or brighter areas, and the shadows, or darker areas. In high-contrast light, such as direct sun, light generally falls directly on the subject from the light source. Contrasty light is defined by clearly delineated bright highlights and deep shadows that reveal strong textures in the subject. The shadows are well defined, making a sharp definition of tones between shadows and highlights. High contrast is typically used to convey a rugged, outdoors feeling or for dramatic effect. The smaller the light source in relation to the subject, the higher the contrast. For instance, though the sun is very large, it is so far from Earth that it provides a relatively small point-source of light and a great deal of contrast. If a large cloud passes in front of the sun, it scatters the light rays from the sun, effectively becoming a much larger light source itself. Light from a large cloud in front of the sun therefore produces less contrast than the direct sun. Furthermore, if the entire sky is cloudy, then the expanse of the sky becomes a very large light source and produces very low contrast, or flat, soft light that makes differences between light and dark tones or areas less obvious. These same principles apply if you use a light in a room. A bare bulb produces a higher contrast light than one with a shade to diffuse it. One common form of high contrast light is light produced by a direct flash from a camera.

Soft or Low-Contrast Light. Scattered light is diffused light and is soft in terms of contrast. As mentioned earlier, sunlight behind a bank of clouds is a good example of soft light. Light also can be diffused by bouncing it off a wall or light-toned umbrella, or shooting it through a soft-light box or a cloth. Bouncing the light enlarges the size of the light source and decreases contrast. With soft light, highlights tend to be less bright and harsh, and shadows are open, or less deep, so that you can more easily distinguish details in dark areas. The transition between highlight and shadow typically flows from one tone to another without a strong line of differentiation between them. Soft light is often used to give the subject a romantic or sensual feel or to make portraits of people more flattering.

Direction

Side Light. Light coming from the side of the subject throws shadows on the nonlit side of the subject. Photographers use side light to add a sense of depth, to accentuate contrast and texture, and to increase drama in the scene. Bright, high-contrast light from the side of the face leaves the darker side in deep shadow, adding mystery. Soft, low-contrast light from the side leaves the shadow open and draws the viewer into the image to explore both the light and shadow detail.

Back Light. Light that originates from behind the subject generally appears like a rim of light outlining the subject and throwing shadows on the front (camera side) of the subject. This light usually is high contrast and dramatic and can create a complete silhouette to accentuate the subject's outline. A back light is often used with a front or side light to add drama and to make the subject stand out from the background. This is called rim lighting.

Front Light. Light from or close to the camera position tends to light the subject fairly evenly, showing details throughout the subject area. However, front light tends to diminish the sense of depth, texture, and contrast, and it can impart a sense of being invasive or revealing in an unflattering way.

Fill Light. A less-intense light from the front or side to provide some detail on the front of the subject. The source can be natural, such as window light, or added with a reflector or flash.

Color

Understanding how photography, film, and video production work with color requires knowledge of *light theory*. *Light* is the visible part of the *electromagnetic spectrum*, a range of radiation frequencies, wavelengths, and energies including radio waves and gamma waves. The part of the spectrum that humans can see ranges from shorter wavelengths of about 400 nanometers for violet to longer wavelengths of about 700 nanometers for red (see Color Plate 27). In light theory, all the colors together make *white*. When you see an object as *white*, you are seeing all colors reflected from that object. When the object absorbs all colors of light, you see it as *black*.

Film and digital cameras are manufactured to respond to the *additive colors* of light: *red*, *green*, and *blue*, known as *RGB*. If you are working with *color-balancing filters*, you are using principles related to the *subtractive colors* of light: *cyan*, *magenta*, and *yellow*, CMY. Color filters allow their own wavelengths to pass through and reflect other wavelengths. Note that additive and subtractive colors are *complementary*: cyan is the complement of red, magenta the complement of green, and yellow the complement of blue. In offset printing, black (K) is added as a fourth ink, resulting in the *CMYK* designation.

Figure 10.16. Pop and Matt, by Rick Williams. Note that the shot required a fast enough shutter speed to freeze the action of Pop getting up from the table and a wide enough aperture to record the natural but relatively low window light. The more distinct shadow of the plant leaves on the table top is caused by a bright overhead light.

When working with color in photography, film, and video production, professionals also use another system of measurement. *Color temperature*, measured in *degrees Kelvin*, uses a scale developed by the mathematician and physicist Lord William Thomson Kelvin, who is credited with discovering the law of thermodynamics, the system is based on comparing the visible colors of a blackbody radiator as it is heated. Counter intuitively and counter to the electromagnetic spectrum scale, when using the Kelvin system, reddish light has a lower color temperature than bluish light, which has a high color temperature.

Color temperature becomes particularly important when working with light-recording technologies. Film, for example, is manufactured to respond to different color temperatures. If you shoot regular, daylight-balanced film indoors under a typical household tungsten light, it will record the light with a reddish cast because tungsten light has a lower temperature (about 3,000 K) than average daylight (5,500 K). Different fluorescent bulbs, on the other hand, can emit light ranging in color temperatures from less than 3,000 K up to 6,500 K. Before the days of digital imaging, professionals working with color film often relied on color-temperature meters for measuring the light so they could fine-tune choices of film and color-balancing filters. Now, digital photographers can adjust the color balance of their images by using their cameras' white-balance settings or even after shooting by using computer software such as Photoshop. However, understanding the basics of color temperature and light theory can greatly help a photographer get the color results he/she wants with minimal post-shooting work.

Camera Controls

Shutter Speed Controls Light and Motion

In most single-lens-reflex (SLR) cameras, the *shutter* is a device directly in front of the film or digital sensor. When you press the shutter release button, the shutter opens and then closes for a specific amount of time to let the proper amount of light reach the film. By opening and closing for specific lengths of time, the shutter controls how long light can strike the film or light-recording area. This exposure varies according to the sensitivity or ISO of the film or sensor and the intensity of the light. Shutter speed also controls the creative effect of freezing or blurring motion. Shutter speeds are measured in seconds and parts of a second. A typical shutter-speed scale ranges from 1 or 2 seconds to 1/2, 1/4, 1/8, 1/15, 1/30, 1/60, 1/125, 1/250, 1/500, 1/1000, 1/2000, 1/4000, and 1/8000 of a second. A rapidly moving subject will appear to be blurred in a 1/2-second exposure because the shutter is open long enough to record the movement of the subject. If you choose a shutter speed of 1/4000 of a second, the subject will appear frozen in action, because the shutter is open only long enough to record a tiny slice of the subject's motion. Think about it. One-half second is a good bit longer than 1/4000 of a second, just as one half of a pie is much larger than 1/4000 of a pie. Although shutter speeds were once problematic with digital cameras, models now match the capability of film cameras.

F/Stop Controls Light and Depth of Field

Most lenses house an *aperture* that opens and closes to create a hole of a specific size for light to pass through. By providing different size openings, a lens

Figure 10.17. Nava Christmas Eve, by Julianne Newton. A quiet moment between Doña Margarita and her great-granddaughter at midnight on Christmas Eve took place in a dimly lit room. The image, shot with Tri-X 400 ASA film, required a flash bounced from a ceiling/wall intersection: f/5.6 @ 1/60, 28 mm lens.

aperture controls the amount of light striking the film or sensor but in a manner different than the shutter speed, which controls the time light can strike the film or sensor. At the same time, the aperture controls the size of the light rays that strike the film. When the aperture is larger, the entering light rays are larger and overlap on the film or sensor. When the aperture is smaller, the entering light rays are smaller and appear more distinctly on the film or sensor.

Apertures are called *f/stops* when they refer to the specific size of the lens opening. The term *f/stop* refers to a ratio between the width of the lens opening and the length of the lens (how far the light has to travel through the lens before striking the film).

In addition to controlling light, the size of the aperture controls something called *depth of field*. This refers to the area in your picture that looks *sharp from foreground to background*. Areas of the picture outside the depth of field will look *blurry*. When you focus on a certain spot, a specific distance in front of it and behind it will look sharp. The area that looks sharp (*depth of field*) is controlled by the size of the aperture. A typical aperture scale is designated in f/stops as f/2.0, f/2.8, f/4, f/5.6, f/8, f/11, f/16, f/22, and f/32. The numbers can be confusing at first. An aperture of f/2, for example, refers to a larger lens opening than an aperture of f/16. Just remember that the numbers refer to ratios: the larger the opening (smaller f/stop numbers), the less the depth of field. The smaller the opening (larger f/stop numbers), the larger the depth of field.

To master photographic exposure, the photographer must learn to control the shutter and f/stop together to get the correct exposure, desired motion control, and depth of field.

Working Shutter Speed and F/Stop Together

If both f/stop (for example, f/8) and shutter speed (for example, 1/125) control light, and thus exposure, why bother with both? In addition to controlling exposure, each also offers a different creative effect. As explained above, shutter speed controls motion. Aperture controls depth of field. This interplay of motion and depth of field are creative trade-offs that integrate the function of photography with the aesthetics of photography — the rational and the intuitive. Skilled photographers consider these options each time they take a picture.

For example, each time you increase the depth of field by using a smaller aperture, you decrease the amount of light reaching the film and thus you must increase the amount of time the light exposes the film by using a slower shutter speed. This slower shutter speed diminishes your ability to freeze motion and may cause blur. The faster the shutter speed you use to freeze motion, the less depth of field you will have. Consequently, photographers not only must constantly monitor how they use these controls to gain correct exposures but also be aware of how those choices are affecting the final images in terms of motion and depth of field.

As a creative tool, increased depth of field can be used to include foreground and background sharply in focus and to place the subject in context by including the surrounding area in sharp focus. Decreased, or shallow, depth of field

Figure 10.18. Cowboy Art, by Julianne Newton. To make this image, the photographer used a 55mm macro, or closeup, lens. Note how the wide aperture resulted in shallow depth of field, with sharpness extending from about two inches in front of the art to three inches behind the art. Photographing the tiny work of art in the palm of the artist's hand gives viewers a comparative sense of scale.

can also be used creatively to place foreground and background out of focus. This isolates and emphasizes the primary subject by making only the main subject look sharp while other areas appear blurry.

Motion control can be used creatively to freeze the action of a baseball leaving a bat, a tennis ball leaving a racket, or a gymnast flipping in midair. It can also be used to blur a race car while leaving the stands and track in focus or to blur any dancer in a ballet who is moving when the shutter is released. Look at the images in this chapter to see how these controls were used creatively.

These choices alter both the appearance and the meaning of photographs. They also illustrate why it is important to practice technique so that it becomes natural and second nature. If you spend too much time trying to figure out the technical controls before you take a specific picture, you may well lose the decisive moment and thus the aesthetic power of the image. Like meditating, drawing, or dancing, once you have learned the rational technique you can transcend or blend technique with intuitive aesthetics. In the next section, we discuss some other creative decisions that photographers make in this symphony of cognitive balance.

Lenses

The length of a lens — its *focal length* — is measured in millimeters (*mm*). Length refers to the actual distance from the rear nodal point of the lens to the focal plane of the camera when the lens is focused at infinity. If you are not familiar with millimeters, a rough approximation is 25 millimeters to 1 inch. Hence, a 50 mm lens has a focal length of about 2 inches. Compare that to a 200 mm lens, which would have a focal length of about 8 inches, and you will understand why a 200 mm lens is called a long lens. A 50 mm lens is considered a normal lens for a 35 mm camera because it provides an angle of view between the left and right edges of the frame that is approximately the same as your eyes see, without including your peripheral, or side, vision.

Digital cameras often use sensors that are actually smaller than the film size of a 35 mm camera. This causes the focal length of their lenses to operate as longer lenses than they would on a film camera — generally by about 1.5 times. This means that a 35 mm lens would be the normal, or 50 mm-equivalent lens on a digital camera, but this is generally not true on high-end professional digital cameras. It is important to know this before you buy lenses for your digital camera. Lenses are generally divided into wide angle or telephoto lenses on each side of normal or medium focal lengths.

A *wide-angle lens* is shorter in focal length than a normal lens. Typical wide-angle lenses for a 35 mm camera include 35 mm, 28 mm, 24 mm, and 20 mm. The lower the number, the wider the angle of view. A wide-angle lens has an angle of view that is significantly greater than your eye and tends to include a lot of the foreground and background around the subject. Wide-angle lenses have the effect of making viewers feel present with the subject, as if they could step into the scene. Photographers like to use wide-angle lenses in small spaces because the lenses can take in a great deal of area, even at close proximity. You might also use a wide-angle lens to capture an expanse of land and sky or to exaggerate or distort a close-up subject.

A *long, or telephoto, lens* is longer in focal length than a normal lens and has a narrower angle of view. The higher the number, the narrower the angle of view. Typical telephoto lenses for a 35 mm camera include 85 mm, 100 mm, 150 mm, 200 mm, 300 mm, 400 mm, and 600 mm. Telephoto lenses generally do not include as much foreground or background around the subject as wide-angle lenses, and they have the effect of isolating the subject from its context. They also make subject elements appear compressed, or closer together than they are. A sports photographer would want to use a long lens, such as a 600 mm lens, to make images that look as though they were taken extremely close to the athlete. She would choose a wide-angle lens, such as a 28 mm, if she wanted to include an expanse of the playing field or stands. That's one reason you often see sports photographers with two or three cameras dangling from their shoulders: changing lenses takes time and could mean missing the picture!

A *zoom lens* is designed so that a photographer can change from one focal length to another simply by turning or sliding a ring on the lens or pushing a button on the camera. Typical zoom lenses for a 35mm camera include 17–35 mm, 28–70 mm, 28–200 mm, and 70–200 mm. Zoom lenses are more expensive than single focal-length lenses, but usually not as expensive as buying all of the lenses in the zoom range. They also have the advantage of not having to

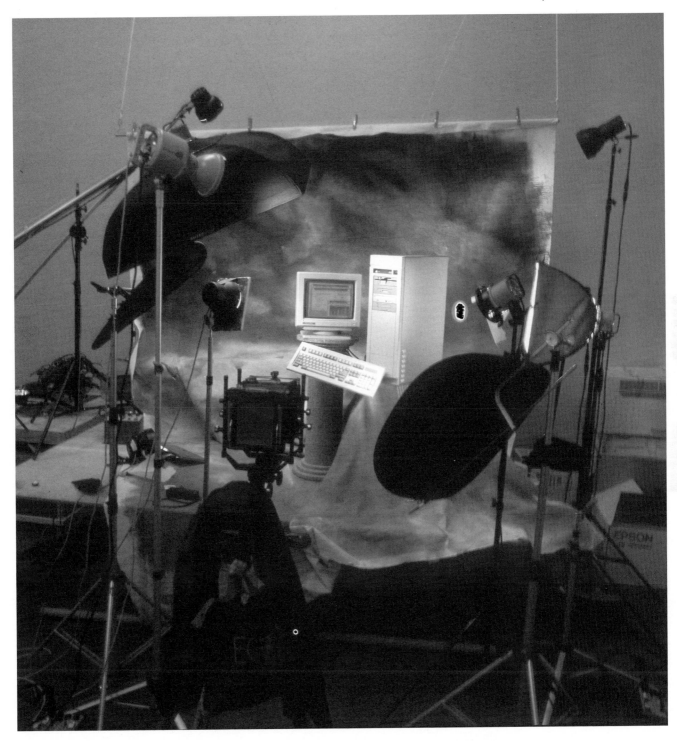

Figure 10.19. Studio setup for computer company catalog, by Rick Williams.

change the lens to change the focal length. This can save a great deal of time and help a photographer get shots he would miss while changing lenses. On the other hand, the ability to change focal length requires more complex use of

Visual Communication: Integrating Media, Art, and Science   229 glass elements, making the lens heavier and harder to hold steady — an important factor when shooting in low light at a slow shutter speed.

Adding Light

Photographers have a number of options for adding artificial light sources to enhance a scene. Single-use and point-and-shoot cameras often have built-in *flashes* with limited ranges of between four and 15 feet. Older cameras have a *hot shoe*, or a device on top of the camera for attaching a flash unit. *Wireless* technology allows using flash units off camera, either as *direct flash* aimed at the subject or as *bounce flash* aimed at a reflective surface to throw diffused light at the subject. Flashing light directly at the subject can make a person look washed out, overexposed, or too bright, contrasted against an underexposed, dark background. Flash placed directly in front of the subject so that light enters the iris and bounces off the retina causes what is commonly known as *red eye* because it reveals blood vessels at the back of the eye. Some photographers, such as Mary Lee Edwards (see Figure C8.1), perfect direct-flash technique to give the effect of harsh reality. Other photographers prefer to bounce flash off a wall, ceiling, or ceiling/wall corner (see Figure 10.17) to achieve a softer, more natural effect.

Manufacturers rate flash units using *Guide Numbers*, which indicate the capacity of the flash to cover a certain distance. The higher the guide number, the more powerful the flash.

Beyond direct-versus-bounce effects, several technical concerns are critical when using flash. Newer flash models use through-the-lens (TTL), remote firing, and auto-exposure systems to make flash use relatively simple when compared with 20th-century technologies, such as flash bulbs. Nevertheless, best results come from understanding a few basic principles:

• *Light rays travel in a straight line* (unless refracted).
• *Inverse Square Law* — Light from a point source falls off inversely to the square of the distance. Moving the light from 10 to 20 feet away results in 1/4 the intensity. Light from a flash falls off dramatically the further the subject is from the flash. Conversely, subjects close to the flash receive the most light and can be overexposed easily.
• *Law of reflection* — Angle of reflection is equal to the angle of incidence: Light is reflected at the same angle from which it came, but in the opposite direction.
• *Distance* = how far the light travels, NOT the distance between the camera and subject unless a flash is on the camera and aimed directly at the subject.
• *f/stop* = Guide Number divided by distance.
• *Shutter speed* varies depending on whether the photographer is trying to balance light from the flash with ambient light or dominate the scene with light

from the flash. Shutter speed must be equal to or slower than the *flash synch speed* for a particular camera in order to avoid non-exposure of part of the frame.

Professional photographers become expert at adding multiple sources of light when working in studios and on location. A flash meter, light kits, stands, tripods, backdrops, and power packs are common accessories. Digital camera technology, with increased capacity to capture images in low light, has decreased the need for adding artificial light in many instances.

Tripods

Photographers often use three-stemmed support devices called *tripods* to make sure their images will be sharp when using slow shutter speeds. If light is very dim, for example, one would attach the camera to a tripod to avoid the blurry effects resulting from even slight camera movement while using a slow shutter speed. When photographers use medium- and large-format cameras, they usually use tripods to support the extra weight. The great landscape photographer Ansel Adams said he used the largest, heaviest camera and tripod available to get the quality of larger-size film. Sports photographers often support their long lenses with monopods — single-legged support poles — that allow them relative freedom of movement. Photojournalists, however, eschew both tripods and large cameras because they want maximum flexibility of movement, exposure, and lens. Advances in lens and camera technology also are making possible equipment with image stabilizing functions, which can control motion blur from both photographers and subjects.

Constantly Changing Technology

Ironically, just about the time film technology advanced to the point of making cameras and lenses smaller and lighter weight, new technologies once again required photographers to carry massively heavy gear. By the end of the 20th century, in addition to multiple cameras and lenses, a professional news photographer might have carried a laptop computer for downloading and transmitting images immediately from the scene of an event to the editor in the newsroom. A typical backpack of gear weighed 50 to 60 pounds. Fortunately, as digital technology improved, the size of equipment decreased again. As wireless technology became more common, transmitting pictures became less problematic.

Walter Curtin, a Canadian photographer who lived through most of the 20th century's technological changes, once said he was waiting for the day when he could simply wink an eye and then touch his fingertip to a reception device to produce a photograph. Regardless of technological advances, *what matters most in photography are the eye, heart, and mind of the seer.*

Figure C10.1. The Touch, by Rick Williams.

CREATIVE TEN
Image Insights:
Photography from the Inside Out

The Goal: Translating Seeing Into Images

Your goal is to see through a camera lens, put frames around parts of the real world, and produce a visually interesting set of images and words.

What You Need

1. *Camera.* Any camera you know how to use is fine, including a cardboard throwaway camera you can buy at any photo or drug store, a digital point-and-shoot (must have *at least a 3.3 megapixel sensor*), or a professional camera. Camera phones usually do *not* produce images of sufficient quality.

2. *Film* (if using film). Use a roll of 24-exposure color print film (not slide/transparency film). We suggest ASA/ISO 200 or ASA/ISO 400. You may use black-and-white film if you can make prints or have them made. *A note about film processing*: One- and two-hour turn around for color-negative film processing and printing is available at commercial processors.

However, BEFORE you leave your film with a processor, or your digital files with a service bureau, be sure you know when your prints will be ready and what the final product will be (number and size of prints, scanned to CD, proof sheet).

3. *At least an hour of free time* for shooting and additional time to deliver and pick up film or download digital images, edit images, and write.

4. *Allow extra time for things to go wrong.* When working with camera equipment, film, commercial processors, computer equipment, labs, and so forth, the number of problems you may have to solve increases.

Part I — Seeing and Creating Photographs

1. Go somewhere you enjoy being and that is visually stimulating to you.

2. Spend at least the first 10 minutes using the best technique for you to shift into the intuitive mode. You might listen to music with your eyes closed, meditate, draw, do a blind contour drawing, or simply relax and daydream.

3. When you have made the shift, get up and move around. Look, see, feel, experience the environment around you. Look at the quality of the light. Consider the contrast range and the angle. Notice what the light reveals and what it hides — how it draws you in or shuts you out. When you see something that interests you visually, take a picture of it. Look at it from different angles and through the lens to consider what you want in or out of the frame. What draws your eye? How does putting a frame around what you're seeing affect how you see it?

 These images should be mostly spontaneous, coming from your feeling mode. Consider appropriate technique as well as you can to produce compelling photographs, but don't dwell on technical issues to the point of interrupting the flow of your seeing, framing, and picture taking.

Shoot at least 24 different pictures before you stop. You may shoot several angles of the same subject, but shoot at least four different subjects.

4. If you're shooting film, take it to a processor for developing and printing. Ask for a small proof sheet or CD. [One 3 x 5-inch or 4 x 6-inch print of each picture is fine. You may also want to ask the processor to scan the negatives into digital form and make a CD. Not all processors have such capability, and it may cost extra. Download digitally captured images to a CD, make prints of your three favorite images, and print out a proof sheet of all your images.

Part II — Seeing and Creating Word Images

Pick at least three of your images and use them to inspire a poem or piece of creative prose. Write one poem or short piece of creative prose for each of the three photographs you have selected as your best/most appealing images.

Part III — Preparing Your Work for Presentation

1. Arrange the three pictures and accompanying words in a creative manner. This is a good opportunity to practice using page-design software, but you may do the design manually (for example, pasting the images neatly on a piece of paper on which you have printed your words).

Summary

- Read the instructions carefully and get your camera and supplies ready.
- Think carefully about where you will photograph and the time of day you choose. Will the light be sufficient for good exposures? When is the light best where you plan to shoot? Will the visual characteristics of the surroundings be appealing and creatively stimulating?
- Spend time relaxing before you start photographing.
- Shoot at least 24 exposures of at least four different subjects.
- If you're shooting film, take it to a processor for developing and printing. Ask the processor to make a proof sheet. One 3 x 5" or 4 x 6" print of each picture is fine. You may also want to ask the processor to scan the negatives into digital form and make a CD for you. Note that not all processors have such capability and that it may cost you more. Download digitally captured images to a CD, make prints of your three favorite images, and print out a small proof sheet of all your images.
- Pick your three favorite images. Indicate the three images on your proof.
- Write a poem or creative prose for each of your three chosen images.
- Design and prepare the presentation of your photographs and accompanying words.
- Reflect on and write an assessment of your overall experience.

Examples

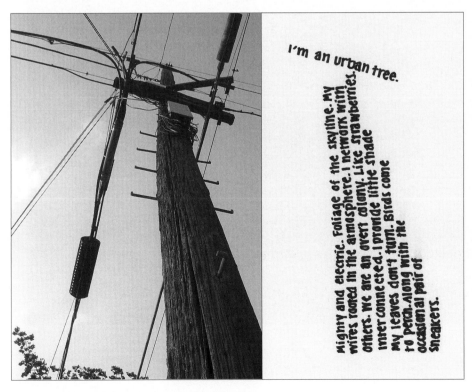

Figure C10.2. Urban Tree, by Andrea Scheider.

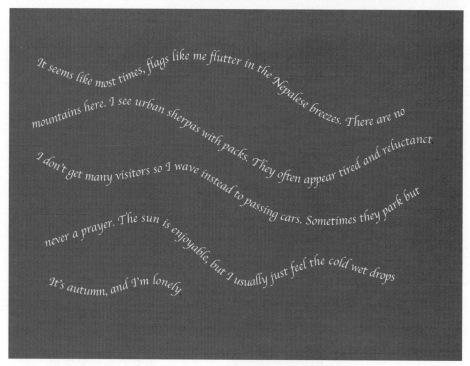

It seems like most times, flags like me flutter in the Nepalese breezes. There are no mountains here. I see urban sherpas with packs. They often appear tired and reluctanct. I don't get many visitors so I wave instead to passing cars. Sometimes they park but never a prayer. The sun is enjoyable, but I usually just feel the cold wet drops It's autumn, and I'm lonely

Figure C10.3. Flags, by Andrea Schneider.

a has a serif
　　that likes to sit on bowls
really expensive ones
in really expensive shops
　　　and then laugh at the people who buy them
　　which is mean and judgmental

maybe people really like those bowls
and don't want them sat on
and don't want to laughed at by a stupid serif
that only likes to sit on bowls

Above: Figure C10.4. Photograph and poem by Ally Burguieres.

Who needs a square robe anyway?
                                    And a square pillow
                                    And a square blanket
                  In a round chair
And they take up the whole chair anyway
So no one else can sit in it
Except for the Squares and all the other Squares in the Square club.

Above: Figure C10.5. Photograph and poem by Ally Burguieres.

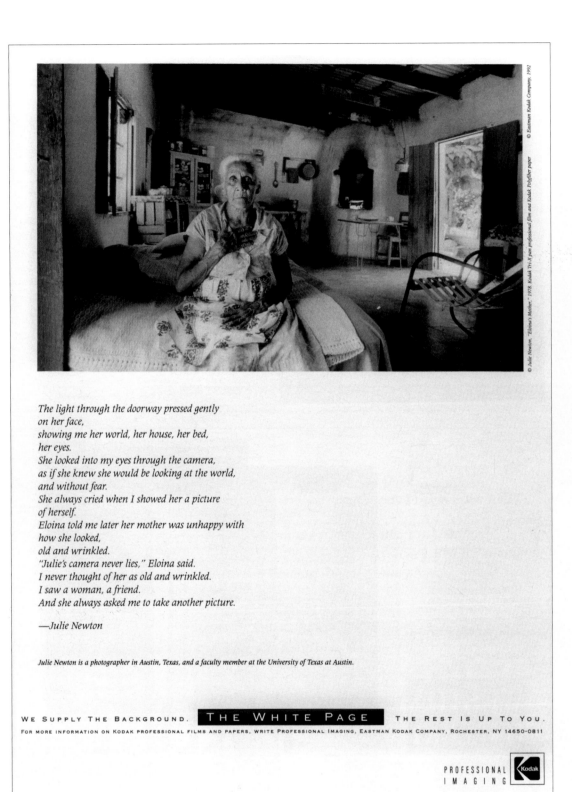

The light through the doorway pressed gently
on her face,
showing me her world, her house, her bed,
her eyes.
She looked into my eyes through the camera,
as if she knew she would be looking at the world,
and without fear.
She always cried when I showed her a picture
of herself.
Eloina told me later her mother was unhappy with
how she looked,
old and wrinkled.
"Julie's camera never lies," Eloina said.
I never thought of her as old and wrinkled.
I saw a woman, a friend.
And she always asked me to take another picture.

—Julie Newton

Julie Newton is a photographer in Austin, Texas, and a faculty member at the University of Texas at Austin.

WE SUPPLY THE BACKGROUND. THE WHITE PAGE THE REST IS UP TO YOU.
FOR MORE INFORMATION ON KODAK PROFESSIONAL FILMS AND PAPERS, WRITE PROFESSIONAL IMAGING, EASTMAN KODAK COMPANY, ROCHESTER, NY 14650-0811

PROFESSIONAL
IMAGING

Figure C10.6. Eloina's Mother, photograph and poem by Julianne Newton. From The White Page fine art campaign, Eastman Kodak, as published in Aperture, 40th Anniversary Issue, Fall 1992. Compare this cropped version of the photograph with the full-frame version in Figure 1.4. Designers should not crop art photographs and should take great care to avoid altering meaning or diminishing aesthetic quality when cropping any photograph. When in doubt, consult the photographer.

Figure 11.1. Magazine cover design by D.J. Stout, Pentagram.

CHAPTER ELEVEN
Designing for Meaning

Fundamental to visual and intuitive literacy is understanding the basic principles visual communicators use to inform, inspire, and persuade both our conscious and nonconscious minds. These principles derive from within and without — from within through the basic structures of matter and life, and from without through millennia of human cultivation of symbol systems. The 3rd-century BCE mathematician Euclid laid the geometrical framework for many of the theories and visualizations that bridge science, math, and art today.

Those who study and teach design use terms such as contrast, harmony, balance, proportion, rhythm, movement, color, repetition, dominance, and unity. Peter Stebbing, a German design and visualization educator, devised what he calls a universal grammar: contrast, rhythm, balance, and proportion, or CRBP for short. Stebbing analyzed how many times key terms were used in the tables of contents for 50 books by leading visual design authors. Stebbing believes humans, and perhaps other primates, share "a basic sense of composition":

> The adaptation of our perceptual system to the recognition of the principles of organic organization (as perceptual primitive) has resulted in our favoring the same principles for aesthetic composition. This knowledge provides a strategy for art and design educators, because what has appeal for us has been determined by our evolutionary past. We have apparently evolved a cognitive fluidity for responding to organic novelty based on permutations of universal principles — Contrast, Rhythm, Balance and Proportion — that are simultaneously embedded in our own biology. (p. 69)

Stebbing grounds his conclusion in theories of evolution and ecology, asking why humans "possess a sense of visual composition" and "from what ability did this sense evolve" (p. 67). Key to this idea is research indicating that "the recognition of complex form takes place through the perception of simple patterns" (p. 67). Other contemporary theorists, such as Gunther Kress and Theo van Leeuwen, have articulated in verbal terms an intricate grammar of visual design to encompass the complex ways visuals work in contemporary media. You will recall from chapter 9 that psychologist Carl Jung believed humans share a "collective unconscious" rooted in "archetypes," or primordial patterns. This ability to perceive patterns is fundamental to contemporary research in neuroscience (see chapter 6). As we've discussed earlier, we need not comprehend the origins of human visual perception or the intricacies of how and why we see to appreciate that creating and interpreting imagery is central to 21st-century communication.

We begin here with a discussion drawing on basic elements of visual literacy pioneer Donis Dondis outlined as components of images. Then we add work from other theorists and practitioners to extend the discussion where appropriate.

A *visual element* is a unit we perceive when we see. It can be as simple as a speck of dust, a dot in a newspaper photograph, or a brushstroke of color in a class painting. In combination, visual elements can be as complex as the intricately arranged details of a movie set; the carefully constructed scenario of a video game; or the expanse of meadows, rivers, valleys, sky, and clouds we see when we stand atop a mountain peak. In *The Way of the Earth*, T. C. McLuhan explored the idea that the land on which we live and evolve — whether coast or plains, mountains or valleys, forest or desert — affects the ways we develop our symbol systems. Our eyes and brains organize visual elements into groups or patterns that have evolved within the structures of life and the physical world. Recall our brief introduction to the idea of the gestalt in the introduction to this book: the whole is more than the sum of its parts. Barry stressed the relational aspect of the parts within that whole: "A gestalt implies a configuration that is so inherently unified that its properties cannot be derived from the individual properties of its parts" (p. 42). In this chapter we break down the whole into parts to help you understand how to construct and interpret designs.

A *design* is *an arrangement of visual elements, or parts, into a whole.* Design can be conscious or nonconscious in origin. Design can be effective or ineffective. *Good design* is an *effective* arrangement of visual elements, meaning that the arrangement of visual elements communicates or evokes feeling. Good design can be defined as the *artful arrangement of elements within a frame to create a unified or meaningful whole.* Artists and designers use basic elements to create patterns of meaningful design. As we first discuss the basic elements of graphic design, we use very simple illustrations that help you see how easily elements fit together to form meaning. Then we show you how artists and visual communicators use these same processes in more sophisticated ways.

The Basic Elements

Point

The first and most basic element of visual design is the *point* or *dot*. Designs are built from this simple element. The moment you press your pen to the surface of paper or point the cursor and click the period symbol on your computer keyboard, you create a point. In the illustrations below, you see that a simple point within a frame can be used to attract attention; indicate direction; carry meaning, emotion, or weight; or look like something:

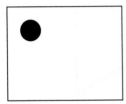 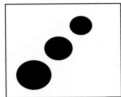  

Line

The second basic element of design is a *line*. When you extend a point or connect points, you create a line. Lines can be long or short, thick or thin, curved or straight. Lines can even be implied by a series of dots. Written language evolved from patterns of points in combination with lines. When used together, lines can indicate look and shape; they can have quality, emotion, and movement; and they can convey meaning.

Plane/Shape

The third basic element of design results from extending a line to create a *plane* or *shape*. You can also connect lines to make a shape. Lines form three basic shapes — *square*, *circle*, and *triangle* — as well as irregular shapes. Each shape has its own character and elicits particular emotional responses.

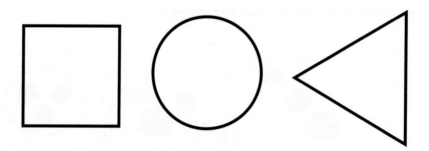

A *square* tends to have a character that is honest, solid, static, and straightforward. A *circle* suggests a continuum and feelings of warmth, perfection, and nurture. A *triangle* is dynamic and suggests action, conflict, and tension. A basic plane or shape has *two dimensions*: *height* and *width*. The square, circle, and triangle are two dimensional.

Volume

By extending a plane along both the width and height axes, you create the illusion of the *third dimension*, or *depth*, and we tend to perceive that shape as having *volume*. If you look closely at the extended cube, you see how the front and back of the cube seem to shift back and forth, depending on how you look at the figure. This classic is known as a Necker Cube. Your eyes shift focus between the cube's front and back planes.

Point, line, plane, and volume are four of the five basic elements at the heart of design. As you can see, these simple elements convey visual meaning and can evoke feelings and ideas. They also express a basic property of visual communication: *Visual elements represent meaning.*

If we add *tone* or *color* to any visual elements, we can further influence how viewers interpret their meaning. For example, if we add different shades of gray to the

different planes of the Necker Cube, you perceive a third dimension more easily, enhancing the illusion of volume and depth, within what really is only a two-dimensional plane.

Filling a simple rectangle with black makes the rectangle look solid, heavy, and as though it has depth or substance. Without the tone, the rectangle looks empty — unless you stare at it long enough to begin perceiving the white tone within the rectangle as carrying substance, or visual *weight*. Notice also how the black-filled rectangle appears to be a different size though both are the same size. We can take the same shape, add *texture* or *pattern*, and vary the communication in an infinite variety of ways.

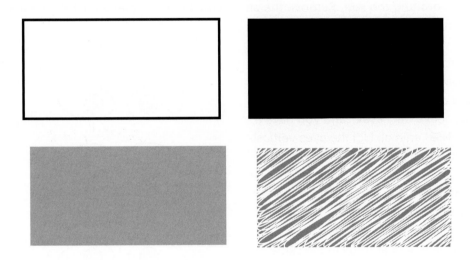

We can take a set of shapes, adjust the basic shapes, arrange them, add tone or color, and suggest different meanings. What meanings can you create with these three elements?

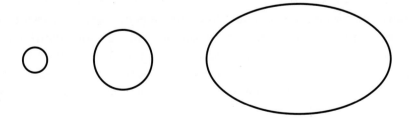

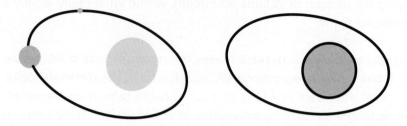

Rearrange them, tilt and elongate the large oval slightly, add tone to two of the circles, and *overlap* the large oval with the smaller circle. You begin to convey a planet orbiting the sun. Remove the small smaller circle and adjust the oval a bit, and you have a fried egg.

Duplicate the oval with the circle and flip one set horizontally, and you can see a pair of animal eyes. Add heavy lines above the "eyes" and you have a perplexed animal. Flip the eyes vertically and you have a worried animal. Use two pieces of paper to cover all but one set of eyes if you find it difficult to interpret expressions conveyed by the eyes. The mind works to *relate* visual elements that appear to be in the same group. Previous experiences with similarly arranged elements also affect how people interpret visual elements.

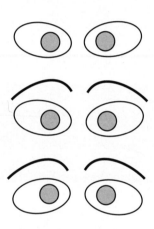

Frame

Another way to think of a group of visual elements is to envision them surrounded by a *frame,* the fifth basic element of visual design. Any shape also can be a frame. Frames have *shape, size,* and *direction.* Horizontal frames tend to have left to right direction. Vertical frames tend to have top to bottom direction. Notice how we intuitively relate the three sets of "eyes" above into a vertical organization with an implied frame. Square frames evoke more of a circular direction. You also can frame subject matter within another frame for emphasis or pattern. A door can frame a person. A building can frame a door. A tree can frame a building. Frames help add a sense of dimension and direct the viewer's eye to the subject.

Frames create meaning because they *include.* They wrap up elements within them causing the brain to search for ways to relate those elements. Frames also create meaning because they *exclude*. They cut out elements outside the frame so that we pay attention to the elements within the frame. In the eye sets above, each oval frames a smaller circle, which is filled with gray. The brain relates the ovals, circles, and arcing lines because they are close together and look familiar. This causes us to organize the visual information, relating the elements into patterns and interpreting the patterns as eyes. Notice that the brain intuitively completes the face around each set of eyes, even though a face frame is not drawn, as it is below. One of the first things we learn as new-borns is to recognize our mothers' faces. Newborns are drawn to simple

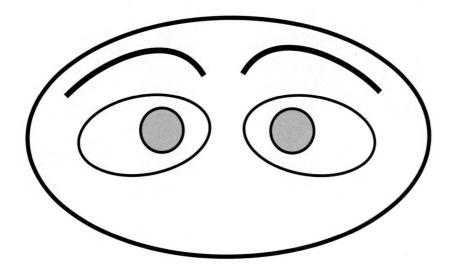

shapes, especially when their combinations resemble faces.

Notice that the large oval above appears to be in the background, whereas the "eyes" and "eyebrows" appear to be in front of the large oval. As you learned when completing Creative Four, this is seeing *figure* and *ground*.

This logo design, with which you worked in Creative 5, was created by Maggie Macnab for Maddoux-Wey Arabians and evokes the classic figure/ground rela-tionships of the ancient yin-yang symbol. As we noted earlier, visual experts tell us we cannot see both figure and ground at the same time. What seems to be simultaneous viewing of both may be rapid reversal. The same phenomenon was true when you looked at the Necker Cube — but it probably was harder to see both the front and back of the cube reverse as quickly. To see how Maggie came up with her design, turn the page and study her sketches and explanations.

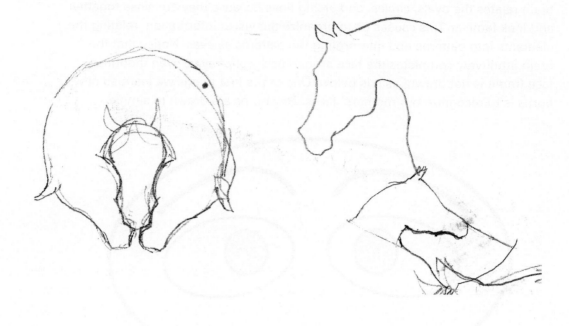

Figures 11.2-5: Maddoux-Wey Arabians logo by Maggie Macnab.
The Arabian horse logo, a variation on the ancient symbol yin-yang,
represents the intrinsic role of relationship and duality in the universe.

The underlying symbolism of this mark refers to cross-breeding opposites
and the long standing relationship we have had with this animal
to help us horsepower civilization.

Indeed, civilization would not exist like it is today without
the work and fleet transport these animals provided.

Appropriately, the Middle East, where these small-boned and large-lunged horses
run over desert sands, is considered the cradle of civilization.
Arabian horses are known for their endurance, grace, and intelligence.

The shape also visually supports the signature arch of an Arabian's neck
and the dished face, which structurally lets them breathe more effectively in sandstorms.

The whole of these rather intricate concepts when seamlessly integrated
creates a multi-metaphoric, yet simple, symbol.

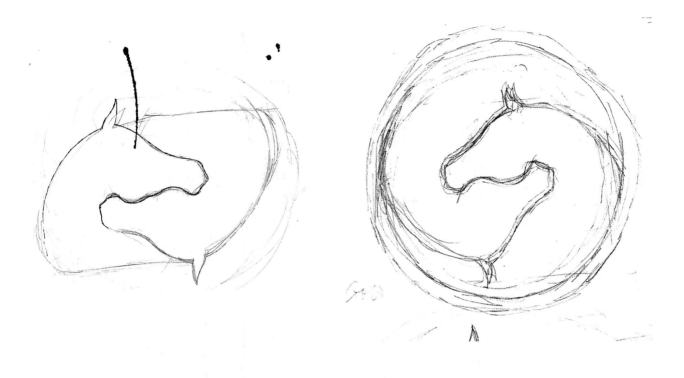

Here is how I arrived at a simple symbol that says so much.

From Far Left: Figure 11.2. Intuitively, my initial drawings begin with the circle
and showing relationship in the most visually obvious way: touching closely.

Figure 11.3. I then explore relationship in another way: the mare with foal at her side.
I begin to see the Escher-esque opportunity of working equally with negative and positive space.
This creates the oppotunity to use the jawline to communicate maximum information
with minimum detail.

Figure 11.4. It doesn't take long from here to see where I'm going.
I needed to bring it back full circle.

Figure 11.5. Herein lives an eternal symbol which creates an effective and enduring logo.
There is no attachment to style in the essential work of a concept development —
just attention to the substance of the true communication and skilled execution.
Branding provides the opportunity to stylize, but even this design's support collateral,
created more than 20 years ago, is viable and vibrant today.

Now, return to our ovals and lines. Let's change the size and shape of the large circle so that it no longer frames the eyes but becomes the base of the face. Note that changing only one visual element causes a shift in our perception of all elements.

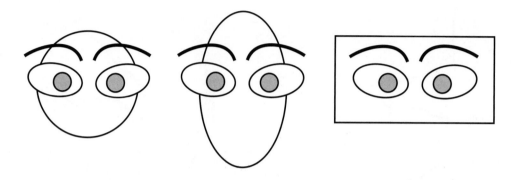

Typically, frames are rectangles rather than circles, in part because we are used to seeing that way and in part because of conventions in industrial manufacturing. The 35 mm photographic frame is said to have been created by Oskar Barnack for the Leica camera because the frame approximated a classic Golden Rectangle, which we discuss later in this chapter.

What happens if we reverse the background tone (also called *white space* or *negative space*) to make the eyes and eyebrows (*figure*) stand out against the background (*ground*) in a different way? Note that we turned the small ovals vertically. Now, if we add pattern to the eyes, we create yet another meaning: These simple illustrations show how easy it is to shift the meanings we perceive by reconfiguring the same basic visual elements. Imagine the infinite number of possible meanings we can communicate given more visual elements, more time, and creative thinking. For instance, notice how the artists used points, lines, shapes, the illusion of three dimensions, and frames in some of your favorite artwork or media images.

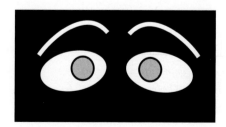 

Williams and Newton

Figure 11.6. Bennie Roping, by Rick Williams. Draw a thumbnail sketch of the elements and analyze what is included, excluded, and related by the photographic frame.

Summary of Key Points

- The five basic visual elements are point, line, plane (shape), volume, and frame.
- We can add such characteristics as tone or color, texture, and pattern to enhance the meaning an element conveys or evokes.
- Frames have size, shape, and direction.
- Frames include, exclude, and relate visual elements.
- Visual elements can be viewed as figure, ground (positive or negative space), or both.
- We can arrange and combine the elements in different ways to communicate and evoke feeling.
- If we change one element in a design, it changes the whole of the design.

The Core Principles

To understand how designers integrate the basic elements in graphic design, we focus on Stebbing's four organizing principles as the *core principles of design — contrast, rhythm, balance, and proportion.*

Contrast

Contrast refers to an emphasis or difference in size, shape, placement, or color in relationships and suggests meaning. For instance, contrast might visually relate things that are large and small, black and white, in front of and behind, above and below.

Representational contrast might relate concepts such as young and old, male and female, or happy and sad. In music, contrast might be expressed through loud and soft sounds, or fast- or slow-moving sequences. Contrast generates and suggests attention and importance. It can create tension among the various elements.

Rhythm

Rhythm is achieved by repeating or contrasting visual elements. Rhythm can convey pattern and a sense of movement or direction. We might see rhythm, for example, in the repeating pattern of light and shadow made by the sun shining through leaves of a tree or by the repeating circles a pebble makes when it strikes the surface of water.

Balance

Balance is the arrangement of elements in terms of *symmetry*, or regularity. In design, we describe balance as either *formal* or *informal*.

In *formal balance*, also known as *symmetrical balance*, compositional elements are arranged equally on both sides of an imaginary middle axis. Formal balance generates feelings of stability, formality, sophistication, and elegance.

In *informal* or *asymmetrical balance*, there is no formal balance or attention to equally dividing space on either side of an *axis*. An *axis* can be clearly visible as a line separating parts of the frame, or it can be perceived or sensed through the arrangement of elements in the frame. Informal balance is dynamic and can generate a sense of energy, change, or tension.

Proportion

Proportion is a ratio of one part of a frame to another part. Proportion defines how dimensions of the frame itself (width and height) relate to one another. Proportion also establishes the relative relationship between visual elements or

Williams and Newton

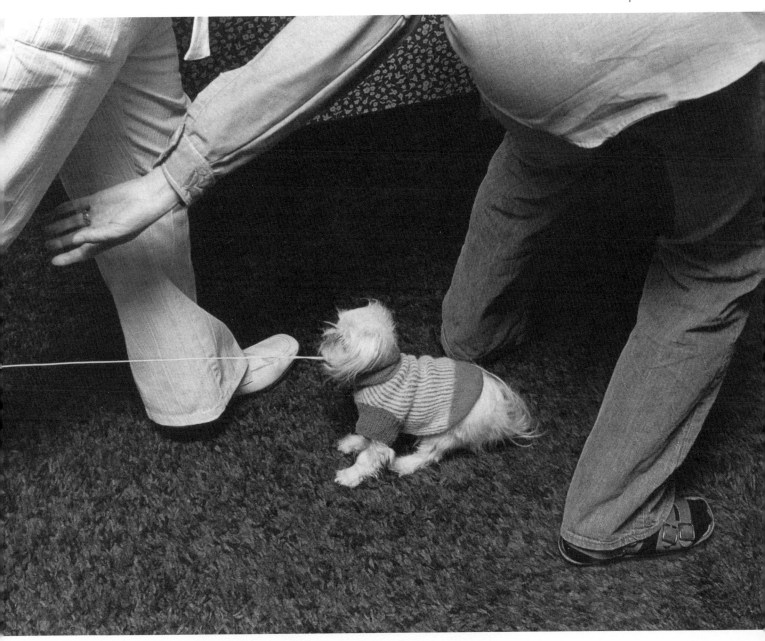

Figure 11.7. *Couple with Dog, by Ave Bonar. Contrast the small dog with the large people, or the light tones of the dog against the dark background. Notice the movement communicated by the lines of the arm and hand, and the rhythm of the folds in the pant leg or the shapes of the background and foreground. Although you can draw a line vertically through the center of the picture, balance is informal with the weight of elements in the right side of the frame assymetrically balanced by the movement toward and space in the left side of the frame. Proportion can be interpreted as 1:1 (divided vertically down the middle) or as a 3:1 (divided vertically at the dog's tail). Close your eyes for a few seconds. Now open them and look at the image again. Your eyes likely settle on the dog, determining center of interest in the frame, and are directed leftward by the visual vectors of the dog's body, the taut leash, and the extended arm.*

between an element or group of elements and the design as a whole. Here are a few frequently used proportions:

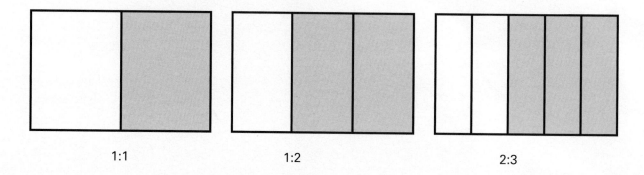

| 1:1 | 1:2 | 2:3 |

One of the most frequently used proportions is found repeatedly in nature and is variously known as the Golden Ratio, Golden Rectangle, *Golden Section*, the Golden Mean, the Golden String, or the *divine proportion*. Some would go so far as to say the Golden Section is the only universal design principle. The Golden Section, found in such patterned natural objects as conch shells, leaves, and pinecones, is expressed in human creations through music, art, mathematics, architecture, and product design. The mathematical expression, known in one form as the Fibonacci series, is especially helpful when trying to understand and verbalize the intuitively sensed Golden Section. The numbers in a Fibonacci series begin with 0, 1, 1, 2, 3, 5, 8, 13, and so on. They are obtained by adding the last two to get the next: 2 + 3 = 5, 5 + 8 = 13, for example. The rectangle below is a golden proportion because a:b as b:c.

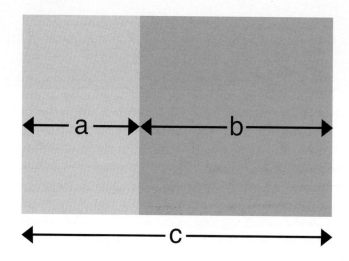

Williams and Newton

Figure 11.8. Chasing Strays, by Rick Williams. While riding a horse during a roundup on the Green Ranch, Rick intuitively framed this shot in a classic golden proportion (envision reversing the a and b parts of the figure at left). Also notice Rick's point of view (see chapter 10) and the contrasting sizes of cattle and horse head, an illusion of scale achieved through use of foreground/background framing (spatiality). Balance is informal, with the dominant visual elements on the right balancing the open but rhythmically patterned space on the left. The frame also can be divided horizontally by imagining a line between the lower half, ending at the top of the horse's left ear, and the top half with the cattle. The horizontal directionality of the frame is enhanced by visual vectors, which convey the illusion of movement toward the upper right of the frame.

Additional Terms of Graphic Structure

Learning a few other terms of graphic structure will help you create and analyze designs. These terms are related to the characteristics of tone, color, pattern, and texture, which we discussed above.

Movement

Movement is generated by a sense of rhythm or direction in a design. Line establishes movement visibly and rationally, as in this frame with the arrow, or intuitively, as in the frame with the dots:

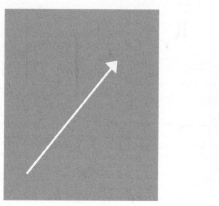 

Note how the arrowed line at left appears to ascend, directing your eye to the upper right-hand portion of the frame, whereas the two dots in the frame at right form a pattern you read as a line that appears to descend, directing your eye toward the lower right-hand side of the frame. These are *visual vectors*, which visual communication theorist Herb Zettl defined as *forces with direction and magnitude*. Lines and shapes help move our eyes around the frame of an image or composition. These vectors can direct our eyes toward certain areas in a frame or toward objects that convey meaning or feelings.

Center of Interest

Key subjects that attract your eye within a composition are referred to as *centers of interest*. There may be single or multiple centers of interest, but typically one or two centers dominate the others and are considered primary. A secondary center of interest can make a composition more interesting and help direct eye movement. Using compositional elements in the frame to create diagonal lines helps direct the eye from one center of interest to another as a form of visual vector. Including too many focal points can diminish the composition.

Williams and Newton

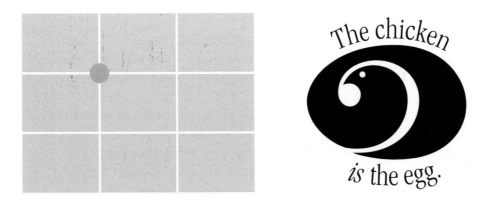

Figures 11.9-10. Left: Rule of Thirds illustration by Janet Halvorsen. Right: Logo design by Maggie Macnab.

Rule of Thirds

The *Rule of Thirds* divides the frame into thirds vertically and horizontally. The four points where the lines cross are primary points of visual interest for subject placement because these are points where the eye naturally falls.

Note how the Rule of Thirds relates to the core principles of balance and proportion. One way to achieve effective *asymmetrical balance* is to place the most important visual element at one of the intersecting points. This also establishes a proportion of 1:2. Dividing a frame in half, or 1:1 proportion, results in *symmetrical balance* if the elements in each half mirror. Centering the principal subject is another way to focus attention on an element but also can be static and boring unless used sparingly and purposefully.

Scale

Scale is the relation in size between shapes and objects of unknown size with those of known size. Scale helps us discern how large or small something is. Scale carries emotional impact, such as the relationship of a small child's hand in the hand of a very large man. Exaggerated scale can be used to emphasize importance or power and to establish contrast.

Spatiality

Spatiality is the way elements (the figures) are arranged within the frame in terms of the area (the ground) surrounding them. Spatiality evokes attitudes. Typically, a lot of white space evokes attitudes of class, wealth, uniqueness, and room to breathe. On the other hand, crowded pages with little white space seem cramped or pinched and tend to represent inexpensive products or sale items. Pushing the edge of the frame can imply a cramped setting with a larger world beyond. Yet a crowded composition can also be dynamic and convey a sense of action.

Perspective

Perspective establishes a sense of depth and conveys point of view. In two-dimensional representation, depth refers to the way visual elements appear to have dimension through the use of shadowing, size, and position in the frame.

Using linear perspective in drawing or within a photographic frame makes lines appear to converge, establishing an illusion of depth in the frame. Closer objects appear smaller, and distant objects appear larger. Perspective as *point of view* refers to how we look at something — are we directly in front of it, or above or below it? This is also called *angle of view*. In photography, selecting an angle of view that places the camera eye below and looking up at the subject tends to give a sense of importance or power to the subject. Selecting an angle of view that places the camera above and looking down on the subject tends to diminish the importance of the subject and make it appear more submissive or less powerful. Conceptually and ideologically, perspective refers to the individual point of view each individual has as a result of unique cultural experiences and biological characteristics.

Light and Color (related to tone)

Light (see also chapter 10, Photography), the visible part of the electromagnetic spectrum, is a form of energy that illuminates visual elements in our field of view. Light, or the effect of light, sets the emotional mood and feeling by illuminating shape, texture, and specific parts of the subject while leaving other parts in shadow. *High-contrast light* with deep, dark shadows and bright highlights and colors can create a sense of drama and toughness and generate feelings of fast-paced action and bright sunlight. *Diffused,* or *low-contrast light*, is soft with open shadows that flow smoothly into medium highlights and produce more pastel colors. This light is used to generate sensual, friendly, or young and peaceful feelings.

Light is also described in terms of *hue, saturation,* and *brightness. Hue* refers to the actual color or specific tone, as in primary red, yellow, or blue. *Saturation* is the strength, intensity, or purity of the color from gray to vivid. *Brightness* refers to lightness or darkness of a color, ranging from black to white.

Light also is described as being *warm* or *cool.* Natural sunlight changes color from morning to evening. Light is measured in degrees Kelvin (K) with cool, bluish, morning sunlight measuring about 5,500 degrees K and warm, red and orange afternoon sunlight measuring in ranges from about 3,600 K to 4,600 K. The colors of light also carry emotional overtones, as do cultural colors such as a white or black hat or the colors of a nation's or organization's flag. Still photographers and cinemaphotographers often use color gels over their lights or flashes to simulate natural daylight colors.

Context

Perceiving can be ambiguous until we know the circumstances or situation into which visual elements fit. For instance, a pistol on a white backdrop has little or no context for interpretation. A pistol under the seat of a car has a different context, and thus a different meaning, from a pistol in a police officer's holster. One technique that advertising uses is to produce images in which the context is not completely clear so that the meaning can be whatever the viewer imagines.

Figure 11.11. Melvin at the Longhorn Cafe, by Rick Williams. Note the strong side light from the window on Melvin's face, contrasted with the shadows on his shirt. What is the center of interest? Does the Rule of Thirds apply to this photograph? Is the photograph symmetrically or asymmetrically balanced? How is the space in the frame handled? How does the bright light affect the overall communication of the moment? How does scale work in the frame?

Tying it All Together

Principles of the Gestalt

Finally, we come to four key concepts brought forth by the German perceptual psychologists Koffka, Köhler, and Wertheimer in the 1930s. Recall that the basic idea of gestalt is that an arrangement of visual elements means something more than any one of the elements alone — *the whole is greater than the sum of its parts* — a 1 + 1 = 3 effect.

The primary principle, the *Law of Prägnanz*, stated that a "psychological organization will always be as 'good' as the prevailing conditions will allow" (Koffka, p. 110). Koffka admitted that the principle was "somewhat vague." The concept of *good*, though undefined, embraced "such properties as regularity, symmetry, simplicity and others" (p. 110). Barry said it another way: "As the principle which unifies perceptual elements into a single harmonious whole, this Law of Prägnanz is the early twentieth-century counterpart of Aristotle's concept of 'common sense,' the Gestalt essence of which is efficiency achieved through simplicity, regularity, and symmetry" (p. 47).

Four sublaws follow:

- *Law of Proximity* — we perceive grouped elements as belonging together
- *Law of Similarity* — we perceive similar elements as belonging together
- *Law of Good Continuation* — we perceive a line as continuing beyond its ending point
- *Law of Closure* — we will complete unseen parts of a shape

Unity

All of these elements, terms, concepts, and principles come together through *unity*, a concept similar to gestalt expressing the sense that all visual elements in a design work together to form a whole that communicates. That whole may not be harmonious and, in fact, may not "work" well. *Fragmentation* can occur if all of the elements do not relate or are working against each other. Fragmentation provides a psychological feeling of incompleteness or tension, as if the elements are coming apart. Fragmentation can be disturbing but can also be dynamic and exciting, depending on context and meaning.

Cultural Biases

It is important to remember that this chapter is heavily influenced by traditions of Western European design. Although we have stressed basic elements, principles, and terms that some scholars argue are understood by all humans, different people in different cultures can and do apply and interpret them in different ways to construct and discern different meanings. Kress and van Leeuwens

Figure 11.12. Pies at a Psychiatrists' Convention, by Ave Bonar. How do the Law of Prägnanz and the four sublaws of Gestalt psychology affect the way you interpret the photograph? Do you have a context for interpreting the image, or do you supply your own (see * below)? Can you see how gestalt perception affects your understanding of the images?

argued that "visual language is not transparent and universally understood, but culturally specific" (p. 3). Yet we began this chapter with Stebbing's idea that humans perceive the universal principles of contrast, rhythm, balance, and proportion. Both approaches are useful when learning to understand and create visual design. We discuss these issues more fully in chapter 12.

For now, we invite you to explore the visual through your own "design for meaning."

*They really are pieces of pie at a pyschiatrists' convention.

Figure C11.1. Heiress Series ad, Sims girl's snowboard (original in color) in Transworld Snowboarding.

CREATIVE ELEVEN
Graphic Visions: Looking for Meaning

The Goal: Understanding the Frame

Use a creative exercise such as visualization to help relax and enter a state of conscious seeing and reflection. Allow yourself plenty of time. Although the exercise may at first seem tedious to work through, the potential rewards are great. The goal is for you to gain a clear understanding of how design communicates meaning in a purposefully constructed visual message with persuasive intentions. Read the instructions carefully.

Look through a magazine or newspaper to find two advertisements: one that appeals to you and in which you think the design works, and one that does not seem to work as well. Note the name and date of the publication and the page numbers of the ads for your records. Note any information identifying models, photographers, designers, or agencies. Although such information is seldom made available, it is important to think about the people who were involved in creating the ad.

Now, sketch the ad in two ways.

First, draw a *thumbnail-size frame* — a small, simple rectangle (or other shape if appropriate) 1 or 2 inches wide — in the basic shape of the ad's overall frame. Sketch in the three to five primary visual elements of the ad. Use simple lines to represent the type and other visual elements in the ad.

Consider how each of the *five basic visual elements* (*point, line, plane, volume,* and *frame*) studied in chapter 11 is used in the design of the ad. Make notes to use later.

Second, draw a *quarter-page* frame (about 4″ wide) in the basic shape of the ad's overall frame. Sketch in the three to five primary visual elements in the ad — this time with more detail. Use lines or simple, overall shapes to represent the type in the ad. You may draw these two sketches on the same piece of paper if you wish. What you are doing is practicing the process a graphic designer might use to originate the design for the ad. You are simply doing it in reverse order, meaning you are starting the finished design and working backward so you can evaluate and interpret the design rather than starting with simple sketches and working forward to fine-tune your design ideas.

Now, using your two sketches to guide you, consider again how each of the five basic visual elements is used in the ad design. Think about the lines or blocks of type as design elements rather than individual letters and words. Squinting your eyes and looking at the ad through the blur of "half vision" sometimes can help you discern what visual elements stand out in an image. Make notes about what you see.

Work your way through the following questions, making notes as you go. You may find drawing additional thumbnail-size sketches to address each question will help you break down the design to understand how it works visually to communicate its meaning.

- How are the *five basic elements of visual design* (point, line, plane, volume, and frame) used in the ad?

- Which visual elements stand out as *figure*? How is *ground* used in the ad?

- How are the *design characteristics* of tone or color; texture; and pattern used in the design?

- How are the *four core design principles* (contrast, rhythm, balance, and proportion) achieved in the ad? Are some of the principles more obvious or do some work better than others?

- How do other *aspects of graphic structure* (movement, vectors, centers of interest, Rule of Thirds, scale, spatiality, perspective, light, context) discussed in chapter 11 work in the design? Discuss at least three.

- How do the *five gestalt principles* (Law of Prägnanz, Law of Proximity, Law of Similarity, Law of Good Continuation, Law of Closure) work in the ad?

- How is *unity* achieved?

- What *cultural biases* do you discern in the ad?

Now, using your notes and sketches to guide you, write an essay addressing these questions and discussing how the design of the ad communicates the meaning of the ad visually.

Now, draw a thumbnail sketch of the second ad and make notes about why it is not as effective as the "well-designed" ad. Write a paragraph about the design of the second ad, addressing what does not work well and including suggestions for how to improve the second ad.

Conclude your essay with a paragraph comparing the two ads.

Reflect on and write an assessment of what you learned and of your overall experience.

Summary

- Spend time relaxing before you start to work.
- Read the instructions carefully.
- Choose two different print advertisements from a magazine or newspaper. Choose one ad that you think uses good design and one that you think uses poor design. Note the name and date of the publications, page numbers of the ads. Note any information identifying models, photographers, designers, or agencies.
- Work first with the well-designed ad.
- Draw a thumbnail sketch and a quarter-page sketch of the main visual elements in the ad. Sign and date your sketches.
- Use your drawings to help you assess the graphic design of the ad. You may need to do additional drawings to help you see various design elements, principles, graphic structure, and gestalt principles.
- Evaluate the ad in an essay as described above. Be sure to address all the questions.
- Draw a thumbnail sketch of the poorly designed ad. Sign and date your sketch. Write a paragraph for your essay evaluating the design and suggesting how to improve the design.
- Conclude the essay with a paragraph comparing the two ads.
- Reflect on and assess your overall experience.

Example by Andrea Schneider

The first ad I chose was one from *Transworld Snowboarding* magazine for a Sims girl's snowboard called the "Heiress Series." It is marketing to an atypical snowboard buyer, a more high maintenance girl in particular. The ad works and communicates the message because of its effective design. All the elements cooperate and support each other to sell a board for a girl who, although stereotypically girlish, still has an edge.

Points in the ad include the girl's face, the dogs (especially the one peeing), the board's graphic of the dog, the logo and the text image. The logo in the upper left, the board, and the text image are distinguished by the color pink and are emphasized. The dog collars are also pink and draw attention to those elements.

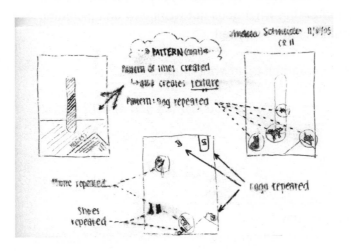

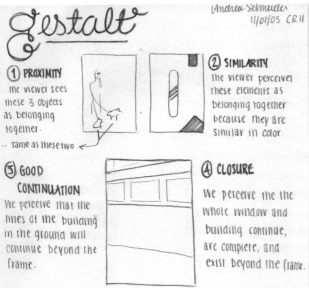

Figures C11.2-4. Analysis of visual design for first ad critiqued by Andrea Schneider.

There are lines that run through the board's graphics and they are repeated in various ways throughout the design. The direction of the text in the lower right corner follows these lines and is also echoed by the texture of the sidewalk in the ground. The lines in the building in the ground help move the reader's gaze from left to right across the page. If you were draw a line connecting the two point of the dogs, this line would run parallel to the same lines of the board graphic. All these lines help to create a movement, especially to the upper-right hand corner of the ad where the Sims logo is.

The variety of shapes creates a tension of different emotions in the ad. There is warmth created by the circular shapes and curves in the snowboard and the girl. The word Heiress is also very round. A triangular shape of energy can be seen more in the dogs, the logo, and the text block image. Relationships between different elements within the design seem to form triangles.

Different planes and levels exist within the ad. The graphics seem to sit on top of the overall image, while the snowboard also seems to exist on its own plane. The location of the girl with her two dogs in front of her staggered different distances also creates depth with the ground of the building falling to the back of the ad.

Tone and color are very active in distinguishing, emphasizing and relating different elements. The board, logo, and text graphic grab the viewer's attention and seem to be related because of the pink, the flatness, and tone. The girl and her dogs are related because they are more muted and have more depth. The pink collars of the dogs help relate them to those elements first mentioned. In contrast, the ground is very monochromatic and recedes. It acts as negative space for the ad. The abundance of negative space evokes a feeling of wealth in this instance, and the design echoes that of a fashion ad rather than one for sporting equipment.

The frame contains the main elements in mid-range without cutting any of the images off and still leaving some space to let the viewer's eye wander across the ad to the logo and text.

Patterns can be seen with the lines in the snowboard graphic echoed with the sidewalk texture and direction of the text. Other elements are also repeated throughout the design. There are two dogs on a leash but there is also a pink silhouette of a dog incorporated into the text image in the lower right-hand corner. An even smaller dog is in the snowboard graphic itself along with the same text "Heiress." The girl in the picture is talking on her cell phone and wearing stilettos and both those can be found again as pink silhouettes in the text image. The Sims logo appears in a pink box in the upper right-hand corner of the design but also makes the tag of the dog's pink silhouette and is inscribed in the building in the ground. Texture isn't used that effectively in the ad and seems to be most abundant in the ground.

The ad does effectively contrast different elements. The most recognizable contrast is with color. A few items share the same color pink and it is the only real notable color in the ad (aside from some green stripes). The rest of the ad is more muted in an almost grayish sepia hue. Elements also contrast in that flat, bold images grab attention. As a whole there is a contrast in proportion and balance where the right side has more of the key elements of the ad. More in regard to the message of the ad itself, there is a contextual contrast where the snowboard seems out-of-place in its environment. In this same sense the image of the fashionable girl seems to contrast the stereotype of a snowboarder and that's played upon with this "classy" girl and her high maintenance dog peeing on the snowboard. While this contrast exists, it also relates the girl and the snowboard; the "Heiress" is both the snowboard and the girl.

Rhythm is a successful element in communicating the ad's message because relationships, line, and movement create continuity. There is rhythm created by the relationship of both size and placement of the girl and the snowboard. The three dominant figures to the right create rhythm balanced by the girl and her two dogs on the left. By connected each set of these three elements, a triangle is formed. The same occurs in the bottom third of the ad with the two dogs and pink dog silhouette. Together these elements and their relationships also create and informal balance or asymmetry that still has fluidity.

Within the ad there seems to be an approximate 2:1 ratio. The attention grabbing elements on the right seem to occupy two-thirds of the design. It appears the designer created this ad without particular regard for the rule of thirds. Most elements fall outside the focal points created by the three squared lines. Instead the snowboard sits central and the other elements lie out at outward directions from it. Regardless, I feel that the design was still successful with its nontraditional arrangement.

The perspective of the ad seems to be from an angle below center. That way the snowboard and the girl appear higher on the page but are also very large and important looking. This technique reflects the message and attitude of the "Heiress." Even the small dogs don't look meek and obedient, but are regal and mischievous.

Gestalt principles help the viewer perceive the intended message by creating relationships and meaning. The rule of proximity allows the viewer to group the girl and the two dogs because they are close together. The law of similarity helps the receiver of the message group the other three main elements on the right of the page including the logo, snowboard and text box image. This correlation is aided because the objects are similar. They all have similar color and appear bolder and flatter than others in the ad. The ad successfully uses the different design elements in conjunction with the process of seeing and relating to communicate the message. It uses stereotypes to help identify and reach the market, but uses humor to help sell the product.

Ad #2 Critique and Comparative Discussion

Although the product is similar, the Sims ad is much more effective than the House Boardshop ad. The Sims ad effectively uses different visual elements and structures of design that are absent in the other ad. One particular success of the Sims ad is its use of color. The designer used pink to emphasize certain elements and create rhythm, movement, line, and relationships through the gestalt law of similarity. Pink also conveys the message of the creator. In contrast, the House Boardshop ad uses color in a distracting way. No one element grabs your attention. Instead the eye darts around the page trying to determine a hierarchy.

Color type and type blocks themselves also create line but result in a sort of wavy, haphazard movement across the page. Other elements, like the logo and snowboard are subjugated due to their lack of color. Red text and blue background do not organize the design effectively, especially because the creator switched the use of color. Sometimes the text was in color; sometimes the block behind was in color and other times text was outlined in color.

The Sims ad also uses space effectively. The abundance of negative space contributes to the message by conveying a wealthy and fashionable attitude. In the House

Figure C11.5. House Boardshop ad (original in color).

Boardshop ad, objects and text are crowded and jumbled, giving the ad a cheaper and chaotic look. The negative space itself is colored and takes away from other more important elements in the ad.

Although some balance from left to right is created by placement of the snowboard and snowboarder on either side, an effective informal balance was not achieved. The Sims ad had similar elements but achieved balance because of the relationships with other parts. There is no rhythm, and the way the text was presented doesn't evoke any type of cohesion. It's also harder to determine which elements are related in the ad. Red seems to signify type and the style groups certain text together, but the text doesn't work together and fights for attention. The House Boardshop ad doesn't use effective proportion. In fact, I'm not even sure how to determine proportion in this ad.

GROUND

The blue background seems to be acting as ground. There is little negative space and the design feels crowded with little organization.

POINTS

☆ There are many points, but a single one doesn't grab your attention because there are other distracting elements.

All text boxes also act as FIGURE

Main points
⇨ also comprise FIGURE

The blue ground distracts

Seemingly important images have little or no color and recede

Figures C11.6-7.
Top: Small
thumbnail.
Left: Larger sketch
of key visual elements.
Ad Critique #2 by
Andrea Schneider..

Were I trying to improve this ad, I would start by deciding what I wanted to be a focal point. The text I wanted to stand out I would perhaps make red and then find another structure to organize the rest of the type. I would also choose to emphasize the logo by also making it red. Instead of having a distracting blue negative space, I would make it a neutral color, such as beige and that would help both my text and my images come forward. I would try to open the ad up a bit by having more ground. Arranging some of the text in horizontal lines instead of waves might help me accomplish that. Making a few of these simple changes would improve the design in other ways by creating more contrast, better movement, informal balance, and rhythm.

Figure C11.8. Hot Springs, Big Bend National Park, 1979. Photograph © Frank Armstrong.

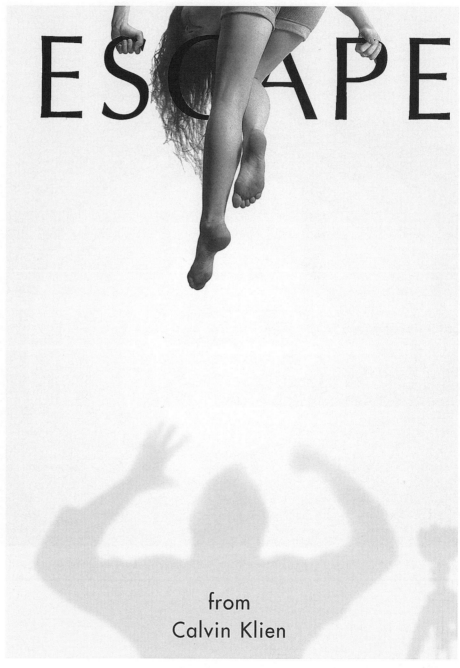

Figure 12.1. What are the signs conveyed in this spoof ad from Adbusters.org? What is signifier and what is signified?

CHAPTER TWELVE
Embedded Meanings:
Learning to Look Behind the Mirrors
and Beyond the Windows

magery created by and delivered to us by the media is the basis of the most prolific, pervasive, and effective popular art in history. By *effective*, we mean that media images fulfill the purpose for which they were designed. Media images, particularly those developed for advertising and public relations, are most often created from a strategy of persuasion. Yet even news and entertainment imagery use communication strategies with specific intentions: to inform you; to grab and hold your attention; to increase television ratings; to sell the newspaper or magazine; to make money through box office sales, video rentals, and Internet advertising; and, perhaps most important, to provide an audience for advertisers and sponsors.

These strategies use visual images to generate psychological and physiological responses that encourage us to do whatever the imagemaker has in mind: get especially excited about watching an upcoming sports event, crave a juicy bacon cheeseburger, buy a greeting card that says "just the right thing in just the right way," enjoy a movie so much that you will tell your friends to go see it — and will later rent it or buy it (and related products) to watch again. Beyond all of these fairly obvious consumer-oriented prompts, it is even more significant that media use visual images to create a sense of what is normal and acceptable in terms of our values, lifestyles, and related behaviors. In effect, media images often urge us to adopt an impossible reality as our own.

Advertising is by far the most sophisticated producer and user of intuitive media messages. Advertising professionals and educators use the work of neuroscientists, psychologists, and media scholars to understand precisely what images, sounds, phrases, movements, and combinations of intuitive processes are most effective in establishing emotional and psychological associations with their messages of persuasion. Though the educational system as a whole may marginalize the significance of intuitive intelligence, schools of advertising, media, art, and communication study it as the core of the integration of creativity and persuasion. The advertising industry was expected to spend close to $600 billion worldwide in 2006 (Coen, 2005). It costs more to produce 30 seconds of a major television ad than it does to produce the same amount of time in a blockbuster sci-fi movie. And advertising concepts are incorporated into all media, including TV sitcoms, children's programming, video games, and your favorite movie. It is estimated that the average U.S. citizen sees as many as 4,000 media-generated images every single day.

The cumulative effect of all of these messages — whether or not we take the specifically intended action — can be seen as a kind of collective memory, one based on media-generated images and events rather than on interaction with real people. Ultimately, that collective memory shapes our perceptions of reality and guides our behaviors in real life by defining the culture in which we live. This collective memory based on shared media experiences is related to but differs from Carl Jung's idea of a collective unconscious. Collective memory is not media dependent — people can be thrown together during a major event, for example, and share memories of a unique experience — but it often is the result of sharing experiences with millions of people via mass media. Jung's collective unconscious focuses on sharing universal understanding of basic life patterns because we are part of the same species.

Because media imagery blends sophisticated rational and intuitive cognitive processes in visual components, competence in creating and understanding visual and media messages is now requisite for contemporary viewers. It is important here to distinguish between visual literacy and media literacy. *Visual literacy* encompasses the ability to interpret and create visual messages of all kinds — from dreams and poetic imagery through virtual reality. *Media literacy* is a component of visual literacy that focuses on learning to interpret and use forms of mass media, such as newspapers and television, in intelligent ways. *Intuitive literacy* means the ability to use intuitive intelligence to complement rational intelligence, thus enhancing both visual and media literacy.

Although most of us can see to a degree when we are born, infants still must learn to focus and recognize shapes, colors, and such patterns as their parents' faces. As noted earlier, seeing is more than the physiological act of gathering light rays and sending signals to other parts of the brain. In fact, "seeing" is only 1/10th physical in terms of eye functions. The other 90% of the process of visual perception is mental, or cognitive. This refers to the processing the brain goes through to make meaning and store visual information into memories that are mostly nonconscious. So, when we speak of the mind's eye, we are really talking about mental experience that operates on both rational and intuitive levels.

In the chapter on language, we explored the rational and intuitive aspects of language. We suggested that a word stands for a meaning that we share, at

Williams and Newton

least to a basic extent. As an example, we offered the idea that when we say the word *mother*, we all share the meaning that a mother is the female parent of a child. We may also have varying, culturally learned descriptors for a mother, such as nurturing, caring, intelligent, and successful. These represent our basic rational or logical concepts of who a mother is.

We also discussed another type of cognition related to the word *mother* that represents an intuitive cognitive response based in our interior, personal, emotional, psychological, and physiological experiences and interactions. This intuitive process touches our deepest feelings, values, and emotions, and it often moves us toward a physiological response, such as a small shudder, smile, feeling, or the desire to talk with one's mother.

If a simple word, such as *mother*, can elicit such strong mental imagery and emotional responses, imagine what kind of response an external visual image that has been carefully designed to influence your deepest feelings, values, and emotions can elicit.

Culture and Making Sense of What We See

Most media images use both visual imagery and value-laden, emotional language. Many media images also use sound, music, and movement to affect our perceptions and shape our behaviors. Consider, for example, a television advertisement of a man and woman, whom we interpret as a mother and father, sitting together on a comfortable, colorful sofa in a beautiful home filled with warm afternoon light. Dad puts his arm around Mom, and the two of them smile tenderly as he reaches for the phone to make a call. The screen splits, and a young man, whom we interpret as their son, in a college dormitory room looks up from his books and picks up his cell phone. When he hears his dad's voice, he smiles and moves to the cozy comfort of his bed, as the same afternoon light that shines on Mom and Dad shines through his window to warm him. The son happily talks and connects with his parents as the voice over suggests that you "reach out and touch someone." The intended message is that talking on the phone connects parents with their children in college in the same way that being with them would. The intended behavior is that viewers will *associate* talking on the telephone with the visual and emotional impact of actually being with (touching) beloved family members, as in this dreamlike scenario.

Mediated messages such as this have been produced to attract our attention, touch our emotions, and move us to act. As noted earlier, the average U.S. citizen sees 4,000 such messages every day. These estimates are probably low if we include the thousands of colorful boxes and wrappers we see in a single stroll though a store (about eight per second). Then there are the logos on clothing worn by people we pass on the street, magazines and newspaper ads we think we don't notice as we browse publications in a waiting room, the covers of magazines on a newsstand, products carefully arranged in store windows, posters taped to a telephone pole, pictures on envelopes and stamps in our mailboxes, huge billboards on the sides of road and buildings, the television that lulls us to sleep, the flashing Internet banners that divert our attention from news stories, and the ever-present television screens in airports and sports bars. Of course, we cannot simultaneously attend to all of these images on a conscious level. However, our intuitive cognitive processes, synthesizing across space and time, take in more information than we consciously note and retain a sense of many of these messages in nonconscious memory. Here, they are used as a standard of reality against which new perceptual information is weighed as our nonconscious mind creates nonconscious biases that guide our behavior.

On a conscious level, we think we select what we "see." However, we our nonconscious memories and predispositions guide us in this editing process. What we choose to note, or bring into our rational consciousness from the seeing process, depends on such factors as:

- What catches our attention — The bright colors and movement of a banner or news crawl running across the bottom of the television makes us want to read it.
- What we know — Leaves turn red and gold in the fall, so we think of changing seasons when we see brightly colored leaves.
- What we believe — We don't like a political candidate, so when we see him speak on television, we "see" him as looking arrogant or stupid and we interpret what he says as deceitful.
- What we want — We see a beautiful model wearing a coat in an ad and think, "I don't need a new coat, but the coat in that ad is really cute . . . maybe I could use another coat."
- Our physical or emotional state — We're tired from studying most of the night, so we drift off during class, daydreaming about taking a nap when we get home.
- Memory — We saw a political ad on television that we consciously recognized as misleading. The images stick in our memory, however, and we use them later, perhaps nonconsciously, as evidence for voting against the candidate.

Figure 12.2. The Oregonian, March 21, 2006. Images of photojournalism differ from many other media images in that their purpose is to visually convey truthful information about real events that happen to real people. Their messages also carry deep symbolic meaning and invite viewers to connect with people they meet through the images. Unfortunately, we often view the images so quickly that we do not stop to consider their multiple meanings. Serious photojournalism often becomes lost in a sea of ads and entertainment imagery. This makes appropriate interpretation especially challenging. Which one of these photographs, highlighted with others here on a newspaper picture page, most catches your attention? Why? Consider that image in terms of the six personal editing factors listed above.

NEWS FOCUS

EXAMINING WORLD, NATIONAL AND REGIONAL EVENTS

Three years in Iraq: A visual record

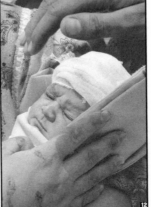

1. Shock and awe: Smoke billows from a presidential palace compound in Baghdad on March 21, 2003. U.S.-led forces launched the war with a massive air assault.
RAMZI HAIDAR/AGENCE FRANCE-PRESSE

2. Fallujah fight: Marine Lance Cpl. James takes a smoke break Nov. 9, 2004, on the second day of a battle to rout insurgents from Fallujah.
LUIS SINCO/LOS ANGELES TIMES

3. Burning wells: Kuwaiti oil workers try to extinguish an oil fire March 27, 2003, near Rumaila, Iraq. Retreating Iraqi troops set several wells ablaze.
MARIO TAMA/GETTY IMAGES

4. Heading to Baghdad: A Marine convoy passes a dead Iraqi on April 8, 2003, after crossing a bridge over the Diyala River. U.S. forces swarmed into the Iraqi capital the next day.
JAMES HILL
NEW YORK TIMES NEWS SERVICE

5. Running the country: L. Paul Bremer, then the civilian administrator in Iraq, consults tribal leaders June 14, 2003, in Hillah, in south-central Iraq.
BULLIT MARQUEZ
ASSOCIATED PRESS

6. Grieving: An Iraqi man is consoled by another on Nov. 21, 2005, at a Baqouba hospital after his family was killed when U.S. forces fired on their vehicle.
MOHAMMED ADNAN
ASSOCIATED PRESS

7. Oregon Guard: Sgt. 1st Class Daniel Moran of Parkdale, Ore., dances March 6, 2005, with members of the Iraqi police and army in Laylan, near Kirkuk, before a meeting in the village to promote better relations. Moran is with Alpha Company, 3rd Platoon, 3rd Battalion, 116th Cavalry, Oregon Army National Guard.
RANDY L. RASMUSSEN
THE OREGONIAN

8. Saddam on trial: Former Iraqi President Saddam Hussein says in court March 1, 2006, that he ordered the trial of 148 Shiites in Dujail who were eventually executed. But he insisted he had the right to do so because they were suspected of trying to kill him.
BOB STRONG/ASSOCIATED PRESS

9. Prison scandal: A hooded Iraqi prisoner, attached to electrical wires, stands on a box at Abu Ghraib prison in fall 2003. The image was one of dozens made public in early 2004 of abuses by U.S. guards at the prison west of Baghdad.
COURTESY OF THE NEW YORKER

10. Proud voter: A woman in Zubayr shows off her purple finger after voting Jan. 30, 2005, in the country's first free elections in half a century. Iraqis voted again Dec. 15, 2005, to choose the 275-member Council of Representatives that met for the first time last week.
ANDREW PARSONS/ASSOCIATED PRESS

11. Sewer work: A U.S. soldier stands guard at a sewage treatment plant June 14, 2004, in Baghdad. By the end of last year, the United States had contributed $18.44 billion to repair Iraq's infrastructure, but sabotage has hindered rebuilding efforts.
SHAWN BALDWIN/NEW YORK TIMES NEWS SERVICE

12. Civilians hurt: Four-day-old Miriam Jabber, injured by flying glass, is brought by her mother to a Baghdad hospital on July 13, 2005. A suicide car bomb exploded as U.S. soldiers distributed candy to children, killing at least 27 people, including a dozen children.
KHALID MOHAMMED/ASSOCIATED PRESS

To learn more: "Journey to Iraq," a slideshow of photos by The Oregonian's Randy Rasmussen, who has traveled to Iraq twice to cover the Oregon National Guard: www.oregonlive.com/special/oregonian/iraq/

By the time we bring images into the conscious mind, they have already affected behavior on intuitive levels. They have become part of our nonconscious memory that helps to shape our perceptions of reality and guide our behavior. Thus, it is critical to our understanding of ourselves and how we interact with others that, in our highly visual and mediated world, we learn how to better understand and use visual communication both intuitively and rationally.

We can approach the study of visual communication in a number of ways. In this chapter, we explore several analytical techniques for studying visual media images.

Traditional Ways to Study Visuals

Researchers use five categories of techniques for studying the media: survey research, experimental design, content analysis, historical/comparative analysis, and field research. Although a great deal of the media research conducted in the 20th century was statistically oriented, or quantitative, the last 30 years have seen a rise in the use of methods that rely more on verbal analysis than on numbers. Increasingly, researchers are finding they need to use more than one type of method for trying to answer their questions or test their ideas.

Key concepts in research underlie the credibility of any study. First, has the research been conducted in a *systematic* manner? A systematic method of study refers to a careful, reasoned process that the researcher can clearly explain. Second is the research *valid* — that is, does it study or measure what it says it does? A third key concept in research is *reliability* — that is, will we obtain the same result in repeated studies conducted in the same way?

You are probably most familiar with *survey* research, in which randomly selected individuals are questioned about their thoughts, opinions, feelings, and behaviors. Public opinion polls and Nielsen television ratings are examples of survey research. Surveys are useful for giving us an idea of trends, such as how many people plan to vote a certain way or what people are thinking. However, people often act differently from what they say they do. People usually underestimate the amount of food they eat in a day, for example. In addition, unless they are very careful, survey researchers can bias the phrasing of questions in such a way as to elicit certain responses.

The only method that can reliably establish *cause and effect* relationships is an *experiment* in which researchers carefully control the conditions to which subjects are exposed. In one classic and often-repeated experiment, called the Stroop Task, researchers ask people to sit in front of computer monitors and indicate the color of a word on the screen. That doesn't seem so hard to do. However, we know from repeated experiments that if the word names a color (such as the word *red*), and the color of the *type* is different than the *name* of the color the word indicates, people have a difficult time responding quickly and correctly. So, if the word "RED" is shown in the color *green* on the screen,

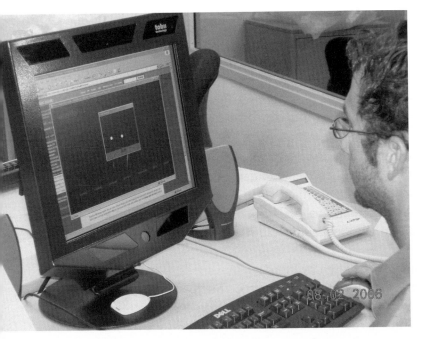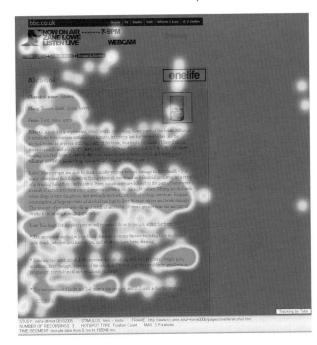

Figures 12.3-4. Testing patterns of eye travel on the Internet. Researchers Nora Paul and Laura Ruel in the Digital Storytelling Effects Lab, a joint project of the University of Minnesota and the University of North Carolina, are studying effective presentation forms for online storytelling. Left: The two dots in the middle of the screen show the user's eye position, which is tracked with an in-monitor camera. Right: Heat map imaging indicate viewing patterns for an HTML page about alcohol use. Researchers determined that users enjoyed and spent more time with an interactive presentation but considered more materials in an "encyclopedic-type reference" presentation and found it easier to navigate.

people find it difficult to say the word "RED." We have learned a great deal about human behavior by testing how people respond and behave in experimental situations. The question then becomes: Will people act the same way outside of the laboratory, in real-world situations? We've even learned that people will act differently in a laboratory setting to please the researcher.

Social scientists sometimes use quasi-experimental design, or experiments conducted in real-world settings, to increase the validity of their studies. An example of a quasi-experimental design is a study in which the social psychologist Stanley Milgram observed how people walking along a sidewalk responded to different kinds of photographic situations. He learned that when the photographer looked more professional, the passersby tended to walk around the photographic scene rather than walk between the photographer and subject, as they might do when the photographer looked like a tourist. The sidewalk experiment was one of a series Milgram conducted to test his theory that when someone takes a picture, it is a "photographic event."

Mass communication researchers use *content analysis* to study images as well as text. In quantitative content analysis, a researcher might count the number of times news stories address a certain topic, measure how much space is given to particular kinds of photographs in a magazine, or time how long news broadcasts report about an issue. Qualitative content analysis often requires subjective judgment rather than objective counting or measuring.

Historical/comparative research examines documents and trends across time and geography.

Field studies use such techniques as interviews, case studies, and participant observation, through which the researcher seeks to understand a community by living in the community. Journalists use field methods to gather both visual and verbal material for their stories. In some ways, you have been conducting this kind of research your entire life. Social scientist Earl Babbie wrote that field research

> is constantly used in everyday life, by all of us. In a sense, we do field research whenever we observe or participate in social behavior and try to understand it, whether in a college class-room, in a doctor's waiting room, or an airplane. Whenever we report our observations to others, we are reporting our field research efforts. (p. 28)

Yet, as Babbie also pointed out, being a good researcher, who obtains valid and reliable information, requires honing these "natural" abilities into thoughtful

Figure 12.5-6. Children pose with Polaroid images of themselves. Giving photos to study participants shows them what the visual researcher is seeing and can enhance both communication about the project and the quality of image content. Photographs by Julianne Newton.

skills that dig below quick conclusions. The key to being a good researcher is questioning one's own preconceptions as well as the preconceptions of society.

We have offered this cursory introduction to research methods to give you an idea of the many different ways scholars and professional communicators try to determine what is true and what is not. Ultimately, we cannot determine with absolute certainty what is true. However, we can work hard to determine what is *reasonably true* (Newton, 2001), given our best efforts to dig beneath the often misleading messages others send our way. If we are genuinely seeking to understand visual images and how they work, we must use different ways to seek that understanding in order to increase the likelihood of determining what is reasonably true.

In that spirit, we introduce you to several techniques that we find especially useful in uncovering the most "reasonable truth" of visual messages.

Other Methods to Study Visuals

A *rhetorical analysis* is an approach to studying a text or image by critically examining the goals of the writer or imagemaker and how they created the message in their effort to achieve their goals. If a Hallmark Cards commercial stirs your emotions, for example, you might ask, "Why did Hallmark want to affect me in this way? What strategies did Hallmark's advertisers use to affect me?" Messages with strong intentions and points of view are not unique to contemporary media, however. People have been using and analyzing rhetorical strategies for at least 2,400 years. Consider this from Plato:

> Socrates: The fact is, as we said at the beginning of our discussion, that the aspiring speaker needs no knowledge of the truth about what is right or good. . . . In courts of justice no attention is paid whatever to the truth about such topics; all that matters is plausibility. . . . There are even some occasions when both prosecution and defence [*sic*] should positively suppress the facts in favor of probability, if the facts are improbable. Never mind the truth — pursue probability through thick and thin in every kind of speech; the whole secret of the art of speaking lies in consistent adherence to this principle.
> Phaedrus: That is what those who claim to be professional teachers of rhetoric actually say, Socrates. (Plato, p. 272)

Although Plato was referring to words in the above scenario, his classic allegory of "The Cave" addressed the challenges of looking beyond the illusion of shadows cast on a cave's wall. A developing field of scholarly study is *visual rhetoric*, in which researchers examine the underlying purposes, meanings, effects, and processes of images, as well as the contexts of image use.

Discourse Analysis is a related method through which researchers study how visual and verbal materials are organized and produced, looking for meanings lying beyond the surface of the obvious content of language. Critical discourse analysis is particularly concerned with how messages exert power over audiences through practices that appear transparent (easy to interpret accurately), yet are actually manipulative.

Psychoanalysis seeks to uncover the underlying processes of the mind by studying people's dreams, thoughts, feelings, fantasies, and behaviors. In psychoanalytical therapy, a person meets regularly with a psychologist or psychiatrist to work through a problem or crisis in the person's life. A classic visual method of psychoanalysis is the Rorshach test, in which an ambiguous inkblot image yields insights about the viewer's mental associations.

Projected Interviewing asks people to look at photographs and talk about them. Photographic historian Zoe Smith, for example, showed images by documentarian Donna Ferrato to women and asked them to tell her what they felt or saw in the images. Ferrato's images were of abused women, and the women viewing the images were either social workers or had themselves suffered abuse. The result was insight into both the credibility of Ferrato's photographs and the lives of those viewing the photographs.

A similar technique is a *focus group*, in which individuals selected for a range of characteristics are invited to discuss a topic, question, or presentation as a group. Focus groups often work best when used to generate ideas that can then be studied through quantitative approaches.

Semiology, or the study of signs, seeks to take apart an image and trace "how it works in relation to broader systems of meaning," wrote Gillian Rose (p. 69). Closely related to *semiotics*, this method examines units of meaning, or signs, which can be "anything that has meaning," ranging from verbal texts, such as news stories or novels, to visual images, such as photographs and films (p. 74). The field of semiotics is so complex that various thinkers have devised different systems for studying *signs*. Two early scholars usually credited with developing this approach are Ferdinand de Saussure and Charles Sanders Peirce, who wrote entire books explaining the way each theorized that signs work. We present only the key terms from their theories with simplified defini-

Figure 12.7. In a semiotic analysis of this ad, Israeli Prof. Amir Hetsroni wrote that this "ad for VISA shows the Mona Lisa, and the text affirms that this is a 'signature smile.' The word signature has three different meanings here — one that relates to the painting, one that signifies the solid position of the credit company and supposedly gives assurance to consumers, and a third meaning that stands for the cardholder's signing on the back of the card" (pp. 62–63). What are the signs in the ad? Are they iconic, indexical, or symbolic? What system of meaning did the designers use to encode the ad's message? Is the design using association or an analogy? Image courtesy of BBDO Denver, Colorado.

the signature smile

our signature card

VISA SIGNATURE

it's not just **everywhere you want to be**
it's everything you ever wanted

you can make reservations at nearly impossible-to-reserve
restaurants with tables held for Visa˚ Signature cardholders

you can get room upgrades and late checkouts at
spectacular places such as Le Méridien Hotels & Resorts

you can get tickets to Disney's *The Lion King* on Broadway

you can play Visa Signature events at Pebble Beach

you can choose from numerous reward partners

you can enjoy remarkable purchasing power and acceptance
at millions more places worldwide than American Express

visit *visa.com/signature* to find out more about the
Visa Signature Card and its premium benefits

tions to introduce you ways of studying images using semiotics. In some instances, we use definitions and examples from Rose, from Daniel Chandler's Web site *Semiotics for Beginners*, and from Arthur Asa Berger. The terms are complex, and we offer only the simplest versions of definitions here.

Sign — anything that stands for something else: picture, word, sound.

Signifier — the form a sign takes.

Signified — the concept a sign represents. If you see an *Open* sign in a shop window, the word *open* is the signifier, and the idea that the shop is open for business is the signified concept.

Icon — a sign that looks like or resembles the thing it stands for. A drawing of a cat is an icon of a cat.

Index — a sign that is logically connected to what it represents. A footprint in the sand is an index to a person.

Symbol — a sign that does not resemble what it represents but that we learn represents a thing or concept. A dove can be a symbol for peace.

Code — A system of symbols that we learn to make sense of signs. The clothes we wear are part of a fashion code that cues other people to our personal characteristics.

Encoding — Using one or more systems of meaning to create a message.

Decoding — Interpreting the image through one or more meaning systems. If you look at a CD cover of a music star, you may use the code of the music genre to respond to the image.

Association — Linking the meaning of one thing with the meaning of another. In a car ad with a Mercedes parked in front of a mansion, we associate the meaning of good taste, wealth, or class with the car.

Simile — Comparing two things using like or as: When Bob Dylan sings "Like a Rollin' Stone," he is using a simile.

Metaphor — Comparing one thing to another directly: When Shakespeare wrote, "All the World's a Stage," he was using a metaphor.

These terms are not mutually exclusive — you will note overlapping categories when you apply them to interpreting visual messages. However, they do provide a vocabulary for helping you analyze and discuss an image. Visual communication scholar Sandra Moriarty has developed a theory called *visual semiotics* that applies these terms to media images such as ads. Moriarty (1995) used visual semiotics to study Apple computer's classic "1984" ad. In a quasi-experimental design, she showed 200 students the ad and then surveyed their responses. Moriarty determined that, although more viewers recalled iconic signs (such as the television screen) than symbolic (inmates and runner) or indexical signs (the hissing wind sound accompanying the explosion was associated with cause and effect), symbolic signs may have created "greater impact" than others (npn). For example, although the running figure was an icon for a woman runner, viewers interpreted her as symbolic for "a new age, new way of life, or new era" (npn).

People who design media messages such as the "1984" ad are expert *encoders,* according to Stuart Hall et al. They are skilled professionals who study research, observe how people respond, and design messages using highly effective codes. People who view media messages learn *codes* for viewing. We learn, for example, how to skip advertisements in magazines if we're reading an article or that a television program will resume after a series of commercials. We learn to *decode* media messages so that we can understand the plot of a movie or distinguish between an advertisement and a newspaper article. However, few people other than those training to become professional communicators learn how to encode information into sophisticated media messages. The result is that people think they are adequately decoding media information, when, in fact, they know only a functional basis for the codes! *This is precisely why we wrote this book: to teach you as much about these codes as we can so that you can more fully understand what you see and how it affects you.* You also will better appreciate the importance of designing messages that communicate in socially responsible ways.

Here is another critically important point about codes. People develop codes consciously and unconsciously. The code that tells you (or leads you to assume) that someone is male or female is in part a dress code developed over centuries through the development of civilization. Dress codes vary by country, function, economic, and social status, to name but a few causes of variations. Some of those codes have developed without a great deal of conscious thought. People who live in Texas in the summer wear shorts and lightweight clothing to make themselves a little cooler in extreme heat. But whether someone wears short-shorts or knee-length shorts more often is a matter of conscious personal choice. Taking the example further, we also know that fashion designers consciously change the length and style of shorts in an effort to sell more clothes. A person selecting which shorts to wear might then unconsciously select shorts that look more in keeping with new designs and unconsciously promote that style of shorts by wearing them.

A phrase that can help you understand the difference between conscious and nonconscious encoding is "it's your air." That means that, if something is so familiar or comfortable to you that you are not aware of it, it is like the air you breathe. You can't see it; you seldom think about it; you just breathe. That's how the actions underlying racism, sexism, and many other negative "isms" work. Learning to decode your beliefs is key to becoming a well-educated, enlightened citizen of the 21st-century world. Learning how to understand visual messages and how they affect your behavior is one way to begin.

The next two pages feature Figure 12.6, an Adbusters spoof ad titled "Joe Chemo." Practice analyzing the ad by using visual semiotic theory.

Next Page: Figure 12.8. Spoof of Joe Camel ads (original in color). Courtesy of Adbusters.

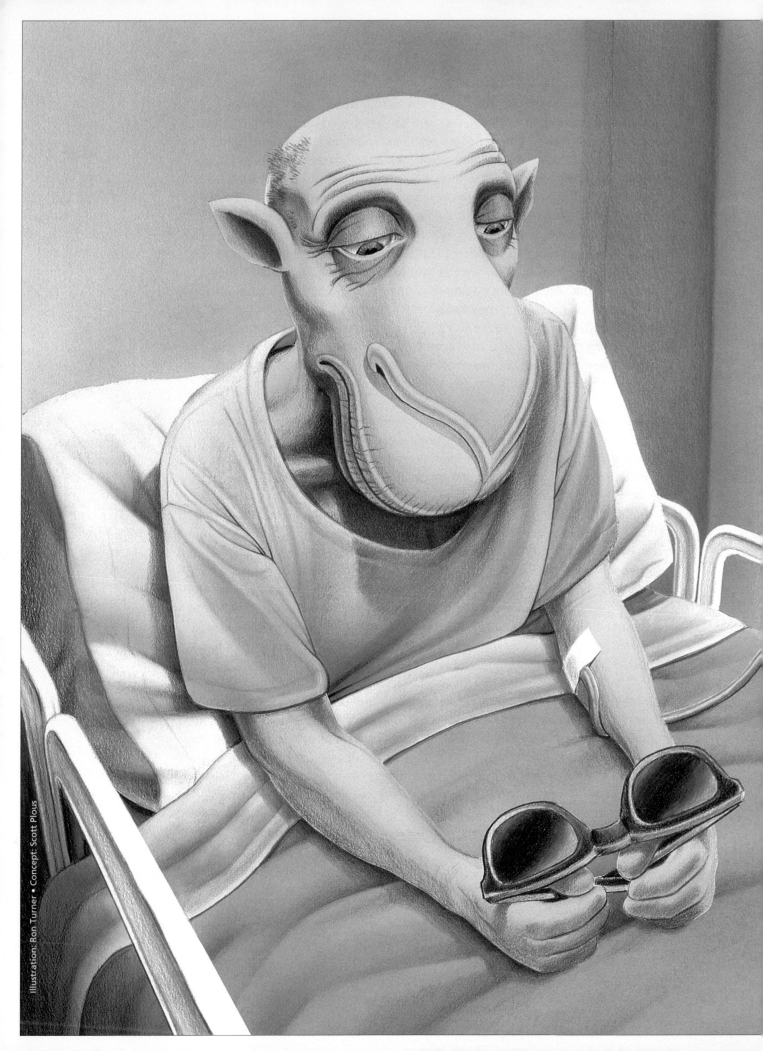

Joe CHEMO

THE SURGEON GENERAL WARNS THAT
SMOKING IS A FREQUENT CAUSE OF
WASTED POTENTIAL AND FATAL REGRET.

Six Perspectives

Another useful method for analyzing images is Paul Lester's (2006) Six Perspectives. You will note that the method combines a few approaches that are key to methods we've already discussed in this chapter. The method also adds other approaches. A photographer, philosopher, and visual theorist, Lester developed this system in his book *Visual Communication* (pp. 111-112) to help people become intellectually involved with the images they study and to encourage viewers to base conclusions about images on rational rather than emotional responses. In some instances, we have adapted Lester's definitions. The six perspectives follow:

1. Personal Perspective — Your subjective response to the work, based on your opinions and feelings. Lester suggested that personal perspectives are superficial, are of limited use, and tell more about the person than the image. He also suggested that a viewer who rests a conclusion about an image on personal perspective denies the chance of perceiving the image in a more meaningful way. Thus he provided five more rationally centered perspectives. We fully discuss Rick Williams's Personal Impact Assessment (PIA), included in Lester's book as one way to explore the personal perspective, in chapter 13.

2. Historical Perspective — examining the work in the context of media or other chronological perspectives. You might discuss the history of newspaper photography when examining a photojournalism image, for example. Or you might discuss the history of visual stereotyping of women when examining a television program.

3. Technical Perspective — exploring how the work was produced and how it is presented. In photography, for example, you might explore the relationships among quality of light, film characteristics, the way the photographer framed the image, and how the image was printed in a magazine.

4. Ethical Perspective — considering the purposes and potential consequences related to a work. You might reflect on the motivations a designer had for creating a logo such as the Nike Swoosh, for example. Then, you might consider how Nike uses the Swoosh logo to sell its products and possible effects of its manufacturing systems and advertising strategies. A few ethical approaches (adapted and expanded from Lester, 2006, pp. 115–117):

> *Teleological* — Goal oriented. The end justifies the means.
> *Deontological* — Principle oriented. Duty and adherence to basic principles matters more than consequences.
> *Categorical Imperative* — Kant - Consistent, unconditional rules.
> *Utilitarianism* — Bentham/Mill - The greatest good for the greatest number of people.

Hedonism — Aristippus - Maximize pleasure without concern for the
    future.
Golden Mean — Aristotle - Find middle ground between two extremes.
Golden Rule — A principle found in most religions and spiritual tradi-
    tions, interpreted variously as "Act toward others the way you want
    them to act toward you."
Veil of Ignorance — Rawls - All people are equal. Imagine you respect
    everyone equally and have no knowledge of class or other human dif-
    ferences, and act accordingly.

5. Cultural Perspective — exploring how parts of the work convey meaning
within a particular society at a particular time. While studying images of pro-
testers, for example, you might consider that the presence of flags could convey peace as patriotism at an anti-war rally or going to war as patriotism at a
pro-war rally. Or you might examine the image in regard to its representation
of race or gender.

6. Critical Perspective — exploring a work in the context of issues of power,
politics, and economics. For example, if you studied television broadcasts
about the United States' attack on Iraq in 2003, you might examine how the
political power of the United States is represented in comparison with the political power of Iraq.

One way to practice visual literacy is to apply apply Lester's six perspectives
and other terms discussed in this chapter to the images included. "Joe
Chemo" is a great place to begin.

Conclusion

Most media images have been especially created for public consumption. They
are meant to be seen and read and to have specific functional meaning and
impact. Traditionally, the kinds of methods we have discussed here are used on
a dominant rational/logical level to decode visual imagery as it is processed by
the conscious mind. These methods categorize and label the significant information about our conscious understanding of images and their meanings.
In this chapter we have presented a number of different ways you can system-
atically, rationally study visual images. Important to note is that these methods
are usually word or number based. That is, they are ways researchers have
devised to try to *translate* visual forms of human expression into words or
numbers. Given the rational, word-biased nature of contemporary, industrialized culture, this is not surprising. Remember, we believe rational analysis is
necessary, but it is only a PART of the process of understanding visuals.

We know that visual communication is also highly intuitive and that a great
deal of visual communication takes place on nonconscious levels. Thus, both

the production and the consumption of imagery involve the nonconscious, intuitive cognitive processes of both the *creator* of the communication and the *user* of the communication. We can only speculate about the nonconscious motivations of the creators of visual communication, and it is unlikely that we could consciously decode all of our own nonconscious visual cognition. However, these nonconscious visualizations are perhaps even more significant to our decision making than the images of which we are conscious.

It is advantageous to develop ways to bring these nonconscious visual motivators to consciousness. By learning about imagemakers' motivations and techniques, you can learn how images affect you and influence your behavior. In the next few chapters, as we discuss different kinds of visual media, we teach you methods that balance both intuitive and rational processing techniques.

The goal: *for you to be both a wise user and an ethical creator of visual media.*

Figure 12.9. Washington Post Readers (original in color). Photograph © Andrew Glickman.

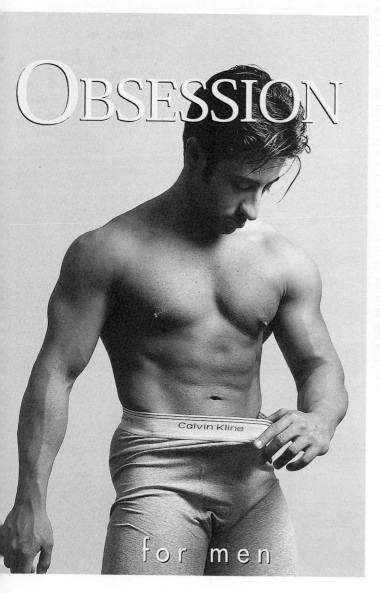

Figures C12.1–2. These ads are part of Adbusters's culture jamming series, which uses ad campaigns from tobacco, fashion, food, alcohol, and other companies to challenge the way signs are used and misused to motivate product purchase and use. From Adbusters.org.

CREATIVE TWELVE
Thinking Systematically about Images

The Goal: Focusing on the Rational

Look through a magazine or newspaper to find an advertisement that grabs your attention. Then, use semiotics, Six Perspectives, and field research to analyze the ad. As always, read the instructions carefully before you begin.

Part I. Semiotic Evaluation of an Image

Using the definitions and information in chapter 12, analyze the image using a semiotic perspective. Be sure to address the following points:

1. List all of the *signs* you see in the ad.
2. Select and note the *three most important signs.* One way to do this is to close your eyes, then open them, and pay attention to which three signs grab your attention first. Another way is to draw a thumbnail sketch of the ad.
3. Decide whether each of the three most important signs is *iconic, indexical, symbolic,* or a *combination. Discuss why* you think so.
4. *Discuss the code* or codes you the think the *image creators used* to *encode* the meaning of the image.
5. *Discuss the code* or codes *you are using* to help you *decode* the meaning of the image?

Part II. Analyzing an Image Using Six Perspectives

Now, apply each of the Six Perspectives to help you analyze the same ad. Write several lines using each perspective to explore the image.

Part III. Using Field Research to Study an Image

Using the same ad, *interview at least five different people* about their interpretations of the image. You may interview people together in a group (called a *focus group)* or privately. Avoid conveying your own ideas about the ad. Simply show the ad to people and ask them to talk to you about it. This is called *projected interviewing.* If a person doesn't know how to begin, you might ask him to point out the most important parts of the image and to tell you why he thinks the parts are important. That usually will get people started talking. You might ask the person to tell you what each part she selects means in the image, and then what the overall image means. *Either tape record (ask permission first) or take good notes about the interviewees' comments.*

After the interviews, summarize the main points each person made.

Part IV. Overall Self-Assessment

Reflect on and assess your experiences in completing the exercise. What did you learn from doing each part? Which part was most effective in helping you understand underlying meanings of the ad? Include a discussion of how you conducted your interviews and how the interviewees' interpretations of the ad compared or contrasted with your own interpretations. Conclude with a summary of your final interpretation of the ad and if/how your understanding of the ad shifted as you worked through the methods.

The Exercise

- Read the instructions carefully.
- Select an ad published in a magazine or newspaper.
- Use the same image for Parts I, II, and III of the exercise.
- Follow instructions for each part carefully and thoroughly.
- Reflect on and write an assessment of your experiences.

PART III.
THE PUBLIC AS ART AND IMAGE
The Academy, The Media, and Visual Persuasion

Part III extends the application of integrative mind into discussions of media, introducing basic technical information about each medium as a basis for using and understanding media images. Finally, the book concludes with a discussion of visual ethics and a systemic approach to understanding and using the visual.

*Figure 13.1. G. Cardona: "I was born in Corona, Queens, November 19, 1979.
My family is from Colombia. I love Colombia but I'm not just stuck on Colombia. I do music
for everybody: Cuban, Puerto Ricans, Centro America, Sur America. Everybody."
G. Cardona flew to the Bahamas in 2003 to film his first video, "Donde Están mis Latinos?"
(Where are my Latinos?). "We try to keep it as Latin as we can 'cause we are doing it for the Latinos.
But it's definitely still New York. You gotta have that balance and give everyone what they want."
Photograph by Luís Salazar, from Hip Hop en Español in New York City.*

CHAPTER THIRTEEN
Stopping Time and Framing Space

By now you have a basic understanding of the complexities of visual communication. The first two sections of this book explored the role of subconscious processing in creating knowledge. Part 2 also began our discussion of fundamental symbol systems, from the development of language, to our increased awareness of the significance of dreams in our lives, to an exploration of ways humans have extended themselves beyond the body through photography and graphic design, and finally to focusing your attention on ways we enhance our understanding of our external and internal worlds through systematic observation and careful analysis.

Now we move full force into media, those extensions of body and mind through which we express ourselves and connect with others. They can be as subtle as the air we breathe — and as overwhelming as a virtual environment that seems so real our minds cannot discern it is a machine projection.

Still Media Defined

Our first project in this section is to study ways we control time and space — and hence our perception and behavior — through still media. By still media, we refer to all of those forms that do not convey motion. These include print publications (such as books, hand-prepared journals, photo albums, fliers, newspapers, magazines, and billboards); fine and applied art (such as oil, acrylic, pastel, watercolor, sculpture, pottery, tapestry, photographs, and digital media; products of various kinds, as well as their containers; ways we adorn the body (such as tattoos, jewelry, hairstyles, and clothing); artifacts of medical technologies (such as X-rays, CT scans, MRIs); landscape (home, city, countryside); and architecture. Our bases for selecting media for this category are these:

- the object **does not move** unless attached to another moving object
- its **contents are stationary** and static once created
- the object may be **two- or multi-dimensional**
- the object may be **material or immaterial**

A computer, then, would not be considered a still medium. Even though the container may be stationary, parts within the container move. Its production contents — data — are fluid, constantly changing, and ephemeral. Holders of its production results — a printed page or a CD — are tangible, however. A computer screen fits both still and moving criteria. The perimeters of the screen, for example, are fixed, controlling the space into which we look and which we fill with words, images, and multiple frames. Some of those images move, however, through digital video technology. And even the words move as we create them by typing the keyboard to inscribe them on the digital page on the screen.

Williams and Newton

Left: Figure 13.2. Mae.
Above: Figure 13.3. G. Cardona.
Photographer: "How have you supported your art?"
G. Cardona: "I always hated nine to five. I've been a hustler all my life. And thank God I've been lucky."
Photographer: "What'd you do?"
G. Cardona: "The streets, you know? That's what really got me by up to now. But it's all about my music right now. That's all I'm trying to sell now. I ain't trying to sell nothing else."
Photographs by Luís Salazar, from Hip Hop en Español in New York City.
Note how Salazar's photographs play with the concept of frame.

In this way, a computer screen is a transitional medium, not still, yet retaining aspects of the static. As we became more skilled at creating complex media, such as motion pictures, video, holograms, virtual reality, ultrasound, robotics, vehicles of various kinds, our understanding of the fluidity of knowledge has become clearer.

Let's move now into a few of the specifics about still media that are important for you to know. We begin with the frame, the fifth element of visual design. As we discussed in chapter 11, the way we put a frame around a group of visual elements, or the way we fill that frame with visual elements, determines what we understand about the contents of the frame. Combining elements with surfaces and frames directly affects the way we understand the meaning in seeing and touching them.

For example, when humans first noticed an animal paw print in the earth, that print had an outline shape and a degree of texture, depending on the surface material earth and the weight of the animal. That outline shape was a kind of frame, containing a pattern that was an index sign of the animal whose paw had made it. The outline shape also may have been framed by a path in the forest and, in sequence, became a line, or visual vector, leading the human to follow. Our eyes do much the same work as early humans' did when we notice a pattern in a book, such as a letter, and follow the lines of letterforms across the page and back again as we read.

Figures 13.4-6. Pentagram designer D.J. Stout created this cover and interior spreads for MFOH Today, magazine of the Museum of Fine Arts of Houston, to highlight the exhibition "African Art Now." The cover image (left) is by Nigerian J.D. Okhai Ojekere, who says, "Without art, life would be frozen." The first spread below shows Elizabeth Gilbert's documentary photographs of disappearing traditions of Kenya and Tanzania Massai, who used ostrich feather headdresses to frighten enemies and wore hats made of lion manes. The second spread (below right) features the museum's sub-Saharan art collection. Although most of these pieces date to late 19th or early 20th century, the third figure from the right is a fragment of sculpture produced by the Nok civilization, the first sub-Saharan group to create sculpture. Note that each spread is its own frame encompassing two pages the size of the cover.

Williams and Newton

Formats of the Frame

We begin the breakdown of still imagery by expanding discussion of the frame. Remember that a frame can be any shape and size and that it conveys a sense of direction. Consider, for example, the images that often come to mind when we think of humankind's first images: those on cave walls. One of the earliest images is a handprint, either made by an impression on a wall surface, or through a tracing of fingers and palm contours. Archaeologists date some hand images back 60,000 years. British scientists working in Zambia have discovered paint-grinding equipment and pigments they believe are between 350,000 and 400,000 years old. The scientists think these early human ancestors used paint on their bodies during rituals, thus creating *moving images* (see chapter 14 for more about the body as a moving medium). Early still frames likely were stones, clay forms, or walls on which were drawn simple shapes (see chapter 8 for a discussion of the development of oral and written language). Signs and images drawn or chiseled into objects and walls took on the character of the surface and required ways of viewing that are different from today. Cave painting, a more sophisticated form of imaging that scientists believe they can date back about 40,000 years, had to be viewed by daylight, where accessible, or by firelight, which would directly affect what was seen and when it could be seen.

A frame does not have to be a rectangle. A hand or face — even a fingernail — a shell or piece of stone, a tree trunk or spot in the sand, our view of a mountain peak meeting the sky, a cloud — any shape in any size can be a frame. In this way, plates and vases frame patterns; arches and beams frame the tops of

doorways and rooftops; petals and stems frame parts of flowers; and lips frame the mouth. In this way, we have created conventions for designing forms of mass media within still frames.

Many frames we use in print publications have standard sizes and shapes developed to work well with the technologies of printing. A typical book format is 6 x 9", though printed books range in size from less than 1 millimeter square to a 133-pound 5 x 7' book. One such enormous book was designed by MIT scientist Michael Hawley, who believed it was the best way to portray the colorful life of Bhutan through photographs. "What I really wanted was a 5-by-7-foot chunk of wall that would let me change the picture every day," Hawley said. "And I thought there was an old-fashioned mechanism that might work. It's called the book" (Guinness, para. 7). Brewster Kahle, the inventor of the

Figures 13.7-8. Tim Jordan, art director for Oregon Quarterly, designed this four-page spread featuring photographs of Singapore photographer Russel Wong and a story by University of Oregon Prof. William Ryan. Note that Jordan varied columns, using one column surrounded by white space on the open page, two columns on the second page, and three columns on the fourth. Traditionally, designers maintain the same column widths after the opening spread. Here, Jordan used less formal style within the 17 x 11" frame of two 8.5 x 11" magazine pages to design as creatively as Wong photographed. Take a close look, too, at how Wong applied the basic elements of visual design within a square photographic frame to portray celebrities in creative ways.

RUSSEL WONG:
THE "RICHARD AVEDON OF ASIA"

BY WILLIAM RYAN · PHOTOS BY RUSSEL WONG '82

IT'S DIFFICULT TO DETERMINE WHERE RUSSEL WONG'S HOME ENDS and his studio begins. Photographs are *everywhere*. They hang all over the roomy colonial bungalow on Holland Road, a main thoroughfare in the "little Bohemia" section of Singapore. Some images are propped against a teak bookcase lined with photography monographs. Framed work is bubble-wrapped and stacked in deep rows against the walls throughout the house.

I am visiting Wong just after his twenty-five year retrospective at the Singapore Art Museum — *Russel Wong: Photographs 1980–2005*. The exhibit, which occupied four galleries, broke attendance records and had to be extended two weeks to accommodate more than 72,000 visitors. Wong has been invited to hang most of the show at the 2006 Venice Film Festival.

A framed, symmetrically composed image of the temple at Angkor Wat dominates the living room wall. The photograph's golden tint adds to its understated beauty. A muted, large-screen TV

Russel Wong

FACING PAGE: *Oliver Stone, Heaven and Earth, Phuket, 1992; Robert Downey, Jr., Los Angeles, 1986; Marcus Miller, Capitol Studios, Hollywood, 1988;* ABOVE: *Zhang Ziyi, Hero, Hengidam, China, 2002*

sits inside a maple cabinet to the immediate left of the Cambodian print. An English soccer championship game flickers silently. It seems surreal and out of place amid the quiet grace and beauty of Wong's images. The set remains turned on throughout the interview.

This is the first clue that Russel Wong is — along with being one of the most sought-after photographers in the world — a sports fanatic.

In fact, it was track and field that brought him in the late Seventies to the University of Oregon from Singapore—not the UO's academic reputation. While a student, Wong ran the

Prefontaine trail along the millrace and through Hendricks Park daily. A self-described "track nut," Wong loved to run.

"I hung out every day at the track. Ran 10K and Butte-to-Butte," Wong says. He sought out and befriended legendary UO track coach Bill Bowerman.

But Russel Wong had another passion — photography. Using a low-end 35mm Topcon camera his father had given him, he began his career by shooting what he loved, track and field. That turned out to be a great combination.

In 1979, Nike offered Wong a pair of running shoes in exchange for a photograph he shot of storied British middle-

Internet Archive project, bought a copy of the book and noted that its size causes a reader to approach the "book in a fundamentally new way... .You meet it eye-to-eye, like a person" (Guinness, para. 9). Hawley cautioned that his book is not one to read in bed, "unless you plan to sleep on it" (Guinness, para. 2). The largest previously published book was Audubon's 40 x 30" *Birds of America*, four-volumes of 435 hand-colored, life-size images completed in 1838.

MIT scientists Pawan Sinha and Pamela R. Lipson developed a method for reproducing a book about the size of a pencil eraser. The process uses computer software and a font with letterforms about four microns high to write the 180,000-plus words of the New Testament in 24-karat gold on a crystalline silicon chip. Yet the book is not digital: "If the PC goes out of vogue, you'll still be able to read this [with a microscope, that is]," Lipson said (Flaherty, npn).

As noted in chapter 10, photographic frames come in a variety of sizes. Most common is the 35 mm frame, which measures 24 x 36 mm. The world's largest camera, built in 1900 for the Paris Exposition, used a glass plate measuring 8 x 4.5'. The smallest film camera on record is the 1958 Japanese Petal camera, measuring 29 mm in diameter and 16 mm thick (about 1.25" round), and producing 6mm circular images on a 25 mm diameter film disc. The largest photograph in the world is said to be an 18 m x 272 m image of Elton John made in 2002. A traditional, full-sized newspaper page, called a broadsheet, typically is about

Jackie (Chan) Deconstructed, 2004, six-color silkscreen and lithograph on Aquarelle Arches Satine and Plexiglas. Created in collaboration with the Singapore Tyler Print Institute, where Wong was artist-in-residence for 2004.

distance runner Sebastian Coe. One year later, he received a call from the editor of *Track & Field News*, who offered him $160 to use the Coe image on the publication's cover.

Wong kept up his sports photography and the shoes-for-shots arrangement but received no press pass from Nike. Meanwhile, the *Oregon Daily Emerald* turned him down for a photography position. So — lacking proper credentials and getting tired of being bounced (often multiple times for the same meet) — he used his own ingenuity to wriggle into Hayward Field.

His story is interrupted when the ceiling of his living room suddenly sounds like a chorus line of tap dancers gone amok. "My dogs," he says, smiling. His four golden Labrador retrievers are scrambling across the marble floor above us.

He continues, "So, one Saturday, I struck up a friendship with one of the marshals who assumed I had a pass, and I was in." For nearly three years, Wong

successfully "jumped the fence" at that corner of the stadium. Eventually his portfolio would include such sports luminaries as Carl Lewis, Mary Decker, and John McEnroe.

After graduating with a finance degree from the UO, Wong accepted a photojournalism internship at *The Straits Times* — the Singapore newspaper of record. Then he fulfilled his two-year national service obligation by working as a photographer for *Pioneer*, Singapore's armed services magazine. That was his "day job." In the evenings, he experimented with fashion photography. Wong studied the work of master photographers such as Richard Avedon, Irving Penn, and Herb Ritts. He admired their "stripped-down, timeless style." He also reflected on how much he enjoyed shooting the fashion work and portraits he'd done for Nike and the "Life" section of *The Straits Times*.

In 1984, he saw the portfolio of an old friend who had recently graduated from the Art Center College of Design in Los Angeles. "That cemented it. I knew I needed to go there for the technical grounding. The training was amazing."

Wong shoots a quick glance to the soccer game on TV, but doesn't miss a beat. "They were *hardcore* at Art Center. The entire first year we worked on 8x10 view cameras. That's about the time I began shooting celebrities." Since then his lens has captured myriad celebs including Michael Jackson, Isabella Rossellini, Paloma Picasso, Pavarotti, Andrew Lloyd Weber, Glenn Close, David Lynch, and Bruce Willis.

The following year, he spent four months in Milan, Italy, taking in the trendy cafes where he met fashion designers and photographers the likes of Paul Jasmin and Antonio Lopez. They encouraged him to continue his fashion photography and portraiture. Heeding their advice, Wong framed a who's who of the fashion world, including supermodels Cindy Crawford, Claudia Schiffer, and Naomi Campbell, as well as designers such as Kenzo and Anna Sui.

Aishwarya Rai: Lotus Dream, 2004, ten-color silkscreen, lithograph and gold leafing on Rives BFK Tan paper and TGL handmade light blue paper. Created in collaboration with the Singapore Tyler Print Institute.

Today, Russel Wong has ten *Time* magazine covers to his credit and many exhibitions, and he has received a litany of awards for his editorial and commercial work — including a Clio and other international advertising awards. But his true love is still black and white portraiture.

His celebrity portraits have earned him celebrity status. He is heralded as "the Richard Avedon of Asia" — an association Wong doesn't seem to mind.

Like Avedon, Wong creates stunning portraits that are minimal, dramatic, and brilliantly composed. However, his photographs lack the cool indifference and stiffness of Avedon's work; instead, the imagery is warm, personal, engaging.

Where does that gift come from? "It's difficult to explain," he begins. "When I shoot someone, I feel like I'm dancing. The idea I'm working with is equivalent to the melody I hear in my head . . . then I improvise with that song's ups and downs. I often try something really wild at the end."

But great dancing is also born of trust

Joan Chen, Los Angeles, 1989

— not an easy thing with photography, a medium that is notorious for being invasive, particularly among celebrities.

"Photography is a very intrusive medium. We come into your life. We come into your home, your hotel room. We take your photograph," he explains. "But I feel rather than taking a photograph, I'm giving you an image." He stops in mid-thought.

Outside, the cicadas are buzzing loudly. Their drone rises and mixes with the late-morning traffic. He continues, "You know, I give a print to every single person I shoot."

Wong stands up and shuts the jalousie windows behind the couch to muffle the noise. One of the dogs changes into the room and nuzzles me.

"Sidney, cool it," he says. Sidney's tail is wagging wildly as he moves away.

Wong picks up another thought.

"You know some people find it strange I started at Oregon. Occasionally, people will ask me why I just didn't go to Art Center. Me? I wouldn't change a thing. If I hadn't gone to the UO, I wouldn't have the Coe cover or all my work with Nike. The sports stuff sharpened me."

He hesitates. "And I've so many great memories of Oregon." Wong pauses, and then speaks very intently. "The Swensons were my host family; they took me in from scratch. . . . I was one of their kids. Because of them, I got to see and feel the American psyche from the inside out. I still call them every Thanksgiving.

"They had season tickets for everything. They explained the whole culture of sports there — put me on to baseball, basketball, football. Showed me where Pre lived, where he ran . . . where he died near Hendricks Park. Took me to

football games at Autzen, to basketball games at Mac Court." He checks out the TV and looks back. "You know what? I was the first one to sneak a live duck into Mac Court. Let it go during a UCLA game." We both laugh.

Wong shifts gears and begins to talk about future projects. "I'd like to continue my landscape work" — he gestures at the Angkor Wat image. "Actually, that wasn't shot for show; it's personal work — all done in 8x10 — and it's therapeutic. It's like back to basics and very peaceful for me. The exhibition invitation came out of the blue." (The image is one of a series he shot that exhibited along with pieces by Ansel Adams two years ago at a gallery in New York City.)

"The Venice Film Festival is in the works. I'll continue to document popular culture, work on film sets, and do the portraiture of course." Wong also has plans to direct a film for a script he's been writing and working on a more protracted project documenting the different cultures, races, and people of Singapore — whatever "excites" him.

To Wong, the work is all one continuum: "Everything I've ever done adds to what I do right now. People try to pigeonhole me, but I don't care. Light is light for me, you know? I shoot. That's all I do."

He glances quickly at the soccer game and back again. "Actually, we let ducks go in Mac Court twice. They couldn't catch us."

Bill Ryan is an associate professor in the UO School of Journalism and Communication. He holds a doctorate in media systems and has received Mellon, Kellogg, and Fulbright fellowships. Ryan is author of Graphic Communication Today, 4th Edition, and is currently on sabbatical leave and living with his wife, Jan, in Singapore where they are working on two books for Thomson Publications.

The Oregonian

Science

Recovery and discovery: Trees grow taller, elk abound, and the volcano is covered with new high-tech instruments scientists developed to stay ahead of the geologic activity. **Pages D12-13**

INSIDE
COMICS, D14-15
WEATHER, D16

WEDNESDAY • MAY 18, 2005   SCIENCE EDITOR: VICKI MARTIN • 503-221-8313 • VMARTIN@NEWS.OREGONIAN.COM   **D9**

MOUNT ST. HELENS: 25 YEARS LATER

Volcano threat is never over

MOUNT ST. HELENS AND OTHER CASCADES PEAKS SUCH AS HOOD REMAIN CANDIDATES FOR ERUPTION

By RICHARD L. HILL
THE OREGONIAN

Mount St. Helens had been asleep for 123 years when scientists got the first alarm.

An earthquake set off the only seismometer positioned near the volcano. The magnitude 4.1 quake, strong enough to be felt nearby, sent snow avalanches tumbling down the mountain.

That was March 20, 1980, two months before the big blow — just the beginning.

More than 10,000 earthquakes rattled the mountain from that day forward. Hundreds of explosions blasted a crater into the summit, and rising magma shoved part of the north side upward in an ominous bulge.

When the big one hit, at 8:32 a.m. May 18, it was the most lethal eruption in recorded U.S. history. Within minutes, 57 people died, including Spirit Lake innkeeper Harry Truman and geologist David Johnston.

CLAUDIA J. HOWELL/THE OREGONIAN

▲ **May 18, 1980:** Ric Cole, director of emergency services in Yakima, brushes off his windshield after a cloud of ash from Mount St. Helens turned the city completely dark at noon.

▼ **May 3, 2005:** Steam pours from Mount St. Helens, the youngest of the Cascades volcanoes, which began to erupt again last fall. Spirit Lake and Mount Rainier are visible to the north.

The mountain didn't blow its top in a single burst, but in a nine-hour-long cataclysm that left 230 square miles of once-green forests a gray wasteland.

"It was worse than the worst-case scenario," said seismologist Steve Malone of the University of Washington. "We weren't able to predict that eruption on a time scale that was socially useful, meaning hours or a day or so ahead. There was no indication that was going to take place."

Today the mountain is active again, not only heightening awareness of its massive dome-building activity but also intensifying scientists' scrutiny of other Cascades peaks, among them Rainier and Hood, that also could become monsters.

Though they are dormant, Rainier and Hood are perilous volcanoes because they are filled with rock weakened into soft clay by centuries of exposure to hot, acidic fluids in their plumbing systems. An earthquake, oversaturation from intense warm rains, a high rate of glacial melting or even gravity could trigger a collapse of the weakened rock.

Rainier, the highest Cascades mountain at 14,410 feet, is considered the most dangerous. A decade ago, a National Academy of Sciences report on Rainier warned that a major eruption or debris flow could kill thousands of residents and cripple the economy of the Pacific Northwest. More than 150,000 people live on ancient mudflow deposits from the volcano.

Please see **THREAT**, *Page D11*

BRUCE ELY/THE OREGONIAN

The boom that (almost) nobody heard

SOUND WAVES THAT BOUNCE OFF EARTH'S ATMOSPHERE MISS PORTLAND BUT HIT THE COAST AND MONTANA

By RICHARD L. HILL
THE OREGONIAN

Clara Fairfield and her husband were enjoying the sunny, quiet morning near the coastal town of Netarts when a jolting noise like a barrage tore through the air.

"The initial sound was very loud — it

would have awakened the dead," she said, remembering back 25 years. "Then there were five or six more booms following that. I looked at my watch, and it was 8:32."

Minutes later, a phone call from her daughter on Skyline Boulevard in Portland revealed the startling news: Mount St. Helens had exploded. Even more surprising, Fair-

field's daughter had not heard the blast although she was only 50 miles away and could easily see the ash plume.

That intrigued Fairfield, a curator and exhibit designer at the Oregon Museum of Science and Industry. When she returned from her vacation home to work the next day, she and her colleagues launched a survey asking people whether they had heard the eruption. More than 1,200 people replied.

The results revealed two striking findings: Hardly anyone from Albany north to Olympia reported hearing the eruption, but hundreds who were more than 100 miles

away did.

Fairfield, who described the results later that year in Oregon Geology magazine, said the sound was heard as far as Montana, Idaho, Northern California, and the Canadian provinces of Alberta and British Columbia.

"One letter I got later was from a ship's mate on a freighter 500 miles off the Oregon coast," Fairfield said. "They heard it, and they couldn't imagine where it was coming from."

The "loudest zones" in Oregon were along the coast from Tillamook to Newport, in Central Oregon from Redmond to La Pine, and in

Please see **BOOM**, *Page D11*

ST. HELENS MEMORIES

Where were you when the mountain blew?

An invitation to share memories of May 18, 1980, brought nearly 400 e-mails and letters from readers. Many of them are online at: www.oregonlive.com/special/mtsthelens/

CHARLIE CRISAFULLI/U.S. FOREST SERVICE

ELAINE THOMPSON/ASSOCIATED PRESS

INSIDE THE SECTION

Scientists study fish at Spirit Lake (left); now as clear as it was before the eruption. **Page D10**

The new glacier is squeezed and nearly pinched in two. **Page D10**

By the numbers. **Page D10**

Red-legged frogs (right) and other wildlife have returned to Mount St. Helens. **Page D11**

MORE ON THE MOUNTAIN

◆ The U.S. Forest Service on the 25th anniversary and tourist information; a "volcano cam" shows the crater from Johnston Ridge Observatory: www.fs.fed.us/gpnf/msh25

◆ The U.S. Geological Survey's Cascades Volcano Observatory's updates about the volcano, photographs and information about other Cascades peaks: http://vulcan.wr.usgs.gov

◆ The Pacific Northwest Seismograph Network at the University of Washington about earthquakes: www.pnsn.org

◆ Weyerhaeuser, the largest private landowner affected by the eruption, on reforestation: www.theforestreturns.com

Figure 13.9. Science Section Front, The Oregonian, May 12, 2005.
What are the lines of eye travel? How do the type and columns vary?

17 x 22" when folded in half and is cut from massive rolls of newsprint. In order to cut costs, broadsheet newspapers have moved toward trimming page sizes. A standard magazine page is 8.5 x 11", opening to create a 17 x 11" frame for two-page spreads. In contrast, an outdoor billboard can be as large as 48 x 14', the size you might see while driving down a freeway.

Print publications often are designed using a base skeleton called a *grid*. Newspapers and magazines often work with a six-column grid, which allows them to vary the width of their columns across one to six grids.

Designing Well within the Frame

Print publications often use combinations of type blocks and images that fit together as frames within frames. This sometimes results in unfortunate juxtapositions of news stories and advertisements because page designers often view these elements separately rather than as parts of an entire frame of a page. Readers, too, learn to see them separately but subconsciously take in more than the items on which they consciously focus.

Print publication designers have different methods for beginning their designs. Some still prefer to draw thumbnails by hand. Others prefer to begin by plugging visual elements into a page grid via computer page layout and illustration software. Whichever you prefer, the first elements to draw you in are the visual images. Research indicates that readers' eyes go first to photographs, then to headlines, captions, and news stories, in that order. So, it makes sense to begin with the visual element that first grabs the attention of the reader.

When selecting a photograph for a page layout, the designer should keep the following factors in mind:

- Which image best communicates the idea or story?
- Which image do you want viewers to remember?

Only after selecting an image based on its content should a design focus on the visual appeal of the image. All too often, designers work in the opposite manner: They select an image for its visual appeal, and then think about its message content. In another common scenario, designers lay out the text first and then look for images to illustrate it — the opposite of what a designer who wants to maximize potential for reader attention and understanding should do.

Eye tracking research with newspapers indicates that readers process or pay attention to 75 to 80% of artwork and photographs, according to Garcia and Adam. They process 56% of headlines, 52% of advertising, about 30% of briefs and cutlines, and about 25% of text. It makes sense then that designers and editors should take seriously the content of the elements that dominate readers' attention.

"To be honest, I felt like just being here was stripping me of everything, my iden
And to be honest, I don't think that hurt will ever go away."

DAMON STOUDAMIRE

Stoudamire:
Says Blazers don't appreciate his skills

Continued from Page C1

Stoudamire knows there are more than a fair share of fans who would love to tell him what to do: Leave Portland. Now. Today. Yesterday, if he could.

And he knows there are just as many who would plead, eyes welled up with tears, for him to shun free agency and remain a Blazer.

Quite simply, he is the most hotly debated Blazers player since the franchise drafted Sam Bowie ahead of Michael Jordan in 1984.

His detractors say he has been a defensive liability because of his height (he's listed at 5-foot-10; he says he's 5-9); that he has embarrassed and handicapped the franchise with three marijuana-related incidents in three states in the past two years; and that the offense stagnates because he dribbles too much.

His supporters counter by saying if he's allowed to play his freewheeling style, he is electric, as evidenced by the 54 points he scored this season at New Orleans, which broke a 32-year-old franchise record. And they say he has rid himself of marijuana after completing a rehabilitation program last summer, an assertion he backs up by filing documentation of his weekly drug tests. And at a time the Blazers are fumbling with public relation experiments, Stoudamire is the real deal, extensively woven into the fabric of the community, providing free youth summer camps, making charitable donations and privately covering funeral costs for families in need.

"I would like to think that I have been through a lot, to where people have ridiculed me," Stoudamire says. "And I have also been able to overcome a lot, to where people have to respect me. I have been through so much, this decision for me is the easy part."

Easy, if only his mind wasn't telling him one thing and his heart another.

Everything in his life is neat and in order.

The top shelf in his refrigerator looks like any other: a carton of egg whites, four bottles left in a six-pack of Heineken, three bottles of Starbucks Frappuccinos, a carton of 2 percent milk. But the lower shelves would make his college teammates, who teased him about ironing his socks, smile: neatly stacked Tupperware containers, three high, with typed labels taped to the blue lids: Chicken. Spaghetti. French fries. Pizza.

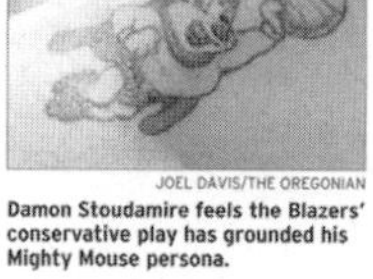

JOEL DAVIS/THE OREGONIAN

Damon Stoudamire feels the Blazers' conservative play has grounded his Mighty Mouse persona.

Upstairs, he breezes by the playroom for when his two sons, ages 3 and 5, visit, declaring it "a mess" . . . after all, three plastic balls have straggled out of a basket, and a foam claw from Blaze, the team's mascot, lies on the floor.

Down the hall, a room featuring a fully stocked, L-shaped bar is where Stoudamire says he "kicks it" with his friends. But the bar is used only when Stoudamire hires a bartender from a Pearl District restaurant . . . of course, to eliminate the potential for a mess.

And in his office, a room lined with memorabilia, including his 1996 Rookie of the Year trophy, he watches his soap operas intently, his attention broken only by various plaques, which must be adjusted.

So understand, then, how the loose ends of his future, dangling in this summer's free-agent winds, create the most untidy of scenarios for Stoudamire.

He could establish order now by listening to what his mind says: Strip his 10,000-square-foot home of everything and send it to Houston. Take the African American art, the painting of a squatting, enchained slave with a trade ship in the background, the ceramic figurine of a black father and son hugging on a golf course; take the cars, the clothes, the video games; take it all and leave.

The way Stoudamire sees it, nobody has ever appreciated him here, anyway. They traded for him that February day in 1998, knowing full well his strengths and his weaknesses, then proceeded to suffocate him in a plodding, get-it-into-the-post system that plays away from his strengths. While they were at it, they magnified his weaknesses, making a spectacle of him by benching him down the stretch of games for defensive reasons.

He has told himself a thousand — no, a billion — times: But these were the people who wanted him, right? They traded for him, right? He didn't ask to come here.

And that's when the pain comes back. Every time he looks back, it's pain. Pain laced with anger.

To stop the throbbing, he goes deep into a stack of papers in his office, and there they are, the pictures. Color shots, of him, Michael Jordan, Charles Barkley, Jason Kidd, Michael Finley. They were in Tokyo for Nike, traveling, promoting the game, posing with Sumo wrestlers. The league's stars. But that was back when he was unbridled, playing with Toronto, averaging 20.2 points and 8.7 assists.

Since he has come to Portland, where he feels they took his game away and stifled it in a wave of conservatism, he has become irrelevant. Nike? It still gives him free shoes, but there's no more Tokyo, no more posters, no more Mighty Mouse.

Now, it is a bunch of so-so statistics, playing on a team of yo-yos. Now, not only had his game been taken away, so had his reputation. He was a dope user, busted not once, not twice, but three times with marijuana.

The first time — the police searching his house (a search later ruled to be illegal) while responding to a burglar alarm as he played a game at the Rose Garden — still irks him as an invasion of privacy.

The second time — the driver of his yellow Hummer being pulled over for speeding in Washington after Stoudamire was smoking joints with Rasheed Wallace — was "ignorance," he says.

"That's just me thinking I can't be touched. Me thinking I'm above it all, and all the cliches that goes with it," Stoudamire says. "But the whole time, I'm thinking, 'Damon, you have done and gone something stupid.' "

The third time — walking through a Tucson, Ariz., airport metal detector with a wad of marijuana rolled in tinfoil — was simply, as Stoudamire put it, "a cry for help."

That's when the pain of not feeling wanted, the anger of not being able to play his way, the frustration of the Blazers bringing him to play, then not playing him, and the loneliness of isolating himself from criticism, all combined to overwhelm him.

"I had everything on the surface, but I was a lonely guy and empty inside," Stoudamire says. "I was a lonely guy. And there was anger, man. To be honest, I felt like just being here was stripping me of everything, my identity, everything. And to be honest, I don't think that hurt will ever go away."

So go downstairs and load the rack of jerseys of his favorite players — the one with the red Indiana Hoosiers No. 11 of Isiah Thomas, the No. 22 Emmitt S All-Pro, the pinstriped Pirates No. 8 Willie Stargell, the two Blazers, Bon Wells and Wallace. And load the ga ball from the 54-point game — still wrapped in protective cellophane – the black-and-red shoes he wore, a send them to Houston. But wait. He something. There is a tug.

BRUCE ELY/THE OREGONIAN

Damon Stoudamire knows there are quite a few people who want him to leave, but there are just as many, such as these Rose Garden fans, who want him to stay.

"My heart tells me I have unfinish business here," he says.

It's March 1, and as Blazers playe straggle onto the court to warm up before a game with the Detroit Pist group of kids from North Portland a brought courtside to meet then-coa Maurice Cheeks.

As Cheeks signs autographs and speaks to the kids, Jerry Moss, the B ers' energetic director of communit reach, introduces players as they en from the locker room.

"Here's Nick Van Exel," Moss says nobody says anything as the Blazers eran taps a couple of heads before t the court to warm up.

Throughout the next 15 minutes, players meander out, each with an duction, and each time the kids kee eye on Cheeks approaching to sign graphs, and the other eye on the ch of getting a high-five from a Blazers er.

Then, before Moss can even call the player's name, it's chaos.

"DAMON! DAMON! YO, DAMON WHAT'S UP, MAN?"

But these are not awestruck screa from seeing celebrity. These are fan remember-me hellos. As if they had him yesterday, and maybe they had their smiles and their eyes oozed re and idolization.

The kids cram the aisle to get clos Stoudamire, who is hugging and sla ping hands.

Cheeks? Totally irrelevant.

DAMON STOUDAMIRE'S YEARS WITH THE BLAZE

Feb. 13, 1998: Stoudamire is traded by Toronto with Carlos Rogers and Walt Williams to Portland for Kenny Anderson, Gary Trent, Alvin Williams and two first-round draft picks, one second-round pick and cash.

THE OREGONIAN/1998

Damon Stoudamire's first game as a Portland Trail Blazer, Feb. 17, 1998.

Feb. 23, 2002: After responding to a burglar alarm at Stoudamire's Lake Oswego residence, police enter through an open door and find more than a pound of marijuana. Fifteen miles away at the Rose Garden, Stoudamire is scoring 24 points with 11 assists against Denver.

April 15, 2002: Six days before the playoffs, Stoudamire is informed he is being investigated for felony drug possession as a result of the February search. The investigation weighs on Stoudamire, who shoots 5 of 22 from the field while the Blazers are swept in the first round of the playoffs in three games by the Los Angeles Lakers.

THE OREGONIAN/2002

May 8, 2002: Stoudamire is charged with one count of felony drug possession. Six days later, he enters a not guilty plea in Clackamas County Circuit Court.

Nov. 15, 2002: Stoudamire is told by coach Maurice Cheeks he no longer is the Blazers' starting point guard. As it turns out, it is more than just a demotion: Stoudamire plays sporadically the rest of the season, including 23 games in which he is benched for the entire game.

Nov. 22, 2002: Stoudamire and Rasheed Wallace are cited for marijuana possession when Stoudamire's Hummer, in which they are passengers, is stopped for speeding on Interstate 5 near Chehalis, Wash., on the way back from a game in Seattle. Marijuana is found in the vehicle.

Dec. 12, 2002: Stoudamire donates $250,000 to the Portland Interscholastic League to help save spring sports.

March 20, 2003: Stoudamire is given 12 months' probation and ordered to complete alcohol/drug rehabilitation school after appearing in Lewis County District Court for marijuana possession charges stemming from the Nov. 22 incident.

July 3, 2003: Stoudamire is cited for marijuana possession at Tucson (Ariz.) International Airport after marijuana wrapped in tinfoil in his pant leg sets off airport metal detectors as he prepares to board a flight to New Orleans. He still was on probation from the Washington case at the time of his arrest.

July 7, 2003: Blazers President Steve Patterson fines Stoudamire $250,000 and suspends him indefinitely.

Oct. 1, 2003: After undergoing voluntary drug rehabilitation in Houston over the summer, Stoudamire is reinstated by the Blazers and his $250,000 fine is dedicated to Portland's Albina Head Start program. Stoudamire also pledges $100,000 to Head Start.

March 5, 200 Stoudamire m good on a pro John Canzano, columnist at T Oregonian, and a surprise dru after a practic Cheeks as a wi Stoudamire pa the drug test.

ything.

Photo composite by BRUCE ELY/THE OREGONIAN

Cheeks says. "What the heck
...?"
...players? Puhleeze.
...no need for the kids to cram,
...udamire squeezes himself
...e rows of seats and makes his
...to touch every one of them.
...s well reach through their rib
...ouch their hearts.
...lly can't place a value on that
...doesn't show in the statistics
...n't show in a column that
...tes are measured by," Moss
...it's the one ingredient all
...chises try to get, or try to in-
...ith Damon, he treats it as if it
...ng you carry around like a cell
...comb. It's just natural to him.
...ees young people, he sees
...rently than you or I see them."
...aire knows most of the kids,
...all by name, but he has seen
...s free summer basketball
...r them at Head Start, has seen
...lf Enhancement Inc., or spon-
...teams at Peninsula Park,
...r called themselves "The Wild-
...nor of Stoudamire's college
...Arizona Wildcats.
...all of them," Stoudamire says.
...lot of those kids I know their
...eir daddies . . . come on, Port-
...that big. But me knowing
...being me. But I think the dif-
...tween me and other guys is
...are in your hometown, you
...he park and not be intimidat-
...e shoot, you grew up in that
...But that's the best part of be-
...situation: You can touch peo-
...at."
...s Portland. Portland knows
...o the Blazers know Damon?
...nire doubts it. It goes back to
...g he gets from the franchise,
...rappreciated snub. And really,
...That's what it is. All he wants

is for the Blazers to reach out and say
they appreciate him. That they want
him.
If they do that, he would melt.
"I think it's more important to me to
see how they view me," he says. "Not just
as playing for the Blazers, but after I'm
done playing for the Blazers."
He's not talking specifically about a
front office job — although the idea is
appealing — but more in general terms,
more along the lines of what his legacy
will be. He wants that bit of acknowl-
edgement that what he has done here
was noticed: the leadership in the locker
room, the practicing every day, the community outreach, playing through injuries.
"I want them to look at me and say,
'You mean more than people give you
credit for meaning to this team,' " he
says. But he isn't very hopeful that will
come. He says not one mention, one
word, one intimation has been made toward getting him back. He guesses the
writing was on the wall last summer,
when he was stung after hearing the
team gave Theo Ratliff a three-year, $35
million extension. Not one red cent was
offered to him.
And as he laces them up today at the
Rose Garden, the penultimate time he
will wear a Blazers home uniform this
season . . . and perhaps ever . . . he will
continue to go back and forth. Stay. Go.
And he will think of a recent magazine
article he read about Boston's Antoine
Walker, who was traded back to the
Celtics this season.
"The gist was that sometimes an organization doesn't realize what it's got until
it's gone," Stoudamire said. "And that's
how I feel about Portland. It just might
be too late before they realize it."

*Jason Quick: 503-221-4372;
jasonquick@news.oregonian.com*

HOW THE IMAGE WAS MADE

This composite was made by combining about
60 of the 276 images The Oregonian's Bruce Ely
took during the Trail Blazers' game against the
Dallas Mavericks on Thursday night at the Rose
Garden. Ely photographed guard Damon
Stoudamire's movements during the game from
the same location in a corner of the arena with
a 200mm lens and a Nikon D2H digital camera.
He then patched together the pictures using
Adobe Photoshop. Ely was inspired by a similar
photograph of former Utah Jazz guard John
Stockton taken by Salt Lake Tribune photographer
Trent Nelson and published in Sports Illustrated
in 2003. The black areas are sections of the stands
that weren't photographed.

**HOW STOUDAMIRE
RANKS AS A BLAZER**

Where Damon Stoudamire stands in the Blazers'
record book (through Friday):

POINTS IN A GAME
1. Damon Stoudamire, 54 at New Orleans,
Jan. 14, 2005
2. Geoff Petrie, 51 at Houston, Jan. 20, 1973,
vs. Houston, March 16, 1973

THREE-POINTERS IN A SEASON
1. Clifford Robinson, 178 (1995-96)
2. Damon Stoudamire, 176 (2004-05)
3. Damon Stoudamire, 156 (2003-04)

THREE-POINTERS, ALL-TIME
1. Terry Porter, 773
2. Damon Stoudamire, 712

ASSISTS, ALL-TIME
1. Terry Porter, 5,319
2. Clyde Drexler, 4,933
3. Damon Stoudamire, 3,000

MINUTES PLAYED
1. Clyde Drexler, 29,526
7. Jim Paxson, 18,398
8. Damon Stoudamire, 17,388

GAMES PLAYED
1. Clyde Drexler, 867
10. Kevin Duckworth, 527
11. Damon Stoudamire, 526

STEALS
1. Clyde Drexler, 1,795
T-9. Rasheed Wallace, 555
T-9. Damon Stoudamire, 555

2004: ...ame in
...toudamire
...d of his
...osition by
...the heels
...nber
...lump (21 of
...not going to
...d cry
...Stoudamire
...n't no

Jan. 14, 2005: After regaining his starting job four days earlier, Stoudamire scores a franchise-record 54 points at New Orleans, breaking Geoff Petrie's mark of 51 set in 1973. Stoudamire makes 20 of 32 shots, including a franchise-record-tying eight three-pointers.

March 16, 2005: An Oregon Court of Appeals decision lets stand a lower court ruling that marijuana found in Stoudamire's home in February 2002 was the result of an illegal search. Unless the Oregon Supreme Court reverses, Clackamas County prosecutors will have to drop drug possession charges against Stoudamire.

April 6, 2005: Stoudamire has his second triple double as a Blazer, finishing with 13 points, 12 rebounds and 10 assists in a loss to Golden State.

ASSOCIATED PRESS

ASSOCIATED PRESS

Eye-tracking research also revealed that readers are more drawn to color than to black-and-white designs. Color is so important to readers that even the *New York Times*, traditionally known as "the good gray *Times*," and the *Wall Street Journal*, known for long columns of type and small visuals known as stipples, underwent redesigns that included the addition of color to their front pages. But they did so cautiously, with reader habits in mind.

Readers become accustomed to a publication's design. Design scholar Kay Amert calls this the *contract of literacy*, meaning readers learn to expect a particular form of visual presentation in a publication. When publications change their design — even for the better — it is often upsetting to readers.

Readers also respond best to clearly organized pages that help them determine what is most important to view. A well-designed newspaper page has a clear, dominant entry point for the reader. Mario Garcia, known for his successful redesigns of U.S. newspapers, stressed that a newspaper front page should have one visual that is at least three times larger than other visual elements on the page.
Editors should choose the words they use in headlines and captions with great care to make the best use of space and the knowledge those readers may never get to the body of a story. Type is a key element in print media, and key to processing type is the designer's selection of typeface.

Figure 13.10. Bruce Ely combined 60 images he took of guard Damon Stoudamire during a Trail Blazers' game against Dallas in Roco Garden to make this composite illustration for a broadsheet doubletruck (center pages designed as one layout in a regular-sized newspaper), The Oregonian, April 17, 2005.

Figure 13.11. *Special Food Section front, The Oregonian, February 10, 2006. Note the sanserif type, text wrap, and fun illustrations. Compare with the serif type, formal design, and serious photojournalism of the science special in Figure 13.9.*

Figure 13.12. Casts of Korean bronze type, 1406. Koreans used wooden types embedded in wax in shallow wooden trays. In 1397, the king of Korea set up a foundry to produce metal types, which were wedged into place with narrow strips of bamboo between each vertical row. Printing was done by inking the type and taking an impression on paper by gently rubbing on the back. These movable types antedate Gutenberg's invention of movable type in Western Europe by more than a century. Science Museum/Science and Society Picture Library.

Characteristics of Type

Although type refers to words, it is important to remember that you perceive the words you read on a printed page — as these you are reading now — through visual means. We have become so accustomed to reading them that we forget the significance of their visual characteristics (see chapter 8 for an earlier discussion of this subject). We are not born reading words — we must learn first how to distinguish letterforms and then how to recognize sets of letters put together into words and sentences. In fact, it is estimated that thousands of oral languages in the world have yet to be recorded in written form.

The Chinese, Japanese, and Koreans printed from movable type well before the Western world discovered the art in the 15th century. In the 11th century, the Chinese developed type characters from hardened clay. Koreans had cast type through a method widely used in China and Japan. The oldest known text printed from movable type was created in 1397. In spite of this history of invention in Asia, Johannes Gutenberg of Mainz, Germany, is generally credited with the invention of printing from movable type between 1440 and 1450. Historians believe his invention consisted of the combination of a number of existing processes. Gutenberg's major contribution probably was the making of adjustable metal molds for casting types of different sizes accurately and in large quantities. By the end of the year 1500, printing presses had been set up in more than 250 cities throughout Europe, a sign of a mass movement of literacy that would shift the control of words — and therefore ideas — in an unparalleled fashion until the diffusion of the personal computer in the late 20th century.

Figure 13.13. Printing, 1574. Woodcut illustration by Jost Amman from "De Omnibus Illiberalibus Siue Mechanicis Artibus...Liber" by Hartmann Schopper, published in Germany. Schopper's book, written in Latin, detailed a variety of trades. Here, two men in the foreground are shown inking type and preparing paper on a printing press, while in the background men are seen selecting and setting the type to be printed. Science Museum/Science and Society Picture Library.

Parts of a Letterform

At this point, we want to introduce you to the basic vocabulary of type and typography in common use today.

stroke — lines of a letterform

serif — finishing marks on the ends of strokes

bowl — the outside of a letter that contains space within it, such as *a* or *d*

counter — the inside of the bowl

lowercase — no capital letters

uppercase — capital letters

x-height — the vertical dimension of a lowercase *x*

ascender — the part of the letterform extending above the x-height, in letters such as *l* or *f*

descender — the part of the letterform extending below the x-height, in letters such as *p* or *y*

size — the vertical dimension of a letterform measured from the bottom of the descender to the top of the ascender

point — the smallest unit used to measure letterforms vertically; 72 points = 1 inch. Type measuring 36 points high is about a half-inch high.

pica — units used to measure line length and width and depth of visual elements and spacing; 12 points = 1 pica, 6 picas = 72 points = 1 inch.

Figures 13.14-15. Top left: Measuring type in points and picas with one inch comparison, illustration by Janet Halvorsen. Top right: Three Ws cast in movable hot metal type, sitting on rows of metal type. © iStockphoto.com/D.S.L. Zgorzelec.

em — the square of a type size. Seventy-two-point type has an em that measures 72 points vertically and horizontally.

en — one-half the horizontal size of an em. Seventy-two-point type has an en that measures 36 points horizontally and 72 points vertically.

agate — small type used largely in classified ads or tables; 14 agate lines = 1 inch.

leading — line spacing. Designs specify (or spec) type as solid (written 9/9 for lines with no additional leading between them, 9/11 for lines with two points spacing between them, or 9/7 for minus leading to reduce space between lines, to stack lines, or to overlap lines).

tracking — how the letterforms or words are spaced in a line

kerning — modifying the space between individual letterforms for better appearance and readability

line length — how wide a line is, often determined by the width of a column used in a grid for layout. One formula for determining the optimum line length

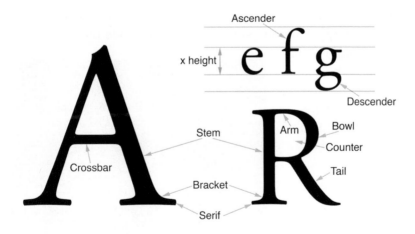

Figure 13.16. Parts of a Letterform. Illustration by Janet Halvorsen.

Figure 13.17. Ludlow line type-casting machine, 1955. Science Museum/Science and Society Picture Library.

for ease of reading is the width in picas of the lowercase alphabet of a font (one typestyle in one size). Use that width as the minimum line length when using that font, and use twice that width as the maximum line length with that font.

flush left — lines of type beginning at exactly the same point on the left side

ragged right — lines of type that are uneven on the right side only

flush right — lines of type ending at exactly the same point on the right side

ragged left — lines that begin at uneven points on the left side only

justified — lines that begin and end at the same point on both the left and right side

centered — when lines of type are spaced exactly in the middle of a type block; both sides will be uneven.

text wrap — when body type is formed around a graphic

Figure 13.18. Lines of hot metal type with metal shim leading between lines (typeset in Swedish). © iStockphoto/Monolinea.

Williams and Newton

abcdefghijklmnopqrstuvwxyz1234567890
-=,./;'[]`\!@#$%^&*()_+<>?:"{}~|

abcdefghijklmnopqrstuvwxyz1234567890
-=,./;'[]`\!@#$%^&()_+<>?:"{}~|*

Figures 13.19-20. Each of the above sets is one font when using the traditional definition based on hot type (or metal). The top one is 14 point Electra LH Regular. The second one is 18 point Ekectra LH Cursive. Digital type (cold type) uses the term font to refer to a general family name, such as Bodoni, and all of its varieties, such as 12-pt Bodoni Bold or 36-pt Bodoni Bold Condensed.

Palatino 6 point

Palatino 8 point

Palatino 10 point

Palatino 12 point

Palatino 14 point

Palatino 18 point

Palatino 20 point

Palatino 24 point

Palatino 30 point

Palatino 32 point

Palatino 36 point

Palatino 48 point

Palatino 72

Figures 13.21. Standard type sizes. Note that the type is set flush left, ragged right.

You will find different names for different kinds of type, but general typefaces fall into six basic *groups* based on shared graphic characteristics:

Blackletter or Text — ornate, angular letterforms created with dominant, thick strokes flourished with thin strokes. Many newspaper nameplates continue to use their original blackletter type as a sign of authority and tradition. These typefaces are associated with medieval times in Europe and the Bible. The Oregonian nameplate (or flag) in Figure 13.23 is set in a blackletter typeface.

Here is an example of a *Blackletter* typeface called Wilhelm Klingspor Gotisch:

Roman — classic letterforms with strokes of varying width and ending with small finishing marks called serifs, originally used to cover strokes made imperfectly with chisels or brushes.

Three subgroups of Roman typefaces are *Old Style*, which uses angled axes, some contrast in stroke width, oblique serifs on some letters (such as the low-ercase *d* or *I*), and bracketed serifs with small indentations, or humps, on the bottom; *Transitional*, which has only slightly angled axes, more stroke-width contrast, bracketed by cleaner serifs with no humps; and *Modern*, which uses vertical axes, increased contrast in stroke widths, and thin, hairline serifs that seldom are bracketed.

This version of Georgia is an example of *Old Style Roman* type:

Old Style Roman

This version of Baskerville is an example of *Transitional Roman* type:

Transitional Roman

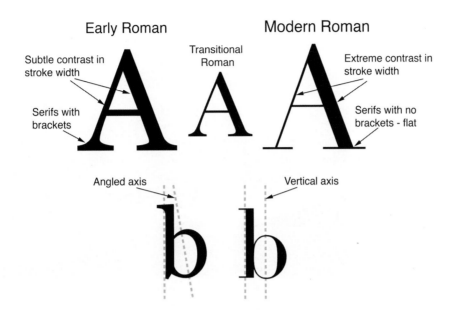

Figure 13.22. Ways to distinguish Early Roman (Old Style), Transitional Roman, and Modern Roman typefaces. Illustration by Janet Halvorsen.

Bodoni is an example of a *Modern Roman* type:

Modern Roman

Sans serif — clean, even strokes with no finishing marks, or serifs.

Many sans serif typefaces are *geometrically* styled with uniform strokes that show little or no variation. Others, more *calligraphically* styled, are based on the subtle variations in stroke widths of calligraphy, offering a more graceful appearance. The body type for this book is set in 10-point Univers, a *Geometric Sans Serif* type.

The Oregonian

SATURDAY
JULY 22, 2006

NORTHWEST
FINAL

PORTLAND, OREGON

VOICE OF THE NORTHWEST SINCE 1850

108 State's highest temp, in Hillsboro and the Dalles

104 Record-breaking temp at Portland airport at 4 p.m. Previous record set in 1994, when the temperature reached 101 degrees.

2 Truckloads of ice being brought in this weekend to keep the Oregon Zoo's three polar bears – Conrad, Tasul and Yugyan – cool

$600 Sales of gelato by Friday afternoon at Mio Gelato's store in the Pearl

Tax-cut initiative joins the fall lineup

Election | The measure would reduce most middle-income filers' bills by about $140 per exemption

**By BETSY HAMMOND
and DAVE HOGAN**
THE OREGONIAN

An initiative that would cut state income taxes by about $140 a person for most Oregonians is the second measure to make the Nov. 7 ballot, elections officials announced Friday.

The measure, championed by anti-tax activist Russ Walker and bankrolled primarily by millionaire entrepreneur Loren Parks, would lower income taxes for nearly all middle-income taxpayers.

It would cost the state more than $400 million a year in lost tax revenue by 2008, state officials say. That would translate to an estimated 6 percent cut in the state budget, which funds schools and other services.

The measure needed 75,630 valid signatures to qualify, and backers collected 79,176, elections officials said. They based that figure on a sampling of signatures reviewed by elections officials in each county during the past two weeks.

Walker says the measure is "a family-friendly" way to give all but the

Please see TAX, Page A3

Colleges ride stars' shirttails to the bank

Ethics | Some athletic departments, including Oregon's, auction game-worn jerseys

By RACHEL BACHMAN
THE OREGONIAN

Bored with buying the same college football jersey everyone else has? Looking for something unique? How about the No. 5 jersey Reggie Bush wore all the way to the 2005 Heisman Trophy?

USC has joined a handful of other universities, including Oregon, in auctioning off jerseys of current and former players. The auctions raise money for athletic departments and give fans one-of-a-kind souvenirs.

But they also test the spirit of NCAA rules, which discourage schools from exploiting athletes while prohibiting players from profiting from their star status. School officials say they are merely using innovative means to generate revenue, but others aren't so sure.

"It's the symbolism of it that is as concerning as anything," said Peter Roby, director of the Northeastern University Center for the Study of Sport in Society.

"You know, it's like, 'We haven't been able to benefit enough from this athlete being here. Let's go and take the shirt right off his back and sell that, too.'"

The auctions practically guarantee

Please see JERSEY, Page A3

Bush
USC Heisman winner's jerseys on block soon

Oh, yeah, we feel the burn

A lone rider takes advantage of Friday's record-breaking temperatures by racing on the Willamette River.

BENJAMIN BRINK/THE OREGONIAN

When it's triple-digit hot out there, let's face it: Oregonians can't take the heat

By STEPHEN BEAVEN
THE OREGONIAN

Yes, another story about the heat.

Because it was hot Friday — a record-breaking 104 in Portland. It's going to be hot again today. And everywhere, it seems, Oregonians act like we're approaching the End Times.

It's crazy: TV reporters go outside and actually sweat. Newspaper editors plot big stories for the front page. And otherwise hardy souls who've endured blazing summers elsewhere turn soft as cheese,

DOUG BEGHTEL/THE OREGONIAN

As temperatures soared past 100 in the Willamette Valley and in Eastern Oregon, Oregonians flocked to the Coast to enjoy breezes that cooled the air to the mid-70s. Tate Waidbillig , 1½, had a taste of the sand at D River Beach near Lincoln City while visiting from Redmond with his parents Friday.

right in front of us.

"What has impressed me is what a wimp I've become since I moved here," says Dr. Don Rosen, a psychiatrist at Oregon Health & Science University who used to live in Topeka, Kan.

The heat here didn't used to bother him, because it wasn't nearly as bad as Kansas. But now Rosen is a true Oregonian. He's having a book club meeting tonight at his house because the previously scheduled hosts don't have air-conditioning.

Please see HEAT, Page A8

Forecast
Saturday: high around 100 degrees, mostly sunny
Sunday: mostly sunny, high around 95
Monday: mostly sunny, high around 90; slowly cooling down next week

For complete weather, see **B6**

Inside
Utilities say they have enough juice to keep the lights on and the air conditioners humming despite surge in electricity usage. **Business, B1**

» Online: Watch a video of Portland fountains creating community and fun in the sun at www.oregonlive.com/news/multimedia

Because of the threat of wildfire, Gov. Ted Kulongoski declares a state of emergency, Page A8

Israel aims more troops at Lebanon

Mideast | As the U.S. warns it won't back a cease-fire that falls short, a ground invasion seems imminent

**By EDWARD CODY
and JOHN WARD ANDERSON**
LA TIMES-WASHINGTON POST SERVICE

BEIRUT, Lebanon — The Israeli military called up reserve troops Friday and broadcast urgent radio warnings for civilians of battered southern Lebanon to leave "immediately" for relative safety north of the Litani River, adding to the growing indications that Israel is planning a large-scale ground operation to root out Hezbollah guerrillas and their missile caches.

Hezbollah, for its part, continued sending rockets into northern Israel on Friday, causing damage and injuries but no deaths.

In Washington, meanwhile, Secretary of State Condoleezza Rice announced plans to travel to the region next week for talks with Israeli and Palestinian leaders, and for a conference on the crisis in Rome on Wednesday with officials from Arab countries and the European Union.

DAVID GUTTENFELDER/ASSOCIATED PRESS

Israeli tanks and troops mass near the Israeli town of Avivim on Friday in preparation of a likely ground invasion into Lebanon.

But she warned that the United States will not support a cease-fire that falls short of fully disarming Hezbollah and restoring Lebanese government control throughout Lebanon.

In Israel, columns of armored vehicles and troops assembled on the border. The Israeli army confirmed that small units have been operating in Lebanon

Please see MIDEAST, Page A7

Eco-saboteur apologizes

Portland woman admits role in Vail arson and other fires, but says she realizes mistakes. **Metro, D1**

Copyright © 2006
Oregonian Publishing Co.
Vol. 154, No. 52,388
74 pages

7 14170 00072 1

BREAKING NEWS AT
WWW.OREGONLIVE.COM

Figure 13.23. Page One, The Oregonian, July 22, 2006. Note how the page designer used different type-styles, sizes, tones, column widths, rule lines, and images to organize the day's news.

Helvetica is another example of Geometric Sans Serif type:

Geometric Sans Serif

Optima is an example of *Calligraphic Sans Serif* type:

Calligraphic Sans Serif

Note the different visual effects of Helvetica and Optima. One is bold, the other more graceful. In these two examples, Helvetic carries more visual weight. Optima is more elegant.

Square serif — uniform strokes with blocky, slablike serifs and a massive, strong-appearing structure. Princetown is an example of *Square Serif* type:

SQUARE SERIF

Script or Cursive — letterforms that resemble handwriting. Script letterforms connect. Cursive letterforms do not (remember the useful trick: curse them because they're not connected). Edwardian Script is an example of *Script* type*:*

Script type

Savoye is an example of *Cursive* type:

Cursive type

Novelty — each typeface in this group has unique characteristics associated with the meaning of the message the type conveys. Jazz is an example of *Novelty* type:

Novelty type

This is Bearpaw:

NOVELTY TYPE

Other Terms

However, our adventure with type does not stop with basic groups. Typeface details are identified by:

- *family* names, such as *Edwardian Script ITC*, Palatino, or **Jazz**
- *style*, which includes such variations as
  — weight (**bold** or light)
  — width (expanded/extended or condensed)
  — posture (*italic/oblique* or upright, also known as Roman)
  (for example: **Baskerville Semibold** or **Optima Bold)**
- *series*, which refers to all the sizes in a particular family of type, as in

6- through 108 -point sizes

- *font*, which refers to all characters for one size and one style of a family of type (such as 10-point Baskerville). Note, for example, that both samples of novelty type above are typeset in 54 point. Yet **Jazz** takes up more vertical and horizontal space than BEARPAW, even though **Jazz** is set in upper- and lower-case and BEARPAW is set in all caps (in 10 point here).

Contemporary use of the word *font* has changed since the term was originated. In the early days of type design, one font filled an actual drawer in a bureau of drawers, each filled with different sizes and styles of the same basic family of type. So, for example, *each size* of the lowercase alphabet, numbers, and punctuation marks for 18-point **Baskerville Semibold** was *one font*.

Before the invention of the Linotype, a machine that melted bars of a lead alloy for formation into lines of letters, a typesetter had to hand select letter blocks and put them together in a form to print even one line of type. For three-fourths of the 20th century, typesetters still hand-set display type, large-size type for headlines and advertisements but used Linotype machines to cast the main text or body of type. As computers took over the processing of words, print shops gradually shifted from using physical type, also known as hot type because of the molten metal used, to cold type, or type that was digitally coded and could be set using software programs such as Microsoft Word. Because of the ease of making type any size and any style one desired, the meaning of font has shifted to refer to the basic names of a typeface.

Practical Guidelines for Effective Design

Designers make many choices beyond frame dimensions, image selection, and type. Other factors, too numerous to name in their entirety in this brief introduction to print publications, include the surface or material that carries the design (the kind of paper, cloth, stone), how the visual elements are inscribed on that surface (offset printing, screen printing, hand application), quantity (one original or millions of reproductions), and distribution (handed from person to person or mailed en masse). Designers' choices are as large as the overall goal of a project — and as small as how to place each visual element, including letterforms, within the frame of the page or object.

Even so, following a few simple practices can help beginning designers produce effective publications that readers can easily read.

- Clarify purpose of the design.
- Know your audience.
- Use a grid for consistency.
- Select visual and verbal content based on the meaning conveyed.
- Use color when possible and appropriate to content.
- Use type wisely.
  - Select type style to convey publication image and content.
  - Mix typefaces sparingly and cautiously.
  - Only vary type styles within the same family when in doubt.
  - Select column width for readability.
- Consider the entire frame, not just individual frames on a page. This means considering the publication with pages open as a whole frame.

More than Appearances

Are these guidelines primarily about appearances — making sure your publication looks good? Hardly. Good design can make the difference between a publication that is picked up or not, read or not, sold or not, and understood or not. Furthermore, design can carry elements of racism, sexism, classism, ageism, any "ism" you can imagine. Lucy Ganje (1998), professor of visual communication at the University of North Dakota, conducted research on the ways American Indian populations perceive design in newspapers. Lakota culture, for example, holds four colors as sacred: red, black, yellow, and white. Black Elk described how ribbons on his sacred pipe stood for the four directions:

> The black one is for the west where the thunder beings life to send us rain: the white one for the north, whence comes the great white cleansing wind: the red one for the east, whence springs the light and where the morning star lives to give men wisdom; the yellow for the south whence come the summer and the power to grow. (npn)

Stressing that "language, culture, and thought are interrelated" and that "layout is a form of expression," Ganje recommended editors use "cultural empathy" through attending to shapes, colors, patterns, directions, numbers, and symbols of unique significance to American Indian readers. She wrote:

> A culturally sensitive layout can be accomplished by relating the precepts of the culture to the design and layout of the publication. Newspapers continue their struggle to attract minority women and younger audiences. There are many barriers to overcome for those from oral tradition cultures who may not operate as well within print-oriented mainstream society. The newspaper should not keep people from the news but guide them through it using familiar signs and landmarks. This map can be accomplished by recognizing that the most effective composition comes from within a culture or community.

As we become aware of the remarkable diversity of human life, even as we shorten distances among us through technology, it is important to remember that the visual resonates deep within the human mind. The way we design, the way we arrange elements within a frame for publication or other use, communicates more than we realize.

Stopping time and framing space are powerful tools in the creation and communication of ways of seeing and knowing. As you can now see, the subtlety and nuance of the many elements of graphic design and visual production techniques create highly intuitive visual communication products using print media. Often, the rationally dominant instruments that we use to assess and understand visual media do not account for the effective use of intuitive techniques to shape our perceptions and persuade us toward specific behaviors. That is why it is so important to understand visual communication from a variety of perspectives that include both rational and intuitive processes.

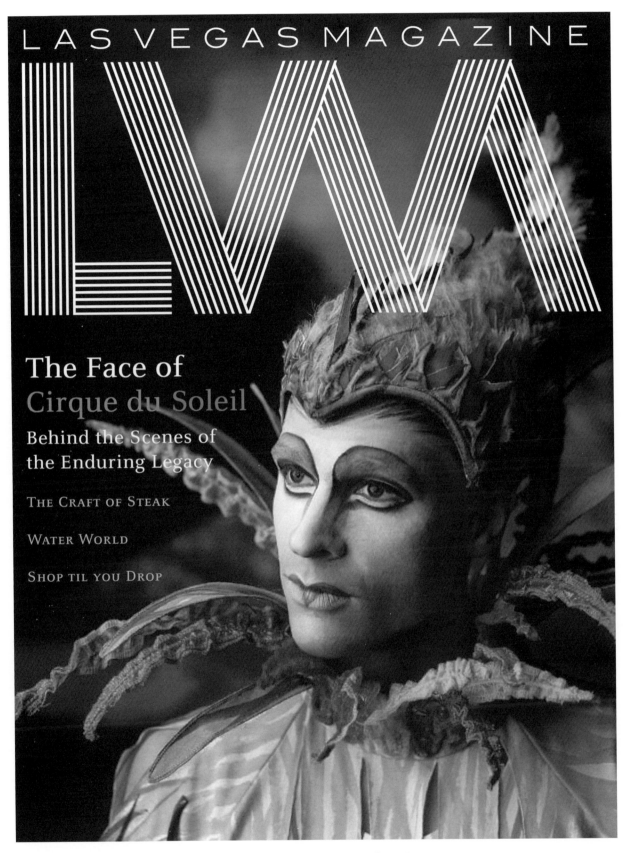

Figure 13.24. LVM cover design by Pentagram (original in color). Courtsey of D. J. Stout.

Figure C13.1. Jovan Musk ad, Coty.

Williams and Newton

CREATIVE THIRTEEN
Personal Impact Assessment: Understanding Images from Intuitive and Rational Perspectives

The Goal: Understanding How Still Media Images Communicate

As we have seen in preceding chapters, the techniques that contemporary media use to convey their messages are visual, musical, and metaphorical flights of fantasy and magic, similar to our dreams. They are processed in the brain using the same intuitive cognitive processes that are used to develop knowledge and memory. These stimuli follow LeDoux's and Damasio's neurological paths through the thalamus, amygdala, and prefrontal lobes to bypass reason. We usually are not even aware that we have been seduced by compelling imagery.

Media imagery is similar to dreams in format, content, and nonconscious memory processing. Because of the intuitive aspects of media communication, the more discursive, rationally biased instruments that we have used to understand media communication, such as semiotics and the Six Perspectives, can never completely access the deeper meanings and influences of mediated imagery. A classic process of dream interpretation, however, can be useful to understand media images from an intuitive perspective.

As noted earlier, Personal Impact Assessment (PIA), an instrument that was adapted by Williams from a Jungian dream interpretation technique allows us to understand media imagery in ways that redirect their persuasive intent toward self-awareness. Working through the process of PIA helps reveal the motivations of the creator of the image and explores the influence of the media-delivered motivations of others on the viewer. This self-awareness is critical to understanding and guiding the effects of those motivations on your behavior in both intrapersonal and interpersonal relationships. This is significant to you on three levels.

First, if you are to guide your own behavior in ways that are individually and culturally advantageous, it is critical that you understand the motivations driving your behavior. As Freud suggested, bringing one's own unconscious motivations into consciousness and integrating that understanding with reason allows a person to consider more fully and critically the outcome of a particular response to those motivations. That, in turn, helps an individual guide that response in ways that are consistent with personal values and beliefs. Using PIA to assess one's own imagery — including dreams, meditations, drawings, paintings, photographs, and metaphorical writing — from an intuitive, synthesistic perspective can help you become more aware of the intrapersonal motivations that have generated the imagery. This is a direct method of integrating the unconscious and conscious toward greater self-awareness.

Second, it is clear that most media images are permeated with messages designed specifically to bypass reason. With symbolic, archetypal power beyond logic, they communicate to our interior feelings, values, needs, and desires in ways that shape our beliefs and direct our decision making and external actions. Similar to waking dreams, media images speak to the whole mind instantaneously, leaving powerful memory suggestions in the unconscious. Because our unconscious memory processes do not differentiate between mediated and real experiences in terms of cognition and decision making, these symbolic memories become more powerful motivators of behavior. In this virtual, visual culture, it is critical to the individual and to society that we learn to recognize and develop means of defense against media seduction and manipulation. In fact, it is critical to our survival as self-aware, self-determining individuals — and to the survival of our planet — that we learn to reverse the effects of these messages of consumerism on the psyche. We can learn to reverse the subsequent, unbridled development of the consumer culture that is itself consuming our self-identities, our resources, and our environment.

Third, whatever your professional aspirations may be, learning to respect the power of visual communication to affect behavior is essential. To be ethically based, that respect must be well grounded in full knowledge of potential consequences of message forms and content on individuals and society. The better you understand how media images affect you on a personal level, the better prepared you will be to create and disseminate socially responsible media images.

To this end, any process that helps integrate the whole mind toward greater awareness of personal values, beliefs, and motivations is worth pursuing. PIA is one such instrument, and it was developed for these purposes. PIA integrates the work of Freud and Jung on the unconscious mind with contemporary media theory, psychology, and cognitive neuroscience. It addresses media ecology issues relating to visual meaning, media learning, and the effects of media. Individuals report that PIA helps them understand more about their motivations and actions, particularly in relation to media effects.
We believe that individuals and groups can also use PIA to reverse the manipulative impact of media messages. By using the information in those very mes-

sages to gain intrapersonal insights. Increasing social awareness and active response to imagery also can help societies develop balanced and sustainable educational, scientific, economic, and cultural systems for living.

How to Begin

This exercises applies the PIA process to a print advertising image. Note the publication name and date and the page number for the ad. Note any credits supplied for photographer, design, model, and so forth. Below we have listed the seven steps in the PIA process with a brief explanation of how to complete each step. The steps may seem linear and tedious at first, but remember, these steps trace a pathway to the unconscious through intuitive, as well as rational, means. Reaching the unconscious mind with a conscious process is not always simple. Even Jung suggested there were only two primary ways: dreams and meditations. Cognitive psychologists and neuroscientists are using functional Magnetic Resonance Imaging and Positron Emission Tomography to observe brain responses to media images. We believe that PIA offers a particularly relevant and readily available way for anyone to access his or her own nonconscious responses to visual media. This in turn can help you assess your contemporary visual culture and its potential effects on you and your life. Remember to read the instructions all the way through and to do a creative activity that helps you relax before you begin.

The Seven Steps of Personal Impact Assessment

1. *Choose and View the Image.* Select an advertisement to assess from a newspaper or magazine published in the last 3 months. Note publication name, date, ad page number, and any available credits. Spend a few minutes just looking at the image and letting your eye and mind wander around the different parts. Notice the light, its direction, contrast, and feel. Notice the primary points of interest and where they are placed. Notice lines, curves, and basic design elements, and how they help or hinder your eye movement. Notice the grain structure. Notice the range of tones and colors and how they affect your feelings. Notice how the image makes you feel. Does it draw you in or keep you out? Does it tell a clear story or does it stimulate your imagination to develop your own ideas or stories?

2. *List Primary Words.* List a single word that describes each of the significant parts of the image that seem significant to you — characters, places, things, colors/tone, feelings, and so on — in a column at the left side of a blank sheet of paper. Leave enough space around each word on the list to write a number of other words.

3. *List Associative Words.* Look at each of the primary words you have written, one at a time. Start with the first word and, beside or in a circle around that

word, write other words (word associations that come into your mind as you think about the first word). Finish all of the associations for the first word before you move on to the next word. We suggest that you list at least three associative words for each primary word. Listing more words is fine.

4. *Select the Most Significant Associative Word.* When you have completed the list of word associations, go back to the first primary word and mull its associative words over in your mind. Again, start with the first primary word and its associative words and go down the list. Try to intuit which is the most significant associative word for each primary word and draw a circle around it or underline it.

Do not overthink this; just say the associative words to yourself until one seems most significant. Do this for each group of associative words you have listed, one at a time. There are no right or wrong answers. Simply pick the word that seems most appropriate to you as you read the words. If more than one word seems correct, then circle both.

5. *Make a list of the most significant associative words. Reflect on the associative words and relate each to an inner part of yourself.* Look at each word in the "significant word association" list and consider what part of your inner self that word represents or symbolizes. Write that part of yourself to the right of the "significant word association." To identify the inner parts of yourself, it may be helpful to say "my inner_____ self," for example, my inner *vulnerable* self, my inner *trusting* self, my inner *fantasy* self. Again, there are no right or wrong answers for these Inner Symbols of your self. This is your personal interpretation.

6. *Review the Inner Symbols.* Look over these word symbols of your inner self and see if there is some clear connection or story that arises about yourself from the interaction of the inner symbols from the image. This story, connection, or meaning may be simply a feeling, or it may come to you in a flash, or as an ah-haaa-type response. It will often reveal the inner conflicts, emotions, values, or feelings that are behind your personal, intuitive creation of or attraction to the image.

7. *Write down the story or insight.* Think about how it applies to your attraction to the image, or how it offers insights about your own life relative to the image. Also consider how associating the product or service advertised in the image with fulfillment of these inner desires and values might establish unconscious biases and motivations. Consider how these unconscious motivations might influence your desire for the product or for things the image associates with the product (for example, a sexual relationship, physical perfection, love, freedom, or luxury) and how this desire might influence you to adapt your behavior in some way. As usual, conclude the exercise with an overall assessment of your experiences.

The Exercise

- Read the instructions carefully, all the way through.
- Spend time relaxing before you start.
- Choose a print advertising image that attracts you.
- Note publication name, date, ad page number, and any available credits.
- Analyze the ad using Personal Impact Assessment as described above.
- Take your time completing the exercise. Remember to pause and relax into an integrative state before beginning.
- Complete the PIA by writing a story using the feelings and self understandings revealed through the process.
- Write an assessment explaining how this process worked for you and what you learned about the image and about yourself. Explain how you might use this information for self-awareness, personal growth, and more informed use of media images.

Example PIA of Jovan Musk Ad

Step 1. The Image

This example examines the Jovan Musk Ad at the beginning of this exercise.

2. Primary Words

BLACK	WHITE
GRAY	SEXY
KISSING	BODIES
LIPS	SOFT
PERSONAL	TOUCHING
CLOSENESS	SKIN
HAIR	TASTE
SMELL	EMBRACE

3. Primary Words with Associative Words

romantic
dark   **BLACK**   contrast

revealing
light   **WHITE**   contrast

dream-like
fantasy   **GRAY**   shadows

longing
desire   **SEXY**   beauty

soft
passionate   **KISSING**   intimate
wonderful

warmth
naked   **BODIES**   closeness

soft
luscious   **LIPS**   tender
big

warmth
content   **SOFT**   skin

closeness
content   **PERSONAL**   private
trust

desire
excitement   **TOUCHING**   warmth
closeness

warmth
caress   **CLOSENESS**   love
relationship

soft
naked   **SKIN**   smooth

sexy
messy   **HAIR**   long, flowing
soft

passion
lips   **TASTE**   desire
tongue   love

happy
animalistic   **SMELL**   desire
scent   closeness

closeness
desire   **EMBRACE**   warm
love

4. *Most Significant Associative Words*

        romantic   revealing
<u>dark</u>   BLACK contrast   light   WHITE   <u>contrast</u>

        dream-like   longing
fantasy GRAY   shadows   <u>desire</u> SEXY   <u>beauty</u>

        soft   warmth
passionate KISSING <u>intimate</u>   <u>naked</u> BODIES closeness
        wonderful

        soft   warmth
luscious LIPS <u>tender</u>   content SOFT   <u>skin</u>
        big

        closeness   desire
content PERSONAL private   <u>excitement</u> TOUCHING warmth
        <u>trust</u>   closeness

        <u>warmth</u>   soft
caress CLOSENESS love   naked SKIN   <u>smooth</u>
        relationship

        sexy   passion
<u>messy</u> HAIR long, <u>flowing</u>   lips TASTE   <u>desire</u>
        soft   <u>tongue</u> love

        happy   <u>closeness</u>
<u>animalistic</u> SMELL desire   desire EMBRACE warm
        scent   closeness   love

5. *Significant Associations*		*Inner-self Associations*
Dark		Inner-self
Contrast		Fantasy self
Dream-like		Fantasy self
Fantasy		Make-believe self
Beauty		Feminine self
Desire		Wanting self
Intimate		Vulnerable Self
Naked		Vulnerable Self
Tender		Maternalistic, loving self
Skin		Naked, exposed self
Trust		Trusting Self
Excitement		Wild, impulsive self
Warmth		Loving, content self
Smooth		Extreme sensitive self
Messy		Impulsive self
Flowing		Feminine self
Desire		Intimate, sexual self
Tongues		Highly sensitive self
Animalistic		Sexual, wanting self
Closeness		Content, trusting self

6 and 7. Story

I think this ad drew me in immediately because it had aspects that appealed to me. It looks like a <u>dream</u> or a <u>fantasy</u> and I <u>wanted</u>, for a second, for that <u>fantasy</u> to be me. I envisioned myself in the bed with the handsome man kissing gently, then more <u>passionately</u>. It appealed to my <u>vulnerable</u>, <u>gentle</u>, <u>trusting</u>, <u>loving self</u> and to my <u>impulsive</u>, <u>wild</u>, <u>animal-like</u>, <u>desired self</u>. I felt all of those feelings at once. At the same time the woman radiates <u>beauty</u>, <u>femininity</u>, and <u>sexiness</u> all at once. I would *love to look like her just for that one moment in my dream [emphasis added]*.

Comments on Example PIA

In the student's story, we underlined all of the words that are also found in the Significant Associations and Inner-self Associations lists. This comparison makes clear not only what exists below the surface of the obvious sexual attraction implicit in the ad but also how persuasive messages can resonate deeply with an individual's inner sense of self needs and values.

Most individuals can take a quick look at the image and logically reject the idea that using the product will fulfill their sexual desires as suggested in the ad. Through this sense of logical understanding, the viewer may feel he/she has not only understood but also countered the effect of the ad. The viewer may never be aware of how the image has seduced them on deep personal and emotional levels through the visual system. The image and its associated feelings and desires become part of the viewer's nonconscious memory and intuitive decision-making process. However, when a person spends time reflecting, using a process such as PIA, he/she can become aware that the initial rational analysis neither revealed the ad's effects nor provided any real defense against its eloquent seduction. With deep reflection, one can begin to comprehend the potential for repeated viewing of persuasive media images to affect one's attitudes and behaviors.

The PIA process is designed to help unmask a sophisticated intuitive messaging system that, on nonconscious cognitive levels, associates product use with the fulfillment of deeply held personal and primal needs, desires, and values. The student in this example associated the ad's carefully constructed visual elements fulfillment of her needs for love, tenderness, contentment, beauty, trust, relationship, maternalism, sensitivity, and vulnerability, as well as her desire for passion, fantasy, impulsiveness, animalistic expression, sexuality, and wildness.

With this new understanding of the self, an understanding that reveals some of the innermost desires, values, and needs of the individual, this viewer is now armed to reverse the manipulative intent of the original message by using the new information for self awareness and self direction. She can consider what actions she might take in her life to address her needs in ways that are real, enriching, and supportive.

The ethical media professional can use PIA to become aware of the need to discontinue using powerfully persuasive messages to encourage external product consumption as a false fulfillment of deep human needs. Persuasive messages can use socially responsible design to encourage authentic, sustainable living in 21st-century culture.

Reflect deeply — then act.

Figure 14.1. Bird Girl, by Rick Williams. Note how motion is implied in the frame through the visual vectors from the woman's hands, the girl's eyes, and the birds' flight paths. The movement of the girl's hair and the wings of the birds was frozen with a relatively fast shutter speed, though the blur of one bird's wing (far left) indicates the wing was moving faster than the camera's shutter.

332   Williams and Newton

CHAPTER FOURTEEN
Images That Move and Sound

Our discussion of images that move — and images that move us — begins with the first creatures of the earth, or perhaps even earlier, as light and fire, wind and water moved in their own ways in their own time. As best we know, the first entities that moved of their own volition were microorganisms deep within the seas of the earth. One has only to view the exquisite flowing beauty and variety of Monterey Bay Aquarium's "Living Art" exhibit of tiny jellyfish to envision an endless array of moving beings — living images — constantly shifting the stillness of time and space.

From there, we must leap to our primary concern in this book — humans, who have worked to extend their multiple dimensions beyond body through tools of their own design since they first could think, act, and create. Today, some 6 million years later, we have yet to replicate completely the multiple, communicative capacities of the body. If a medium is anything that conveys stimuli, and if *multi* refers to more than one, then the body is the core multimedia form among living entities. One living cell, for example, can start a chain of action that can literally result in the life or death of an organism. That one living cell can replicate itself, merge with another cell, or transmit a message that will ripple throughout the body. Combined with other cells, it is part of the multimedia system of any creature, making possible the movement of chemical substances along neural pathways that ultimately result in moving parts of the body or producing aural and visual stimuli to be perceived by other creatures.

Moving Media: Transcending Time and Space

In the last chapter, we dealt with the human ability to stop time and bind space through the frames of different still media. In this chapter, we focus on moving images, again difficult to describe and categorize discretely. We first must bow to quantum physics, a field in which discoverers have led us to understand the constant activity of all things — even when they appear to be still. We necessarily move beyond physics to discuss observable action, movement that we can perceive through our eyes or other senses in space and time. This category

Figure 14.2. Jellyfish, Boston Aquarium. © iStockphoto.com/Xianstudio, llc.
Jellyfish are pulsing, moving images entire to themselves.

of the perceptible moving image then includes not only such media forms as film and television but also gesture, dance, theater, music making, digital imaging, and the basic moving properties of light and material forms.

Our bases for selecting media for this category are these:

- the object itself **may move** by its own or external power.
- or its **contents may move.**
- the object may be **two- or multidimensional.**
- the object may take **material or immaterial** form.

Vocabulary learned in discussions of still images in chapter 13 carry over into discussions of moving images, especially in terms of basic design elements and principles and basic typography and layout. We consider a number of moving image forms, apply terms and concepts from still images where appropriate, and build on that understanding by adding information that is key to the study of moving media. We discuss moving images in similar ways: formats, terms, underlying structure, strategies, and effects. We start with moving elements of earth and space, the body, and finally mass media.

The formats of the earth and the universe around us are the most basic structures of all: the spheres of planets, moons, stars, orbits; the spiral of the wobbling sun through time and space; the concentric circles created by a stone breaking the surface of a smooth lake; the line of a shooting star or comet through the sky; the arcs and peaks of ocean waves; the line of the horizon meeting the sky; the symmetry of an ovum or of a snowflake. Their motion is sometimes obvious; sometimes hidden; sometimes caused by wind or water; sometimes the result of being a growing, living thing.

Watch the patterns of leaves and branches blowing against a dusky sky or the swirling of a whirlpool at the foot of a waterfall. Heraclites said we cannot step into the same river twice. What a beautiful, amazing thought, with both literal and metaphorical implications. Sit still, holding your own body motionless for a time, and watch a river flowing by, completely unaware — and unconcerned — by your presence.

Artist Andy Goldsworthy is a master of visual commentary on the organic patterns and textures of natural land- and waterscapes. One of his works, documented in a panoramic photograph exhibited at the San Francisco Museum of Modern Art, is a cone titled "Ice left by the tide/Stacked and frozen/Worked quickly before the tide, 1999." Other works celebrate a line of poppies that "became windy" or a chain of hazel leaves "gently pulled by the river /Out of a rock pool" (Roland Collection). One gallery commentary on Goldsworthy's artistic process explained that he "works one on one with nature, using nature as both the canvas and the medium. His work is as impermanent as nature's moods; wind, sun, or rain can scatter, melt, or dissolve Goldsworthy's natural masterpieces"(Sweet Briar, npn). Goldsworthy himself said,

> Movement, change, light, growth and decay are the lifeblood of nature, the energies that I try to tap through my work. I need the shock of touch, the resistance of place, materials and weather, the earth as my source. Nature is in a state of change and that change is the key to understanding. I want my art to be sensitive and alert to changes in material, season and weather. Each work grows, stays, decays. Process and decay are implicit. Transience in my work reflects what I find in nature. (Center for Global Environmental Education, npn)

The significance of Goldsworthy's work to our current discussion lies in his sense of a transitory aesthetic, a way of perceiving the constantly changing environmental elements of the earth. We have learned through time and experience that the media of nature change: roses grow from tiny buds into full blossoms whose leaves ultimately drop to the ground, the brightness of day and the darkness of night come and go and affect our daily rhythms, rain falls and forms tiny rivers on a hillside. We accept these phenomena, yet it often takes a painting, poem, or film to call them to our attention for a few preciously aware moments. Media images, on the other hand, constantly vie for our attention, with color, sound, movement, visual effects, and words to turn our heads.

Many of us moving quickly through our time here on 21st-century Earth are caught within the pulsing stimuli of media life in a global culture. Humans living earlier in this millennium appear to have integrated the natural world in their daily lives. Consider the ancient Maya, who constructed the Caracol, an observatory in the spiral shape of a conch shell, with windows placed in relation to astronomical events. At Chichén Itzá, site of a once-thriving Mayan city in the Yucatan, people still gather to view a Mayan moving image: At the equinox, light from the sun gradually shines on stairs of a great pyramid, creating the effect of a slithering serpent.

Living a hemisphere away from Plato's metaphorical cave, the Maya created other moving images by building their own caves (a format) with openings (frames) designed to observe astrological events related to the Sun, Venus, Mars, Jupiter and Saturn. After careful study of Mayan inscriptions and astronomical phenomena, Aveni and Hotaling concluded that some structures likely "were intended to mark staged celebratory events that required the proper astronomical backdrop, such as Venus high in the sky, morning star returning toward the sun, or Jupiter in retrograde" (p. 364). The authors also suggest that "royalty may well have programmed" key dramatic events in public plazas to coincide with "major sky events" (p. 364). Was this an early form of media framing intended to enhance public association of royalty with the power of the gods? The Maya developed a sophisticated culture, including an accurate annual calendar and a written language, dating from about 2600 BCE. Six million Mayan people continue cultural traditions today.

Consider also the fact that archeologists now realize the remarkable images painted on cave walls some 30,000 years ago could only be seen by natural light entering openings in the cave or via torches stationed near by or carried along the cave path, or by the flickering flames of firelight, which would be joined by the shadows of people and animals. Either source provided its own shifting aesthetic of movement to viewing the images.

The Body as Moving Image

One of the first moving media forms was the body itself. Facial expressions and gestures express 80 to 90% of the message when humans communicate face to face. The fluidity of some facial expressions can be so subtle that they are not consciously detected in day-to-day conversation. Yet, like the subtle

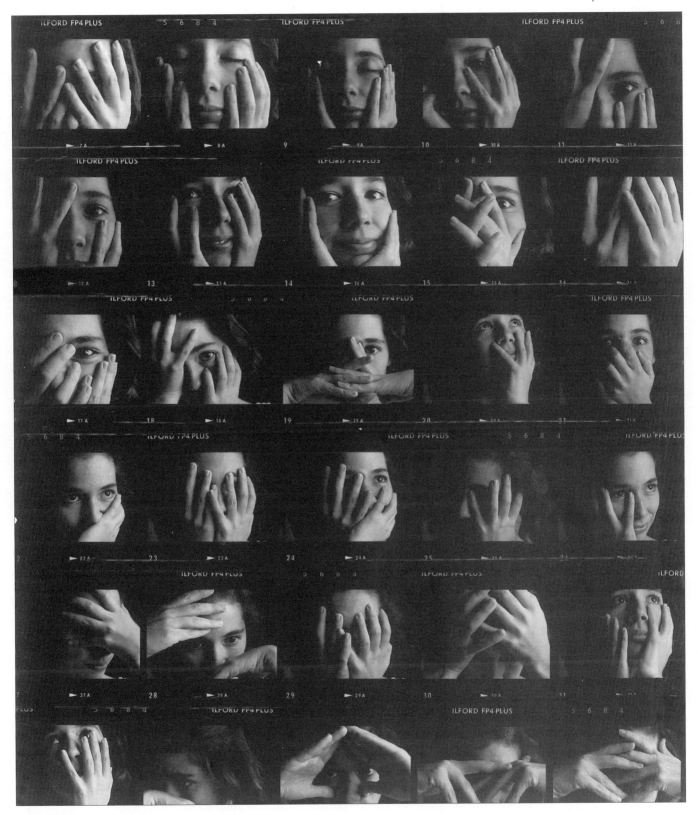

Figure 14.3. Self-Portrait Series, photographs and contact sheet made with 8x10 enlarger by Kristine Wolf.

Figure 14.4. Dancing at Lane, by Rick Williams.

intonations of voice, the minute movements of face and body can communicate so powerfully and quickly that another person will alter his response instantaneously.

Think also about how you visually recognize someone you know well from afar. Before you can make out his facial features and details of his body, you can pick him out quickly from among a group of people by his movements, by the way he carries his body, gestures, and gait. Add to those almost subliminal communications from another person the more overt signs, such as clothing and hair, which they use to distinguish themselves (or not) from others. As mentioned in the previous chapter, archeologists now believe they have evidence that our ancestors ground natural materials such as ochre to make a powder they could use to decorate their bodies as early as 350,000 years ago. We still enjoy donning elaborate costumes for theatrical, dance, or operatic performances, and tattooing and body piercing have become more popular than ever.

These human media forms emphasize the point that media do not have to take the forms of mass news or entertainment. Our bodies also are media through which we visually communicate our sense of self, our moods, feelings, needs, and desires. Media are not entities without connection to human organisms. Media of all kinds have roots in the organic processing of human rational and intuitive thought, as well as in human action — that is how media come to be. An us/them mentality about mass media disconnects us from sources of media, which begin with people. We create media. We use them. We pay for them. We choose them. But we need to fully understand media on rational and intuitive levels to create, choose, and use them appropriately and in ways that bring a healthy balance to our lives.

The ultimate extension of the idea of body as medium may well be cosmetic surgery. Brought to popular culture via the premier in 2004 of such television programs as *The Swan,* a production chronicling what is, in essence, a redesign of 16 self-described ugly ducklings into swans. After 3 months of cosmetic surgery, dental work, dieting, exercise, and self-esteem therapy, each redesigned woman emerged to compete for a spot in a beauty pageant, at which one woman would be crowned The Swan.

French artist Orlan puts a different twist on body as medium (see Figure 15.28). She has for years videotaped performances of a surgeon physically altering her facial structure: "I can observe my own body cut open, without suffering!," Orlan said in her "Carnal Art Manifesto." "I see myself all the way down to my entrails; a new mirror stage" (npn).

Ultrasound has been recording the movements of fetuses in the womb for some time, and physicians regularly use endoscopy, colonoscopy, and other specific techniques to diagnose medical problems they could not detect otherwise. Medical technologies using tiny video cameras extending increasingly high-quality probing eyes into the body. One of the latest inventions is a wireless color video camera that is placed in a capsule and swallowed by the patient so examiners can study "video capsule movies" to detect disease (Sadovsky).

Beyond the body, early moving media included horses for carrying people and mules for carrying objects, then wagons, then cars and trucks, airplanes, space shuttles, and robotized space probes. Recent probes have beamed back images of new planets and solar systems, extending our perspective on the earth and the place of humans in the universe. And — though we forget they are there — surveillance satellites orbiting the earth have cameras so powerful that they can read the newspaper over your shoulder. In fact, Chicago plans to use motion-sensing software and 2,000 remote-control cameras throughout the city to watch for suspicious activity. As Chicago Mayor Richard Daley said, "Cameras are the equivalent of hundreds of sets of eyes. They are the next best thing to having police officers stationed at every potential trouble spot" (Howlett, npn).

All of these media extend the body beyond its physical time and space. As McLuhan suggested, they help us create a "global village" by extending ourselves to places far away and by bringing the sights and sounds and experiences of those places home to us. Whether those experiences are generated in the Middle East or in an advertising agency or TV studio in New York, media machines we have created extend and link our bodies to real and virtual times and spaces. We have learned how to make machine media produce images that are as real to us as bodily experiences. In fact, we extend our bodily experiences through the very media we have created. When we add motion and sound to media images, we enhance the likelihood that we will experience those images the way we experience real life.

Technological History

Although scholars still disagree about whether human symbolic communication originated through gesture or through verbal language, a bit of history about the development of the moving image technologies will help explain how these technologies have integrated such elements as gesture, voice, and light into the sophisticated mass media that affect our perceptions of what is real, important, and normal. We discussed the development of written language, paper, print publications, photography, and art forms in previous chapters. Now we discuss a few highlights about the development of moving image technologies as a basis for understanding how and why we engage respond deeply to forms of moving images.

Among the earliest forms of moving images created by humans were "intricately perforated and painted" leather shadow puppets. These were lit from behind, manipulated by rods, and viewed through a translucent screen (National Museum of Photography, Film & Television, para. 4). Historians often cite a 17th-century device known as a *magic lantern* as the earliest slide projector. In one tabletop mechanism, glass slides were mounted on a circular disk, then turned in front of a light to give the illusion of movement. By the late 18th century, more complicated setups entertained audiences looking through a large rectangular window onto painted scenes moved with pulleys and enhanced with lighting and sound effects. Called the Eidophusikon and described as "Moving Pictures, representing Phenomena of Nature," the open-

Figure 14.5. Early Javanese shadow puppet.
Photograph by Julianne Newton.

Figure 14.6. The Eidophusikon of Phillippe-Jacques de Loutherbourg, ca. 1782, watercolor by Edward Francis Burney (original in color). © The Trustees of the British Museum.

ing season featuring a sunrise, as well as a storm and shipwreck (Yale, 2005, para. 2). Burney's watercolor of the Eidophusikon in Figure 14.6 illustrates a production of Milton's *Paradise Lost*. "The scene depicted Satan arraying his troops on the banks of the fiery lake, with the rising of Pandemonium" (Yale, 2005, para. 3).

During the early 19th century, Daguerre, whom we discussed in chapter 10 in relation to the invention of photography, developed these techniques into the diorama — complete with a revolving floor, three stages, and huge rectangular canvases. The canvases were painted with scenes on both sides that appeared to dissolve into one another through the manipulation of light. "Parisians were treated to the sight of an Alpine village before and after an avalanche, or

Figure 14.7. Chronophotograph made on moving film consisting of twelve frames showing a cat falling, by Étienne-Jules Marey, 1893. National Museum of Photography/Science and Society Picture Library.

Midnight Mass from inside and outside the cathedral, accompanied by candles and the smell of incense," wrote contemporary historian Adatto (p. 7).

Optical toys such as the kaleidoscope and the thaumatrope, a painted double-sided disk controlled with strings, entertained viewers with moving images. Others experimented with point of view, even hauling large cameras into balloons to photograph cities from above. Nadar (Gaspard Félix Tournachon), who made the first photograph from a balloon in 1853, was among a number of photographers and scientists exploring the idea of motion by combining a series of still images. Nadar made portraits of himself rotating from back to front and back again (Lucassen, 2004).

One of the most significant investigators of movement in the 19th century was Étienne-Jules Marey, a French physician whose early studies, which included tracking the movement of blood through the body and the movement of the heart muscle, led him to invent and improve tools for tracking and recording motion. Marey advanced development of the sphygmographe, an instrument for recording the pulse. He also invented a method for visually tracing the beating of an insect's wing and for optically tracking the flight of a wasp in a figure eight. And he

Williams and Newton

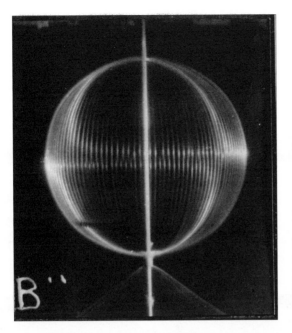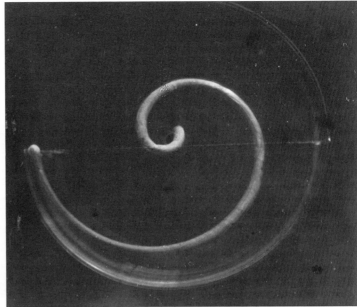

Figures 14.9-10. Geométrie 1 and 2, Figure géométrique engendrée par vibration, chronophotographie sur plaque fixe, vers 1890, Etienne-Jules Marey, Musée Marey-Beaune. © J. Cl. Couvals.

advanced chronophotography, a method for recording moments of movement on one surface. "Once he had explained the internal movements of the body," wrote historians Mannoni and Rollet, "Marey extended his investigations to the motion of the body as a whole: a walking human being, a flying dragonfly, a swimming ray, a falling cat. . . . Tireless, this brilliant visionary stopped the passage of time, accelerated it, slowed it down to 'see the invisible,' and re-created life through images and machines" (npn). Marey also experimented with traces of human motion; the movement of smoke; and geometric forms achieved with black backgrounds, light, points, lines, and curves.

Marey's observations of motion led him to theorize in an 1873 book that a galloping horse lifted all four hooves off the ground at the same time. Although scholars challenged his theory, a former governor of California, Leland Stanford, hired photographer

Figure 14.8. Saut de l'homme en blanc (The man doing the broad jump), chronophotographie sur plaque fixe, vers 1887, Étienne-Jules Marey, Musée Marey-Beaune. © J. Cl. Couval.

Figure 14.11. The Transverse-Gallop: one stride. From Animals in Motion. Photograph, 1887, by Eadweard Muybridge. Image Select / Art Resource, NY.

Leland Stanford, hired photographer Eadweard Muybridge to test the idea. In a form of not-so-instant replay, Muybridge set up an elaborate 12-camera system to produce the images that made the theory fact (see Figure 14.11). Marey and Muybridge later met and collaborated on their studies of motion and uses of multiple cameras and lenses.

Basic Elements of Moving Images

Now let's take a look at the basics of producing and interpreting moving images as we work through key issues regarding contemporary film and video. Noting that content is fundamental, media scholar Herb Zettl believes the aesthetic that create and structure meaning in moving image messages. "Because the process of clarification, intensification, and interpretation of events is based on selection and a specific use of aesthetic elements, the recipient's perceptions are indirectly and, more often, directly manipulated," Zettl wrote (p. 15).

Zettl identified five aesthetic image elements of video and film:

1) light and color
2) two-dimensional space
3) three-dimensional space
4) time/motion
5) sound

You may want to review the discussion of light and color, as well as the basic visual elements and principles of design outlined in chapters 10 and 11, before moving on in this section. The discussion that follows builds on those discussions.

And what does sound have to do with images that move? Not much, if you're watching the gentle dance of jellyfish through an aquarium frame. But a lot, if you're watching film and video. Hearing is based on the physical movement of soundwaves, which ears sense and translate into electrical signals for your brain to interpret. Sound accompanying images — even a series of still photographs — can dramatically alter the way we interpret the meaning of the images and the way the images affect us.

Light and Color

Although light is defined as the visible part of the electromagnetic spectrum, what we usually see is the result of light being reflected from a surface or transmitted through something. This is especially important for understanding the use of lighting equipment, whether in still photography, film, video. As Zettl said, "Lighting is the deliberate control of light and shadows" (p. 20). Refer back to the section on "Photography and Light" in Chapter 10 for basic information on contrast, direction, and color. Two additional terms especially useful in film and video work are *chiaroscuro* lighting, which uses dramatic contrast of light and shadows to enhance visual appeal, and *flat* lighting, which seeks to produce even tones with minimal shadows to enhance visibility.

Television cameras and some digital cameras must be adjusted to the light in a shooting situation. This is called *white balancing*, a process in which you give the camera a reference for a *true white* in the lighting environment in which you are working. Although some video cameras have an automatic white-balance function, professional video cameras usually have manual white-balance buttons. Balance is achieved by filling about 80% of the viewing frame with a true-white subject, such as a white card, setting appropriate exposure and focus, and activating the white-balance function on your camera. Your color television set or computer monitor also vary according to different standards for color temperature.

Two-Dimensional Space

Television and film images are defined by screen space, the horizontal and vertical frame surrounding the area on which images are projected. Screen space is determined by aspect ratio, the relationship of the width of the screen to the height. Remember that in still images, the frame has variable shape, size, and direction (see chapter 13). Television and film screens typically are manufactured with a horizontal orientation, which, as Zettl noted, is similar to the human view of the world. Traditional film and television screens use a 4:3 aspect ratio, or 4 units wide to 3 units high. Film has widened the horizontal dimension, shifting the aspect ratio more dramatically toward a wide format. High-definition television compromises with wider-screen film formats by using a 16:9 aspect ratio. The differences affect not only the viewing of wide-screen films on television sets but also the ways in which camera angles portray content within the frame, particularly with close-ups and environmental shots.

Other factors about the screen directly relate to many of the things you learned about basic design and still images. The moving content within the frame often gives the effect of magnifying principles of the gestalt. Visual vectors, for example, take on increased visual power through camera movement. Figure/ground principles can be shifted for dramatic effects.

Three-Dimensional Space

Those who work with film and video have created a number of techniques for giving the illusion of extending the frame of the screen beyond two dimensions. One technique is to portray people as if they are looking outside the

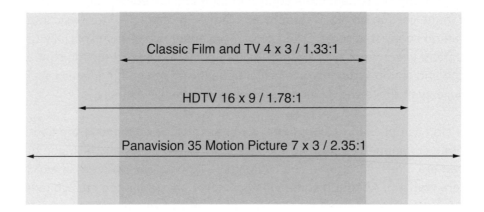

Figure 14.12. Three common screen aspect ratios expressed in two ways.
Illustration by Janet Halvorsen.

screen. When images from multiple cameras are edited together, this can give the viewer the impression that he is looking at more than one dimension.

Another technique is working with *z* axis vectors, achieved by giving the viewer the sense that she is looking directly toward or directly away from the camera. To envision the *z* axis, think about the *x* axis as the horizontal dimension or width of the screen, and the *y* axis as the vertical dimension or height of the screen. The *z* axis identifies the illusion of depth, typically giving us the sense that we are perceiving visual elements moving away from the screen, yet within the two-dimensional plane of the screen. This is a similar effect to the techniques of drawing linear perspective within a two-dimensional frame. The effects of moving the camera above or below the subject area; changing the angle of view (or focal length) of the lenses used; overlapping or layering of visual elements and type in figure-ground combinations through use of foreground, middle ground, and background; and including frames within frames are all intensified when the camera and lens are recording stimuli in motion, rather than completely stopping time and space within the frame. Critical in moving image production, however, is to control the placement of visual elements along the *z* axis, a process called *blocking*.

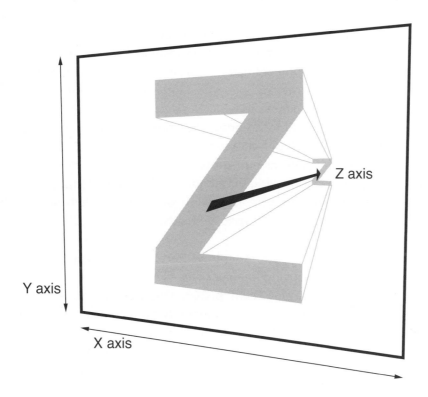

Figure 14.13. The illusion of a third dimension, called the Z axis, is achieved in film and television by recording motion toward or away from the viewer. Illustration by Janet Halvorsen.

Along with the challenges of portraying long periods of time through construction and editing of moving images, come complex decisions about the variety of ways moving images can show us the world. Establishing an effective narrative with film and video techniques can require careful visualization of scenes through multiple still frames or drawings, a process called *story-boarding*. Zettl wrote,

> We do not know what time is. All we really know is how to experience time in the form of duration, recurring phenomena, cycles, rhythm, and motion. We can measure it. We live, love, have children, suffer, and die with it and through it, but we do not exactly know what it is. . . . The philosopher gives us one set of answers, the physicist another. . . . Artists may be concerned only with the aspect of time that best suits them in their quest to clarify and intensify experience within a specific medium." (p. 225)

As we noted in chapters 10 and 11, photographers, designers and other visual artists can give the sense of stopping time by using a fast shutter speed to freeze action or by drawing a specific pose and expression. With moving images, however, time passes as the viewer watches. Whether it is a 15-second television commercial or a 3-hour movie, the image demands the viewer's attention for a particular length of time to be perceived. Zettl distinguished among objective time, which he defined as measurable, clock time; subjective time, or felt, psychological time; and biological time, a kind of internal clock that regulates behavior. The degree to which an event or production involves us in these different kinds of time via projected images, whether live or recorded, is determined not only by content but also by the structure of the medium and the artists' production choices and knowledge of the power of media. Production techniques for conveying time and motion include lengths of shots and scenes, pacing and rhythm, camera motion and zooms, cuts from one shot to another, dissolves and fades, and special effects.

Establishing *continuity* through attention to vectors, camera placement, and color during the editing of moving images helps viewers make sense of what they see through mental mapping (Zettl, p. 285). One way to maintain continuity through camera placement and subsequent editing is to establish an index vector following the converging lines of sight of individuals in the scene. This vector line is variously called the *180-degree rule*, the *line of conversion or action*, or *the line*. Figure 14.16 illustrates appropriate placement of three cameras in relation to the index vector established by two individuals. Figure 14.15 illustrates potential visual effects achieved when following the 180-degree guideline properly and improperly.

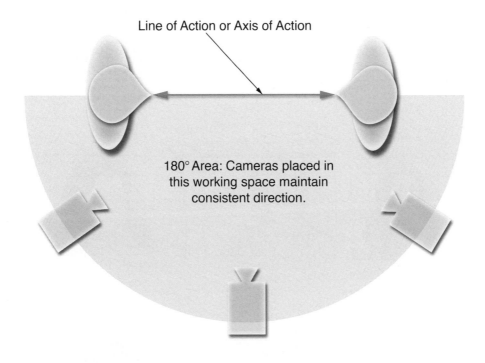

Line of Action or Axis of Action

180° Area: Cameras placed in this working space maintain consistent direction.

Figure 14.14. The index vector line or 180-Degree Rule. Illustration by Janet Halvorsen.

Complexity editing, on the other hand, uses such techniques as montage, through which separate images are juxtaposed to intensify the communication and evoke viewer emotion. Complexity editing might cut quickly from an image of a china-and-silver-embellished dining table loaded with luscious foods to one of a bare wooden tabletop bearing a loaf of bread to contrast wealth and poverty — or ostentation with simple elegance, depending on visual details, narrative context, and point of view.

Film and video convey motion through an illusionary phenomenon of human perception called stroboscopic or apparent motion. Early theorists believed the phenomenon, which results in our perceiving the content of multiple, rapidly moving but separate image frames as movement, was the result of an after-image being burned into the retina. Though we still do not have a definitive description of the phenomenon, contemporary theorists believe the brain does not differentiate the gaps "between the film's frames" (p. 17). In other words, we perceive "an illusion of apparent movement," which is known as the *phi phenomenon* (Winston, p. 17). When Gestalt theorists produced the illusion of movement by flashing "side-by-side light sources . . . at a particular interval" (Zettl, personal communication), they evolved the foundation for their ideas:

ECU Henry

CU Sophia

CU Henry

MCU Sophia

2 SHOT Henry & Sophia

2 SHOT Henry & Sophia

MCU Sophia

CU Henry

CU Sophia

ECU Henry

2 SHOT Henry & Sophia

MCU Sophia

CU Henry

CU Sophia

ECU Henry

Figures 14.15. Top: Attending to the line of action so viewers can easily follow cuts from one person to another. Middle: An appropriate continuation of the sequence, adhering to the 180-degree rule. Bottom: Violating the 180-degree rule — note that in the final frame at right, Henry faces away from Sophia rather than toward her. In this series, the scene moves inductively from the specific closeup of Henry through the general medium shot of Henry and Sophia together. Scenes also can progress deductively from the general to the specific. Illustration by Janet Halvorsen.

"that the key to perception lay in relationship — in something different from what is found in separate sensations" (Barry, pp. 43–44). Today's films show us 24 still frames every single second. Because of the phi phenomenon the brain perceives these frames as moving images.

Television, on the other hand, is created by electron beams that are constantly changing. "Because the mosaiclike dots of the color television screen light up only temporarily and change their brightness according to how hard they are hit by the electron beams, the television image is never complete. While some of the screen dots are lighting up, others are already decaying," Zettl wrote (p.

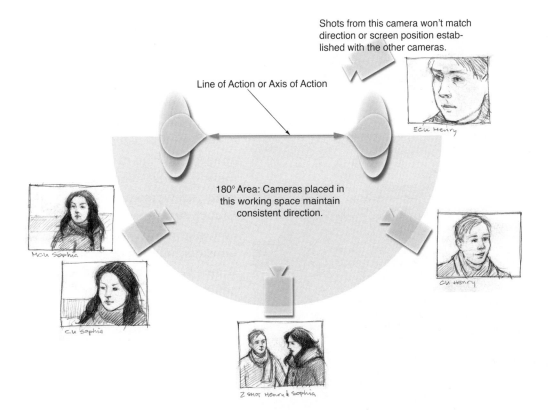

Shots from this camera won't match direction or screen position established with the other cameras.

Line of Action or Axis of Action

180° Area: Cameras placed in this working space maintain consistent direction.

ECU Henry

CU Henry

MCU Sophia

CU Sophia

2 shot Henry & Sophia

Figure 14.16. Diagram of appropriate camera placement, as well as inappropriate camera placement for one closeup of Henry (upper right). Illustration by Janet Halvorsen.

230). The complete television frame is created as the electron beams scan two fields of alternating lines that interlace in a constant, repeated pattern on the screen. Liquid crystal displays (LCDs) and plasma displays operate by activating many pixels with an electric charge or ultraviolet light. As a result, they display a "relatively stable picture" until "something moves," when "the various dots light up and decay in rapid order similar to that of the television image."

In all cases, the size of the frame — the screen — affects the way we perceive the images. Screen size not only affects the intensity of our responses, affecting our attention, arousal and memory but also influences how real we perceive the image content to be (Grabe, Lombard, Reich, Bracken, and Ditton). The larger the screen, the more real the images seem to us (Aiken & Bracken).

We also have learned that such aesthetic effects as slow motion, achieved by increasing the number of frames per second in film but decreasing the number of frames scanned in television, affect our judgment of image content. A controlled experiment measuring viewer response to slow motion and standard

Figure 14.17. Cover of The Daily Show host Jon Stewart's book America. Cover design by Pentagram. Courtesy of D. J. Stout.

speed news footage indicated three findings: a) viewers are more likely to blame suspects shown in slow motion than those shown in standard speed motion; b) slow motion video makes news stories seem less fair, less informative, and more sensational; and c) slow motion video magnifies already negative news stories, making viewer experiences of bad news feel worse (Barnett & Grabe). And remember: Perceptions affect behavior. Consider the case of Rodney King, whose beating by Los Angeles police was videotaped by a civilian who happened to witness King's arrest. Watching the videotape in real time, or as it actually unfolded, leaves little doubt about the viciousness of the beating. Yet when prosecutors slowed down the video and froze frames for jurors during the trial, a different perception of the event resulted, one which probably contributed to the verdict of an acquittal for the police officers who were charged with the beating.

Sound

Sound communicates on both rational and intuitive levels. Voice, for example, uses pacing, tone, and inflection to create mental images and draw on memories in the mind's eye. In addition to voice, music and sound intensify the perceptual experience of visual stimuli, enhancing both the emotional involvement and the visual imagination of the viewer/listener. Music also can bring structure to what otherwise might appear to be unrelated visual images.

Zettl distinguished sound from noise: although both "are audible vibrations (oscillations) of the air or other material," sound is purposefully organized, and noise is random (p. 327). Early films were made before including recorded sound was technologically possible. The result was a form of acting that exaggerated gesture to emphasize the intention of the visual communication. Live musicians in an orchestra pit below the screen stage played complex scores composed specifically to "supply a rhythm to the loosely sequenced visual images" and to enhance emotional response (Zettl, personal communication). If you've not experienced this unique phenomenon, we recommend it. Hearing and sensing the presence of live musicians interacting with visuals through the cues of a gesturing director adds a degree of spontaneous energy that shifts the entire perception. Early filmmakers even considered sound detrimental to the visual communication and artistic creation of a film. Even today, the audio component of a film is handled separately and merged during the final edit.

Television, on the other hand, quickly established the practice of simultaneously recording, processing, and broadcasting sound and images. This critical technological difference underlies our perception of the medium of film as primarily *visual* and the medium of television as *audiovisual*. Such technological advances as surround sound and large-screen film — balanced to some extent by high-definition video, larger screens, and high-definition audio in television — have increased attention to sound quality in both media.
Interestingly, sound has its own form of semiotics, carrying meaning through audio signifiers. For example, literal sounds, also called *diegetic sounds*, refer to specific sources, such as conversation, vehicles, and nature. Nonliteral sounds, called *nondiegetic sounds*, are not connected with a specific, identifiable source. These are used to convey the energy of a scene and to evoke feelings in the viewer. Examples of nondiegetic sounds are music and sound effects.

Sound has five basic elements:

1. **pitch** — the frequency, or vibrations per second, of a sound indicated through highness or lowness relative to an agreed-upon scale
2. **timbre** — tone quality or color of a sound, created through overtones, which are frequencies vibrating in addition to a particular pitch
3. **duration** — how long the sound lasts
4. **loudness** — the dynamic strength of a sound
5. **attack/decay** — how fast a sound rises to a level of loudness (attack or crescendo), how long the level is sustained, and how fast the level declines (decay or diminuendo). The sound envelope refers to the entire process of attack, duration, decay, and final release.

Zettl stressed the importance of matching the historical/geographical, thematic, tonal, and structural effects of both pictures and sounds to create a reinforcing, synergistic communication.

This overview of technical aspects introduces principal terms and concepts you can use for analysis and to begin creating your own moving media. To deepen your understanding, we suggest you study a key resource such as Zettl's *Sight, Sound, Motion*. To really learn, you must do.

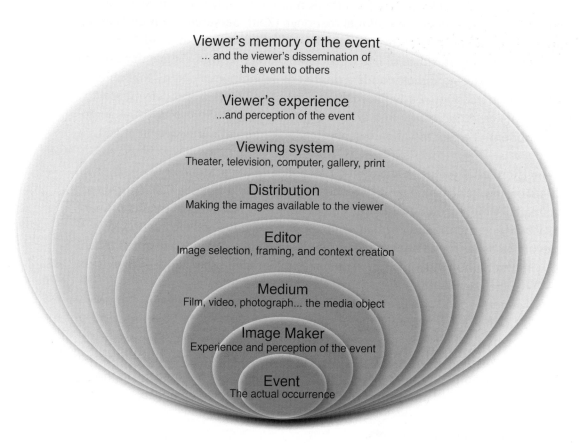

Viewer's memory of the event
... and the viewer's dissemination of
the event to others

Viewer's experience
...and perception of the event

Viewing system
Theater, television, computer, gallery, print

Distribution
Making the images available to the viewer

Editor
Image selection, framing, and context creation

Medium
Film, video, photograph... the media object

Image Maker
Experience and perception of the event

Event
The actual occurrence

Figure 14.18. Levels of understanding an event. Illustration by Jan Halvorsen, adapted from Zettl (1973).

Returning to Content

It should be clear to you at this point that the technical and aesthetic characteristics of moving media forms convey content in ways that both parallel and exceed the techniques of still media. They accomplish this through conventions of communication that have become "our air," or that are so familiar to us that we do not notice how they operate — or even that they are operating. We perceive their communication through intuitive processing using visual, aural, bodily kinesthetic, and psychological intelligences.

At the same time, what the media convey through these means has a level of content directly related to the purposeful communication of ideas. We perceive some of these ideas through attention to a story or narrative, to violent or sexual behavior, to humorous or tragic experiences, or through informative, entertaining, and artistic formats. A great deal of scholarly and popular literature about media, whether still or moving, focuses on rational critique and deconstruction of manifest content (denotative meaning) and latent motivations (connotative meaning). We have tried to focus attention on the inherent properties of particular media — characteristics that operate through intuitive communication.

This communication occurs through continual shifts in our perceptions, a moving aesthetic in constant flux, dynamically affecting us, as we create and affect it. Figure 14.17 is one way to envision the filters through which a report of even the simplest event must pass on its way to becoming part of your memory. We talk more about this shifting aesthetic and about new media in chapters 15 and 16.

Especially significant are moving media whose overt function is to report reality — information about local and world events that we call *news*. Each medium has its own way of packaging news for dissemination in mass form. Broadcast news historically has been viewed as a credible source of immediate information about breaking and ongoing events. Increasingly blurred boundaries between news and entertainment media, accentuated by economic pressures to maintain large audiences, underscore the challenges of communicating actual occurrences. Cinema scholar Bill Nichols described the problem well:

> Inevitably, the distinction between fact and fiction blurs when claims about reality get cast as narratives. We enter a zone where the world put before us lies between one not our own and one that very well might be between a world we may recognize as a fragment of our own and one that may seem fabricated from such fragments, between indexical (authentic) signs of reality and cinematic (invented) interpretations of this reality....Studies offer structure; they organize and order the flux of events; they confer meaning and value. But stories are not a phenomenon occurring naturally. They are themselves a product of history and culture....The occurrence does not announce its own beginning or end, its predecessors or consequences, its implications or significance. Only those who look back upon it can provide such things, and inevitably, more than one tale can be told for any one occurrence" (p. *ix*).

When television news workers use archived video from past events to illustrate new events and hold viewers' attention, they cross a reality line that is even more significant than the 180-degree line of action. The nonconscious mind of the viewer does not stop to consider whether the moving images on the screen actually relate to the words the anchor reads. The nonconscious mind perceives and stores the images as if they are current and real.

Television producers monitor research about viewer attention and memory to determine effective advertising and entertainment programming. The informed viewer should do the same. With as many as 30 billion cumulative viewers taking in such events as the 2006 World Cup (Roxborough), the stakes are high. Not only is economic profit at stake but also the perceptions and behavior of people across the globe.

More than 160 years ago, Alexis de Tocqueville wrote in his *Democracy in America*, "Nothing but a newspaper can drop the same thought into a thousand minds at the same moment."

What would de Tocqueville say now?

Figure 14.19. Watching television in the 1950s. NMPFT/Daily Herald Archive.
A coin-operated television receiver was displayed for the first time in New York City in 1946,
and this was also the first time that most people viewing it had seen a television.
This photograph was probably taken in the early 1940s or early 1950s in order to promote
television use in Britain. © Science and Society Picture Library.

Figure C14.1. Scene storyboard, by Colin Elliot. Can you guess the film Colin analyzed?

CREATIVE FOURTEEN
Film Clip Analysis

The Goal: Understanding How Moving Images Communicate

Creative 14 is designed to extend your understanding of basic design elements and principles from still images to moving images. The idea is to watch a film and analyze a scene in rational and intuitive ways.

How to Begin

1. *Choose and view a film.* You may select any kind of film you wish as long as you can replay the film at will. Watch the entire film, looking at the images and letting your eyes, mind, and heart wander around and through the movie.

2. *Write a summary of the overall film.* A brief paragraph of four to five lines will be sufficient. Do not, however, copy a synopsis from the Internet.

3. *After at least 24 hours, watch the movie again, this time taking notes.* Start and stop the video as needed, replaying scenes to make notes. Describe:

- direction, contrast, and feel of the light in various settings
- how lines, curves, and basic design elements help or hinder your eye movement
- camera movement and cuts from one image to another
- how the range of tones and colors affects your feelings
- how the images in different scenes make you feel (for example, do they draw you in or make you feel afraid?)
- how the music and dialogue affect you at different times in the movie
- how close-ups and wide shots are used
- how scene settings are communicated.

4. *From the movie, select one scene on which to concentrate.* The best way to do this is simply to think of what moment in the film first comes to your mind

when you think about the film. For example, if the film is *Fight Club*, you might select the scene when the skyscrapers collapse. Select a manageable moment from the film: a short, containable fraction of time that can be broken down into a few key visual frames for you to draw and study.

5. *Briefly describe the scene in words.*

6. *Pause to relax and shift into a creative mode.*

7. *Sketch a storyboard of the key images/concepts in that scene.* As with drawing thumbnails of advertisements, drawing a storyboard will help you analyze the film scene. Doing this from memory is the easiest way to help you isolate the critical frames. Draw six to eight panels that communicate the essential moments of the scene. Drawing in stick figures is fine as long as they convey the key visual communication moments of the scene.

8. *Briefly describe and analyze visual techniques used in the scene.* Refer to chapter 14 to help you recall and select techniques to discuss. Write several lines about how each of Zettl's five basic aesthetic elements (light and color, two-dimensional space, three-dimensional space, time/motion, and sound) is applied in the scene. Address how the elements help communicate the content of the scene within the context of the overall film.

9. *Begin a Personal Impact Assessment of the scene.* Analyze the scene as you did the ad for Creative 13.

> *List Primary Words:* List significant parts of the scene on a clean sheet of paper, leaving two or three lines between the words. Each significant part should be described by a single word. Examples of significant parts are people, places, things, colors/tones, and feelings. List the words in one or two columns on the page, leaving two or three spaces between each word.

> *List Associative Words:* Go back over the list. For each primary term, list other words the primary term makes you think of (associative words). Look at each original descriptive term — the parts of the scene — you have written, one at a time. Start with the first term and, in a circle around that term, write other words (word associations that come into your mind as you think about the first word). Finish all of the associations for the first word before you move on to the second, and so forth.

> *Select the Most Significant Associative Words:* When you have completed the list of word associations, go back over the list again and intuitively select and circle (or underline) a key asso-

ciative word for each of the original terms. Again, start with the first descriptive word and its associative words and go down the list. As you go back through the list, mull over the associative words in your mind. Try to intuit which is the most significant associative word for each original term and draw a circle around it. Do not overthink this; simply say the associative words to yourself until one seems most significant. Do this for each group of associative words you have listed, one at a time. There are no right or wrong answers. Simply pick the word that seems most appropriate to you as you read the words.

List the Most Significant Associative Words: On a clean sheet of paper, list the circled or underlined associative words in a column in the order in which they appear in the first list.

Relate Associative Words to an Inner Part of Yourself: On the same sheet of paper, make a second column in which you write a word that stands for a part of your inner self. Look at each word in the "significant word association" list and consider what part of your inner self that word represents. Write that part of yourself to the right of the "significant word association." To determine the inner parts of yourself, it may be helpful to say "my _____ self" (for example, my "vulnerable self," my "trusting self," my "fantasy self").

•*Review the Inner Symbols*: Go back over the two columns looking for related themes, feelings, and concepts. Look over these symbols of your inner self and see if there is some clear connection that arises about yourself from the interaction of the symbols from the scene. This story, connection, or meaning will often come to you in a flash or in an "ah-haaa" response. It will often represent the inner conflicts or emotions or feelings that are behind your attraction to the scene. Consider how the connections among these symbols offer insights about your own life relative to the scene.

•*Write the Story/Interpretation:* On a new page, write what this means to you. Write down the story or connection and see how it applies to your attraction to the moving images or how it offers insight about your own life.

10. *Evaluate your experience.* Reflect on your experiences completing the exercise and write an assessment of them. How did the exercise help you understand techniques, terms, and ideas about moving images. Explain how you can use what you learned to enhance self-awareness.

The Exercise

- Read the instructions carefully
- Choose and view a film. Write a synopsis of the film.
- After at least 24 hours, watch the movie again, taking notes this time.
- Select one scene from the movie and briefly describe the scene in words.
- Pause for a while to relax and shift into a creative mode.
- Sketch a storyboard of the scene (six to eight panels).
- Describe how Zettl's five basic aesthetic elements are used in the scene and how they help communicate the content of the scene and the film.
- Do a Personal Impact Assessment of the scene.
- Write an assessment about your experiences completing the exercise.

Figure C14.2. PIA Parts 2-4, by Colin Elliot.

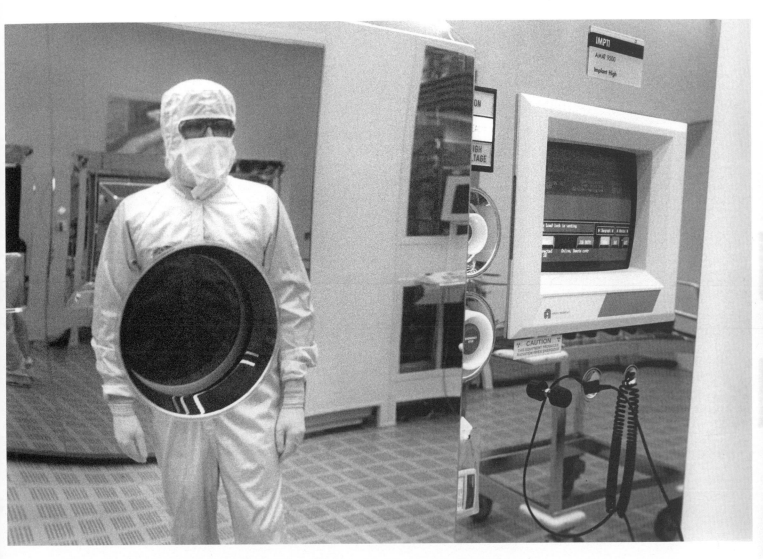

Figure C14.3. Ion Implanter, Applied Materials clean room. Photograph by Rick Williams.

Figures 15.1-2. Brighton Boat, by Jeremy Wood (original in color). Location: Brighton and Hove, East Sussex, UK. Created by riding a bicycle 67.7 km and using Global Positioning System (GPS) Drawing. Wood and Hugh Pryor have developed the new form of drawing, which uses satellite navigation technology, by "treating travel like a geodetic pencil or a cartographic crayon." They use GPS receivers to track their journeys.

CHAPTER FIFTEEN
Living at the Speed of Mind:
Old Media–New Media

Student: Oh, Professor McLuhan, I have the perfect title
  for this show!
McLuhan: What is it?
Student: Learning to live at the speed of light!
McLuhan: Oh no! No! No! That's too slow!
Student: What do you mean?
McLuhan: It's learning to live at the speed of the mind!
  It's the speed of the mind that counts.

So went a scenario at the University of California at Irvine between Marshall McLuhan and a student excited about the possibility of a new student television show (© Matie Molinaro, personal communication, June 7, 2004).

The conversation took place more than 25 years ago. McLuhan would be able to say, "I told you so," were he still living today.

Science has advanced our understanding of the brain a great deal, particularly in the last 20 years. We even know that the speed of mind operates on a scale of milliseconds — in other words, mental speed is measured in thousandths of a second. In fact, it takes 300 milliseconds longer for a signal to travel from the thalamus and to the neocortex than to reach the amygdala, where an emotional response is generated. The brain works so fast that 300 milliseconds is enough time for the amygdala to synthesize that information and generate a response before the rational brain receives the signal.

Researchers are now harnessing this knowledge to create new forms of media systems that use electrical impulses of the brain to move devices outside the body. The systems work by translating brain signals from either an internal sensor implant the size of a baby aspirin or a conductive skull screw that records surface signals into such actions as moving a cursor on a computer screen. Neurobiologists hope their work training rhesus monkeys to control

Figures 15.3-5. To left: To celebrate its 20th anniversary in 2001, the Chaos Computer Club turned the "Haus des Lehrers" (house of the teacher) office building at Berlin Alexanderplatz into a giant interactive computer display. Called Project Blinkenlights, organizers arranged 144 computer-controlled lamps in the windows to produce a "matrix of 18 times 8 pixels." Mobile phone users could play Pong and display loveletters on the building. Photograph by Dorit Günter and Nadja Hannaske. Top middle: How the building looked in the context of the city. Photograph by Tim Pritlove. Top right: In fall 2002, the group transformed Tower T2 of the Biliothéque Nationale de France into a matrix of 20 x 26 windows displaying computer games, pictures, and animations. Photograph by Dorit Günter and Nadja Hannaske.

robotic arms with their thought signals will work with humans. One study recently approved by the U.S. Federal Drug Administration is testing the system with five quadriplegics (Warner).

So much is happening in all the fields related to visual communication that each day seems to bring news of a discovery. Consider these examples:

— Within a decade, you will be able to wear a tie-clip-sized personal life recorder (PLR) containing a microphone and camera lens to record everything you do 24/7 (Maney). Using magnetic random access memory (MRAM), the device is based on controlling and reading the spin of electrons.

— Project Blinkenlights created a giant public message board and interactive display by using a computer to control lamps in eight floors of windows in a Berlin building. People used their mobile phones to play Pong and send love letters via the building. The building display produced images through a matrix of blinking windows equivalent to 18 times 8 pixels (window-sized).

— A new type of video game, *The Sims 2* from Electronic Arts, allows players to develop relationships with characters whose behavior emerges in an unscripted fashion, based on their own artificial intelligence and histories.

— Due in part to new technology, the U.S. softball team won its third straight gold medal in the 2004 Olympics with "an almost flawless romp" that was "just a blink from perfection" (Associated Press). Mike Bonaventura, a Chicago physician, developed equipment to train the players' eyes to see speeding softballs better than the average person. Bonaventura explains that eye muscles "are the same types as in your fingers, arms and hands" and can be trained

(Sanders, para. 5). After learning to see the color of ink and the number on the side of a tennis ball coming at them at 150 miles per hour, team members reported that no matter how fast a ball comes at them, they can now mentally slow it down, see the seams and the rotation — just like ink color and numbers on the tennis ball" (Sanders, para. 8). The result is much improved hand–eye coordination — and better softball.

— You can use a USB Web cam and an Eye Games system to project yourself into a sports or adventure game and control the action with your body (Eye Games).

— Animated media are becoming increasingly successful as technology and art catch up with the sophistication of human capacity to appreciate humor, multiple meanings, and diverse cultural environments. Media watchers note "the tendency of animated characters to speak the unspeakable" about such topics as alcoholism, bigotry, profanity, and politics, in part because animated media "seem so unthreatening" (Carr).

— Researchers have determined that humans remember the details of an event witnessed via a video recording more accurately than an event witnessed live (Ihlebaek, Love, Eilertsen, & Magnussen).

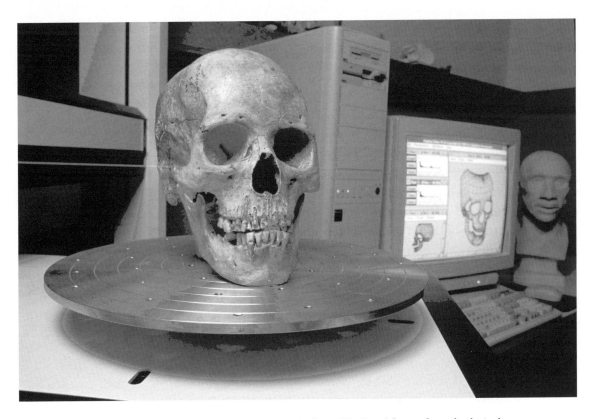

Figure 15.6. A laser (beam at middle left of photo) scans a skull into 3D digital format for archeological research at The University of Texas at Austin. Photograph by Rick Williams.

Figure 15.7. Dog Video Drawing, by Hugh Pryor and Jeremy Wood with Boris and Jemma, Cutteslowe Park, Oxford, 2006 (original in color). The lines were created by using video motion tracking data of the tennis ball and Boris's tail, and the background collage was created using GPS tracking data for alignment. Notice the parabolic trajectory of the tennis ball. "Boris is really enthusiastic about using his tail as a paintbrush," Pryor reported.

— A new breed of cattle carrying a genetic mutation allows their muscles to grow without bodybuilding exercise. Known as Belgian Blues, the "bovine caricatures of Arnold Schwarzenegger" do not effectively use the growth-blocking substance myostatin (Kristof). Physiologists believe injecting myostatin-blocking genes into humans will help people who have neuromuscular diseases such as muscular dystrophy as well as the muscle loss associated with aging. Experiments show the gene therapy works with mice (Pennsylvania Muscle Institute). Kristof worried that athletes will turn to gene therapy, rather than drugs, to improve their bodies' abilities to compete. "The standard human shape would become different, and anyone with money could look like a body builder," Kristof wrote. If you happen to be interested in improving a herd of cattle, check out the British Belgian Blue Cattle Society's Bull Book to select a British Bred Semen Sire. The society's chairperson describes the cattle as "being fine boned, heavily muscled, docile animals with tremendous growth potential, leading to a very high percentage of saleable meat" (Barber)

— Interior design researcher Nancy Kwallek investigates the effects of color on workspaces ranging from everyday offices to space stations (University of Texas Austin). If you want to be more productive in your office, use the right colors. If you are able to "screen out or ignore" your environment, you are likely to work better in a red room. If you are a "low screener," go with blue-green. Kwallek determined that, although "workers made more errors in white rooms, regardless of their screening abilities," all-white environments do not affect performance over time. "The optimal work environment is a combination of the two color extremes — a soft blue-green separated by wainscoting over a soft red," Kwallek said.

— Satellite signals using global positioning system (GPS) technology make it possible for emergency workers to locate people who have dialed 911 on their cell phones (Kanellos). The same technology makes it possible for bosses to track their employees via "'geofences' technology" on their cell phones (Charny). But that's not all. Using the 24 satellites of the GPS network, two British artists are creating art by tracking their journeys by foot, bicycle, car, boat, and airplane with GPS receivers. They draw by "treating travel like a geodetic pencil or a cartographic crayon" (Wood).

— Astronomers, using a powerful radio telescope covering about 20 acres, at the Arecibo Observatory in Puerto Rico have started collecting information in a new project to map the galaxy (Griffiths). An instrument "that is essentially a camera for making radio pictures of the sky" was installed above Arecibo's 20-acre reflector disk, making it possible for astronomers to gather information about seven times more quickly than before (Brand). Information on everything from pulsars to black holes will be compiled in a database available to scien-

Figure 15.8. Spiral Galaxy M81. Spitzer Space Telescope/IRAC, NASA/JPL-Caltech/S. Willner (Harvard-Smithsonian CfA), ssc2003-06c.

Figure 15.9. IPod viewing of "Zenmobile," a video by Don Barth. To view a clip from "Zenmobile,"
which was selected for a mobicapping (Mobile Image Capture for the New Century) international juried
competition, go to http://www.mobicapping.com/index.htm. Photograph by James Henderson.

tists throughout the world via the Internet. The Arecibo Observatory also monitors star systems for extraterrestrial signals (National Astronomy and
Ionosphere Center).

— iPods, camera phones, and other personal electronic media have quickly
become pervasive technology. Their proliferation has prompted new formats,
such as low-resolution movies uploaded to the Internet and podcasting.

— Hip 8-year-olds are "done with Barbies" (La Ferla). The new generation of
multiracial dolls are "anatomically advanced" and "ethnically diverse"
"avatars of urban chic with platform boots," "exploded hair, inflated lips," and
"wardrobes that speak to the aspirations of a nation of third-grade J.Lo and
Beyoncé worshippers." Mattel's Flava line of dolls is billed as "the first reality-
based fashion doll brand that celebrates today's teen culture through authentic

style, attitude, and values. Mattel has created a hot hip-hop themed line that allows girls to express their own personal flava" (Mattel).

— A digital bookmobile is putting free books into the hands of children who have never read, much less owned a book (Dean). Anywhere Books, a non-profit organization, sends a van to such areas as the Buikwe region in Uganda. The van is equipped with a computer, printer, cutter, and bookbinder to print such classics as Peter Rabbit as well as children's own stories.

— Astronomers announced they had photographed "what appears to be a planet orbiting another star . . . the first confirmed picture of a world beyond our solar system" (Britt). The new system is 230 light-years away.

— Déjà vu is not a "Twilight Zone" phenomenon. When we experience the discomfiting feeling that we have seen something before, we probably have. Experiments have proven that information recorded by the unconscious mind — regardless of whether the source of the information is one's own imagination, a novel, or real-life scenarios — can emerge later as an uncanny sense of familiarity with things not consciously remembered (Carey).

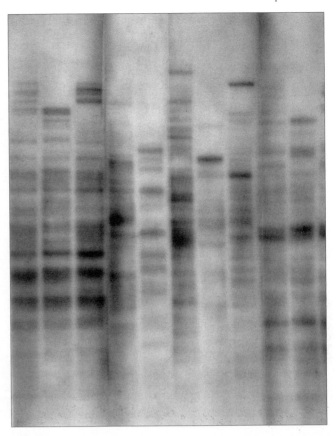

Figure 15.10. An autoradiograph of the first genetic fingerprint prepared by Alec Jeffreys at Leicester University, September 19, 1984. Jeffreys was the first to discover a series of probes to hypervariable DNA sequences. These regions of DNA consist of many repeats of the same sequence (tandem repeats). Since hypervariable DNA differs markedly from individual to individual, the presence of common bands between individuals indicates a relationship. In conjunction with the technique of 'Southern blotting' (named after Ed Southern, its developer), Jeffreys developed a method of analysis by which he could look at these sequences and observe differences between individuals in a population. This technique has wide applications in forensic science. Science Museum/Science and Society Picture Library.

— Our right ears hear differently than our left ears. Researchers now know that the right ear is better at processing speech and the left ear is better at processing music (O'Connor). This is an excellent example of how ideas once thought to be "facts" — such as the assumption that both ears process sounds in the same ways later turn out to be incorrect.

— The ultimate new medium may be cloning. Although highly controversial, embryonic stem cells, which can now be derived from clone embryos, offer keys to managing such diseases as diabetes and Alzheimer's.

Figure 15.11. With 135-miles-per-hour winds, Hurricane Katrina pounded the U.S. Gulf Coast early on August 29, 2005. NASA.

And then consider the following points, which perhaps confirm the truism that for every step forward we take as a society, we take at least one step backward:

— Such corporations as McDonald's, Disney, and General Mills spend some $15 billion a year on immersive advertising, through which they sponsor video games embedded with ads aimed at children (Ha, 2004). One game Web site, neopets.com, has 23 million registered users, and 60% are females.

— Technological advances could neither predict nor prevent the earthquake and ensuing Indian Ocean tsunami that killed an estimated 150,000 people on December 26, 2004. Many parts of the world do not have communication systems in place. Those that do are changing. Even hurricanes, which take time to grow and travel, have forces that transcend any rational process or technology. Although meteorologists, media, and public officials warned residents of the New Orleans area to flee Hurricane Katrina, systems were not in place to facilitate evacuation, resulting in the deaths of more than 1,000 people. As Hurricane Ivan made its way through the Caribbean in fall 2004, meteorologists used satellite images, as well as readings gathered from the storm's eye by diving aircraft — along with pencils and an eraser — to correct their projections of the storm's path. "This is the state of hurricane science in the new century," *New York Times* science writer Revking noted, "a mix of growing skill and persistent uncertainty, of intuition and algorithms, satellites and erasers."

What Does All This Mean?

First, let's relate a few of the terms we've used to describe still and moving images, the primary visual elements and formats, to new media.

In new media, points are pixels — individual bits of information we use to build digital images — and electrons — tiny bits of energy that form the basis of wireless communication. Although living organisms are "old media," the idea of living organisms as forms of media is an unconventional idea in design and visual communication studies. So, let's include the cells of living things in

Figure 15.12. Taking cues from local building materials, Rogers Marvel Architects designed "nogo" sculptures to provide seating and congregating places for pedestrians as well as protecting the Wall Street area from truck bombs. Graeme Waitzkin, designer for Rogers Marvel, believes security and design should and can be integrated into welcoming structures that fit their surroundings. Photograph by Richard Ramsey.

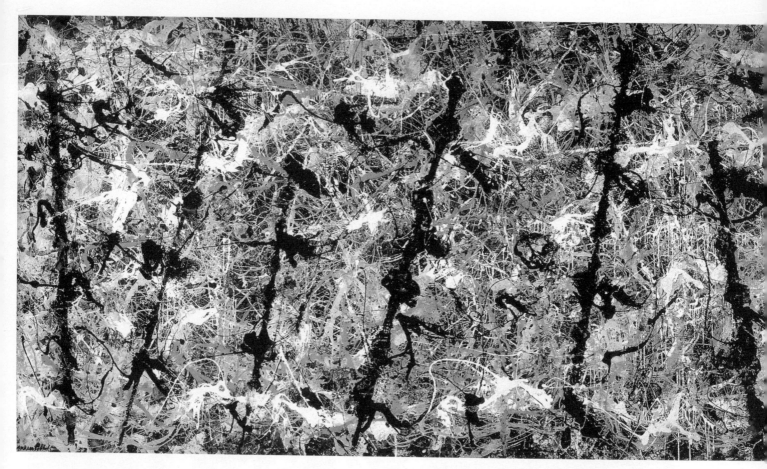

Figure 15.13. Blue Poles, by Jackson Pollock, 1952. Using computer algorithms and graphics software, Richard Taylor and his colleagues determined that the fundamental design underlying Pollock's drip paintings is composed of fractals. Taylor theorizes that Pollock, who was captivated by the natural world, moved in an intuitive manner as he created his art. To learn more about fractals and how the physicists analyzed Pollock's paintings, turn to Figures 15.14-17. To view Blue Poles in color, as Pollock created it, see the Color Plate section in this book. © 2006 The Pollock-Krasner Foundation/Artists Rights Society (ARS), New York. The National Gallery of Australia.

our description expansion of points. Think of cells as living equivalents of pixels in the new media of the body.

In mechanical new media, lines as visual elements are streams of pixels and electrons forming paths of data, energy, and synapses. Shapes leave the limiting traditions of rectangles and ovals to become forms as infinitely varied as fractals. Volume, the visual element that is hardest to represent in two-dimensional media, flourishes through multidimensional digital and holographic layers and projections of objects and organisms. And frames have become both binding and amorphous containers as tiny as quarks — the fundamental components of neutrons and protons — and as expansive as the universe. Just as Copernicus and Galileo changed our perception of the earth's relationship to

the sun, contemporary astronomers and physicists shift our perceptions of the universe with discoveries in both planetary and nuclear science.

In the body as new media, specialized cells transmit perceptual information to the neuron cells of the brain. Visual stimuli create visual images by repeatedly firing neurons across the layers of the primary visual cortex. Studies with Macaque monkeys show a remarkable similarity between a seen shape and the shape of the neural activity in the visual cortex, as shown by Damasio. Thus, a parallel exists between the way pixels and electrons make up images on a monitor or television screen and the way the brain creates visual images in the visual cortex. When this is extended to behavior the body actually becomes a form of electronic media. For instance, an image from television associates a particular product with a particular lifestyle, A Nike Swoosh, for example, may be associated with a buff body seen repeatedly and recorded in the brain as nonconscious cognitive memory system. Later, when something stimulates those same nonconscious visual associations with the unconscious desire to have that buff body, the individual is prompted to purchase Nike to help fulfill this fantasy. Through this process the body assimilates and transforms media messages into human behavior. Furthermore, when the individual wears his new Nike product, he extends the original media image, potentially evoking similar nonconscious associations in other people.

The idea of formats in new media often focuses on such new technologies as digital imaging, the Internet, and wireless transmission. If we want to understand visual communication, however, new media must be inclusive. MRIs, dolls, fashion, surgery, global positioning systems, DNA, and the human body all are part of the new media field.

Our bases for selecting new media for this category are these:

- the medium applies technology (including the technology of the body) via a **new form** or the medium uses an **old form in a new way**
- the medium **shifts** the way a living entity **interfaces** with an object or the medium expresses or **facilitates a new understanding** of self, other, and world
- the medium can be either **material or immaterial** in form
- the medium often is transitory or in a constant **state of flux**
- the medium often makes possible **simultaneous** participation in multiple realities

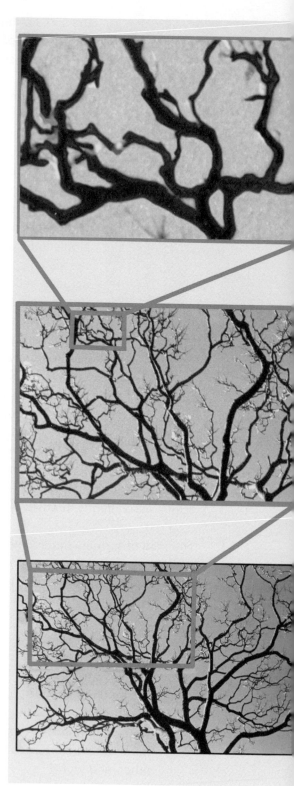

Figures 15.14-18. Many patterns, such as the mountain and waves in the above photographs, are fractals, the intricate shapes that build the natural world. Fractals recur repeatedly when magnified, as illustrated at right in the two sets of tree-branch images (one set from a real tree, the other a simplified drawing of the patterns). The grids at far right show how Richard Taylor and his colleagues analyzed one of Pollock's paintings using computer software to detect fractal patterns. Photographs and illustrations by Richard Taylor.

The individual who wants to learn to create, use, and interpret these multiple forms of communicating will do well to practice the exercises in this book. In some ways, this process is similar to learning to crawl and then walk — it helps to learn to do one before the other. At the same time, it is important that creative thinkers not be restricted by traditions of art, communication media, and science. Remember, for example, that there was a time when great painters knew nothing about perspective drawing. The inverted pyramid, journalism's tradition of putting the most important information in the first paragraph of a news story, was developed to meet the problems of telegraphing information during the days when only a few words or sentences made it through. We're reminded of the old story about the woman who always trimmed the ends off a ham before baking it. She had learned the technique from her mother and thought it was the secret to cooking a delicious ham. When she finally asked her mother why she cooked hams that way, the mother replied that she didn't know — but her mother had always cooked hams that way. When the mother asked the grandmother why, the older woman said it was simply so a large ham would fit in the pan she had. Visual design and patterns of communicating have developed because they work, and some "ways of doing" will always be useful to us. That does not mean, however, that we should avoid exploring new ways of thinking, creating, and working, as well as new ways to understand all media.

What Do We Know?

As new forms of media develop and old forms evolve, we are learning how to create, use, and interpret them better. One of the most useful new research projects is Eyetrack III, a preliminary study of online use of news sites, a format that has existed about 10 years. Researchers studied the movement of people's eyes as they viewed and read prototype news Web sites in this joint effort of The Poynter Institute, a program dedicated to improving journalism; Estlow International Center for Journalism & New Media at the University of Denver; and Eyetools, a commercial company that grew out of a Stanford University's eye-movement and human–computer interface project.

"It's like getting inside of a person's head and watching what they see—with the advantage that a computer is recording every eye movement and fixation for later compilation and analysis" reported the Poynter Institute (2004). Though the researchers stressed that the study examined reading patterns of only 46 people in the San Francisco area and focused on news sites, their findings are helpful for thinking about how to design for the Internet. More important perhaps is that they encourage us to question whether practices that work with one medium, such as print newspapers, are effective in another medium, such as Internet news sites. Here are a few of the key findings of the Eyetrack III project:

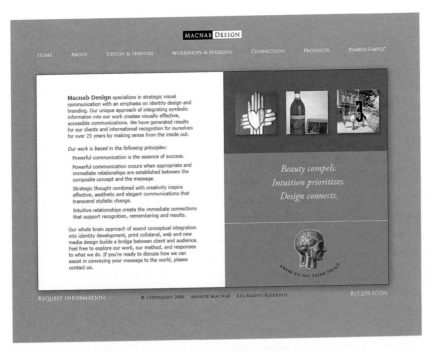

Figure 15.19. Maggie Macnab's opening page for her design web site.

Figures 15.20-21. July 17, 2006, USA Today on-line. Because Internet design facilitates instant design, USA Today could update information throughout the day.

Layout

—People go to the upper left of a page, peruse the top of the page, and then look down the page.
—Dominant headlines get attention first.
—People go to text first and spend more time looking at text. Eyetracking research on print newspapers indicated the opposite — photos ruled.
—Viewers spend more time reading smaller type and tend to scan lighter type.
—Keeping blurbs, which are short summary statements used with headlines, the same type size as the headlines works best.
—The first two words of both headlines and blurbs are most important and determine whether people read on.
—A reader spends less than a second on a headline.
—Though people do scroll down a page, they tend to scan lower sections for something that grabs their attention.
—Navigation elements work best at the top of a home page.
—Article paragraphs should be short—one to two sentences.
—Using one column for articles works best.
—Using introductory, well-written paragraphs with articles is best. People will read them, but they will not necessarily encourage further reading.

Images

—Use larger photos (500x300 pixels or at least 210x230 pixels).
—Use faces—and more than one face—in photos when possible.
—Use well-cropped photos with strong centers of interest.
—Make images link to larger or more images, or to an article related to the photo.
—Content can be more important to reading than format when viewers are interested in the content.

Ads

—Ads draw more attention when placed on the left side of the page.
—Visual barriers such as white space or borders between ads and articles tend to stop viewers from looking at ads.
—When ads look more like article content (visual bleed), people look at them more.
—Common ad types are text, skyscrapers (ads that are narrow and tall), inset, mouse-over, and pop-ups.
—Text ads attract viewers.
—Larger ads draw more intense viewing.
—Inset ads (ads notched into the text of article) tend to work best.
—Ads that expand when the mouse runs over them (mouse-over ads) work better than other banner ads.
—Ads closer to top left work better.

Williams and Newton

—People quickly look at pop-up ads and close them or ignore them, spending a total of 1 second, on average, looking at the ad.

—Compelling ad quality and content draw viewers.

Multimedia

—Include audio-narrated slide shows, video, interactive graphics, animation.

—Use text to increase recall of names, places, and facts.

—Use animated graphics and well-written accompanying text to inform about an unfamiliar process or procedure.

—When graphics, audio, and text conflict, recall may decrease.

—People reread shocking information.

Although the researchers stressed that they need to do more research to verify their findings, these guidelines point to design issues when communicating on the Internet. The complexity of the results from this preliminary study of only one type of new media — online news sites — also illustrates the challenge of

Figure 15.22. Different media, ranging from gelatin silver photographs to digital page design were involved in producing this book in the authors' workspace. Photograph by Rick Williams.

Figure 15.23. Scanogram, by Justin Abbott. Making scanograms, an assignment in Julianne Newton's introductory photojournalism class, combines wet-lab photogram techniques with digital flatbed scanning.

understanding increasingly complex media. That is one of the main reasons — if not the main reason — research about the brain and visual communication is only now beginning to make significant progress.

New media — computer processing, functional magnetic resonance imaging and other medical technologies, electron microscopy, and radio telescopes — have made possible exploring our world in all its forms. Yet, as with fine art and effective writing, mastery of any medium or form of communication takes practice and study. Using both intuitive and rational intelligences in concert facilitates mastery. This is an exciting time to be living, learning, and creating.

Reconceptualizing Media Studies

Past chapters focused on still and moving media. It is time to move beyond such traditional media categories as print and video to reconceptualize our study of media. Print and moving media in familiar forms probably will continue, but we cannot foresee all the changes to come. In the final chapter of this book, we discuss what you can do about this. However, at this point in our discussion, we want to delineate a few characteristics of new media as we see them.

First, new media quickly become old media. When Brazilians meet people who seem like someone they have known all their lives, they use the phrase: "new old friends." Contemporary "new media" are similar. Though they incorporate old media practices, in other ways, they are indeed new. Five years ago, few of us would have believed we could play a game in the windows of a building by using our cell phones — or that we could swallow a capsule video camera rather than go through an endoscopy. But think back on how quickly you have become accustomed to using e-mail, doing research by "googling," talking on the phone with a friend while you're sitting in rush-hour traffic, or feeling comfortable in a sports bar with 30 television sets in front of you. In the industrialized world, our abilities to adapt to new forms of

Top: Figure 15.24. Food Force, a game distributed free by
the United Nations World Food Programme, helps 8- to-13-year-olds
learn about world hunger, where food originates, how emergency teams deliver food,
and how long-term food security helps community development.
Above: Figure 15.25. Food Force characters, from left:
Carlos Sanchez, emergency team manager; Rachel Scott, logistics officer;
and Joe Zaki, nutritional expert.

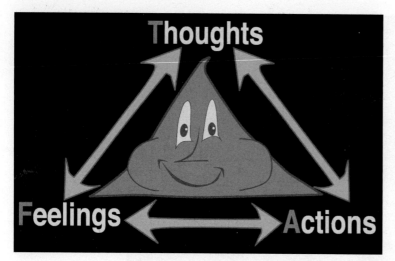

communicating and expressing ourselves are accelerating to the point that we cannot imagine a time when we lived without such forms.

Second, our conscious sense of aesthetics can be as transitory as new media. Aesthetics generally refers to theories of art and responses to art. The term is often associated with beauty or judgment of what is considered beautiful or aesthetically pleasing. This judgment traditionally has carried with it a power to determine what is acceptable, beautiful, or even what art is. New forms of media challenge perceptions about art as well as perceptions about what is beautiful or what is acceptable. The range of expression on the Internet alone validates the idea that "anything goes," as long as people want to share their ideas or images with others and other people respond to those expressive forms. As discussed in past chapters, design, still images, and moving media have cultivated standards for creative formats based on visual elements, color, composition, sound, technical concerns, performance issues, cultural issues, political economic issues, and ethics. The "new aesthetic" embraces an appreciation for visual forms varying from traditional approaches to an "anti-aesthetic." Art critic Arthur Danto wrote, "It is the mark of our period that everything can be regarded as a work of art and seen in textual terms. . . . Contemporary art replaces beauty, everywhere threatened, with meaning" (p. *xxx*). This is what allows us to view women undergoing plastic surgery as a form of performance while also being able to enjoy the unique beauty of a sunset. As McLuhan and McLuhan wrote, "The etymology of all human technologies is to be found in the human body itself: they are, as it were, prosthetic devices, mutations, metaphors of the body or its parts."

Third, new media are our environment. They are more than receiving and transmission devices of mass media. They are more than multimodal attempts to extend the human organism. They are a kind of living, constantly evolving ambience, much like the body itself, both surrounding and affecting life.

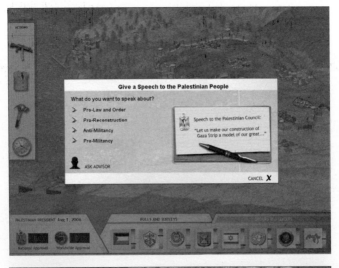

Figures 15.27-29. *PeaceMaker: A Video Game to Promote Peace by ImpactGames, which was founded by Eric Brown and Asi Burak while they attended Carnegie Mellon University.*

Figure 15.30. Orlan. The cover image of the French performance artist's 2004 book, Orlan: Carnal Art, conveys her assertion that her performance "transforms the body into language" (2006, para. 4). Orlan wrote, "Carnal Art loves mockery and the baroque, the grotesque and other neglected styles since it opposes itself to social pressures the burden of which is carried by both the human body and the work of art" (2006, para. 9).

Fourth, new media are at once personal and impersonal. They are tailored to individual needs and preferences while also meeting (or creating) the needs and preferences of every human in a world that is simultaneously known and anonymous.

Fifth, new media are at once connected and disconnected. They facilitate rapid communication with an increasingly wide array of people and sources. Yet they also isolate the body within spaces of aloneness.

Sixth, the real new (and old) medium is the self. As an evolving entity influenced by biology and culture, each of us moves through life creating and responding to the many forms of media we encounter, including other humans. In that process, those of us who can see, speak, hear, smell, touch, and taste, form our truths and our sense of ourselves as we go. The mind is indeed the ultimate medium.

Seventh, new media are increasingly reflexive. That means two things: a) they encourage us to become more self-aware, even as they encourage us to reach beyond ourselves, sometimes to become someone else; and b) they are self-referential, meaning they play games on themselves — and on us. As evidence, consider the increasingly self-referential character of comedy. As *New York Times* media critic David Carr, wrote,

> There are cartoons about movies — and movie producers, with Robert Evans doing the voice for his own mini-me in a forthcoming Showtime series called "Kid Notorious" — cartoons about television shows, and cartoons about cartoons. Everybody, including the characters, is in on the jokes, which sometimes even poke fun at animation's hoariest clichés. In . . . Shrek 2, a conniving feline interlopes on the relationship between the ogre and his trusty donkey sidekick. "I'm sorry, the position of annoying talking animal has already been taken," the donkey explains. (npn)

Eighth, our ability to perceive the world visually is increasing exponentially. Contrary to many educators and media critics, we believe children and young adults are more sophisticated than previous generations precisely because of their exposure to and use of the many new forms of external media available to their incredible internal communication systems. Each generation may think the succeeding generation is "going to the dogs," or hopelessly lost within the moral abyss of changing cultures and societies. We believe the divide between older and new generations we currently are experiencing is indeed larger than that faced by previous generations — change is occurring faster and with more dramatic effects. Our challenge, however, is not to revert to 15th-century modes of educating the young — modes based on linear thinking and mastery of the written and spoken word. Our challenge is to face a world that has always been diverse and multifaceted, but that now is aware of itself. In their classic book, *The Global Village*, McLuhan and Powers addressed these challenges as 21st-century transformations that required acknowledgment of simultaneous, multidimensional ways of knowing and living.

Only by embracing these changes as equal and complementary ways of knowing and being will we learn to use them appropriately to build sustainable communities for the future.

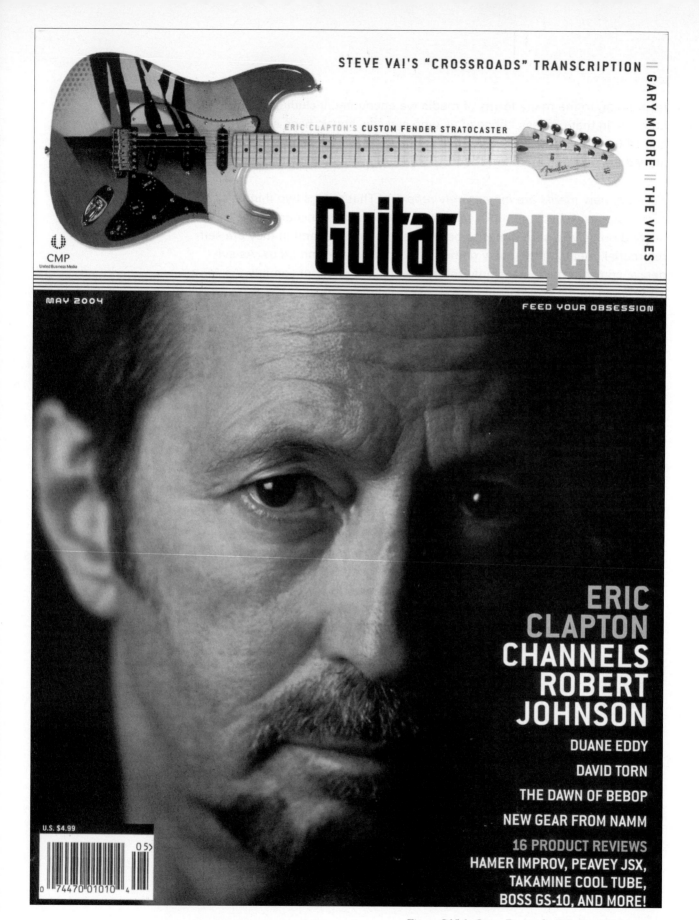

Figure C15.1. Cover Design by D.J. Stout, Pentagram.

CREATIVE FIFTEEN
Communicating the Story of a Person

Goal: To tell a story visually with supporting words.

Your task is to produce a picture and word package communicating about a person. You and another person must photograph each other for this exercise. If you are in a class or workshop, a classmate or colleague is ideal for the assignment.

Photographing and being photographed are integral to the assignment. Make at least 48 images each.

Your goal is to communicate — in pictures and in words — the most authentic view of a person that you can. Doing this creative is excellent practice for a career in journalism and communication, as well as other creative media. The personality or human-interest story is one of the most fascinating and frequently published features in newspapers, magazines, television broadcasts, Internet publications, newsletters, and other media forms. If you do this exercise well, you also will have an excellent example of your work to use in your professional and personal portfolio.

Read these instructions all the way through before you begin.

What You Need to Begin

1. *Time* to interview and photograph your photo partner and to produce your picture/word package.

Planning is especially critical to the success of this creative exercise. You must plan your time to meet for interviews and photo shoots. You also must allow time to download your images or have your film developed, edit your photographs, prepare prints to turn in, and prepare text and layout material to accompany the pictures.

2. *Camera.* Any camera you know how to use is fine, including a cardboard throwaway camera you can buy at any photo or drug store, a digital point-and-shoot (must use at least 3.3 megapixels), or a fine professional camera. Camera phones generally do not produce adequate quality for this creative.

Note: You may do this assignment as a video and prepare it for distribution via the Internet or a personal display device if you have the equipment and expertise. Although the instructions detail how to prepare materials for a print publication, the basic process is much the same for various media. This is a great opportunity to practice preparing a multimedia package with images, text, and audio.

3. *Film (if using film):* If you are not shooting digitally, use any brand of color print film (not slide/transparency film unless you are experienced with it and have knowledge and means for scanning and printing) that has at least 24 exposures. Any speed or ASA/ISO is fine, although we suggest ASA/ISO 200 or ASA/ISO 400. You may use black and white if you can make prints or have them made.

4. *A note about film processing:* Two-hour turn around for colo- negative film processing and printing is available in most communities. However, BEFORE you leave your film with a commercial processor, be sure you know exactly when your prints will be ready and what the final product will be (number and size of prints, scanned to CD, proof sheet).

5. *Allow extra time for things to go wrong.* When working with camera equipment, film, commercial processors, computer equipment, labs, and so forth, the number of problems you may have to solve increases.

You will work with many variables — including another person, technical processes, camera equipment, computer equipment and software, and possibly a commercial business. All of these factors can affect the result, quality and timing of your project.

Notes about Picture Editing and Writing Captions

Picture editing occurs before, during and after a photo shoot. Beforehand, you can envision where you will photograph your subject, the time of day, the light, the background, the environment, how close you will get to the person, how you might pose the person, how he/she might pose herself/himself. Drawing thumbnail sketches can help you plan. Plan time for talking with your photo partner, getting to know him/her better, so you can make more authentic extended portraits of one another.

During the shoot, you will make choices, which are a form of editing. Do you include a tree in the frame? Do you move in very close to photograph just the face, or do you stay back a bit so you include head and shoulders? When do you press the shutter? What is the subject doing when you press the shutter? Are you and the person interacting well, or are you tense and awkward with each other? What can you do to help ease the tension? Each of these factors —and others — will affect the content and quality of your resulting photographs.

After the shoot, you have a final opportunity to shape the story you will tell about your subject. Will your story be flattering, negative, fun or sad, or "just the way you saw the person"? Will you pick the happy-looking closeup or the sad one? What does the environment included in the pictures say about your subject? Do the posed shots look posed, or will most viewers think they are candid? In what order will you place the photographs? You can tell "the story" of your photo partner in a number of ways, depending on which photographs you select for your final edit and on the order in which you place the photographs.

Part I. Photographing

Tell the story of a person through pictures. By "story," we mean that you should communicate to those of us who do not know your subject what that person is like. Interview the person about his or her life, activities, major, and goals. Remember: everyone has a story and has interesting things to say and tell you — if you give them time, are genuinely interested, and listen well.

When you are photographing, include the following:

- Close-up portrait
- Full-body portrait
- Environmental portrait (one that shows the person doing something in surroundings that tell us something important about the person)
- Photographer-posed portrait (you tell the person what to do)
- Subject-posed portrait (the person decides what to do)
- Free shoot (whatever works and is fun and creative!)

Part II. Editing

Select the six best shots — one for each of the above categories — and arrange them so they tell a story. You should have more good photos than you can use. This is exactly what you want. *National Geographic* photographers shoot as many as 30,000 shots in order to get the 10- to-15 extraordinary images they and editors will select to publish with an article. We're not asking you to shoot 30,000 — just 48 (though you may shoot more). Then select the six best from among those. *Mark the selected shots on your proof sheet.*

Determine an order of presentation for the six photos. Think about beginning, middle, and end. There will be a number of ways to arrange the photos in order to tell your story. It's often a good idea to begin and end with one of your strongest shots. You might begin your sequence, for example, with a close-up portrait that introduces the person visually. You might end the sequence with a full-body shot of the person walking away.

The images you do not use are called your *outtakes*. You also will submit all of these. If you shoot digitally, submit them in on a CD, along with proof sheets. If you shoot film, submit all your film, prints, and proof sheets.

Part III. Writing

DO NOT make up information and quotes. The captions and text must be true and accurate information.

Write captions for each edited photograph and a brief feature story about your classmate. Telling your story in pictures is more important to this assignment than telling your story in words. You do need to add words, however, in order to insure that we, as your viewers and readers, clearly understand how to read the pictures. Words, in the form of headlines, captions, and story text, usually accompany photographs in media presentations. The great LIFE magazine picture editor Wilson Hicks used to say that, when pictures and words were put together on a page, they brought about a *third effect*, a kind of communication that neither words nor pictures can accomplish alone. This is the Gestalt perceptual principle of perception at work.

Write a 2-3-line caption for each of the six (or more) photographs. Each caption should tell us something we cannot determine from the photos, such as the person's name, age and other relevant details not communicated by the pictures. Write so that captions are not redundant but build on each other to enhance the story with more information. Include some of the person's own words as direct and indirect quotes. Tell us where the person is in the photograph, and add bits and pieces of information about his/her background, job, and interests as you work your way through the picture story.

Don't write the obvious, however. For example, DO NOT tell us the person "smiles at the photographer while posing in the park." DO tell us, for example, that your classmate just found out she won a scholarship to attend UO next year, or that he is struggling to finish the term because he's burned out on school and working two part-time jobs.

Next, write a *short feature story* about your classmate. This should be 300 to 500 words in which you flesh out details you could not include in the captions. This is where you go into more depth, including full direct quotations and paraphrased quotes. Tell us what is unique about your classmate — the "story behind the story." In other words, tell us more than is readily obvious.

The Exercise

- Select a person to photograph, someone who also will photograph you.
- Plan time for completing all aspects of the project.
- Conduct interviews and photograph the person in different settings/time
- Process the images.
- Edit the images.
- Write the story and captions.
- Draw thumbnail designs and produce the layout.
- Prepare the completed picture/word story for submission or presentation. The options are as varied as your imagination, as long as the result is professionally executed and presented.
- Answer the above questions in a short essay.
- Assess your overall experience completing this creative.

Part IV. Designing

Plan a professional presentation of the photographs and captions. Your goal here is to design a magazine spread, a newspaper picture page, a small book, a video, web site, or some other form of publication or distributed package that presents your photographs and words in a polished, professional manner.

Follow these steps:

1. Draw thumbnail layouts of your design. Try different layout designs. Vary the size in which you use the photographs. Which is your dominant, or lead image? How do the images work together? Think about the style and size of type that will best communicate your headline, subheads, captions, byline and text.

2. Review your picture edit. Have you selected the best photos to tell the story visually and to work in the layout? You may need to discard some of your choices and select other images in order to communicate the story most effectively.

3. Review your captions and text. Have you included sufficient quotations and pertinent details to complement the photos and flesh out the story?

4. Type out all of your captions and your story text so you can import them into your digital layout.

5. Scan your images or prepare your digital images for importing into your digital layout.

6. Translate your selected thumbnail design into a digital layout using a computer software program such as InDesign or Quark Xpress. If necessary, an adequately professional layout can be designed using Microsoft Word.

7. Import your image scans and text into your layout.

8. Adjust spacing, sizing, and type as necessary to polish your layout. Do you want to use a rule line around the image? What other changes need to be made to make the presentation look professional?

9. Print out a proof.

10. Proofread your type, check the details of your design, make corrections to the text and captions, and adjust the design where necessary.

11. Print out your final version. Be sure you include variety in your final edit. If you do not use the six required poses in your layout, include a labeled print for each pose not included. You may more images if they are really good. You need not follow this order determine the best order as you edit and do your layout.

Part V. Assessment

Write 1-2 pages discussing the following:

• What challenges did you encounter during the exercise?

• How did you overcome practical problems in completing the

• How and what do your photos communicate about the perso

• Why did you select the shots you did for your best six?

• What is your best photograph? This should be one of your b
  you consider it your best shot?

• What is the most authentic, most representative photograph
  In other words, which one photo would you pick as communi
  truthfully what your subject is like? This should be one of you
  tographs.

• What is the least authentic, least representative photograph? '
  photo communicates the least truthfully what your subject is l
  or may not be one of your five best shots. For example, you m
  tured a hilarious but uncharacteristic shot of your subject in ar
  tion. Or perhaps you posed, or the subject posed herself, hims
  that is completely an act.

• Which one photograph best communicates symbolically? In ot
  which photo tells us more than the obvious? Which photo doe:
  visually describe the person? Which photo makes you feel you
  stand something about the person when you look at it?

• How did you feel photographing your classmate?

• How did you feel being photographed?

• How might your feelings apply to subjects of media photograp

• How did the process of selecting images, choosing words, and
  your layout affect the final story?

• What might you do differently next time?

• What additional reflections do you have about your experiences

The Exercise

- Select a person to photograph, someone who also will photograph you.
- Plan time for completing all aspects of the project.
- Conduct interviews and photograph the person in different settings/times.
- Process the images.
- Edit the images.
- Write the story and captions.
- Draw thumbnail designs and produce the layout.
- Prepare the completed picture/word story for submission or presentation. The options are as varied as your imagination, as long as the result is professionally executed and presented.
- Answer the above questions in a short essay.
- Assess your overall experience completing this creative.

CHAPTER SIXTEEN
The Thousand-Year Project

We began our journey through this book with a parable about a scientist, a theologian, and a shaman who had different interpretations about how a mother bear nurtures her cubs. We want to begin your journey beyond the pages of this book by telling you another parable.

The story begins with the same protagonists, but within another setting. A scientist, a theologian, and a shaman gather around the bedside of a dying patient. Each has known the person well throughout her life. As they stand respectfully beside their friend, they watch her labored breathing, knowing each rise of her lungs may be her last.

The woman is conscious, aware that her friends are with her, and moves her gaze slowly from one to the other, lingering for a moment to look deeply into the eyes of each. Finally, she shifts her gaze to look beyond the three, far beyond through the window at the foot of her bed, into the blue summer sky outside. Her chest continues its slow, deliberate rise and fall with each breath.

Then, in an instant, the rhythm stops. Her eyes continue to stare, but they do not move, not even to blink. All is still.

The scientist looks at the theologian, who looks at the shaman, who looks at the scientist. Each knows what he has observed: A friend has just died. They can sense the absence of her life, no longer emanating through her body.

Yet, only seconds earlier, she was alive. In their grief, they try to explain to one another what has just happened.

"The biochemical processes of her brain ceased to function," says the scientist.

"Her soul has gone to heaven," says the theologian.

Figure 16.1. Untitled, by Jerry Uelsmann.

"What was, is no more," says the shaman. She joins our ancestors in memory and being.

Just as the parable of the She-Bear used symbolism to communicate the significance of balancing rational and intuitive processing, so this parable uses a real-life story to communicate approaches to understanding the nature of life and death. We have spent a great many of the pages of this book discussing cognitive neuroscience, the study of how the brain creates the mind. We also have spent a great many pages on different forms of visual communication so that you can both create and interpret visual images. We do not pretend to have all the answers. What we do hope is that you have learned a few of the most important scientific and artistic approaches to the primary ways of knowing that we call visual communication. Even more important is our hope that by working through the creative exercises, you have learned more about your own unique interaction with the world around you as well as about tendencies you share with others.

It is not critical that you fully understand the intricate workings of the brain — even neuroscientists will readily tell you they know relatively little about the 1 billion neurons that make the brain what it is, much less about how they all work.

Design theorist John Chris Jones, a founder of ergonomic design, supports the idea of intuitive/rational integration. Jones stressed the importance of designing "whole systems or environments" through "an educational discipline that unites art and science and perhaps can go further than either." Jones's idea of going further means "designing 'without a product,'" as a process or way of living in itself." Holder of the Lifetime Achievement Award from England's Design Research Society, he believes the future of design rests in two ideas: 1) that "in the end [design] will be done by everyone" and 2) that we learn "to become ecologically viable human societies." Jones stressed that we are "very unready at present" for that future.

The key to bringing that future to life begins by drawing on visual communication to balance both rational and intuitive abilities across disciplines and practices. Like the square peg in the round hole, integrating cognitive modalities combines science and art into an ecologically sound, whole-mind experience. We believe this generates more balanced individuals and thus more balanced and viable human societies.

Although scientists have not yet determined exactly how humans began to think on symbolic levels, they are beginning to realize that the answers to the future of our species lie in the integration of knowledge rather than in specific kinds of knowledge. Increasingly, those in disciplines across art and science realize the necessity for working together to contribute pieces to the giant puzzle of human knowing.

Williams and Newton

Figure 16.2. Coffee House, by Ave Bonar.

Synthesis

Although there is so much more to tell you, we conclude our book journey now with a proposal for the future. We have suggested that the pervasiveness of visual and intuitive illiteracy throughout our culture empowers the predominantly visual media to become the predominant educational force of our lives. Ultimately, this leads to a question: How can we change an educational system that produces an intuitively illiterate culture, one that supports unbalanced, rationally biased, corporate, economic, and political systems?

As educators and practitioners of communication and art, we believe most educators strive to teach students of art, media, marketing, mass communication, design, photography, and journalism the appropriate roles of media in a society based on free expression. They teach about media effects, critical theories of mass communication, ethics, race and gender politics, and subjective reality. They know that students will need an increasingly sophisticated variety of skills in art, science, communication, and economics.

Yet, in all of this, students seem to emerge only half prepared. So entrenched have we become in facilitating the role of rational intelligence, logic, and theo-

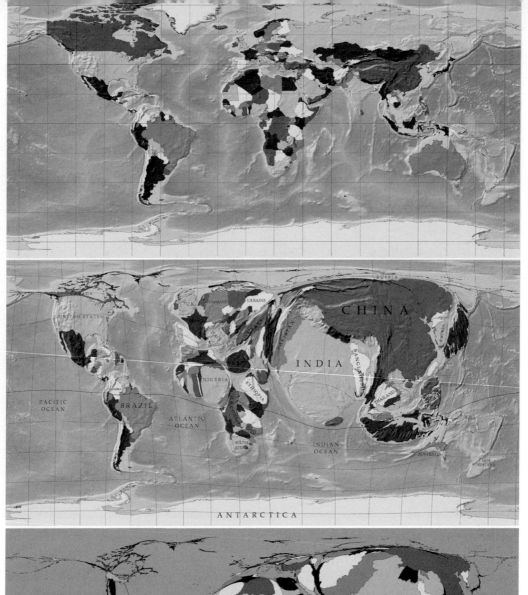

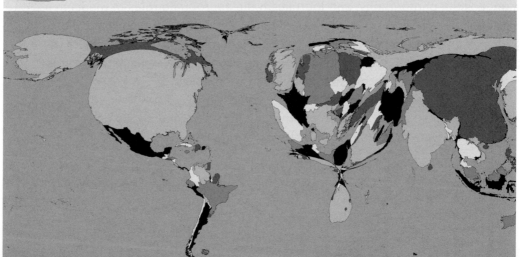

ry in education that we have neglected to fully develop intuitive intelligence. This intuitive intelligence guides the creative, relational, and ethical problem-solving and decision-making processes that generate balance between quality and quantity in our culture. So, as educators teach from a predominately rational perspective, they also support the rational bias of global corporate culture, which emphasizes quantity as the primary goal of work and life. The few relatively unsophisticated abilities we develop through our innate visual intelligence are like intuitive pebbles tossed randomly into a rational sea. They develop little, if any, defense against the "seduction of eloquence" that entices, persuades, and manipulates us using highly integrative media techniques.

The Larger Problem

The basic problem of illiteracy in all its forms is larger than just the media, or even than global corporations. It would be ludicrous to suggest that we do away with honing rational intelligence — just as ludicrous as to assume that intuitive intelligence is unworthy of at least equal development and mainte-nance as rational intelligence. Without the analytical power of the rational processes, we would be little more advanced than Jaynes's bicameral human, existing without conscious choice. An intuitively biased world would surely be as undesirably imbalanced as our rationally biased world is now.

To correct this imbalance, integrative mind theory proposes we begin with two traditional sources of enlightenment — the individual and formal education. An integral part of the solution to the rational bias is found in the teaching of intu-itive intelligence as a complementary and equivalent companion to the teach-ing of rational intelligence. Such a holistic educational system has the potential to help fill the intuitive void, diminish intuitive illiteracy, fulfill the need for cog-

From top left: Figure 16.3. Ordinary map of the world. Roughly speaking, on a map like this, the sizes of the countries of the world are in proportion to their actual sizes on the surface of the planet and their shapes are the same as their actual shapes. The tones in this and the three cartograms below remain relatively consistent to help you identify countries where shapes change a great deal. Figure 16.4. Population cartogram of the world. Cartograms portray geographic or social data by making the sizes countries bigger or smaller to represent a statistic. Here, the cartogram shows coun-try sizes proportionally to represent the human population of a countries in relation to other coun-tries. A country with 20 million people, for example, appears twice as large as country with 10 mil-lion people. Compare the relative sizes of India and China, in which a third of the world's people live, with Canada and Russia, which have smaller populations but are the world's two largest coun-tries by land mass. Longitude and latitude lines are distorted by the growing and shrinking coun-tries. Figure 16.5. Cartogram of child mortality in the world. Figure 16.6. Cartogram of greenhouse gas emissions. Population data are from the International Center for Earth Science at Columbia University. Other cartogram data are from the United Nations Statistics Division and from World Health Organization databases. © 2006 M. E. J. Newman, Department of Physics and Center for the Study of Complex Systems, University of Michigan.

nitive balance, disarm media manipulation, develop individuals with holistically functional minds, and ultimately benefit humanity and the planet as a more sustainable, holistic ecosystem.

To learn how the visual media operate and to develop defenses against manipulation, we must cultivate both intuitive wisdom and a sense of responsibility about images intended for mass consumption. The intuitive mind creates our perceptions of reality and guides our behavior. Developing it taps the potential of the nonconscious mind to live fully in a world of endless images. By exploring visual abilities through visual note taking and drawing, through examining dreams, and through cultivating creative writing and photography, you can develop your own mind as a powerful instrument of communication — both as sender and receiver. You can learn to use mediated messages to gain insight into your own life.

From Ulysses to Artificial Intelligence

It is neither reason nor intuition alone, but a synthesis of both, that has established the dream as a symbol of our quest for freedom, dignity and equality in both our individual and our communal lives.

The dream is an inner vision, a visual voice from the core of our being. From the free-form chaos of our interior unconscious, the dream emerges as an admonitory symbol, a guiding message.

Dreams, the essence of visions, are the inner messengers of the primal, ancient mind of Ulysses, Abraham, and Sitting Bull. They are the origin of the hallucinatory and inner voices of the bicameral mind and the voice of the gods to the Mycenaean people. They represent the intuitive mind that guided all human behavior before the Greek Age of Reason.

Before the logical imperative for scientific proof dominated knowing, dreams expressed reality. After the age of Reason, unfeeling reason severed from reality the validity of the unconscious experience, exchanging the creative quality of vision for the assumed safety and surety of quantification. Imagination became subservient to those phenomena that could be proven, repeated, quantified, and analyzed.

Cogito ergo sum. I think, therefore I am.

The call of reason over the imagination meant the triumph of rationality over the intuition of vision. Ulysses stood on the rocks before the sea, the great symbol of the unconscious, and proclaimed the supremacy of his logic, but the meaning of dreams as he knew them is now lost.

Jung and Freud knew that the nightmare is never literal but instead is a symbolic insight into the ever-emerging unconscious life of the dreamer. And with the age of neuroscience, their ideas have taken on new significance.

Roger Sperry and Joseph Bogen provided evidence that the mind is double, that reason and intuition are twin brother and sister. From their early efforts and the ideas of Jaynes, Edwards, Barry, Ornstein, Capra, Gardner, LeDoux, Wolfe, and Damasio, to mention only a few, we have made progress toward a clearer understanding of our cognitive abilities and hence of our lives.

That complementary cognitive processes, one rational/logical and one synthesistic/global, are integrated and equally significant to the whole mind experience is clear. That the logical is more verbal and the intuitive more visual is

Figure 16.7. Japanese Ulysses. Legend of the grand minister Yuriwaka. Kyoto, Japan, 17th century. MS 2468 Schøyen Collection, Oslo.

Figure 16.8. Texas Wildflowers, by Ave Bonar.

well established. And it is just beginning to become clear what the effects of rational bias have been on individuals and on society. We are just beginning to explore and understand how we might learn to balance our cognitive perspective.

As a part of this effort, we have introduced integrative mind theory, omniphasic thinking, and creative exercises as a model to nurture and develop cognitive balance within educational systems and, by extension, into our cultures.

We live in an amazing world of exciting and powerful imagery and imagination. We are surrounded by images that can enrich our lives and fulfill our needs for quality cognitive experiences of a visually synthesistic, intuitive nature. We have extraordinary advantages and opportunities for visual experiences available to us at a moment's notice. We live in cities and towns full of art museums and galleries, spectacular architecture, gardens and parks, public art, theaters that offer both moving pictures and live productions, bookstores and libraries full of books of photographs and art, and musical spectaculars that are both aural and visual feasts. And of course, we can draw and produce art, write literature and poetry, play music and dance, and meditate and dream in self-guided intuitive experiences. We can sit on a hill and watch the first light

Figure 16.9. Boys Reading, Italy,1999, by Andrew Z. Glickman.
From the series "At the Mall."

or the mist rise like breath breathed from the water. We can turn inward through meditation, dreams, and other processes to seek guidance from our own inner voices.

We are surrounded, without and within, by intuitive, visual opportunities that can enrich our experience of life and impart a sense of wholeness and fulfillment in a way that perhaps nothing else can. And all we have to do is, with self-directed intention, choose to seek out and nurture the intuitive.

The Other Side of the Problem

In direct competition with and in opposition to our self-directed intuitive, visual experiences are the most powerful and pervasive cultural and economic forces of all of history. Mass media, dominated by advertising and corporate agendas and values, work relentlessly to attract, seduce, and direct us, shaping our perceptions, and thereby our lives and our cultures. They offer us, at every turn of the dial, on every street corner, in every facet of life, an alternative to self-directed intuitive experience.

Figure 16.10. Sandra's Birthday, by Julianne Newton.

But it is an alternative without a qualitative sense of wholeness and fulfillment. It is hollow and counterfeit. Commercially mediated people and lifestyles are based in fantasy. They are not attainable and offer no internal fulfillment. Though they appeal to our raw emotions, mediated emotions such as those created by advertising suggest that an external solution can fulfill an internal need. This helps create a society based on lies, false emotion, and counterfeit values rather than on personal completeness, security, and fulfillment.

We need to recognize that our intuitive cognitive processes represent at least half of our consciousness, half of our cognitive abilities, and half of our human experience. It is the half that connects us to a reality larger than ourselves, that is concerned with a global perspective, integrity, caring, nurturing, mystery, creativity, sustainability, and the quality of our lives. Our intuitive intelligence facilitates holistic, powerful cognitive processing that rapidly synthesizes information across space and time. It is more rapid and complex than our logical process. It helps us quickly grasp "the big picture" of a problem and respond creatively before and beyond the slower process of reason. Nonconscious cognitive processes are at the core of creativity, problem solving, and decision making. It taps into our deepest, primal emotions and value systems with the power to transform our perceptions and thus to direct our actions without the need for reason.

Many would argue here that lack of reason causes these problems. Yet, to teach children to successfully negotiate our rational educational and cultural systems, we spend the first 20-odd years of their lives teaching them how to use their minds and their linear talents in areas such as writing, reading, math, philosophy, and science. Allowing for some overlap in the rational/intuitive cognitive paradigm, this educates perhaps 60% of our known cognitive functions, but with a strong linear bias toward logic and toward reasoning processes and systems rather than toward creative problem solving.

Does it not make logical sense that we should give equal attention to the other half of our cognitive abilities? Would we not benefit from such a cognitive balance that enhances creativity, problem solving, and decision making intelligences? We don't know how anyone could answer this question with a negative response. We can only anticipate a resounding response of, "How do we do that?" And that IS the question: How do we nurture and develop our intuitive intelligence in a system that has been and, for the most part still is, hostile to even the concept of intuitive intelligence?

The Plan

First, we must focus on the positive aspects of such an endeavor. The enrichment of our individual and communal lives. The fulfillment of our holistic natures. The balanced development of our minds and of the individual and cultural relationships and systems we develop with them. The enhancement of our creativity and our abilities to solve problems and make decisions in new, exciting, and sustainable ways. The disarming of the media in terms of their ability to exploit our intuitive naiveté. Within this we must also recognize the significance of the rational mind and that a society unbalanced toward intuitive initiatives would still be unbalanced and no more desirable than the current state of affairs.

Second, we must take individual initiative to nurture and develop our own intuitive intelligences by choosing and practicing those intuitive processes that inspire and enrich our lives and cultures. We must redirect our efforts to include, as an integral part of our lives and education, those things that celebrate and nurture the quality of our lives as art — the passion of drawing, creative writing, music, dance, photography, meditation, dream interpretation, and many others that are being discovered or rediscovered daily. There is clearly evidence that those who participate in arts processes enhance their intelligence, improve their academic and professional performance across disciplines, and improve the quality of their lives. Intuitive cognitive processes represent the cognitive core of creativity and problem solving. Arts practices enhance those cognitive abilities. When you participate in art processes, according to Eliot Eisner, you:

- Enhance your creativity
- Learn to transform creativity into a functional, finite form
- Learn to evaluate your work
- Learn to communicate about your thought processes and work

These are life skills that are core to the ability to creatively solve problems and make decisions that are both qualitatively and quantitatively valuable to the individual and to culture. We believe that the practices of intuitive processes through art and other applications will enhance overall intelligence and performance in a more balanced way.

Third we must begin to integrate, into our educational system, omniphasic (balanced) courses that blend the teaching of both the rational and intuitive aspects of the mind through visual communication and art practices. From this base, we expand the integration of intuitive teaching practices that can enrich all learning experiences. First, into the disciplines that welcome them, like architecture, art, literature, photography, film, drama, home economics, anthropology and sociology, mathematics, and physics . . . and then into the more traditionally linear areas of study in business, natural sciences, engineering, and technology.

Through this effort toward holistic cognitive integration, it is imperative that our actions be based on integrative rational and intuitive intelligences. Through the ebb and flow of cognition and life experiences, we will invariably and desirably

Figure 16.11. The Human Store, Arpin, Arkansas. Photograph by Frank Armstrong.

learn to apply the appropriate mind process to the appropriate task, with logic leading at one turn and intuition at another; logic directing the technical aspects of photography, dance and math; intuition facilitating the creative and aesthetically transcendent quality of the experience. We must remember that together we are whole. To educate the whole mind, we must avoid oppressing either the rational or the intuitive. If we do not, we lose the essential quality of life as a unified creative experience and an expression of wholeness. Howard Gardner (1993) said it well:

> Dissatisfaction with the concept of IQ and with unitary views of intelligence is fairly widespread. . . . The whole concept has to be challenged; in fact, it has to be replaced. I would like to present an alternative vision — one that yields a very different view of school. It is a pluralistic view of mind, recognizing many different and discrete facets of cognition. (pp. 6–7)

The techniques we have described in this book are a beginning. According to thousands of our past students, they work. This new approach requires the contributions of many other educators and scholars to fulfill its potential through development, integration, and maintenance of omniphasic practices. It is our hope that, over time, these ideas and techniques will be incorporated into virtually every course of study to prepare students to become more balanced, fully educated, self-determining individuals, who are less susceptible to manipulative media influence and better prepared to apply classroom experience to life experience in ways that will holistically benefit both the individual and society.

Table 15 summarizes the key ideas of this book.

Table 15. Key Ideas

- There are many different ways to learn and many different intelligences to teach.

- Intuitive/synthetic and rational/analytical are two major learning modes.

- It is possible to make a clear correlation between intuitive/synthetic intelligences and between rational/analytical intelligences.

- Rational mode is the dominant learning mode in our schooling and therefore is the predominant tactical tool in our society. This leaves an intuitive void in our intellectual, psychological, and life experiences.

- The dominance of the rational mode sets up a type of rational hegemony that diminishes the expansion of our cognitive abilities and the structuring and enrichment of society.

- Profit-motivated mass media, owned by multinational corporations, have effectively filled the intuitive void through advertising and programming, exploiting our intuitive intelligence toward their own ends.

- It is possible to develop holistic, omniphasic approaches to learning, teaching, and living that equally include all known intelligences and all people. In doing so, we can embrace the whole of our potential as humans to build a balanced society.

- The integration of intuitive and rational intelligences into an educational model for the whole mind can provide balance within the academic world, the lives of our graduates, and the societies that they create.

An Eye to the Future

If we do it right, 1,000 years from now, people will look back on this era as a great equalizer, as we do when we look back on the time of Gutenberg in the 15th century. By Gutenberg's time, writing by hand had been going on at least 2,000 years. Yet most people in Europe still could not read or write in the 15th century. Most people depended on those in power—royalty or religious leaders—to record and recite ideas deemed worthy of the time-consuming and skilled process of writing and printing. People could hear and use the words, but they could not give them permanency. With Gutenberg's press came speed and multiple, exact copies.

The next giant step toward creating a literate and more democratic world came with the hand-held camera. When George Eastman put an easy means of recording the visual world into the hands of nonphotographers, he began a movement toward democratizing visual communication that would have even greater impact on the control of ideas than the printing press. Previously, only the wealthy could afford to have a skilled artist paint their portraits or make real-life renderings of the material world. The spread of photography in the early part of the 20th century led the Bauhaus artist Moholy Nagy to predict, "The illiterate of the future will be ignorant of pen and camera alike" (p. 54). The proliferation of the still camera led to the proliferation of the video camera, and with it, the possibility that anyone with a camera could impact both culture and history.

The third technological innovation to disseminate the power to control ideas was digitization and the computer. Visionaries such as communication scholar Wayne Danielson foresaw in the 1970s that "there would be a computer in every living room" within a few decades. Now, because of digital cameras and the Internet, amateur documentaries can instantaneously inform the global society. Such was the case of photos from Abu Ghraib Prison in Iraq that informed the world of acts of torture in 2004. Because of visual technology, we can see the rings of Saturn.

Six billion people populate 21st-century Earth. Of these, close to 1 billion adults do not know how to read or write. But, as we have discussed, 21st-century literacy means more than knowing how to read and write. According to World Literacy of Canada (WLC), literacy goes beyond reading, writing, and numeracy, to include meeting the basic needs for quality of life. "Illiteracy is linked to poverty, disadvantage and exclusion," notes the WLC Web site, adding, "Literacy is an essential element in the struggle for justice, human dignity and equality" (para. 2). Today, therefore, we must talk about different kinds of literacy: the traditional verbal literacy of being able to read and write words and handle numbers well enough to function in an economically based world and the visual literacy of being able to interpret and create images,

media literacy, emotional literacy, cultural literacy, and now, intuitive literacy. Jacques Delors, former president of the UNESCO Task Force on Education for the Twenty-first Century, asserted that life is based on four pillars: learning to live together, learning to know, learning to do, and learning to be (pp. 20–21). The ability to learn translates into power. As futurist Alvin Toffler predicted, those who can communicate well in various ways are those who will hold power in society.

Our goal with this book has been to empower you to understand, respond, and communicate with your whole mind. You have been taught to read and write words and to handle numbers. You have responded to, and to a less sophisticated extent understood and used, visual images all of your life. Yet most of you have not been taught to integrate the verbal and visual mental-processing abilities in the sophisticated ways you need to help you navigate a complex world.

We want to conclude with several important points about literacy in general:

• *Literacy can be culturally relative.* We cannot assume that a lack of knowledge of one type of literacy means illiteracy in general. Many Haitians, for example, cannot read or write words, but most can tell and understand stories with graphic pictures on fences throughout their communities.

• *Literacy has a cumulative effect.* The more diverse a person's literacies, the more effective he/she can be as a communicator. Consider the power of knowing multiple verbal languages, for example. European children grow up being able to communicate in a number of languages, whereas most U.S. children grow up knowing only one or two. Which children can more easily navigate the world?

• *Literacy does not equal wisdom or ethics.* A person can be a skilled visual artist and an articulate speaker without possessing wisdom. A person who speaks multiple languages can misuse the power.

• *Increased literacy does not guarantee a decreased gap between those who know and those who do not.* You probably have heard the term "digital divide" or "knowledge gap." This gap is growing wider as those who have access to computer technology gain power.

• *Literacy continues to be misunderstood and misapplied.* True literacy includes the ability to both understand and create in the communication forms of one's culture and society.

Figure 16.12. The Storyteller, by Julianne Newton.

Figure 16.13. Mammatus Clouds, by Ave Bonar.

The future is your responsibility. We have the means today to spread integrative literacy to anyone. Literacy can be a tool for good or ill. Literacy can be an equalizer or a divider. It's up to the communicators of the future.

Conclusion

Critical changes in education and culture are about more than words and pictures. They are about thinking, ways of knowing and doing. The shift from an oral tradition has changed the way we tell stories, for example. In centuries past, the storytellers conveyed information through a dynamic, person-to-person process. With the written and printed word, storytelling shifted into a linear, more static process. At the same time, the power of the storyteller to weave emotion and mystery into the tale through creative voices and gestures shifted to media use of highly realistic images capable of manipulating those who watch and listen. As researcher George Gerbner noted, media have replaced our village storytellers, conveying values along with information. Gerbner rightly pointed out that the media constructed "instant history" with their coverage of the 1992 war in Iraq, determining what and how people in the United States would remember the war. Media professionals, in turn, point out that government control of press activities largely constructed the war the press was allowed to portray. During the second war in Iraq, U.S. viewers again saw what mainstream media and government officials wanted them to see — unless they made use of the Internet and other alternative sources for information. Whether our politics are conservative or liberal, we must learn to challenge what we see and hear — whatever the source — and realize the magnitude of media power.

This book has sought to strengthen visual communication abilities as the primary route to intuitive literacy, the fundamental ability of the mind to integrate different ways of processing and conveying information, to solve problems, and make wise decisions. In some ways, human beings have come full circle, moving from a visual age to a verbal age back to a visual age. Yet we also have evolved from the oral, largely intuitive culture of prehistory humans to the verbal, logical age of Aristotle, and now to an age in which we need to balance intuition with logic and pictures with words to communicate in effective ways as a globally literate culture. We are now in a virtual age, an age in which knowledge is so confounded with illusion that it is hard to know what is real. Yet discerning what is authentic is what really matters in this world.

And that's what living at the speed of mind is all about.

We have shown you how to do just that, to take you beyond visual and media literacy to show you how visual information, which directly and powerfully feeds your subconscious mind, guides your thoughts, your dreams, and your actions. By cultivating both rational and intuitive mental processing toward integrative mind, you can become a more powerful communicator and a more integrated and balanced individual.

Figure A.1. Paradise, by Ave Bonar.

AFTERWORD
Ecology in Paradise

*Justice in the life and conduct of the State is possible only as
first it resides in the hearts and souls of the citizens.*

Plato

Moving toward an ecology of the visual, as Julianne Newton calls it, is the primary and most immediate route to developing integrated systems of knowing and understanding ourselves and our world. Better understanding of how the human brain — operating from complex, functionally specific, but integrated cognitive modalities — creates a unified mind is likely to be the most significant contribution that scholars make in this age of the brain. It is no wonder that we grapple with theory, method, and meaning as we strive to understand the cognitive and intelligence functions of the visual as they construct meaning and guide our lives.

The study of the visual is one of the most interdisciplinary of modern scholarly endeavors, drawing from art, communication, media, and anthropology, cognitive neuroscience, psychology, physics, biology, and mathematics. Such technologies as functional MRIs and PET scans unveil and summon the powers of the unconscious, synthesistic, intuitive mind and intelligences to position the visual, with other intuitive processes, as the first-level cognitive informant of knowledge, understanding, and behavioral motivation.

Ironically, all of this new information and empirical evidence about unconscious intuitive intelligence systems is built on models of logic and rationality that, for millennia, have marginalized the unconscious mind and intuitive cognitive synthesis. How do we reconcile that the very science based on reason now suggests that nonrational cognitive functions are the primary source of creativity and advantageous problem solving and decision making?

In a broader sense, the quest for a unified theory to explain the origins and workings of the universe focuses today on this quest to understand and apply integrative mind. It is as old as time uncounted or time measured in cycles of moon and sun and tide.

Through Homer, Odysseus brought to life the dominant mind of the Gods over the mind of logic. Plato reversed the order and subjugated the mind of divine passions to divine reason and behavior to bring about the Greek Golden Age of Reason. Descartes separated the mind's modalities into the dominance of reason over feeling to fuel the ages of industry, science, and technology.

Today, the quest for mind drives art and science to embrace the ecological whole of being. Mathematical equations for fractals predict structures that may represent the underlying logic of the biological and subatomic universe, just as they underlie the intuitive structure of Jackson Pollack's paint splatters on huge canvases. Physicists predict 11 or more dimensions of reality as parallel universes that unify mechanical and quantum physics. Transitory subatomic structures of invisible, vibrating strings of energy that can only be imagined are proposed as the structure of reality itself. Through nanotechnology bioengineers work on molecular and subatomic scales, shifting the balance of grace and power in the human body and shaping the physical and political world at large.

Scientists and mystics alike celebrate the power of intuitive intelligence and the self-aware universe that creative artists have heralded and represented in handprints on cave walls, impressionistic art, and mass media. We stand at the vortex of the integration and balance of creativity and intellect, poised to know and understand the unity of all things seen and imagined.

Because as much as 75% of all of the information that enters the brain is visual, and because all intelligences have significant visual components, both cognitively and functionally, visual theory and applications can be used to understand and enhance the integrative human mind. To deny the cognitive role and power of unconscious, visual knowing as intelligent nonverbal thought is to deny the full power of our creativity and our ability to solve problems in new and fully human ways that are sustainable.

In this age, when the study of the brain melds art and science, it is time for scholars of all disciplines to join forces to solve the integrative puzzle of knowledge and understanding. No matter how we describe it, whether we call it omniphasic or multimodal, unified theory or holistic thinking, rational and intuitive, or integrative mind, we must acknowledge that this is not an "either or" but rather a "both/and" paradigm of the rational and intuitive modalities.

Essentially, our success as scholars turns not on our credentials or our positions but on our willingness to recognize and embrace our own power and wisdom as part of the integrative whole of knowledge and humanity.

Visual and verbal, rational and intuitive represent highly complex cognitive modalities that operate in distinct, independent ways to create perceptions of reality and guide behavior. It is critical that we understand how essential and equal components of whole mind cognition contribute to the kind of creativity and decision-making that can lead us beyond the traditional scientific paradigm to a new ecological worldview. Ultimately, it is the imperceptibly seamless and integrative work of the human brain that can unite us all.

CONTRIBUTORS

We gratefully acknowledge the generous contributions of the individual artists, scholars, educators, and students, as well as institution and company representatives, who made this book a truly integrated visual/word creation by helping us to obtain mages and granting us permission to include their work:

Justin Abbott, alumnus, University of Oregon.

Adbusters Media Foundation.

Collin Andrew , photographer based in Eugene, OR.

Frank Armstrong, fine arts photographer based in West Boylston, MA., and teacher of photography at Clark University.

Artists Rights Society of New York. Marisa Young, rights administrator.

Art Resource Inc., New York. NY. Tricia Smith and Eric Lessing.

Bayerisches Nationalmuseum München, Germany. Angelika Grandi, Dr. Nina Gockerell.

BBDO Advertising, Denver, CO.

Ave Bonar, who embraced the "narrative documentary" tradition of photography early in her career, is a photographer based in Austin, TX.

Marta Braun, author of *Picturing Time: The Work of Etienne Jules Marey*, and teacher of art history, photographic history, and film theory, Ryerson University School of Image Arts, Toronto, Canada.

The Trustees of The British Museum. Axelle Russo.

Robert Roy Britt, managing editor, LiveScience, www.LiveScience.com and senior science writer, SPACE.com, Imaginova Companies.

Ally Burguieres, artist, photographer and doctoral student at Georgetown University.

Beau Cease, graduate student at the Visual Studies Workshop, Rochester, NY., and founder of the Obediah Dogberry Society.

J. B. Colson, professor emeritus and founder of the Photojournalism Program, UT Austin School of Journalism andCommunication.

Randy Cox, director of visuals, The Oregonian, Portland, OR.

Don Barth, assistant professor, Department of Art at the University of South Carolina. His computer-based art explores virtual interactive landscapes.

Michael Broschart, graphic designer, Media Services, The Valley Library.

Brett Crosse, visual and aural storyteller, alumnus of the University of Oregon School of Journalism and Communication, and "dedicated to an unflinching exploration of life."

Binh Danh, who created a process for making unique "chlorophyll prints," was born in Vietnam in 1977, the year his family immigrated to the United States. He is represented by the Haines Gallery, San Francisco, CA.

Prof. Philip J. Davis, Brown University, and Reuben Hersh, University of Minnesota, co-authors of Descartes' Dream.

Mary Lee Edwards, Austin, TX, photographer/poet before her death in 2001.

Colin Elliot, University of Oregon student.

Kristine Wolff Fiskum, free-lance editorial and commercial photographer based in Chicago, Ill.

Roy Flukinger, senior curator of photography and film, and Linda Briscoe Myers, assistant curator of photography, Harry Ransom Center, U T Austin.

Bonnie Fournier, digital fine art painter and photographer in St. Paul, MN.

Andrew Z. Glickman, Bethesda, MD., photographer.

The Global Children's Art Gallery, created in 1997 by Jason Hunt, as part of The Natural Child Project (NCP), Jan Hunt, director.

Grant. Artist, Houston, Texas

Adam Grosowski, instructor of art, Lane Community College, Eugene, OR. His work is represented by Karin Clark Gallery, Eugene.

Janet Halvorsen, designer and artist, teaches at Lane Community college, Eugene, OR.

Germán Herrera, fine art photographer whose images are "felt, not thought."

Amir Hetsroni , senior lecturer, Department of Communication, Yezreel Valley College.

Hitachi America, Ltd. Kenji Nakamura, General Manager / Executive Vice President, and Daniel Lee, Vice President, Marketing, Ubiquitous Platform Systems, Hitachi.

ImpactGames, co-founded by Eric Brown, chief executive officer, and Asi Burak, chief creative officer / executive producer, to explore social and political issues affecting the world.

John Chris Jones, Welsh design theorist, a founder of ergonomic design, and author of Design Methods.

Tim Jordan, art director, Oregon Quarterly alumni magazine, and designer for Creative Publishing, UO.

Igloolik Isuma Productions, Katarina Soukup and Anne Paré.

iStockphoto.com/Xianstudio, llc., Calgary, Alberta, Canada.

The Lambesis Agency, a full-service brand development company headquartered in San Diego, CA. Chad Farmer, President; Vicki Hoekstra, COO, Executive Media Director; Victoria Kudirka, Executive Director, Strategic Planning and Research; Janna Ekholm, Senior Account Supervisor.

Library of Congress Prints and Publications Division. National Archives.

Maggie Macnab, who teaches logo design and "symbols as visual literacy for designers" at the University of New Mexico.

Rogers Marvel Architects, PLLC. Tim Fryatt, Jonathan Marvel, Richard Ramsey, Robert Rogers, and Graeme Waitzkin.

Matie Molinaro, founder of the Canadian Speakers' and Writers' Service Ltd, Canada's first literary agency, and co-editor, with Corinne McLuhan and William Toye, of the Letters of Marshall McLuhan.

Morse Library, Beloit College, Beloit, WI.

National Park Service, National Archives and Records Administration.

Musée Marey–Beaune, Marion Leuba and Delphine Cornuché.

National Aeronautics and Space Administration (NASA), Connie Moore.

Matthew Newton, systems engineer, Micromenders, San Francisco, CA., holds a degree in religious studies from University of California, Berkeley.

Nur, 9, and Abd Al-Rahman, 13, the Sudan. Courtesy of Human Rights Watch, 2005.

Oregon Center for Applied Science, a research-based company creates interactive multimedia programs designed to enhance lives. Carol Horne, senior staff writer; Marta Makarushka, behavioral researcher; Kim Lindquist, graphic artist, musician, and videographer.

Orlan, scholar in residence, Getty Research Institute, Angeles. Professor, National Art School at Cergy, France, and teaches at the Art Center College of Design, Pasadena, CA., www.orlan.net

Erik Palmer, Portland, OR,scholar and artist who examines the relationship between comic book superheroes and other forms of cultural expression.

Nora Paul, Institute for New Media Studies, School of Journalism and Mass Communication, University of Minnesota, Minneapolis, MN; and Laura Ruel, Assistant Professor, Visual Communication and Multimedia, School of Journalism and Mass Communication, University of North Carolina at Chapel Hill. Digital Storytelling Effects Lab, a joint project of the University of Minnesota and the University of North Carolina.

Nancy Pobanz, Eugene artist, combines "the influence of the Oregon high dessert with concealed journal writing" and her own hand-made pigments, papers, and inks to produce one-of-a-kind books, wallpieces, and sculpture.

Project Blinkenlights, an online gallery of public interactive installations, Chaos Computer Club. Photographers Dorit Günter, Nadja Hannaske, and Tim Pritlove.

Hugh Pryor, Graphic Designer and Digital Artist, Oxford, UK., started GPS Drawing with Jeremy Wood.

Luis Salazar, director of communications, Zamorano, a private international university in Tegucigalpa, Honduras. www.zamorano.edu

Andrea Schneider, student, University of Oregon.

Science & Society Picture Library, National Museum of Science & Industry, London, England. Natasha Mulder, image sales coordinator.

Slim Films, New York-based company specializing in covers, illustrations, and animations. Andy Christie.

The Schøyen Collection, Oslo, Norway, a private collection comprising 13,540 manuscript items from throughout the world and spanning more than 5,000 years. Martin Schøyen, owner, and Elizabeth Gano Sorenssen, librarian.

Maggie Steber, international photojournalist and documentarian.

D.J. Stout, graphic designer and partner, Pentagram, Inc., Austin, TX.

Former students who gave us permission to publish their work: Allison Hibbs, Patrick Healy, T. Adams, M. Chrissy, D.A., Michael Stevens, Jaci Sonnenberg, A. Megan, Abel, Beason, Fowell & Harrell, Almeida & Jackson, and Stu Holdren.

Melissa Szalkowski, freelance editorial digital illustration artist in New York.

Maggie Taylor, digital image artist and photographer working in Gainesville, FL.

Richard Taylor, associate professor of physics, psychology, and art, Department of Physics, University of Oregon.

Mike Tsukamoto, Page One photo editor, and Dixie Vereen, USA Today.

Jerry Uelsmann, photographer and artist and retired graduate research professor of art at the University of Florida.

Joshua Williams, director of commercial sales, Alamo Title Company, Austin, TX., holds a bachelor's degree in art from the University of Texas at Austin.

Bill Westheimer, photographer, New York.

Russel Wong, free-lance photographer based in Singapore.

World Food Programme, Rome, Italy. Silke Buhr, Communications Division.

The Worldmapper Team and the Sheffield Group. Mark Newman, professor, Department of Physics and Center for the Study of Complex Systems, University of Michigan. Danny Dorling, professor of human geography, University of Sheffield, UK.

Herb Zettl, professor emeritus, San Francisco State University, and author of *Sight, Sound, Motion: Applied Media Aesthetics*.

Rebecca Zimmerman, promotions/marketing coordinator, Publications Department, The Museum of Modern Art (MOMA), New York, NY.

REFERENCES

Adatto, K. (1993). *Picture perfect: The art and artifice of public image making*. New York: Basic Books.

Altmann, G. T. M. (2001). The language machine: Psycholinguistics in review. *British Journal of Psychology, 92*, 129–170.

Amert, K. (1995). *Rereading the Contract of literacy: Typography and the intellect*. Paper presented to the Visual Communication Division, Association for Education in Journalism and Mass communication, August, Washington, D.C.

Associated Press. (2004, August 23). Nearly flawless, U.S. women win gold. *ESPN*. Retrieved September 26, 2004, from http://sports.espn.go.com/oly/summer04/softball/news/story?id=1865646

Audobon, J. J. (1838). *Birds of America*. Edinburgh.

Aveni, A. F., & Hotaling, L. D. (1996). *Monumental inscriptions and the observational basis of Mayan planetary astronomy: Eighth Palenque Round Table, 1993*. San Francisco: Pre-Columbian Art Research Institute.

Babbie, E. (1998). *The practice of social research* (8th ed.). Belmont, CA: Wadsworth.

Barber, J. (2004). Chairman's introduction. *British Belgian Blue Bull Book*. Retrieved September 26, 2004, from http://www.belgianblue.co.uk/breed/bull_book.html

Barry, A. M. S. (1997). *Visual intelligence: Perception, image, and manipulation in visual communication*. New York: State University of New York Press.

Bechara, A., Damasio, H., Tranel, D., & Damasio, A. (1997). Deciding advantageously before knowing the advantageous strategy. *Science, 275*, 1293–1295.

Berger, A. A. (1998). *Seeing is believing: An introduction to visual communication* (4th ed.). Mountain View, CA: Mayfield.

Boeree, C. G. (1997). *Carl Jung. Personality theories*. Retrieved December 27, 2004, from http://www.ship.edu/~cgboeree/jung.html

Bogen, J. E. (1975). Some educational aspects of hemispheric specialization. *U.C.L.A. Educator, 17*, 24–32.

Bracken, C. C., & Atken, D. (2004). How screen size affects perception of television: A survey of presence-evoking technology in our living rooms, *Visual Communication Quarter, 11*(Winter/Spring), 23–27.

Brand, D. (2004, April 21). Arecibo Observatory gets 7-pixel eye on the sky that will make world's most sensitive dish radio telescope incredibly more sensitive. *Cornell News*. Retrieved September 26, 2004, from http://www.news.cornell.edu/releases/April04/Arecibo.Eye.deb.html

Britt, R. R. (2004, September 10). Astronomers produce photo of possible extra solar planet. SPACE.com. Retrieved September 10, 2004, from http://www.usatoday.com/tech/science/space/2004-09-10-extrasolar-planet-pic_x.htm?POE=click-refer

Burgoon, J. K., Kelley, D. L., Newton, D. A., & Keeley-Dyreson, M. (1989). The nature of arousal and nonverbal indices. *Human Communication Research*, *16*(2), 217-255.

Cane, F. (1951). *The artist in each of us*. New York: Pantheon.

Capra, F. (1991). *The tao of physics*. Boston: Shambhala.

Capra, F. (1996). *The web of life: A new scientific understanding of living systems*. New York: Anchor.

Carey, B. (2004, September 14). Déjà vu: If it all seems familiar, there may be a reason. *New York Times*. Retrieved September 14, 2004, from http://www.nytimes.com/2004/09/14/science/14deja.html

Carr, D. (2003, July 6). Is animated funnier than live? *New York Times*. Retrieved September 7, 2003, from http://www.nytimes.com/2003/07/06/movies/06CARR.html

Cascardi, A. J. (1984). Cervantes and Descartes on the dream argument. *Cervantes: Bulletin of the Cervantes Society of America, 4.2,* 109–122.

Cervantes, M. de (2004). *The literature network. Don Quixote*. Retrieved August 17, 2004, from http://www.online-literature.com/cervantes/don_quixote/ (original published in two parts, 1605 and 1616)

Chandler, D. (1995). *Semiotics for beginners*. Retrieved August 27, 2004, from http://www.aber.ac.uk/media/Documents/S4B/semiotic.html

Charny, B. (2004, September 24). Big boss is watching. *CNET News*. Retrieved September 25, 2004, from http://news.com.com/Big+boss+is+watching/2100-1036_3-5379953.html?tag=sas.email

Coen, R. (2005). *Insider's report*. UniversalMcCann. Retrieved August 26, 2006, from http://www.universalmccann.com/pdf/Insiders1205.pdf#search=%22Coen%20Insider's%20Report%22

Colson, J. B. (1986-1996). Unpublished class notes and personal communication. The University of Texas at Austin.

Coolidge, F. F. (2004). *Dreams of early hominids and the evolution of cognition* [Electronic version]. Retrieved December 27, 2004, from http://web.uccs.edu/twynn/Dreams.htm

Crick, F. (1994). *The astonishing hypothesis: The scientific search for the soul*. New York: Scribner.

Curtin, W. (1985). Presentation to Texas Photographic Society, Austin, Texas.

Damasio, A. (1994). *Decartes' error*. New York: Putnam.

Damasio, A. (1999). *The feeling of what happens*. New York: Harcourt Brace.

Danto, A. C. (2000). *The madonna of the future: Essays in a pluralistic art world*. New York: Farrar, Straus and Giroux.

Davis, P. J., & Hersh, R. (1986). *Descartes' dream: The world according to mathematics*. San Diego: Harcourt Brace & Jovanovich.

Delors, J. (1996). *Learning: The treasure within*. Report to UNESCO of the International Commission on Education for the Twenty-first Century. Paris: UNESCO Publishing.

Deutsch, C. (2004, September 13). New logo and tagline for Xerox. *New York Times*. Retrieved September 14, 2004, from http://www.nytimes.com/2004/09/13/business/media/13adcol.html?8seia

Dondis, D. A. (1973). *A primer of visual literacy*. Cambridge, MA: MIT Press.

Edwards, B. (1979). *Drawing on the right side of the brain* : A course in enhancing creativity and artistic confidence. Los Angeles: Tarcher.

Edwards, B. (1989). *Drawing on the right side of the brain: A course in enhancing creativity and artistic confidence* (Rev. ed.). New York: Putnam.

Eisner, E. (2002). *The arts and the creation of mind*. New Haven: Yale University Press.

Elkins, J. (2003). *Visual studies: A skeptical introduction*. New York: Routledge.

Erdmann, E., & Stover, D. (1991). *Beyond a world divided*. London: Shambhala.

Estés, C. P. (1992). *Women who run with the wolves: Myths and stories of the wild woman archetype*. New York: Ballantine.

Eye Games. (2004). *About us*. Retrieved September 10, 2004, from http://www.eye-games.com/aboutus.html

Ganje, L. A. (1998). Living pictures: Design and the native press. *Newspaper Research Journal, 19*(2), 31–47.

Garcia, M., & Stark, P. (1991). *Eyes on the news*. St. Petersburg, FL: Poynter Institute.

Gardner, H. (1985). *Frames of mind: The theory of multiple intelligences*. New York: HarperCollins.

Gardner, H. (1993). *Multiple intelligences: The theory in practice*. New York: Harper Collins.

Gastner, M., Shalizi, C., & Newman, M. (2004). Maps and cartograms of the 2004 U.S. presidential election results. Retrieved August 17, 2006, from http://www-personal.umich.edu/~mejn/election/

Gazzaniga, M. S. (2005). *The ethical brain*. New York: Dana Press.

Gerbner, George (1991). *The Wayne Danielson Award for Outstanding Contributions to Communication Scholarship, Address by 1991 Recipient, Dr. George Gerbner*, College of Communication, The University of Texas at Austin, November 13, no page numbers.

Goleman, D. (1995). *Emotional intelligence*. New York: Bantam.

Gorny, E. (1995). Between knowledge and understanding. *Creator, 3*.

Grabe, M. E., Lombard, M., Reich, R. D., Bracken, C. C., & Ditton, T. B. (1999). The role of screen size in viewer experiences of media content. *Visual Communication Quarterly, 6*(2), 4–9.

Griffiths, F. (2004, September 3). Scientists begin mapping entire galaxy on Friday. *USA Today*. Retrieved September 10, 2004, from http://www.usatoday.com/tech/science/space/2004-09-03-get-out-the-map_x.htm?POE=click-refer

Grow, G. (1990). *Writing and multiple intelligences*. Presentation to Association for Educators in Journalism and Mass Communication. (ERIC Document Reproduction Service No. ED406643). Available from http://www.longleaf.net/ggrow

Guinness: Scientist creates world's largest book. (2003, December 16). CNN.com. Retrieved August 30, 2004, from http://www.cnn.com/2003/TECH/ptech/12/16/largest.book.ap/

Ha, K. O. (2004, September 14). It's a neo world; popular site for kids stirs controversy. *San Jose Mercury News*. Retrieved September 14, 2004, from http://www.siliconvalley.com/mld/siliconvalley/9658520.htm

Hall, S., Hobson, D., Lowe, A., & Willis, P. (Eds.). (1980). *Culture, media language: Working papers in cultural studies, 1972–79*. London: Centre for Contemporary Studies, University of Birmingham.

Hetsroni, A. (2005). Art in advertising: A cross-cultural examination of ads and creatives. *Visual Communication Quarterly*, *13*, 58–77.

Hill, E. (1966). *The language of drawing*. Englewood Cliffs, NJ: Prentice-Hall.

Holmes, N. (1994). Presentation to Visual Communication Division, Association for Education in Journalism and Mass Communication, Atlanta, GA.

Howlett, D. (2004, September 9). Chicago plans advanced surveillance. *USA Today*. Retrieved September 10, 2004, from http://www.usatoday.com/tech/news/surveillance/2004-09-09-chicago-surveillance_x.htm?POE=click-refer

I Ching or book of changes (R. Wilhelm, Trans). (1950). Princeton: Princeton University Press.

Ihlebaek, C., Love, T., Eilertsen, D. E., & Magnussen, S. (2003). Memory for a staged criminal event witnessed live and on video. *Memory*, *11*, 319–327.

Innis, H. (1951). *The bias of communication*. Toronto: University of Toronto Press.

Jaynes, J. (1990). *The origin of consciousness in the breakdown of the bicameral mind*. Boston: Houghton Mifflin.

Jewett, C., & Kress, G. (Eds.) (2003). *Multimodal literacy*. New York: P. Lang.

Johnson, R. (1986). *Inner work*. San Francisco: Harper & Row.

Jones, J. C. (2004a, March 20). Lifetime Achievement Award Speech. Design Research Society. Royal College of Art, London. Retrieved September 13, 2004, from http://www.dmu.ac.uk/4dd/DDR4/DDR4-frame2.html

Jones, J. C. (2004b, September 11). *What is life?* Retrieved September 13, 2004, from http://www.softopia.demon.co.uk/2.2/digital_diary_04.09.11.html

Joyce, J. (1959). *Finnegans wake*. New York: Viking.

Jung, C. G. (1968). *The archetypes and the collective unconscious* (2nd ed., R. F. C. Hull, Trans.). Princeton: Princeton University Press.

Karabinis, P. (2000). Interview of Jerry Uelsmann at the University of North Florida, 1997. Retrieved on June 25, 2006 from http://www.uelsmann.net

Kellogg, R. (1969). *Analyzing children's art*. Palo Alto, CA: Mayfield.

Koffka, K. (1935). *Principles of gestalt psychology*. New York: Harcourt, Brace & World.

Kostelanetz, R. (Ed.) (1970). *Moholy-Nagy*. New York: Praeger.

Kress, G., & van Leeuwen, T. (1996). *Reading images: The grammar of visual design*. London: Routledge.

Kristof, N. D. (2004, August 24). Building better bodies. *New York Times*. Retrieved August 25, 2004, from http://www.nytimes.com/2004/08/25/opinion/25kristof.html?ex=1096344000&en=506d846cf726c705&ei=5070&th

La Ferla, R. (2003, October 26). Underdressed and hot: Dolls moms don't love. *New York Times*. Retrieved October 31, 2003, from http://www.nytimes.com/2003/10/26/fashion/26DOLL.html?ex=1151467200&en=ef733c5dbaac2cfe&ei=5070

Lark-Horovitz, B., Lewis, H., & Luca, M. (1967). *Understanding children's art for better teaching*. Columbus, OH: Merrill.

LeDoux, J. (1986). Sensory systems and emotion. *Integrative Psychiatry, 4*, 237–243.

LeDoux, J. (1996). *The emotional brain*. New York: Simon & Schuster.

Lester, P. M. (1995). *Visual communication: Images with messages*. Belmont, CA: Wadsworth.

Lester, P. M. (2006). *Visual communication: Images with messages* (4th ed.). Belmont, CA: Wadsworth.

Lester, P. M. (2000). *The zen of photography*. (2000). iUniverse Incorporated (Self-Published).

Logan, R. K. (1986). *The alphabet effect: The impact of the phonetic alphabet on the development of western civilization*. New York: Morrow.

Lowenfeld, V. (1947). *Creative and mental growth*. New York: Macmillan.

Maney, K. (2004, September 8). Every move you make could be stored on a PLR, Cyberspeak. *USA Today*. Retrieved September 8, 2004, from http://www.usatoday.com/tech/columnist/kevinmaney/2004-09-07-plr_x.htm?POE=click-refer

Mannoni, L., and Rollet, G. (2004). Étienne-Jules Marey: movement in light. Trans. Richard Crangle. Maison du Cinéma, Online Exhibition, accessed on September 17, 2004 from http://www.expo-marey.com/ANGLAIS/home.html

Mattel (2004). *Mattel asks girls "what's your flava?" in an all-new line of fashion dolls*. Retrieved September 27, 2004, from http://www.mattel.com/swap_feat/default_flavas.asp

McLuhan, M., & McLuhan, E. (1988). *Laws of media: The new science*. Toronto: University of Toronto Press.

McLuhan, M., & Powers, B. (1989). *The global village, transformations in world life and media in the 21st century*. New York: Oxford University Press.

McLuhan, T. C (1994). *The way of the earth: Encounters with nature in ancient and contemporary thought*. New York: Simon & Schuster.

Merriam-Webster's collegiate dictionary (10th ed.).(1993). Springfield, MA: Merriam-Webster.

Messaris, P. (1994). *Visual "literacy": Image, mind, & reality*. Boulder, CO: Westview.

Messaris, P. (1997). *Visual persuasion*. Thousand Oaks, CA: Sage.

Miller, H. (1965). *Plexus*. New York: Grove.

Moholy-Nagy, L. (1932). A new instrument of vision. In Kostelanetz, R. (Ed.) *Moholy-Nagy*, pp. 50-54. New York: Praeger.

Moriarty, S. (1994). *Visual semiotics and the production of meaning in advertising*, paper presented to Visual Communication Division, Association for Education in Journalism and Mass Communication, Washington, DC. Retrieved July 19, 2006, from http://spot.colorado.edu/~moriarts/vissemiotics.html

National Astronomy and Ionosphere Center. (2004). *Arecibo Observatory accomplishments*. Retrieved September 26, 2004, from http://www.naic.edu/public/discovrs.htm

National Museum of Photography, Film & Television. (2004). *Cinematography, insight: Collections & Research Centre*. Retrieved September 18, 2004, from http://www.nmpft.org.uk/insight/onexhib_cin.asp

Newman, M. (2006). Images of the social and economic world. Retrieved on August 17, 2006, from http://www-personal.umich.edu/~mejn/cartograms/

Newton, J. H. (2001). *The burden of visual truth: The role of photojournalism in mediating reality*. Mahwah, NJ: Lawrence Erlbaum Associates, Inc.

Nichols, B. (1994). *Blurred boundaries: Questions of meaning in contemporary culture*. Bloomington: Indiana University Press.

Nicolaides, K. (1941). *The natural way to draw*. Boston: Houghton Mifflin.

O'Connor, A. (2004, September 14). The right ear is from Mars. *New York Times*. Retrieved September 14, 2004, from http://www.nytimes.com/2004/09/14/science/14ear.html

Orlan (2004). Official Orlan Web site. Retrieved May 27, 2004, from http://www.orlan.net/

Orlan (2004). *Orlan: Carnal art*. Hartney, E., Blistene, B., Buci-Glucksmann, C., & Cros, C. (contributors). Paris: Editions Flammarion.

Orlan (2006). Carnal art. Retrieved September 11, 2006, from http://www.orlan.net/

Ornstein, R. (1997). *The right mind: Making sense of the hemispheres*. New York: Harcourt, Brace & Co.

O'Sullivan, E. (1999). *Transformative learning: Education vision for the 21st century*. London: Zed Books in association with University of Toronto Press.

Paul, N., and Ruel, L. (2005). *HTML versus Flash: What works best — and when*. DiSEL Digital Storytelling Effects Lab Report One. Minneapolis and Chapel Hill: School of Journalism and Mass Communication, University of Minnesota, and School of Journalism and Mass Communication, University of North Carolina.

Peirce, C. S. (1931–1958). *Collected writings* (Vols. 1–8; C. Hartshorne, P. Weiss, & A. W. Burks, Eds.). Cambridge, MA: Harvard University Press.

Pennsylvania Muscle Institute. (2004). *Gene therapy and neuromuscular disease*. Retrieved September 26, 2004, from http://www.uphs.upenn.edu/pmi/graduate/grad_gene.shtml

Plato (n.d.). *Phaedrus* (Trans.). Retrieved August 27, 2004, from http://www.uky.edu/ArtsSciences/Classics/rhetoric.html

Postman, N. (1985). *Amusing ourselves to death: Public discourse in the age of show business*. New York: Viking.

Poynter Institute. (2004). *Eyetrack III: Online news consumer behavior in the age of multimedia*. Retrieved September 27, 2004, from http://www.poynterextra.org/eyetrack2004/faq.htm#1

Project Blinkenlights. (2004, February 1). *Blinkenlights Reloaded*. Retrieved September 13, 2004, from http://www.blinkenlights.de/

The public mind: Image and reality in America. Consuming images. [videorecording]. (1985). With B. Moyers. Alexandria, VA: Public Broadcasting Service.

Rabkin, N., & Redmond, R. (Eds.). (2004). Putting the arts in the picture: Reframing education in the 21st century.

Rohm, W. (2004, January). Seven days of creation: The inside story of a human cloning experiment. *WIRED, 01*, 120–129.

Rose, G. (2001). *Visual methodologies: An introduction to the interpretation of visual materials*. London: Sage.

Roxborough, J. (2006, June 29). World Cup viewers may top 30 billion. *Holly Reporter*. Retrieved on July 18, 2006, from http://www.hollywoodreporter.com/thr/international/brief_display.jsp?vnu_content_id=10 02764101

Sadovsky, R. (2003, February 13). Video capsule endoscopy vs. small bowel radiography. *American Family Physician*. Retrieved September 2, 2004, from http://www.findarticles.com/p/articles/mi_m3225/is_4_67/ai_975925

Sanders, K. (2004, August 19). U.S. softball team uses secret weapon; technology and tennis balls help the players see a pitch to hit. *NBC News*. Retrieved September 26, 2004, from http://www.msnbc.msn.com/id/5761652/

Saussure, F. de (1966). *Course in general linguistics*. C. Bally & A. Schehaye, with A. Riedlinger (Eds.). (W. Baskin, Trans.). La Salle, IL: Open Court. (Original work published 1959)

Schiller, H. I. (1989). *Culture inc.* New York: Oxford University Press.

Schmandt-Besserat, D. (1996). *How writing came about*. [Abridged edition of *Before Writing, Volume I: From Counting to Cuneiform* (1992), Austin: University of Texas Press] Austin: University of Texas Press.

Simmons, S., & Winer, M. (1977). *Drawing the creative process*. Englewood Cliffs, NJ: Prentice-Hall.

Sondheim, A. (2004). *Internet text. Philosophy and psychology of the Internet*. Retrieved September 13, 2004, from http://www.anu.edu.au/english/internet_txt/

Sperry, R. W. (1968). Hemisphere disconnection and unity in conscious awareness. *American Psychologist, 23*, 723–733.

Sperry, R. W. (1973). Lateral specialization of cerebral function in the surgically separated hemispheres. In F. J. McGuigan & R. A. Schoonover (Eds.), *The psychophysiology of thinking* (pp. 209–229). New York: Academic.

Stebbing, P. (2004). A universal grammar for visual composition? *Leonardo, 37*(1), 63–70.

Sweet Briar's Cochran Library. (2004). *Andy Goldsworthy*. Retrieved September 2, 2004, from http://www.artgallery.sbc.edu/highlights/tour.html

Takahashi, D. (2004, September 13). *The not-so-simple life, New Sims game takes leaps in AI technology*. Retrieved September 13, 2004, from http://www.siliconvalley.com/mld/siliconvalley/9651869.htm

Tocqueville, A. de (1980). *Alexis de Tocqueville on democracy, revolution, and society: Selected writings, Stone, J., and Mennell, S. (Eds.)*. Chicago: University of Chicago Press.

Toffler, A. (1990). *Powershift: Knowledge, wealth, and violence at the edge of the 21st century*. New York: Bantam.

University of Texas Austin. (2004). *Color me productive: Research gauges impact of color in the workplace*. Retrieved September 1, 2004, from http://www.utexas.edu/supportut/news_pub/yg_kwallek-color.html?AddInterest=1286

Van Harken, J. (2003, August 20). *Budgets cut student experience*. CNN.com. Retrieved July 8, 2004, from http://www.cnn.com/2003/EDUCATION/08/13/sprj.sch.cuts/

Wakefield, J. (2004, July). Doom and gloom by 2100. *Scientific American, 291*, 48–49.

Warner, J. (2004, April 15). *Brain implants move at the speed of thought. New devices operate on the power of thought alone, testing begins in humans.* WebMd.com. Retrieved September 19, 2004, from http://my.webmd.com/content/Article/85/98694.htm?pagenumber=1

Weismann, D. L. (1970). *The visual arts as human experience.* Englewood Cliffs: Prentice-Hall.

Wilde, J., & Wilde, R. (1991). *Visual literacy: A conceptual approach to graphic problem solving.* New York: Watson-Guptill.

Williams, R. (1995–1999). [Anonymous student course and instructor evaluations]. Unpublished raw data administered by the University of Texas Measurement and Evaluation Center, Austin.

Williams, R. (2000). *Working hands.* Bryan: Texas A&M University Press

Winson, J. (2002, August). *The meaning of dreams. Scientific American: The hiddden mind (special ed.), 12,* 54–61.

Winston, B. (1996). *Technologies of seeing: Photography, cinematography and television.* London: British Film Institute.

Wood, J. (2004). *What is GPS drawing?* Retrieved September 26, 2004, from http://www.gpsdrawing.com/info/guide.htm

World Literacy of Canada (2006). Defining literacy. Retrieved June 27, 2006, from http://www.worldlit.ca/defininglit.html

Yale Center for British Art (2005). *The Eidophusikon.* Retrieved September 10, 2006 from http://ycba.yale.edu/information/pdfs/mediakits/05-cottage-eidotentroom.pdf

Zettl, H. (1973). *Sight, sound, motion: Applied media aesthetics* (1st ed.). Belmont, CA: Wadsworth.

Zettl, H. (2005). *Sight, sound, motion: Applied media aesthetics* (4th ed.). Belmont, CA: Wadsworth.

SUGGESTED READING

Adam, P. S., & Conneen, A. (1999). *Color, contrast & dimension in news design*. Retrieved August 30, 2004, from http://poynterextra.org/cp/colorproject/color.html

Adventures in Cybersound. (n.d.). *Magic machines: A history of the moving image from antiquity to 1900*. Retrieved September 17, 2004, from http://inventors.about.com/gi/dynamic/offsite.htm?site=http://www.acmi.net.au/AIC/MAGIC%5FMACHINES.html

Altick, R. *The Shows of London*

Anywhere Books. (2004). *News & updates*. Retrieved on September 27, 2004, from http://www.anywherebooks.org/home.php

Arnheim, R. (1960). *Art and visual perception: A psychology of the creative eye*. Berkeley: University of California Press.

Associated Press. (2004, August 23). Nearly flawless, U.S. women win gold. *ESPN*. Retrieved September 26, 2004, from http://sports.espn.go.com/oly/summer04/softball/news/story?id=1865646

Barnett, B., & Grabe, M. E. (2000). The impact of slow motion video on viewer evaluations of television news stories. *Visual Communication Quarterly, 7*(3), 4–7.

Berger, A. A. (1998). *Seeing is believing: An introduction to visual communication* (4th ed.). Mountain View, CA: Mayfield.

Boeree, C. G. (1997). *Carl Jung. Personality theories*. Retrieved December 27, 2004, from http://www.ship.edu/~cgboeree/jung.html

Bogen, J. E. (1969). The other side of the brain. *Bulletin of the Los Angeles Neurological Societies, 34*, 73–105.

British Belgian Blue Cattle Society (2004). A register of british bred semen sires [Electronic version]. *British Belgian Blue Bull Book*. Retrieved September 26, 2004, from http://www.belgianblue.co.uk/breed/bull_book.html

Burgin, V. (Ed.). (1982). *Thinking photography*. London: Macmillan.

Camp, J. (1981). *The drawing book*. New York: Holt, Rinehart and Winston.

Center for Global Environmental Education. (1999). Andy Goldsworthy. Retrieved September 2, 2004, from http://cgee.hamline.edu/see/goldsworthy/see_an_andy.html

Davis, H., & Waldon, P. (Eds.). (1983) *Language, image, media*. Oxford: Blackwell.

Debord, G. (1983). *Society of the spectacle*. Detroit: Black and Red.

Dean, K. (2004, September 24). Rural kids print, bind and read. *WIRED News*. Retrieved September 27, 2004, from http://www.wired.com/news/culture/0,1284,64627,00.html?tw=wn_tophead_5

Deutsch, C. (2004, September 13). New logo and tagline for Xerox. *New York Times*. Retrieved September 14, 2004, from http://www.nytimes.com/2004/09/13/business/media/13adcol.html?8seia

Elkins, J. (2003). *Visual studies: A skeptical introduction*. New York: Routledge.

Erdmann, E., & Stover, D. (1991). *Beyond a world divided*. London: Shambhala.

Ewen, S. (1988). *All consuming images: The politics of style in contemporary culture*. New York: HarperCollins.

Ewen, S. (Commentator). (1989). *The public mind: consuming images* [Videotape]. New York: Public Broadcasting System.

Flaherty, J. (2003, June 9). In gold ink on a chip, the world's tiniest book. *New York Times*. Retrieved August 30, 2004 from http://www.nytimes.com/2003/06/09/technology/09TINY.html?ex=1094097600&en=2753d15b93eb95a9&ei=5070

Floch, J. (2000). *Visual identities* (P. Van Osselaer & A. McHoul, Trans.). London: Continuum.

Foer, J. S. (2004). Questions for Jonathan Safran Foer. *New York Times*. Retrieved September 10, 2004, from http://www.nytimes.com/ref/books/foer-answers.html?8bu

Freud, S. (1965). *The interpretation of dreams*. New York: Avon.

Fromm, E. (1951). *The forgotten language: An introduction to the understanding of dreams, fairy tales, and myths*. New York: Rinehart.

Gardner. H. (1997). Are there additional intelligences? In J. Kane (Ed.), *Education, information, and transformation*. Englewood Cliffs, NJ: Prentice-Hall.

Gardner. H. (1999). *Intelligence reframed: Multiple intelligences for the 21st century*. New York: Basic Books.

Gazzaniga, M. S., & LeDoux, J. E. (1978). *The integrated mind*. New York: Plenum Press.

Gernsheim, H., & Gernsheim, A. (1956). *L. J. M. Daguerre: The Daguerrotype and the Diorama*. London: Secker and Warburg

Gombrich, E. H. (1977). *Art and illusion: A study in the psychology of pictorial representation*. London: Phaidon.

Gombrich, E. H (1982). *The image and the eye: Further studies in the psychology of pictorial representation*. London: Phaidon.

Goodman, N. (1968). *Languages of art: An approach to a theory of symbols*. London: Oxford University Press.

Hanson, J. (1987). *Understanding video*. Newbury Park, CA: Sage.

Hill, E. (1966). *The language of drawing*. Englewood Cliffs, NJ: Prentice-Hall.

Hoopes, J. (Ed.). (1991). *Peirce on signs: Writings on semiotics by Charles Sanders Peirce*. Chapel Hill: Univeristy of North Carolina Press.

Howlett, D. (2004, September 9). Chicago plans advanced surveillance. *USA Today*. Retrieved September 10, 2004, from http://www.usatoday.com/tech/news/surveillance/2004-09-09-chicago-surveillance_x.htm?POE=click-refer

Infrared Processing and Analysis Center and SIRTF Science Center, California Institute of Technology. (2004). Discovery of the infared. *Cool Cosmos*. Retrieved September 2, 2004, from http://coolcosmos.ipac.caltech.edu/cosmic_classroom/ir_tutorial/discovery.html

Jung, C. J. (1961). *Memories, dreams, reflections.* New York: Random House.

Jung, C. J., [and others]. (1964). *Man and his symbols.* Garden City, N.Y: Doubleday.

Jung, C. G. (1968). *The archetypes and the collective unconscious* (2nd ed., R. F. C. Hull, Trans.). Princeton: Princeton University Press.

Karabinis, P. (2000). Interview of Jerry Uelsmann at the University of North Florida, 1997. Retrieved on June 25, 2006 from http://www.uelsmann.net

Kanellos, M. (2004, April 9). After years of struggle, GPS is taking off. *News.Com.* Retrieved September 26, 2004, from http://news.com.com/After+years+of+struggle%2C+GPS+is+taking+off/2100-1033_3-5187758.html?tag=nl

Keirsey, D., & Bates, M. (1984). *Please understand me: Character and temperment types.* Del Mar, CA: Prometheus Nemesis Book Company.

Kilbourne, J. (Producer/Narrator). (1987). *Still killing us softly: Advertising's image of women* [Videotape]. Cambridge, MA: Cambridge Documentary Films.

Kilbourne, J. (Producer/Narrator). (1995). *Slim hopes: Advertising and the obsession with thinness* [Videotape]. Northhampton, MA: Media Education Foundation.

Knott, R. (2004). *Fibonacci numbers and the Golden Section.* Retrieved August 24, 2004, from http://www.mcs.surrey.ac.uk/Personal/R.Knott/Fibonacci/fib.html

Langer, S. K. (1942). *Philosophy in a new key.* Cambridge, MA: Harvard University Press.

Langer, S. K. (1953). *Feeling and form.* New York: Scribner's.

Lark-Horovitz, B., Lewis, H., & Luca, M. (1967). *Understanding children's art for better teaching.* Columbus, OH: Merrill.

Levy, J. (1968). Differential perceptual capacities in major and minor hemispheres. *Proceedings of the National Academy of Science, 61,* 1151.

Levy, J. (1974). Psychobiological implications of bilateral asymmetry. In S. J. Dimond & J. G. Beaumont (Eds.), *Hemisphere function in the human brain.* New York: Wiley.

Lubell, S. (2004, September 23). The womb as photo studio. *New York Times.* Retrieved September 23, 2004, from http://www.nytimes.com/2004/09/23/technology/circuits/23ultr.html?ex=1097160189&ei=1&en=b62be85a7465bd04

Lucassen, C. (2004). *Chronophotographical projections.* Retrieved September 18, 2004, from http://web.inter.nl.net/users/anima/chronoph/index.htm

Luke, H. M. (1982). *The inner story.* New York: Crossroad.

McLuhan, M. (1967a). *The mechanical bride: Folklore of industrial man.* Boston: Beacon.

McLuhan, M. (1967b). *The medium is the message.* New York: Bantam.

Miller, M. C. (Commentator). (1989). *The public mind: consuming images* [Videotape]. New York: Public Broadcasting System.

Neihardt. J. (1988). *Black elk speaks.* Lincoln: University of Nebraska Press.

Newhall, B. (1976). *The Daguerreotype in America.* New York: Dover.

Nystrom, C. L. (2000). Symbols, thought, and reality: The contributions of Benjamin Lee Whorf and Susanne K. Langer to media ecology. *The New Jersey Journal of Communication, 8*(2), 8–33.

Peeble, D., & Peeble, S. (1985). *Artforms.* New York: Harper & Row.

Piaget, J. (1952). *The origins of intelligence in children* (M.Cook, Trans.). New York: International Universities Press.

Pollack, A. (2004, September 14). Method to turn off bad genes is set for tests on human eyes. *New York Times*. Retrieved September 14, 2004, from http://www.nytimes.com/2004/09/14/business/14gene.html?th

Postman, N. (1985). *Amusing ourselves to death: Public discourse in the age of show business*. New York: Viking.

Schiller, H. I. (1989). *Culture inc*. New York: Oxford University Press.

Schiller, H. I. (Commentator). (1989). The public mind: Consuming images [Videotape]. New York: Public Broadcasting System.

Sciolino, E. (2004, September 3). Ban on head scarves takes effect in France. *New York Times*. Retrieved September 3, 2004, from http://www.nytimes.com/2004/09/03/international/europe/03france.html?ex=1095195983&ei=1&en=9e7f4708102d07b3

Sondheim, A. (2004). *Internet text. Philosophy and psychology of the Internet*. Retrieved September 13, 2004, from http://www.anu.edu.au/english/internet_txt/

Sperry, R. W. (1968). Hemisphere disconnection and unity in conscious awareness. *American Psychologist, 23*, 723–733.

Tagg, J. (1988). *The burden of representation: Essays on photographies and histories*. Amherst: University of Massachusetts Press.

Toys "R" Us. (2004). ToysRUs.com. Retrieved September 26, 2004, from http://www.amazon.com/exec/obidos/tg/detail/-/B00008XYPX/qid=1096253406/sr=1-2/ref=sr_1_2/102-4083365-6427327?v=glance&s=toys and http://www.bratzpack.com/index2.asp

Weisstein, E. (2004). *Kelvin, Lord William Thomson*. Scienceworld.wolfram.com. Retrieved September 2, 2004, from http://scienceworld.wolfram.com/biography/Kelvin.html

Whorf, B. L. (1956). *Language, thought and reality*. Cambridge, MA: MIT Press.

Williams, R. (1999). Beyond visual literacy: Omniphasism, a theory of cognitive balance, part I. *Journal of Visual Literacy, 19*, 159–178.

Williams, R. (2000b). Omniphasic visual-media literacy in the classroom, part III. *Journal of Visual Literacy, 20*, 219–242.

Williams, R. (2003). Transforming intuitive illiteracy: Understanding the effects of the unconscious mind on image meaning, image consumption, and behavior. *Explorations in Media Ecology, 2*, 119–134.

Williams, R. (2000a). Visual illiteracy and intuitive visual persuasion, part II. *Journal of Visual Literacy, 20*, 111–124.

Wolfe, J. (1983). Hidden visual processes. *Scientific American, 248*, 94–103.

INDEX OF TERMS BY CHAPTER/CREATIVE

Creative Twelve

Chapter Thirteen

Creative Thirteen

Chapter Fourteen

Creative Fourteen

ALPHABETICAL INDEX

What got you here will get you out of here.
Joe Garagiola

Color Plate 1. El veinte de noviembre, Zaragoza, Coahuila, Mexico.
Cibachrome print. Photograph by Julianne Newton.

Color Plate 2. Dancing galaxies captured by NASA's Spitzer Space Telescope. Blue areas are the cores of two merging galaxies, called NGC 2207 and IC 2163, which are twirling around each other. Image courtesy of NASA, ESA/JPL-Caltech/STScI/D. Elmegreen.

Color Plate 3. Winter Oak, composed of 75 photographs, by Bonnie Fournier.

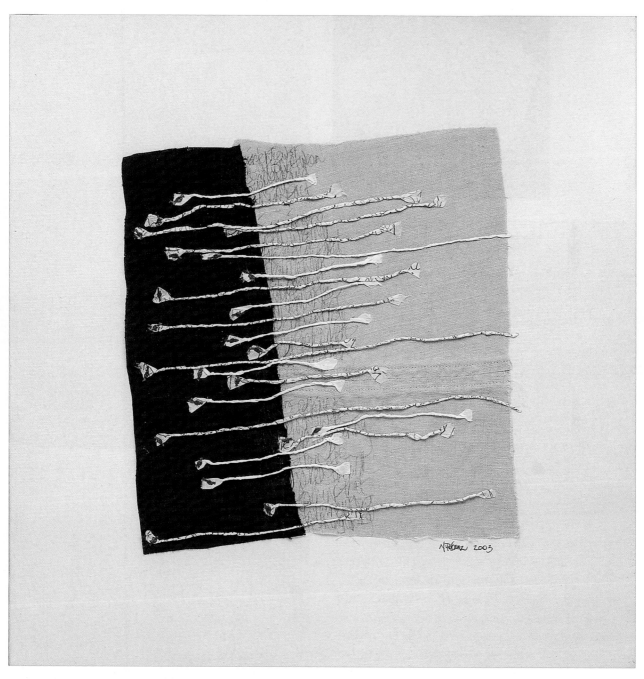

Color Plate 4. Selective Memories, by Nancy Pobanz 2003. All natural fibers and pigments. The strings are rolled pieces of paper on which thoughts have been written.

Color Plates 5-8. Clockwise from top left: Sesh, Hieroglyph of "Scribe." Deir-el-Medina, Western Tebes, 1307-1070 B.C.E. Autograph and self portrait of an artist who decorated tombs in the Valley of the Kings and Queens. MS 1695. ABECEDARY, Greece, ca. 800 B.C.E. From the oldest writing tablets, which were made of copper and strung together to fold like a concertina, described as "an . . . amazing preservation of students' learning of the Greek alphabet at the very inception of its use" MS 108. Gift from the "high and mighty of Adab to the high priestess on the occasion of her election to the temple." Sumer, 26th century B.C.E. MS 3029. Phra Malai; Thai Buddhist visions of heaven and hell, Thailand, ca. 1800, MS 2478. All from The Schøyen Collection , Oslo.

Color Plate 14. The Sower, 1988, by Vincent Van Gogh. Rijksmuseum Kroeller-Mueller, Otterlo, The Netherlands. Photograph by Erich Lessing / Art Resource, NY.

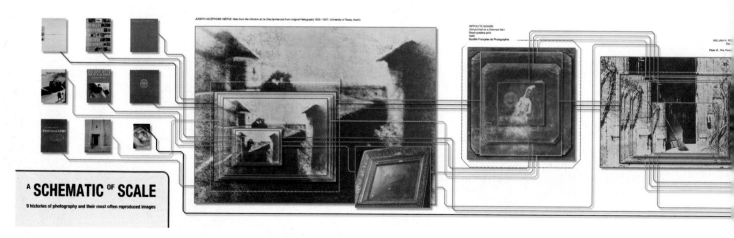

Color Plate 16. A Schematic of Scale, the most prevalent photographs in 9 histories of photography, by Bleu Cease. The image of Photography Until Now is used without the dust jacket.

Color Plates 9-13. Clockwise from left: Hvitebjørn Kong Valemon, William Lunden, Asbjørnsen and Moe: Norwegian folk tales, 1936, MS 2774. Pablo Beaumont: Cronica de Mechoacan, Mexico City, ca. 1820-1830, MS 1072. Apache pictographs and symbols. Southern Plains, USA, MS 4604. Cheyenne drawings. Kansas, 1878-1879, MS 2956/1. Suryaprajnapti Sutra, astronomy, India, ca. 1500, MS 5297. All from The Schøyen Collection, Oslo.

Color Plate 15. The Potato Eaters, 1885, by Vincent Van Gogh. Van Gogh Museum, Amsterdam, The Netherlands. Photograph courtesy of Art Resource, NY.

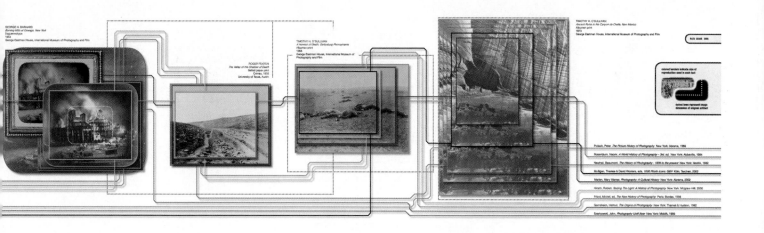

Right: Color Plate 17. Beware of Red, 1940, by Paul Klee. © 2006 Artists Rights Society (ARS), New York / VG Bild-Kunst, Bonn; Erich Lessing/Art Resource, New York. Below: Color Plate 18. Blue Poles, by Jackson Pollock. © 2006 The Pollock-Krasner Foundation / Artists Rights Society (ARS), New York.

Top: Color Plate 19. Young Woman Drawing, by Pablo Picasso. © 2006 Estate of Pablo Picasso/Artists Rights Society (ARS), NY; Scala/Arts Resource NY.
Left: Color Plate 20. Kaufbeuren, Allgäu (Southern Bavaria), 1981, by Herb Zettl. Courtesy the artist.
Above: Color Plate 21. Scout, by Josh Williams (from photograph of Scout take just after he had grabbed a rack of ribs off the barbecue grill). Courtesy the artist.

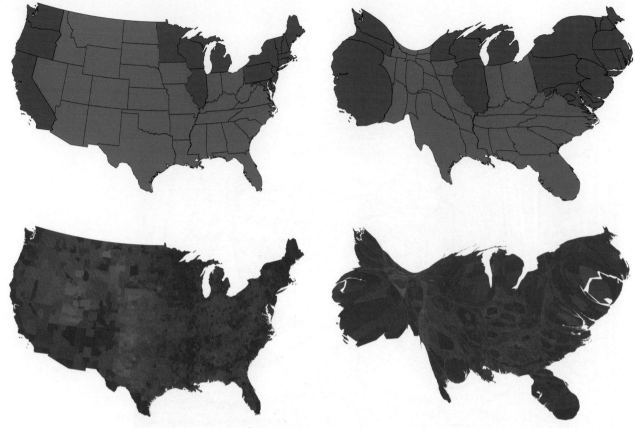

Color Plates 22-25. Representations of U.S. Voting Patterns in 2004 Presidential Election, by Mark Newman. Blue = Democrat. Red = Republican. From top left: Map by states, cartogram bypopulation. Above from left: Map by county, cartogram by county.

Above: Color Plates 26-29. Logodesign for the Heart Hospital of New Mexico by Maggie Macnab.
Right: Electromagnetic spectrum, illustration by Janet Halvorsen.
Top Right: Poster showing cartogram of world toy imports, with U.S. in blue, by Danny Dorling and Mark Newman, The Worldmapper Team.
Far Right: Corporate logo flag, Adbusters.

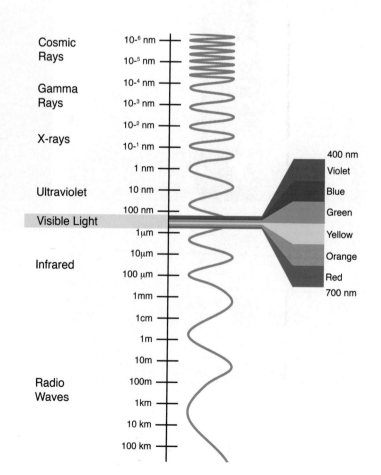

Toy Imports

Most imports of toys (US$ net) are to the United States, followed by the United Kingdom. Toys are fun but not necessities. Thus toy imports give an indication of disposable incomes.

The lowest imports of toys (US$ net) per person are to territories in Africa and also Tajikistan (in the Middle East). Central Africa, Southeastern Africa, Southern Asia and Northern Africa contain the poorest territories in the world.

The highest imports of toys (US$ net) per person are to territories in Western Europe, North America, Asia Pacific and Eastern Europe.

Territory size shows the proportion of worldwide net imports of toys (in US$) that are received there. Net imports are imports minus exports. When exports are larger than imports the territory is not shown.

Land area

Technical notes
- Data source: United Nations Conference on Trade and Development, 2002.
- There were no net toy imports recorded for 33 territories.
- The toys category includes sporting goods.
- See website for further information.

MOST AND LEAST US$ OF NET TOY IMPORTS

Rank	Territory	Value	Rank	Territory	Value
1	Andorra	340	158	Niger	0.03
2	Greenland	57	159	Mali	0.03
3	United States	51	160	Ethiopia	0.02
4	Iceland	48	161	Chad	0.02
5	Norway	48	162	Rwanda	0.02
6	Niue	39	163	Togo	0.01
7	Luxembourg	36	164	Burundi	0.01
8	New Zealand	36	165	Liberia	0.01
9	Cyprus	35	166	Somalia	0.01
10	Canada	33	167	Tajikistan	<0.01

US$ worth of toys imported annually per person living in that territory*

REGIONAL NET TOYS EXPORTS

"Is there a present that a child or family member just has to have and you can't find it in any store?"

Kidsource, 2000

Map 058

Color Plates 30-31. Top: The Director, Photograph by Russell Lee, digital image by J. B. Colson. Above: Found Portraits Collection: from the Cambodian Killing Fields at Tuol Sleng, 2003, by Binh Danh, chlorophyll print and resin, courtesy of the artist and Haines Gallery, San Francisco.

Color Plates 32-33. Top: Peinándose, photograph by Julianne Newton. Right: Dreamstate, double exposure photograph, by Brett Crosse.

Color Plates 34-37. Stills from video advertisement for Hitachi plasma high-definition televisions, by the Lambesis Agency. © 2006 Hitachi.

Color Plates 38-40. Top: Thai Silk, oil pastel, by YodKwan P., age 7, Krabi Province, Thailand. Above: Jake's Garden, finger paint, by Jake L., age 1, California, USA (both from Natural Child Project). Right: Multimedia Mind Show, by Slim Films.